Family Spending
A report on the 2008 Living Costs and Food Survey

2009 Edition

Editor: Rachel Skentelbery
Office for National Statistics

ISBN 978-0-230-57550-9
ISSN 0965–1403 (print), ISSN 2040–1647 (online)

A National Statistics publication

National Statistics are produced to high professional standards as set out in the Code of Practice for Official Statistics. They are produced free from political influence.

About us

The Office for National Statistics

The Office for National Statistics (ONS) is the executive office of the UK Statistics Authority, a non-ministerial department which reports directly to Parliament. ONS is the UK government's single largest statistical producer. It compiles information about the UK's society and economy, and provides the evidence-base for policy and decision-making, the allocation of resources, and public accountability. The Director-General of ONS reports directly to the National Statistician who is the Authority's Chief Executive and the Head of the Government Statistical Service.

The Government Statistical Service

The Government Statistical Service (GSS) is a network of professional statisticians and their staff operating both within the Office for National Statistics and across more than 30 other government departments and agencies.

Palgrave Macmillan

This publication first published 2010 by Palgrave Macmillan.

Palgrave Macmillan in the UK is an imprint of Macmillan Publishers Limited, registered in England, company number 785998, of Houndmills, Basingstoke, Hampshire RG21 6XS. Palgrave Macmillan in the US is a division of St Martin's Press LLC, 175 Fifth Avenue, New York, NY 10010.

Palgrave Macmillan is the global academic imprint of the above companies and has companies and representatives throughout the world. Palgrave® and Macmillan® are registered trademarks in the United States, the United Kingdom, Europe and other countries.

A catalogue record for this book is available from the British Library.

10 9 8 7 6 5 4 3 2 1
19 18 17 16 15 14 13 12 11 10

Contacts

This publication

For information about the content of this publication, contact the Living Costs and Food Survey
Tel: 01633 455282
Email: efs@ons.gsi.gov.uk

Other customer enquiries

ONS Customer Contact Centre
Tel: 0845 601 3034
International: +44 (0)845 601 3034
Minicom: 01633 815044
Email: info@statistics.gsi.gov.uk
Fax: 01633 652747
Post: Room 1015, Government Buildings, Cardiff Road, Newport, South Wales NP10 8XG
www.ons.gov.uk

Media enquiries

Tel: 0845 604 1858
Email: press.office@ons.gsi.gov.uk

Publication orders

To obtain the print version of this publication, contact Palgrave Macmillan
Tel: 01256 302611
www.palgrave.com/ons
Price: £52.00

Copyright and reproduction

Printing

This book is printed on paper suitable for recycling and made from fully managed and sustained forest sources. Logging, pulping and manufacturing processes are expected to conform to the environmental regulations of the country of origin.

Printed and bound in Great Britain by Hobbs the Printer Ltd, Totton, Southampton

Typeset by Kerrypress Ltd, Luton

Contents

	Page
List of tables	v
List of figures	xi
Introduction	xvi
List of contributors	xiv

1: Overview — 1

Overview	2
Household expenditure	2
Household expenditure by income	2
Household expenditure by age	3
Household expenditure by economic activity and socio-economic group	3
Household expenditure by household composition	3
Household expenditure by region	4
Household Income	4
Household income by age	4
Household income by region	4
Household income by economic activity and socio-economic classification	4
Ownership of durable goods	5

2: Housing Expenditure — 7

Background	8
COICOP	8
Analysis	8
Results	9
Housing expenditure over time	9
Expenditure by gross income	10
Expenditure by age of the household reference person	10
Expenditure by region	11
Expenditure by socio-economic classification	12
Analysis of housing costs by renters and mortgage holders	14

3: Equivalised Income — 27

Background	28
Equivalisation Methodology	28
Results:	29
Household composition by income groups	29
Household expenditure by income	30
Household expenditure by household composition and income	31
Sources of income	32

Page

4: Trends in household expenditure over time   59

Background	60
Interpreting EFS/ LCF time series data	60
Household expenditure over time	60

5: Regression analysis of household expenditure and income   70

Background	71
Explanatory Variables for Household Expenditure and Income	72
Testing the Standard Assumptions	72
Multivariate Regression Modelling	73
Results	74
Conclusion	75
Further research	76

Appendix A   79

Household expenditure tables	81

Appendix B: Methodology   183

Section B1	Description and response rate of the survey	184
Section B2	Uses of the survey	186
Section B3	Standard errors and estimates of precision	187
Section B4	Definitions	190
Section B5	Changes in definition, 1991 to 2008	200
Section B6	Weighting	203
Section B7	Index to tables in reports on the FES/EFS in 1999/2000 to 2008	206

List of tables

Page

1: Overview

Table 1.1	Expenditure by COICOP category and total household expenditure	2

2: Housing Expenditure

Table 2.1	Definition of total housing expenditure	9
Table 2.2	Housing expenditure 2006 to 2008	15
Table 2.3	Housing expenditure by gross income decile group, 2008	16
Table 2.4	Housing expenditure by age of household reference person, 2008	17
Table 2.5	Housing expenditure by UK Countries and Government Office Region, 2008	18
Table 2.6	Housing expenditure by socio-economic classification of HRP, 2008	20
Table 2.7	Housing expenditure by household composition, 2008	22
Table 2.8	Expenditure on rent by renters, 2006 to 2008	23
Table 2.9	Expenditure on mortgages by mortgage holders 2006 to 2008	23
Table 2.10	Expenditure on rent and mortgages by renters and mortgage holders by gross income decile group, 2008	24
Table 2.11	Expenditure on rent and mortgages by renters and mortgage holders by UK Countries and Government Office Region, 2008	25

3: Equivalised Income

Table 3.1	Percentage of households by composition in each gross and equivalised income decile group, 2008	33
Table 3.2E	Household expenditure by gross equivalised income decile group, 2008	34
Table 3.2	Household expenditure by gross income decile group, 2008	36
Table 3.3E	Household expenditure as a percentage of total expenditure by gross equivalised income decile group, 2008	38
Table 3.3	Household expenditure as a percentage of total expenditure by gross income decile group, 2008	40
Table 3.4E	Expenditure of one person non-retired households by gross equivalised income quintile group, 2008	42
Table 3.4	Expenditure of one person non-retired households by gross income quintile group, 2008	43

Page

Table 3.5E   Expenditure of one person retired households not mainly
               dependent on state pensions by gross equivalised income
               quintile group, 2008   44

Table 3.5   Expenditure of one person retired households not mainly
               dependent on state pensions by gross income quintile group, 2008   45

Table 3.6E   Expenditure of two adult households with children by
               gross equivalised income quintile group, 2008   46

Table 3.6   Expenditure of two adult households with children by gross
               income quintile group, 2008   47

Table 3.7E   Expenditure of one adult households with children by gross
               equivalised income quintile group, 2008   48

Table 3.7   Expenditure of one adult households with children by gross
               income quintile group, 2008   49

Table 3.8E   Expenditure of one man one woman non-retired households
               by gross equivalised income quintile group, 2008   50

Table 3.8   Expenditure of one man one woman non-retired households
               by gross income quintile group, 2008   51

Table 3.9E   Expenditure of one person retired households mainly
               dependent on state pensions by gross equivalised income quintile
               group, 2008   52

Table 3.9   Expenditure of one person retired households mainly
               dependent on state pensions by gross income quintile group, 2008   53

Table 3.10E   Expenditure of one man one woman retired households mainly
               dependent on state pensions by gross equivalised income quintile
               group, 2008   54

Table 3.10   Expenditure of one man one woman retired households mainly
               dependent on state pensions by gross income quintile group, 2008   55

Table 3.11E   Expenditure of one man one woman retired households
               not mainly dependent on state pensions by gross equivalised
               income quintile group, 2008   56

Table 3.11   Expenditure of one man one woman retired households
               not mainly dependent on state pensions by gross income
               quintile group, 2008   57

Table 3.12E   Income and source of income by gross equivalised
               income quintile group, 2008   58

Table 3.12   Income and source of income by gross income quintile group, 2008   58

Page

4: Trends in household expenditure over time

Table 4.1 Household expenditure based on the FES classification,
1992 to 2008 at 2008 prices 64

Table 4.2 Household expenditure as a percentage of total expenditure,
1992 to 2008 based on the FES classification at 2008 prices 66

Table 4.3 Household expenditure based on the COICOP classification,
2002-03 to 2008 at 2008 prices 68

Table 4.4 Household expenditure as a percentage of total expenditure,
2002-03 to 2008 based on the COICOP classification
at 2008 prices 69

Table 4.5 Household expenditure 2002-03 to 2008 COICOP based
current prices 70

5: Regression analysis of household expenditure and income

Table 5.1 Potential key variables to explain household expenditure
and income 72

Table 5.2 Regression models used for analysis 74

Table 5.3 House expenditure regression results 77

Table 5.4 Household income regression results 78

Appendix A

A1 Components of household expenditure, 2008 81

A2 Expenditure on alcoholic drink by place of purchase, 2008 91

A3 Expenditure on food and non-alcoholic drink by place of
purchase, 2008 92

A4 Expenditure on selected items by place of purchase, 2008 94

A5 Expenditure on clothing and footwear by place of purchase, 2008 95

A6 Household expenditure by gross income decile group, 2008 96

A7 Household expenditure as a percentage of total expenditure
by gross income decile group, 2008 98

A8 Detailed household expenditure by gross income decile
group, 2008 100

A9 Household expenditure by disposable income decile group, 2008 110

A10 Household expenditure as a percentage of total expenditure
by disposable income decile group, 2008 112

A11 Household expenditure by age of household reference
person, 2008 114

Page

A12 Household expenditure on main items as a percentage of total expenditure by age of household reference person, 2008 115

A13 Detailed household expenditure by age of household reference person, 2008 116

A14 Household expenditure by gross income quintile group where the household reference person is aged under 30, 2006 and 2008 121

A15 Household expenditure by gross income quintile group where the household reference person is aged 30 to 49, 2006 and 2008 122

A16 Household expenditure by gross income quintile group where the household reference person is aged 50 to 64, 2006 and 2008 123

A17 Household expenditure by gross income quintile group where the household reference person is aged 65 to 74, 2006 and 2008 124

A18 Household expenditure by gross income quintile group where the household reference person is aged 75 or over, 2006 and 2008 125

A19 Household expenditure by economic activity status of the household reference person, 2008 126

A20 Household expenditure by gross income quintile group: the household reference person is a full-time employee , 2008 128

A21 Household expenditure by gross income quintile group: the household reference person is self-employed, 2006 and 2008 129

A22 Household expenditure by number of persons working, 2008 130

A23 Household expenditure by age at which the household reference person completed continuous full-time education, 2008 131

A24 Household expenditure by socio-economic classification of the household reference person, 2008 132

A25 Expenditure by household composition, 2008 134

A26 Expenditure of one person retired households mainly dependent on state pensions, by gross income quintile group, 2006-2008 134

A27 Expenditure of one person retired households not mainly dependent on state pensions, by gross income quintile group, 2006-2008 137

A28 Expenditure of one person non-retired households by gross income quintile group, 2006-2008 138

A29 Expenditure of one adult households with children by gross income quintile group, 2006-2008 139

Page

A30	Expenditure of two adult households with children by gross income quintile group, 2006-2008	140
A31	Expenditure of one man one woman non-retired households by gross income quintile group, 2006-2008	141
A32	Expenditure of one man one woman retired households mainly dependent on state pensions by gross income quintile group, 2006-2008	142
A33	Expenditure of one man one woman retired households not mainly dependent on state pensions by gross income quintile group, 2006-2008	143
A34	Household expenditure by tenure, 2008	144
A35	Household expenditure by UK Countries and Government Office Regions, 2006-2008	146
A36	Household expenditure as a percentage of total expenditure by UK Countries and Government Office Regions, 2006-2008	148
A37	Detailed household expenditure by UK Countries and Government Office Regions, 2006-2008	150
A38	Household expenditure by urban/rural areas (GB), 2006-2008	160
A39	Government Office Regions of the United Kingdom (map)	161
A40	Income and source of income by household composition, 2008	162
A41	Income and source of income by age of household reference person, 2008	163
A42	Income and source of income by gross income quintile group, 2008	163
A43	Income and source of income by household tenure, 2008	163
A44	Income and source of income by UK Countries and Government Office Regions, 2008	164
A45	Income and source of income by GB urban/rural area, 2008	164
A46	Income and source of income by socio-economic classification, 2008	165
A47	Income and source of income, 1970 to 2008	165
A48	Characteristics of households, 2008	166
A49	Characteristics of persons, 2008	168
A50	Percentage of households with durable goods, 1970 to 2008	169
A51	Percentage of households with durable goods by income group and household composition, 2008	170
A52	Percentage of households with cars by income group, tenure and household composition, 2008	171

		Page
A53	Percentage of households with durable goods by UK Countries and Government Office Regions, 2008	172
A54	Percentage of households by size, composition and age in each gross decile group, 2008	174
A55	Percentage of households by economic activity, tenure and socio-economic classification in each gross income decile group, 2008	176
A56	Average weekly household expenditure by OAC supergroup, 2008	178
A57	Average weekly household expenditure by OAC group, 2008	180
A58	Average gross normal weekly household income by OAC supergroup, 2008	182

Appendix B

B1	Percentage standard errors of expenditure of households and number of recording households, 2008	188
B2	Percentage standard errors of income of households and number of recording households, 2008	188
B3	95 per cent confidence intervals for average household expenditure, 2008	189
B4	The effect of weighting on expenditure	204

List of Figures

Page

Overview

Figure 1.1   Household expenditure by income decile group, 2008   2

Figure 1.2   Expenditure on selected items as a proportion of total spending by age of HRP, 2008   3

Figure 1.3   Household expenditure by region, 2006–2008   4

Figure 1.4   Percentage of gross weekly households income by source of income, 2008   4

Housing Expenditure

Figure 2.1   Housing expenditure, 2006–2008   10

Figure 2.2   Expenditure on selected items by gross income decile group, 2008   10

Figure 2.3   Expenditure on selected items by age of household reference person, 2008   11

Figure 2.4   Housing expenditure by region, 2008   11

Figure 2.5   Percentage difference compared with UK average for net rent by UK Countries and Government Office Regions, 2008   12

Figure 2.6   Percentage difference compared with UK average for mortgage payments by UK Countries and Government Office Regions, 2008   12

Figure 2.7   Housing expenditure by socio-economic classification of household reference person, 2008   13

Figure 2.8   Expenditure on selected items by socio-economic classification of the household reference person, 2008   13

Figure 2.9   Expenditure on net rent by UK Countries and Government Office Regions, 2008   14

Figure 2.10   Expenditure on mortgages by UK Countries and Government Office Regions, 2008   14

Equivalised Income

Figure 3.1   Percentage of households with children in each gross income decile group, 2008   30

Figure 3.1E   Percentage of households with children by gross equivalised income decile group, 2008   30

Figure 3.2   Percentage of retired and non-retired households by gross income decile group, 2008   30

Page

Figure 3.2E   Percentage of retired and non-retired households by gross
               equivalised income decile group, 2008   30

Figure 3.3   Expenditure on food and non-alcoholic drinks by gross and
               equivalised income decile group, 2008   31

Figure 3.4   Expenditure on clothing and footwear by gross and
               equivalised income decile group, 2008   31

Figure 3.5   Percentage of total expenditure on selected items by
               equivalised income decile group, 2008   31

Figure 3.6   Sources of income by gross income quintile group, 2008   32

Figure 3.6E   Sources of income by gross equivalised income
               quintile group, 2008   32

Trends in household expenditure over time

Figure 4.1   Total household expenditure based on COICOP classification,
               2002-03 to 2008, at 2008 prices.   61

Figure 4.2   Household expenditure based on COICOP classification,
               2002-03 to 2008, at 2008 prices   61

Regression analysis of household expenditure and income

Figure 5.1   Histogram of total household expenditure, 2008   72

Figure 5.2   Histogram of gross normal household income, 2008   72

Figure 5.3   Histogram of log-transformed total household expenditure, 2008   73

Figure 5.4   Histogram of log-transformed gross normal household
               income, 2008   73

Symbols and conventions used in this report

xiii

[ ]	Figures should be used with extra caution because based on fewer than 20 reporting households.
..	The data is suppressed if the unweighted sample counts are less than ten reporting households
-	No figures are available because there are no reporting households.
Rounding:	Individual figures have been rounded independently. The sum of component items does not therefore necessarily add to the totals shown.
Averages:	These are averages (means) for all households included in the column or row, and, unless specified, are not restricted to those households reporting expenditure on a particular item or income of a particular type.

Period covered: Calendar year 2008 (1 January 2008 to 31 December 2008).

List of contributors

Editor:	Rachel Skentelbery
Authors:	James Boyde
	Martina Aumeyr
	Laura Keyse
	Louise Skilton
	Sarah Skinner
LCF Team:	Karen Carter
	Debbie Curtis
	Steven Dunstan
	Joseph Hawthorne
	Tracy Lane
	Gareth Powell
	Scott Symons
	Karen Watkins
	Sarah Whitehead
	Linda Williams
	Sian Wilson
	Sian-Elin Wyatt
	Field Team and Interviewers
	Coders and Editors
Reviewers:	Karl Ashworth
	Andrew Barnard
	Denise Blackmore
	Mike Prestwood

Acknowledgements

A large scale survey is a collaborative effort and the authors wish to thank the interviewers and other ONS staff who contributed to the study. The survey would not be possible without the co-operation of the respondents who gave up their time to be interviewed and keep a diary of their spending. Their help is gratefully acknowledged.

Introduction

This report presents the latest information from the Living Costs and Food Survey for the 2008 calendar year (January to December). The Expenditure and Food Survey (EFS) was renamed as the Living Costs and Food Survey (LCF) in 2008 when it became a module of the Integrated Household Survey (IHS).

The current LCF is the result of the amalgamation of the Family Expenditure and National Food Surveys (FES and NFS). Both surveys were well established and important sources of information for government and the wider community, charting changes and patterns in Britain's spending and food consumption since the 1950s. The Office for National Statistics (ONS) has overall project management and financial responsibility for the LCF while the Department for Environment, Food and Rural Affairs (DEFRA) sponsors the specialist food data.

The design of the LCF is based on the FES and the same questions were asked of the respondents. The survey continues to be primarily used to provide information for the Retail Prices Index; National Accounts estimates of household expenditure; the analysis of the effect of taxes and benefits, and trends in nutrition. However, the results are multi purpose, providing an invaluable supply of economic and social data.

The 2008 survey

In 2008 5,271 households in Great Britain took part in the LCF survey. The response rate was 51 per cent in Great Britain and 54 per cent in Northern Ireland. The fieldwork was undertaken by the Office for National Statistics and the Northern Ireland Statistics and Research Agency.

Further details about the conduct of the survey are given in Appendix B.

The format of the Family Spending publication changed in 2003-04 so that the tables of key results which were found in the main body of the report are now in Appendix A. This year's report includes an overview chapter outlining key findings, two detailed chapters focusing upon expenditure on housing and the impact of equivalising income when calculating results, a fourth chapter looking at trends in household expenditure over time and finally a chapter modelling income and expenditure using regression analysis.

Data quality and definitions

The results shown in this report are of the data collected by the LCF, following a process of validation and adjustment for non-response using weights that control for a number of factors. These issues are discussed in the section on reliability in Appendix B.

Figures in the report are subject to sampling variability. Standard errors for detailed expenditure items are presented in relative terms in Table A1 and are described in Appendix B, section B6. Figures shown for particular groups of households (e.g. income groups or household composition groups), regions or other sub-sets of the sample are subject to larger sampling variability, and are more sensitive to possible extreme values than are figures for the sample as a whole.

The definitions used in the report are set out in Appendix B, section B4, and changes made since 1991 are described in section B5. Note particularly that Housing Benefit and Council Tax Rebate (rates rebate in Northern Ireland), unlike other social security benefits, are not included in income but are shown as a reduction in housing costs.

Income and Expenditure Balancing

The LCF is designed primarily as a survey of household expenditure on goods and services. It also gathers information about the income of household members, and is an important and detailed source of income data. However, the survey is not designed to produce a balance sheet of income and expenditure either for individual households or groups of households. For further information on the balancing of income and expenditure figures, see 'Description and response rate of the survey', page 184.

Related data sources

Details of household consumption expenditure within the context of the UK National Accounts are produced as part of Consumer Trends (http://www.statistics.gov.uk/statbase/Product.asp?vlnk=242). This publication includes all expenditure by members of UK resident households. National Accounts figures draw on a number of sources including the LCF: figures shown in this report are therefore not directly comparable to National Accounts data. National Accounts data may be more appropriate for deriving long term trends on expenditure.

More detailed income information is available from the Family Resources Survey (FRS), conducted for the Department for Work and Pensions. Further information about food consumption, and in particular details of food quantities, is available from the Department for Environment, Food and Rural Affairs, who are continuing to produce their own report of the survey (http://statistics.defra.gov.uk/esg/publications/efs/default.asp).

In Northern Ireland, a companion survey to the GB LCF is conducted by the Central Survey Unit of the Northern Ireland Statistics and Research Agency (NISRA). Households in Northern Ireland are over-sampled so that separate analysis can be carried out, however these cases are given less weight when UK data are analysed.

Additional tabulations

This report gives a broad overview of the results of the survey, and provides more detailed information about some aspects of expenditure. However, many users of LCF data have very specific data requirements that may not appear in the desired form in this report. The ONS can provide more detailed analysis of the tables in this report, and can also provide additional tabulations to meet specific requests. A charge will be made to cover the cost of providing additional information.

The tables in Family Spending 2009 are available as Excel spreadsheets.

Anonymised microdata from the Living Costs and Food Survey (LCF), the Expenditure and Food Survey (EFS) and the Family Expenditure Survey (FES) are available from the United Kingdom Data Archive. Details on access arrangements and associated costs can be found at www.data-archive.ac.uk or by telephoning 01206 872143.

Overview

This chapter presents the key findings of the 2008 Living Costs and Food Survey (LCF), formerly the Expenditure and Food Survey. The chapter is structured to provide an overview of general household income and expenditure, characterised by different types of household and by region, as well as a summary of the ownership of a limited range of durable goods.

All of the tables (except Table 1.1) referred to in this chapter can be found in Appendix A of the report (page 79).

Household expenditure

Table 1.1 shows total weekly household expenditure in the United Kingdom (UK) by the 12 Classification of Individual COnsumption by Purpose (COICOP)[1] categories. Average weekly household expenditure in the UK in 2008 was £471.00, compared to £459.20 in 2007. As in previous years, spending was highest on transport at £63.40 a week, followed by recreation and culture (£60.10) and housing, fuel and power (£53.00). The average weekly expenditure on food and non-alcoholic drinks was £50.70 a week.

Table 1.1

Expenditure by COICOP category and total household expenditure, 2008

COICOP category	£ per week
Transport	63.40
Recreation and culture	60.10
Housing, fuel and power	53.00
Food and non-alcoholic drinks	50.70
Restaurants and hotels	37.70
Miscellaneous goods and services	35.60
Household goods and services	30.10
Clothing and footwear	21.60
Communication	12.00
Alcoholic drinks, tobacco and narcotics	10.80
Education	6.20
Health	5.10
Total COICOP expenditure	386.30
Other expenditure items	84.60
Total expenditure	471.00

Totals may not add due to the independent rounding of component categories

Of the £63.40 spent on transport each week, close to half (50 per cent) was spent on the operation of personal transport (£31.80 a week), the majority of which was spent on petrol, diesel and other motor oils (£21.00 a week). This represented a 15 per cent increase in the average weekly expenditure on petrol, diesel and other motor oils since 2007 (£18.30). Households spent £10.50 a week on average on transport services, including rail, tube and bus fares (see Table A1).

Almost a quarter (24 per cent) of the expenditure on recreation and culture each week was spent on package holidays (£14.70 per week), most of which were holidays outside of the UK (£13.60). Spending on sports admissions, subscriptions, leisure class fees and equipment hire accounted for £4.80 a week, £1.90 was spent on admissions to the cinema, theatre and museums etc, and £3.20 was spent on gambling payments. On average, £4.80 was spent per week on TV, video and computers, a slight decrease from expenditure of £5.40 per week in 2007 (Table A1).

Of the £50.70 spent on food and non-alcoholic drinks each week, £10.90 was spent on meat, £3.70 on fresh vegetables, £3.00 on fresh fruit, and £4.00 on non-alcoholic drinks (Table A1). Almost three-quarters (72 per cent, £36.50 per week) of food and non-alcoholic drinks were purchased from large supermarket chains (Table A3).

Alcohol bought and consumed on licensed premises accounted for slightly more than half (54 per cent, £7.20) of all expenditure on alcoholic drink (£13.40 per week). The remaining £6.20 was spent on alcohol bought at large supermarket chains or off-licence outlets (Table A2).

Household expenditure by income

Household incomes have been ranked in ascending order and divided into decile groups, with households with the lowest income in the first decile group, in order to examine expenditure patterns between different income groups. Average weekly household expenditure ranged from £153.70 in the lowest of the ten income decile groups to £1044.90 in the highest (Figure 1.1, Table A6).

Figure 1.1

Household expenditure by gross income decile group, 2008

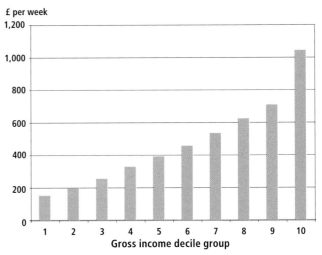

Households in the lowest income decile groups spent a larger proportion of their expenditure on housing, fuel and power (24 per cent), and food and non-alcoholic drinks (17 per cent), than those in the highest income decile groups, 7 and 8 per cent respectively (Table A7). However, households in the highest income decile group spent almost twice as much (15 per cent) on transport than those in the lowest gross income decile group (8 per cent) (Table A7).

Household expenditure by age

Average weekly expenditure varied significantly by the age of the Household Reference Person (HRP). Households whose HRP was aged 30 to 49 years had the highest average expenditure (£581.90 per week) while those with an HRP aged 75 years and over had the lowest average household expenditure (£216.80 per week). It should be noted that households with an HRP aged 30 to 49 years contained an average of 3.0 people, compared with 1.4 among households with a HRP aged 75 years and over (Table A11).

The proportion of spending on food and non-alcoholic drinks increased with the age of the HRP, from 9 per cent among households with an HRP aged less than 30 years to 16 per cent among households with an HRP aged 75 years and over. The pattern was reversed for spending on restaurants and hotels where the proportion of spending fell from 9 per cent of all weekly expenditure among households with an HRP aged less than 30 years, to 6 per cent among households with an HRP aged 75 and over. Expenditure on recreation and culture, as a proportion of total spending, increased from 9 per cent among households with an HRP aged less than 30 years to a maximum of 18 per cent among households with an HRP aged 65 to 74 years (Figure 1.2, Table A12).

Figure 1.2

Expenditure on selected items as a proportion of total spending by age of the HRP, 2008

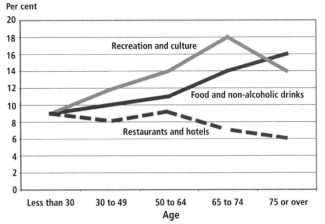

Household expenditure by economic activity and socio-economic classification

This analysis uses the National Statistics Socio-Economic Classification (NS-SEC), see Appendix B, page 192.

Average weekly expenditure of households where the HRP was in employment (£590.20 per week) was more than twice that of households where the HRP was unemployed or economically inactive (£263.50 and £288.90 per week respectively) (Table A19).

The items households spent most on also varied by the economic activity of the HRP. In households where the HRP was in employment, spending was greatest on transport, and recreation and culture, at £84.20 and £71.10 per week. Among households where the HRP was unemployed, spending on housing, fuel and power was highest (£46.70 per week) followed by food and non-alcoholic drinks (£35.10 per week) (Table A19).

Average weekly expenditure was greater among households where the HRP was in the 'large employers and higher managerial' occupational group, at £900.30 per week. This compared with £386.00 in households where the HRP was in a 'routine' occupation (Table A24).

Household expenditure by household composition

As would be expected, household expenditure generally increased with the size of the household. Thus, average weekly household expenditure was highest among households with two adults and three or more children (£802.00) and lowest among retired one-person households who were mainly dependent on the state pension (£145.70) (Table A25).

Household expenditure by region

Overall, average household expenditure in the UK was £459.70 per week for 2006-2008. There were five regions in which expenditure over this period was higher than the UK average: London, where weekly expenditure was greatest at £544.70, the South East (£512.30), the East (£493.40), Northern Ireland (£479.70) and the South West (£469.20). Spending was lowest among households in the North East (£386.10 per week) (Figure 1.3, Table A35).

Figure 1.3

Household expenditure by region, 2006 to 2008

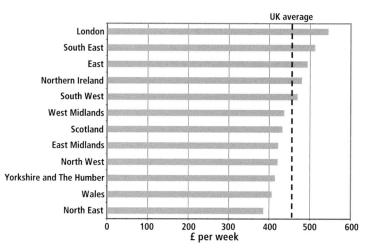

Table A37 shows that spending on transport was highest among households in the South East (£76.40 per week) and lowest among those in the North East (£49.70 per week).

Households in London spent the most on housing, fuel and power, £73.90 a week, compared with the UK national average of £50.80 a week (Table A37). Housing expenditure is looked at in more detail in chapter two.

Households in Northern Ireland and Scotland reported the highest expenditure on cigarettes at £7.50 and £5.10 a week respectively (Table A37).

Households in rural areas had higher overall expenditure (£505.40 per week) than those living in urban areas (£446.70 per week). However, the proportions of household expenditure were comparable, with highest expenditure on transport of £58.10 in urban areas and £76.10 in rural areas, followed by recreation and culture (at £56.00 and £67.40 respectively) (Table A38).

Figure 1.4

Percentage of gross weekly household income by source of income, 2008

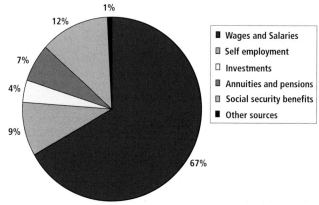

Legend:
- Wages and Salaries
- Self employment
- Investments
- Annuities and pensions
- Social security benefits
- Other sources

Household income by age

On the whole, households with a younger household reference person (HRP) had a higher gross income than their elders, with a maximum of £945 a week among households with an HRP aged 30 to 49. The exception to this is households with a HRP aged less than 30 who had a gross income of £600 per week. Of the £945.00, 78 per cent was obtained through wages and salaries. Households with an HRP aged 75 and over had a lower gross income (£290) with 57 per cent of their income gained through social security benefits (Table A41).

Household income by region

The three regions exceeding the 2006–2008 UK average income of £669 per week were London (£900), the South East (£783) and the East (£712). Overall households in England had the highest gross weekly household income (£683) when classified by UK country, whereas those in Wales had the lowest average income at £570 per week (Table A44).

Income was lowest among households in the North East (£538), who receive the highest proportion of social security benefits (17 per cent) of all the UK regions.

Household income by economic activity and socio-economic classification

Households where the HRP was in the 'large employers and higher managerial' occupational group had an average gross household income of £1,985 a week, more than three times the income of households where the HRP worked in a 'routine' occupation (£544). Whilst the largest proportion of these incomes were gained from wages and salaries (85 and 83 per cent respectively), households with an HRP in the 'long-term unemployed' occupational group obtained 61 per cent of their average gross weekly household income (£285) from social security benefits (Table A46).

Ownership of durable goods

Overall 72 per cent of all households had a home computer and 66 per cent an internet connection. Among households in the highest income group, 98 per cent had a home computer and 96 per cent an internet connection, compared with only 33 and 26 per cent of households in the lowest income group. Households with children were more likely to own a home computer and have an internet connection than those without (Table A51).

Connection to the internet was lowest among households in Northern Ireland (55 per cent) and highest in the South East (68 per cent). Ownership of a mobile phone was lowest among households in Wales (51 per cent) and highest in the East Midlands, West Midlands and South West at 84 per cent (Table A53).

Almost three-quarters (74 per cent) of all households owned a car or van, with 31 per cent owning two or more. Ownership of at least one car or van varied from 29 per cent in the lowest income group, to 96 per cent in the highest (Table A52).

Ownership of a car or van was highest among households in the East and the South West (83 per cent), and lowest among those in London (63 per cent) and the North East (66 per cent) (Table A53).

Notes

1   From 2001-02, the Classification of Individual COnsumption by Purpose (COICOP) was introduced as a new coding frame for expenditure items. COICOP is the internationally agreed classification system for reporting household consumption expenditure. Total expenditure is made up from the total of the COICOP expenditure groups (1 to 12) plus 'Other expenditure items (13)'. Other expenditure items are those items excluded from the narrower COICOP classifications, such as mortgage interest payments, council tax, domestic rates, holiday spending, cash gifts and charitable donations.

Housing expenditure

Background

This chapter presents housing-related costs, including mortgage payments, rent, council tax, home improvements, maintenance and household insurances. Household expenditure on electricity, gas and other fuels, however, is excluded. The first section describes how housing costs are classified using the Classification Of Individual COnsumption by Purpose (COICOP) system and explains why a more comprehensive definition of housing expenditure has been used for the analysis reported in this chapter. The next part examines variations in housing expenditure over time, and by income, region and household characteristics. In the final section, the housing costs for households that pay rent on their properties and for those that pay mortgages, are explored in more depth.

The COICOP definition of housing expenditure

Since 2001–02, the COICOP system has been used to classify expenditure on the Expenditure and Food Survey (EFS). The survey was renamed as the Living Costs and Food (LCF) survey in 2008. COICOP is the internationally agreed classification system for reporting household consumption expenditure within National Accounts. Having an international standard classification facilitates greater consistency between countries in the collection and presentation of data. COICOP is also used on Household Budget surveys across the European Union. These surveys collect information on household consumption expenditure, which is then used to update the weights in the basket of goods and services used in consumer price indices. More information on COICOP can be obtained from the United Nations Statistics Division website at http://unstats.un.org/unsd/cr/registry/regct.asp?Lg=1.

Under COICOP, household consumption expenditure is categorised into the following twelve headings:

1. Food & non-alcoholic drinks
2. Alcoholic drinks, tobacco & narcotics
3. Clothing & footwear
4. Housing (net), fuel & power
5. Household goods & services
6. Health
7. Transport
8. Communication
9. Recreation & culture
10. Education
11. Restaurants & hotels
12. Miscellaneous goods & services

All COICOP classified housing costs except household insurances are contained in the 'housing (net), fuel and power' category, which covers net rent; dwelling maintenance and repair; and water and other service charges. It is important to note, however, that COICOP excludes certain housing-related costs that are considered to be non-consumption expenditure. These costs include mortgage interest payments; capital repayment of mortgages; council tax; domestic rates; housing alterations and improvements; and outright purchases of dwellings.

In addition to the twelve COICOP expenditure categories, the Family Spending tables contained in Appendix A include a category called 'other expenditure items' under which certain non-consumption expenditures can be found. This category includes the following housing-related costs: mortgage interest payments; mortgage protection premiums; council tax; and domestic rates. Housing costs that are not included in either the COICOP definition of housing or the 'other expenditure item' category are captured within the 'other items recorded' category that can be viewed in Table A1 in Appendix A.

For the analysis reported in this chapter all data relating to housing expenditure have been combined in order to facilitate an understanding of total housing costs. The comprehensive definition of housing used for the analysis has therefore been built up from three elements of housing costs:

- Those included within COICOP
- Those included in the 'other expenditure items' Family Spending category
- Those included in the 'other items recorded' category

Table 2.1 shows how the comprehensive definition of housing expenditure has been built up from these elements.

Analysis

The first part of the analysis examined changes in housing expenditure over time and then looked at the variation in housing costs according to region, income, age of the household reference person (HRP) and the socio-economic status of the HRP. For this analysis, expenditure has been averaged over all households, including those reporting nil expenditure on the item in question. All households are therefore deemed to pay a proportion of all housing costs. The impact of this is that all households have been included to calculate average rent and mortgage payments, despite the fact that they are only actually likely to pay one or the other. In order to address this issue, an additional analysis was conducted that examined the expenditure of renters and mortgage payers. The results of this analysis are presented in the last section of the chapter.

Table 2.1

Definition of total housing expenditure

Housing costs which are included in the COICOP classification:

- Actual rentals for housing
  - net rent (gross rent less housing benefit, rebates and allowances received)
  - second dwelling rent
- Maintenance and repair of dwelling
  - central heating maintenance and repair
  - house maintenance and repair
  - paint, wallpaper, timber
  - equipment hire, small materials

- Water supply and miscellaneous services relating to dwelling
  - water charges
  - other regular housing payments including service charge for rent
  - refuse collection, including skip hire
- Household Insurances
  - structural insurance
  - contents insurance
  - insurance for household appliances

Housing costs which are included as 'other expenditure items':

- Housing: mortgage interest payments etc
  - mortgage interest payments
  - mortgage protection premiums
  - council tax, domestic rates
  - council tax, mortgage, insurance (second dwelling)

Housing costs which are not treated as consumption expenditure but which are included here:

- Purchase or alteration of dwellings (contracted out), mortgages
  - outright purchase of houses, flats etc including deposits
  - capital repayment of mortgage
  - central heating installation
  - DIY improvements: double glazing, kitchen units, sheds etc
  - home improvements (contracted out)
  - bathroom fittings
  - purchase of materials for capital improvements
  - purchase of second dwelling

Results

Table 2.2 shows expenditure on the costs included in the comprehensive definition of housing. It also displays total household expenditure, which includes all expenditure items covered by the survey. The total expenditure figure reported here is therefore greater than the expenditure totals shown in the tables in Appendix A, as these exclude certain non-consumption costs. It should also be noted that throughout Family Spending, including this chapter, rent excluding service charges and benefit receipts associated with housing has been used when calculating total expenditure. This convention ensures that rebates, benefits and allowances are excluded from the calculation of total household expenditure on rent.

Under the comprehensive definition of housing, UK households spent on average £143.40 a week on housing in 2008, which equates to just over a fifth (21 per cent) of all weekly expenditure. The narrower COICOP definition of housing incorporated within the 'housing, fuel and power' category gave an average of £34.10 a week on housing (this excludes expenditure on fuel and power) for each household (see Table A1 in Appendix A).

In 2008 spending was highest on mortgages (interest payments, protection premiums and capital repayments) at £57.20 a week, with the next highest expenditure on charges (council tax or domestic rates, water charges, refuse collection and other regular services) at £25.90 a week. This was followed closely by household alterations and improvements at £22.10 per week and net rent at £19.40.

Housing expenditure over time

Table 2.2 provides a comparison of housing costs over the period 2006 to 2008. Expenditure on housing has increased slightly over the past three years, from £138.70 per week in 2006 to £143.40 in 2008. However, spending on housing as a proportion of total household expenditure has remained relatively constant over this period, with housing accounting for just over a fifth of total expenditure in each year.

Figure 2.1 displays the average weekly spend on each category of housing expenditure, over the period 2006 to 2008. The greatest increase was seen in the mortgages category, where spending grew from £47.50 per week in 2006 to £53.30 in 2007, and then grew again to £57.20 in 2008. The average weekly spend on net rent has also risen slightly, from £16.80 per week in 2006 to £19.40 in 2008.

2

Figure 2.1

Housing expenditure 2006 to 2008

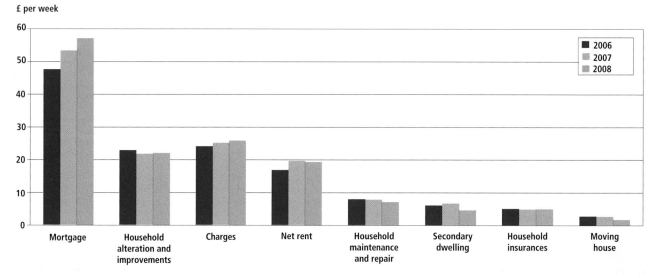

£ per week

Legend: ■ 2006 ■ 2007 ■ 2008

Categories: Mortgage, Household alteration and improvements, Charges, Net rent, Household maintenance and repair, Secondary dwelling, Household insurances, Moving house

Expenditure by gross income

Table 2.3 shows expenditure on housing by gross income decile group. Overall, spending on housing increased with income. The highest income group spent £327.60 per week on housing; more than double the average weekly expenditure for all households (£143.40), and more than eight times that of the lowest income group, who spent £38.40.

The variation in spending on housing according to income was largely due to differences between the income decile groups in terms of expenditure on mortgages, and on household alterations and improvements. Figure 2.2 shows that spending on mortgages increased sharply with income, from £4.20 and £4.00 per week among households in the first (lowest) and second income decile groups to £159.50 among those in the highest income decile group. The pattern was similar for expenditure on household alterations and improvements – the average weekly spend for households in the lowest income group was £2.20 a week compared with £55.60 for those in the highest income decile group.

Expenditure on household maintenance and repair, and on household insurances also increased with income, although the differences between the income groups were less marked for these items. Spending on net rent, however, did not follow this pattern. Households in the ninth (second highest) income group spent the least on net rent at £12.60 per week while households in the eighth (third highest), sixth and fifth income decile groups spent the most (£23.10, £23.00 and £22.80 respectively).

Figure 2.2

Expenditure on selected items by gross income decile group, 2008

£ per week

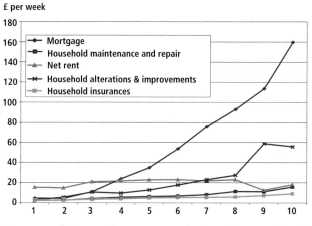

Legend:
- Mortgage
- Household maintenance and repair
- Net rent
- Household alterations & improvements
- Household insurances

Expenditure by age of the household reference person

Figure 2.3 displays the average weekly spend on the top five housing expenditures, by the age of the HRP. Expenditure on net rent declined sharply with age, from £51.70 among households with an HRP under the age of 30 to £7.10 among households with an HRP aged 75 and over. Spending on mortgages, however, followed a different pattern - households with an HRP aged 30 to 49 spent the most on mortgages at £101.80 per week, followed by those with an HRP under 30 (£63.00), while households with an HRP in the 75 and over age group spent the least at 70p per week.

Expenditure on household alterations and improvements was lowest among households with an HRP in the youngest and the oldest age groups (£8.10 for both the under 30 and 75 and over age groups) with these households spending less than half the UK average, which was £22.10 per week. Households with an HRP in the youngest and oldest age groups also spent the least on charges, and on household maintenance and repair, although the pattern was less pronounced for these items.

Figure 2.6 shows that households living in London spent the most on mortgages at £75.80 per week, a third more than the UK average of £57.20. Expenditure on mortgages was also higher than the UK average in following regions: the South East where households spent 27 per cent more (£72.70); the

Figure 2.3
Expenditure on selected items by age of household reference person, 2008

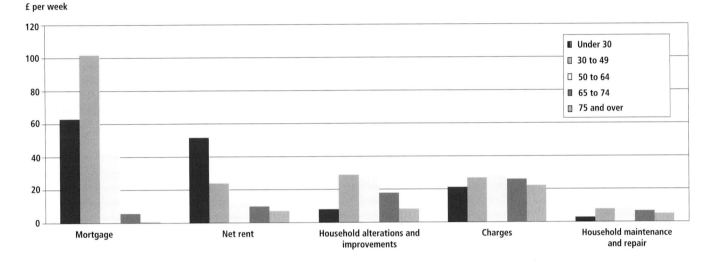

£ per week

Expenditure by region

Table 2.5 and Figure 2.4 show housing expenditure by UK country and Government Office Region. Looking first at expenditure by country, households in Northern Ireland spent the least on housing at £101.80 per week, followed by Wales (£106.30), Scotland (£119.50) and England (£149.70).

There were four regions in England in which households spent more on housing than the UK average of £143.40 per week: London, where expenditure on housing was greatest at £189.50 per week; the South East (£172.30); the East (£168.40) and the West Midlands (£146.40). Expenditure on housing was lower than the UK average for all remaining areas of England.

The regional variation in total spending on housing was largely due to differences between the regions in the average amount spent on rent and mortgages. As shown in Figure 2.5, households in London spent the most on net rent at £43.80 per week, which was 126 per cent more than the UK average of £19.40. The South East had the second highest expenditure on net rent at £24.40, which was 26 per cent more than the UK average. Spending on net rent was lowest in Wales where households spent £12.30 per week (37 per cent less than the UK average), closely followed by the North West of England where households spent £12.60 per week (35 per cent less than the UK average).

East of England where households spent eight per cent more (£61.50); and the West Midlands where households spent four per cent more (£59.30). All other regions spent less on mortgages than the UK average. Expenditure was lowest in Wales, where mortgage costs averaged £39.20 a week, which is just under a third less than the UK average.

Figure 2.4
Housing expenditure by region, 2008

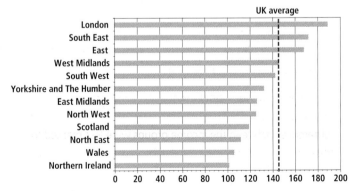

Figure 2.5
Percentage difference compared with UK average for net rent by UK Countries and Government Office Regions, 2008

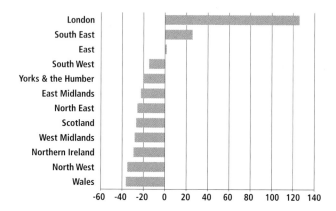

among households classified as 'large employers and managerial'. Expenditure on net rent, however, followed the reverse pattern; households in the 'routine' category spent £37.40 per week on net rent, which was 57 per cent more than the amount spent by households in the 'large employers and higher managerial' group (£23.80).

Figure 2.6
Percentage difference compared with UK average for mortgage payments by UK Countries and Government Office Regions, 2008

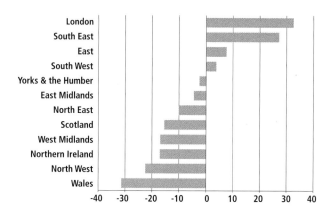

Expenditure by socio-economic classification

Table 2.6 and Figure 2.7 show expenditure on housing by the socio-economic classification of the household reference person (HRP). Households with an HRP in the 'large employers and higher managerial' occupational category spent the most on housing at £309.00 per week, which was more than double the amount spent by households containing a HRP in the 'routine' occupational group (£129.80).

Figure 2.8 shows the average weekly spend on the top five housing expenditures for five different socio-economic groups. Overall, the variation in spending according to socio-economic classification was similar to that described for total expenditure on housing. This pattern was marked for spending on mortgages, where expenditure ranged from £42.70 among households with an HRP in the 'routine' category to £145.10

Figure 2.7
Housing expenditure by socio-economic classification of household reference person, 2008

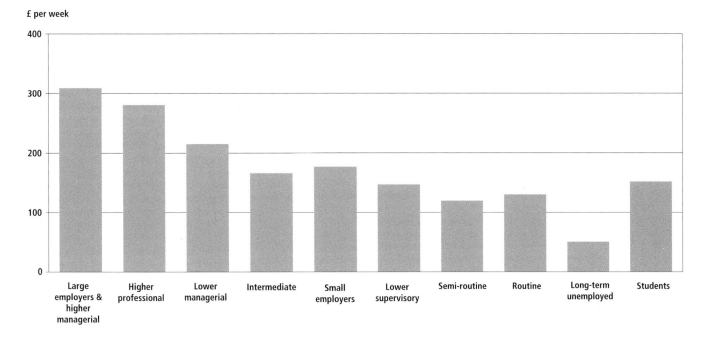

£ per week

Figure 2.8
Expenditure on selected items by socio-economic classification of household reference person, 2008

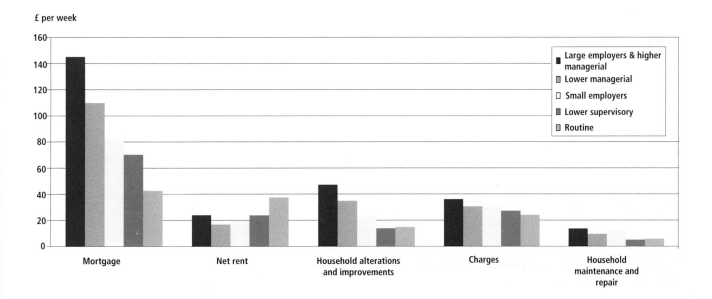

£ per week

Analysis of housing costs for renters and mortgage holders

An additional analysis was conducted on the data relating to expenditure on rent by renters, and on mortgages by mortgage holders. The objective of this analysis was to produce more informative estimates of how much households actually spend on their rent or mortgage each week. This is the only occasion in the Family Spending publication where expenditure has been averaged over just those households that spend money on the item concerned; all other figures in Family Spending are shown as averages across all households.

Table 2.8 shows expenditure on rent for the 1,610 households in the 2008 sample that paid rent while Table 2.9 shows mortgage costs for the 2,210 households that paid mortgages. The analysis showed that among households paying rent, the average net rent across the UK was £66.30 a week. For households paying mortgages, the average weekly spend on mortgage-related costs was £148.50.

Table 2.10 shows the recalculated amounts spent on net rent and mortgages, by income decile group. The analysis based on renters revealed a more consistent pattern of variation in net rent by income level than the analysis that included all households. Expenditure on net rent increased progressively with income from £24.00 among households in the lowest (first) decile group to £301.50 among those in the highest (tenth) decile group. It should be noted, however, that a relatively small number of households in the highest income decile group pay rent. The estimate of net rent costs for this income group should therefore be viewed with caution.

Excluding households in the first (lowest) income decile group, weekly expenditure on mortgages increased with income, from £74.60 among households in the second (second lowest) decile group to £223.10 among those in the tenth (highest) income decile group. The estimate of mortgage costs for the first income decile group should be used with caution due to the low number of households who pay for a mortgage in this group and has therefore been excluded from the discussion of the results.

Table 2.11 and Figure 2.9 show expenditure on net rent among renters by UK Countries and Government Office Regions. Similar to the analysis of all households, London had the greatest expenditure on net rent at £105.10 per week, followed by the South East at £84.00 and the East at £76.90. As in the earlier analysis, spending on net rent fell below the UK average for all other regions. Among households paying rent, average net rent was lowest in the North East at £45.10 per week, followed by the North West at £46.70.

The analysis of mortgage costs for households paying mortgages revealed a similar pattern to the analysis of all households. The most expensive regions for mortgage holders remained London (£216.10), the South East (£186.20) and the East (£165.20). Wales remained the area with the lowest expenditure on mortgages at £110 per week, followed by Yorkshire and the Humber at £114.80.

Figure 2.9
Expenditure on net rent[1] by UK Countries and GORs, 2008

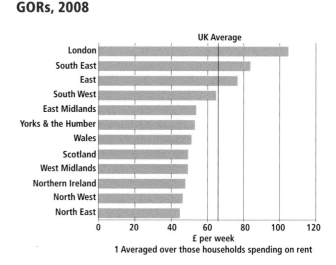

1 Averaged over those households spending on rent

Figure 2.10
Expenditure on mortgages[1] by UK Countries and GORs, 2008

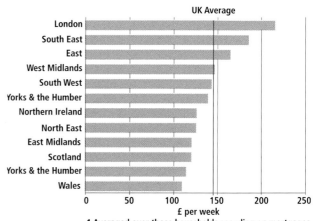

1 Averaged over those households spending on mortgages

Table 2.2

Housing expenditure, 2006 to 2008

	2006			2007			2008		
	£ per week	% of total expend-iture	% of housing expend-iture	£ per week	% of total expend-iture	% of housing expend-iture	£ per week	% of total expend-iture	% of housing expend-iture
Weighted number of households (thousands)	25,440			25,350			25,690		
Total number of households in sample	6,650			6,140			5,850		
Total number of persons in sample	15,850			14,650			13,830		
Total number of adults in sample	12,000			11,220			10,640		
Weighted average number of persons per household	2.3			2.4			2.4		
Commodity or service	Average weekly household expenditure (£)								
Primary dwelling									
Rent	**28.20**	*4*	*20*	**31.40**	*5*	*22*	**31.50**	**5**	**22**
Gross rent	28.20	4	20	31.40	5	22	31.50	5	22
less housing benefit, rebates and allowances received	11.40	2	8	11.80	2	8	12.10	2	8
Net rent[1]	16.80	3	12	19.60	3	14	19.40	3	14
Mortgage	**47.50**	*7*	*34*	**53.30**	*8*	*38*	**57.20**	**8**	**40**
Mortgage interest payments[2]	30.50	5	22	35.60	5	25	37.50	6	26
Mortgage protection premiums	1.80	0	1	1.80	0	1	1.90	0	1
Capital repayment of mortgage[3]	15.30	2	11	15.80	2	11	17.80	3	12
Outright purchase, including deposits	**[5.70]**	*1*	*4*	**[0.20]**	*0*	*0*	**[0.10]**	**0**	**0**
Secondary dwelling	**6.10**	*1*	*4*	**6.60**	*1*	*5*	**4.70**	**1**	**3**
Rent	[0.10]	0	0	[0.00]	0	0	[0.10]	0	0
Council tax, mortgage, insurance (secondary dwelling)	0.40	0	0	0.50	0	0	0.50	0	0
Purchase of second dwelling	5.60	1	4	6.10	1	4	4.10	1	3
Charges	**24.00**	*4*	*17*	**25.10**	*4*	*18*	**25.90**	**4**	**18**
Council tax, domestic rates	17.10	3	12	17.90	3	13	18.50	3	13
Water charges	5.60	1	4	6.00	1	4	6.30	1	4
Other regular housing payments including service charge for rent	1.20	0	1	1.20	0	1	1.10	0	1
Refuse collection, including skip hire	[0.10]	0	0	[0.10]	0	0	[0.10]	0	0
Moving house	**2.80**	*0*	*2*	**2.70**	*0*	*2*	**1.80**	**0**	**1**
Property transaction - purchase and sale	1.40	0	1	1.30	0	1	0.90	0	1
Property transaction - sale only	0.60	0	0	0.60	0	0	0.40	0	0
Property transaction - purchase only	0.60	0	0	0.60	0	0	0.30	0	0
Property transaction - other payments	0.20	0	0	0.20	0	0	0.20	0	0
Household maintenance and repair	**7.90**	*1*	*6*	**7.80**	*1*	*6*	**7.20**	**1**	**5**
Central heating repairs	1.20	0	1	1.20	0	1	1.50	0	1
House maintenance etc.	5.00	1	4	4.60	1	3	3.90	1	3
Paint, wallpaper, timber	1.00	0	1	1.20	0	1	0.90	0	1
Equipment hire, small materials	0.80	0	1	0.80	0	1	0.90	0	1
Household alterations and improvements	**22.80**	*4*	*16*	**21.70**	*3*	*15*	**22.10**	**3**	**15**
Central heating installation	1.00	0	1	1.10	0	1	1.20	0	1
DIY improvements: Double Glazing, Kitchen Units, Sheds etc.	1.20	0	1	1.60	0	1	1.60	0	1
Home improvements - contracted out	19.40	3	14	17.70	3	12	18.10	3	13
Bathroom fittings	0.50	0	0	0.70	0	0	0.50	0	0
Purchase of materials for Capital Improvements	0.80	0	1	0.60	0	0	0.80	0	1
Household insurances	**5.10**	*1*	*4*	**4.90**	*1*	*3*	**5.00**	**1**	**4**
Structure	2.50	0	2	2.40	0	2	2.50	0	2
Contents	2.50	0	2	2.40	0	2	2.50	0	2
Household appliances	0.10	0	0	0.10	0	0	0.10	0	0
Housing expenditure	**138.70**	*21*	*100*	**142.00**	*22*	*100*	**143.40**	**21**	**100**
Total expenditure[4]	**646.60**			**656.40**			**674.10**		

Note: Please see page xiii for symbols and conventions used in this report.

1 The figure included in total expenditure is net rent as opposed to gross rent.

2 An improvement to the imputation of mortgage interest payments has been implemented for 2006 and 2007 data which should lead to more accurate figures. This will lead to a slight discontinuity.

3 An error was discovered in the derivation of mortgage capital repayments which was leading to double counting. This has been amended for the 2006 and 2007 data.

4 This total includes all categories recorded in the LCF, including those outside the 'COICOP' total expenditure

Table 2.3
Housing expenditure by gross income decile group, 2008

	Gross income decile group										
	1	2	3	4	5	6	7	8	9	10	All
Weighted number of households (thousands)	2,570	2,570	2,570	2,570	2,570	2,570	2,570	2,560	2,570	2,560	25,690
Total number of households in sample	550	580	610	630	590	600	590	570	550	580	5,850
Total number of persons in sample	710	970	1,130	1,320	1,380	1,520	1,620	1,640	1,680	1,860	13,830
Total number of adults in sample	600	770	920	1,040	1,070	1,160	1,190	1,240	1,280	1,380	10,640
Weighted average number of persons per household	1.3	1.7	1.8	2.1	2.3	2.5	2.8	2.8	3.1	3.2	2.4
Commodity or service	Average weekly household expenditure (£)										
Primary dwelling											
Rent	**63.40**	**47.90**	**42.00**	**32.50**	**27.40**	**24.10**	**22.70**	**24.20**	**12.70**	**18.30**	**31.50**
Gross rent	63.40	47.90	42.00	32.50	27.40	24.10	22.70	24.20	12.70	18.30	31.50
less housing benefit, rebates and allowances received	48.00	33.20	21.20	10.90	4.60	1.10	0.90	[1.10]	[0.10]	[0.30]	12.10
Net rent[1]	15.40	14.70	20.90	21.60	22.80	23.00	21.80	23.10	12.60	18.00	19.40
Mortgage	**4.20**	**4.00**	**10.60**	**23.50**	**34.60**	**53.50**	**75.60**	**93.00**	**113.30**	**159.50**	**57.20**
Mortgage interest payments	2.70	2.40	6.20	15.10	21.70	33.40	49.70	61.80	76.10	105.90	37.50
Mortgage protection premiums	[0.10]	[0.10]	0.40	0.90	1.50	1.90	2.80	3.20	4.00	3.70	1.90
Capital repayment of mortgage	[1.40]	1.50	4.10	7.40	11.40	18.20	23.10	28.00	33.20	49.90	17.80
Outright purchase, including deposits	–	–	–	–	–	[0.70]	–	[0.20]	[0.10]	[0.10]	[0.10]
Secondary dwelling	–	[0.10]	[0.20]	[0.20]	[0.50]	[0.30]	[0.40]	[13.20]	4.30	27.90	4.70
Rent	–	–	–	–	–	–	[0.00]	[0.10]	–	[0.70]	[0.10]
Council tax, mortgage, insurance (secondary dwelling)	–	[0.10]	[0.20]	[0.20]	[0.10]	[0.00]	[0.40]	[0.00]	[1.10]	[3.30]	0.50
Purchase of second dwelling	–	–	[0.00]	–	[0.40]	[0.30]	[0.10]	[13.10]	[3.20]	23.90	4.10
Charges	**12.10**	**16.00**	**20.80**	**24.60**	**26.10**	**28.10**	**29.00**	**31.00**	**33.00**	**38.70**	**25.90**
Council tax, domestic rates	6.30	9.50	13.30	17.20	18.70	20.60	21.50	23.30	24.80	29.80	18.50
Water charges	4.90	5.40	5.70	6.10	6.20	6.30	6.50	6.70	7.20	7.70	6.30
Other regular housing payments including service charge for rent	0.90	1.00	1.70	1.20	1.10	1.00	0.90	0.70	1.10	1.10	1.10
Refuse collection, including skip hire	–	[0.00]	[0.00]	–	[0.20]	[0.20]	–	[0.30]	[0.00]	[0.20]	[0.10]
Moving house	**[0.20]**	**[1.30]**	**[1.20]**	**[1.20]**	**[1.10]**	**1.40**	**1.90**	**4.00**	**2.60**	**3.20**	**1.80**
Property transaction - purchase and sale	[0.10]	[1.20]	[0.50]	[0.70]	[0.50]	[0.40]	[1.00]	2.20	[1.30]	[1.40]	0.90
Property transaction - sale only	[0.00]	[0.00]	[0.40]	[0.40]	[0.20]	[0.30]	[0.30]	[0.90]	[0.50]	[0.60]	0.40
Property transaction - purchase only	–	–	[0.20]	[0.10]	[0.20]	[0.60]	[0.40]	[0.40]	[0.50]	[0.70]	0.30
Property transaction - other payments	[0.10]	[0.00]	[0.00]	[0.00]	[0.10]	[0.10]	[0.20]	[0.50]	[0.30]	[0.50]	0.20
Household maintenance and repair	**2.10**	**2.50**	**3.90**	**5.20**	**6.00**	**6.60**	**7.90**	**11.20**	**11.00**	**15.60**	**7.20**
Central heating repairs	0.80	0.80	0.80	1.20	1.20	1.50	1.30	1.50	2.50	3.10	1.50
House maintenance etc.	1.10	1.10	1.50	2.70	3.10	3.90	4.80	6.00	5.70	9.20	3.90
Paint, wallpaper, timber	[0.20]	0.40	0.90	0.40	0.80	0.70	1.10	1.60	1.40	1.50	0.90
Equipment hire, small materials	[0.10]	0.20	0.60	0.90	0.80	0.50	0.70	2.00	1.40	1.80	0.90
Household alterations and improvements	**2.20**	**5.20**	**10.20**	**9.30**	**12.50**	**17.40**	**22.70**	**27.20**	**58.60**	**55.60**	**22.10**
Central heating installation	[0.00]	[0.20]	[0.50]	[0.70]	[1.20]	[0.50]	[3.20]	1.70	1.90	[1.60]	1.20
DIY improvements: double glazing, kitchen units, sheds etc.	–	[0.00]	[0.80]	[0.10]	[0.40]	[1.00]	[1.10]	[1.90]	[9.50]	[0.90]	1.60
Home improvements - contracted out	1.00	4.40	8.40	8.20	8.60	14.40	17.30	23.00	44.00	51.20	18.10
Bathroom fittings	[0.00]	[0.10]	[0.30]	[0.20]	[0.60]	[0.00]	[0.90]	[0.50]	[0.80]	[1.30]	0.50
Purchase of materials for capital improvements	[1.10]	[0.50]	[0.20]	[0.00]	[1.80]	[1.40]	[0.30]	[0.20]	[2.40]	[0.50]	0.80
Household insurances	**2.10**	**2.80**	**3.40**	**4.00**	**4.90**	**5.30**	**5.50**	**6.00**	**7.40**	**9.10**	**5.00**
Structure	0.80	1.30	1.60	1.90	2.20	2.70	2.70	3.00	3.90	4.60	2.50
Contents	1.30	1.40	1.70	2.10	2.40	2.60	2.70	2.90	3.40	4.40	2.50
Household appliances	[0.00]	[0.00]	[0.10]	[0.00]	[0.30]	[0.00]	[0.10]	[0.10]	[0.10]	[0.10]	0.10
Housing expenditure	**38.40**	**46.60**	**71.30**	**89.60**	**108.40**	**136.30**	**164.80**	**208.70**	**242.80**	**327.60**	**143.40**
Total expenditure[2]	**160.90**	**219.70**	**291.90**	**388.20**	**491.50**	**608.90**	**741.20**	**908.80**	**1103.00**	**1828.60**	**674.10**

Note: Please see page xiii for symbols and conventions used in this report.
1 The figure included in total expenditure is net rent as opposed to gross rent.
2 This total includes all categories recorded in the LCF, including those outside the 'COICOP' total expenditure.

Table 2.4

Housing expenditure by age of household reference person, 2008

	Under 30	30 to 49	50 to 64	65 to 74	75 or Over	All
Weighted number of households (thousands)	2,530	9,740	6,750	3,140	3,520	25,690
Total number of households in sample	460	2,230	1,590	810	760	5,850
Total number of persons in sample	1,120	6,710	3,480	1,410	1,120	13,830
Total number of adults in sample	800	4,170	3,160	1,390	1,110	10,640
Weighted average number of persons per household	2.4	3.0	2.3	1.8	1.4	2.4
Commodity or service	Average weekly household expenditure (£)					
Primary dwelling						
Rent	**71.00**	**35.40**	**20.90**	**21.50**	**21.70**	**31.50**
Gross rent	71.00	35.40	20.90	21.50	21.70	31.50
less housing benefit, rebates and allowances received	19.30	11.40	9.40	11.60	14.70	12.10
Net rent[1]	51.70	24.00	11.50	9.90	7.10	19.40
Mortgage	**63.00**	**101.80**	**43.90**	**5.70**	**0.70**	**57.20**
Mortgage interest payments	47.40	68.20	24.70	3.40	[0.40]	37.50
Mortgage protection premiums	2.00	3.40	1.40	[0.20]	[0.00]	1.90
Capital repayment of mortgage	13.60	30.20	17.90	2.20	[0.30]	17.80
Outright purchase, including deposits	**[0.20]**	**[0.20]**	**[0.00]**	–	–	**[0.10]**
Secondary dwelling	**[0.20]**	**6.20**	**8.70**	**[0.30]**	**[0.10]**	**4.70**
Rent	–	[0.00]	[0.30]	–	–	[0.10]
Council tax, mortgage, insurance (secondary dwelling)	[0.10]	[1.00]	[0.50]	[0.00]	[0.10]	0.50
Purchase of second dwelling	[0.10]	5.20	[7.90]	[0.20]	–	4.10
Charges	**21.30**	**27.00**	**28.10**	**26.00**	**22.10**	**25.90**
Council tax, domestic rates	14.40	19.50	20.80	18.50	14.50	18.50
Water charges	5.80	6.60	6.60	6.00	5.40	6.30
Other regular housing payments including service charge for rent	1.00	0.80	0.60	1.50	2.20	1.10
Refuse collection, including skip hire	[0.10]	[0.10]	[0.10]	[0.00]	[0.00]	[0.10]
Moving house	**2.70**	**2.40**	**1.60**	**[1.00]**	**[0.50]**	**1.80**
Property transaction - purchase and sale	[1.30]	1.30	[0.90]	[0.60]	[0.20]	0.90
Property transaction - sale only	[0.50]	0.40	[0.30]	[0.30]	[0.30]	0.40
Property transaction - purchase only	[0.70]	0.50	[0.20]	[0.00]	[0.00]	0.30
Property transaction - other payments	[0.20]	0.20	[0.20]	[0.10]	[0.00]	0.20
Household maintenance and repair	**3.10**	**8.10**	**8.80**	**6.70**	**5.00**	**7.20**
Central heating repairs	0.20	1.30	2.00	1.60	1.80	1.50
House maintenance etc.	1.50	4.10	5.20	4.00	2.60	3.90
Paint, wallpaper, timber	0.80	1.20	1.00	0.70	[0.20]	0.90
Equipment hire, small materials	[0.50]	1.50	0.70	0.40	0.40	0.90
Household alterations and improvements	**8.10**	**28.90**	**26.70**	**17.80**	**8.10**	**22.10**
Central heating installation	[0.50]	1.00	1.10	[2.70]	[0.80]	1.20
DIY improvements: double glazing, kitchen units, sheds etc.	[0.10]	1.50	3.20	[0.60]	[0.60]	1.60
Home improvements - contracted out	6.40	24.80	20.80	13.40	6.60	18.10
Bathroom fittings	[0.10]	0.60	0.40	[1.10]	[0.20]	0.50
Purchase of materials for capital improvements	[1.00]	[1.00]	1.30	[0.00]	[0.00]	0.80
Household insurances	**2.80**	**5.40**	**5.80**	**4.90**	**4.00**	**5.00**
Structure	1.20	2.70	2.90	2.40	1.90	2.50
Contents	1.60	2.70	2.80	2.30	2.00	2.50
Household appliances	[0.00]	0.10	0.10	[0.20]	[0.10]	0.10
Housing expenditure	**153.10**	**204.00**	**135.40**	**72.20**	**47.70**	**143.40**
Total expenditure[2]	**585.70**	**877.70**	**750.70**	**427.70**	**246.90**	**674.10**

Note: Please see page xiii for symbols and conventions used in this report.

1 The figure included in total expenditure is net rent as opposed to gross rent.

2 This total includes all categories recorded in the LCF, including those outside the 'COICOP' total expenditure.

Table 2.5

Household expenditure by UK Countries and Government Office Region, 2008

	North East	North West	Yorkshire and the Humber	East Midlands	West Midlands	East	London
Grossed number of households (thousands)	1,260	3,110	2,090	1,970	2,160	2,160	3,040
Total number of households in sample	240	590	490	410	470	530	470
Total number of persons in sample	550	1,420	1,160	970	1,140	1,270	1,130
Total number of adults in sample	420	1,060	880	730	870	960	860
Weighted average number of persons per household	2.4	2.4	2.3	2.4	2.4	2.3	2.5
Commodity or service	Average weekly household expenditure (£)						
Primary dwelling							
Rent	**27.90**	**24.30**	**24.00**	**25.60**	**26.10**	**28.60**	**67.50**
Gross rent	27.90	24.30	24.00	25.60	26.10	28.60	67.50
less housing benefit, rebates and allowances received	13.50	11.70	8.60	10.60	12.20	8.90	23.70
Net rent[1]	14.40	12.60	15.40	15.00	13.90	19.70	43.80
Mortgage	**48.30**	**54.50**	**47.40**	**51.40**	**59.30**	**61.50**	**75.80**
Mortgage interest payments	30.90	33.60	30.70	33.10	35.30	41.50	53.70
Mortgage protection premiums	1.60	2.10	1.80	1.70	2.50	1.80	1.70
Capital repayment of mortgage	15.80	18.80	14.90	16.50	21.50	18.20	20.30
Outright purchase, including deposits	–	[0.10]	[0.40]	–	–	[0.00]	–
Secondary dwelling	**[1.40]**	**[1.70]**	**[16.60]**	**[1.30]**	**[12.70]**	**[12.00]**	**[1.60]**
Rent	–	[0.60]	–	[0.10]	–	–	–
Council tax, mortgage, insurance (secondary dwelling)	[0.40]	[0.40]	[0.40]	[0.70]	[0.10]	[0.20]	[1.10]
Purchase of second dwelling	[1.00]	[0.70]	[16.20]	[0.50]	[12.60]	[11.90]	[0.50]
Charges	**22.30**	**25.30**	**23.30**	**24.20**	**23.90**	**28.50**	**28.60**
Council tax, domestic rates	15.40	17.30	16.30	17.70	17.30	20.80	19.80
Water charges	6.40	7.00	6.40	6.20	6.00	6.60	5.50
Other regular housing payments including service charge for rent	[0.50]	1.00	0.50	[0.30]	0.40	1.00	3.30
Refuse collection, including skip hire	–	[0.10]	[0.20]	[0.00]	[0.10]	[0.10]	[0.00]
Moving house	**[1.20]**	**[1.70]**	**[1.00]**	**3.10**	**[1.70]**	**[2.00]**	**[1.80]**
Property transaction - purchase and sale	[1.00]	[1.20]	[0.80]	[1.90]	[0.60]	[0.70]	[1.10]
Property transaction - sale only	[0.10]	[0.30]	[0.10]	[0.50]	[0.30]	[0.70]	–
Property transaction - purchase only	[0.20]	[0.20]	[0.10]	[0.20]	[0.50]	[0.30]	[0.40]
Property transaction - other payments	[0.00]	[0.10]	[0.10]	[0.50]	[0.40]	[0.20]	[0.20]
Household maintenance and repair	**4.60**	**5.00**	**7.20**	**7.50**	**6.80**	**6.80**	**9.90**
Central heating repairs	1.40	1.40	1.80	1.70	1.30	1.30	1.20
House maintenance etc.	1.50	2.60	3.70	3.30	4.00	3.90	6.80
Paint, wallpaper, timber	1.20	0.60	1.10	1.30	0.70	1.00	0.50
Equipment hire, small materials	[0.60]	0.40	0.50	1.20	0.80	0.60	1.30
Household alterations and improvements	**15.30**	**20.10**	**16.60**	**19.10**	**22.80**	**32.60**	**23.00**
Central heating installation	[0.80]	1.10	[1.20]	[1.30]	[0.70]	[1.60]	[1.10]
DIY improvements: double glazing, kitchen units, sheds etc.	[0.20]	[1.00]	[1.50]	[0.60]	[3.80]	[6.30]	[0.20]
Home improvements - contracted out	14.10	15.70	11.90	16.40	16.70	23.50	19.60
Bathroom fittings	[0.20]	[0.90]	[0.60]	[0.80]	[0.10]	[0.20]	[0.20]
Purchase of materials for Capital Improvements	[0.10]	[1.40]	[1.30]	[0.00]	[1.50]	[1.00]	[2.00]
Household insurances	**4.70**	**4.80**	**4.90**	**5.10**	**5.30**	**5.30**	**5.00**
Structure	2.30	2.50	2.40	2.50	2.60	2.60	2.40
Contents	2.40	2.30	2.30	2.50	2.60	2.60	2.60
Household appliances	[0.00]	[0.00]	[0.20]	[0.00]	[0.00]	[0.10]	[0.00]
Housing expenditure	**112.20**	**125.80**	**132.80**	**126.60**	**146.30**	**168.40**	**189.50**
Total expenditure[2]	**519.40**	**604.70**	**581.90**	**631.00**	**662.80**	**740.60**	**860.10**

Note: Please see page xiii for symbols and conventions used in this report.

1 The figure included in total expenditure is net rent as opposed to gross rent.

2 This total includes all categories recorded in the LCF, including those outside the 'COICOP' total expenditure.

Table 2.5

Household expenditure by UK Countries and Government Office Region, 2008 (cont.)

	South East	South West	England	Wales	Scotland	Northern Ireland	United Kingdom
Weighted number of households (thousands)	2,950	2,530	21,280	1,300	2,440	670	25,690
Total number of households in sample	810	500	4,510	270	500	570	5,850
Total number of persons in sample	1,920	1,150	10,700	600	1,060	1,470	13,830
Total number of adults in sample	1,510	910	8,200	480	880	1,080	10,640
Weighted average number of persons per household	2.3	2.4	2.4	2.3	2.1	2.6	2.4

Commodity or service	Average weekly household expenditure (£)						
Primary dwelling							
Rent	**35.00**	**26.90**	**33.20**	**21.50**	**24.60**	**23.80**	**31.50**
Gross rent	35.00	26.90	33.20	21.50	24.60	23.80	31.50
less housing benefit, rebates and allowances received	10.60	10.50	12.60	9.10	10.50	10.10	12.10
Net rent[1]	24.40	16.50	20.60	12.30	14.20	13.70	19.40
Mortgage	**72.70**	**55.70**	**60.00**	**39.20**	**44.30**	**47.50**	**57.20**
Mortgage interest payments	50.60	36.20	39.60	22.70	28.90	29.20	37.50
Mortgage protection premiums	1.90	2.20	1.90	1.00	1.40	2.80	1.90
Capital repayment of mortgage	20.10	17.30	18.50	15.40	14.00	15.40	17.80
Outright purchase, including deposits	**[0.10]**	**–**	**[0.10]**	**–**	**[0.30]**	**[0.50]**	**[0.10]**
Secondary dwelling	**[3.50]**	**[1.80]**	**5.50**	**[0.10]**	**[0.90]**	**[1.40]**	**4.70**
Rent	–	[0.00]	[0.10]	-	-	[0.10]	[0.10]
Council tax, mortgage, insurance (secondary dwelling)	[1.50]	[0.20]	0.60	-	[0.10]	[0.90]	0.50
Purchase of second dwelling	[1.90]	[1.60]	4.80	[0.10]	[0.90]	[0.50]	4.10
Charges	**29.00**	**28.70**	**26.40**	**24.40**	**26.80**	**11.10**	**25.90**
Council tax, domestic rates	21.40	20.30	18.80	15.90	19.80	10.60	18.50
Water charges	6.30	7.70	6.50	7.10	6.10	[0.00]	6.30
Other regular housing payments including service charge for rent	1.10	0.70	1.10	[0.90]	0.90	0.40	1.10
Refuse collection, including skip hire	[0.20]	–	[0.10]	[0.50]	–	–	[0.10]
Moving house	**2.60**	**[1.40]**	**1.90**	**[0.60]**	**1.90**	**[1.30]**	**1.80**
Property transaction - purchase and sale	[1.00]	[0.90]	1.00	[0.20]	[0.80]	[0.60]	0.90
Property transaction - sale only	[1.00]	[0.40]	0.40	[0.30]	[0.30]	[0.40]	0.40
Property transaction - purchase only	[0.50]	[0.10]	0.30	[0.10]	[0.50]	[0.10]	0.30
Property transaction - other payments	[0.10]	[0.10]	0.20	[0.00]	[0.20]	[0.20]	0.20
Household maintenance and repair	**8.10**	**8.90**	**7.40**	**7.20**	**6.20**	**5.10**	**7.20**
Central heating repairs	2.10	1.60	1.50	0.70	1.50	0.80	1.50
House maintenance etc.	3.90	4.50	4.00	4.50	3.10	3.00	3.90
Paint, wallpaper, timber	1.00	1.20	0.90	1.00	1.00	0.70	0.90
Equipment hire, small materials	1.20	1.60	0.90	1.00	0.60	0.70	0.90
Household alterations and improvements	**26.60**	**24.80**	**22.80**	**17.30**	**20.00**	**16.90**	**22.10**
Central heating installation	[0.90]	[2.80]	1.30	[0.70]	[0.40]	[0.50]	1.20
DIY improvements: double glazing, kitchen units, sheds etc.	[2.10]	[1.40]	1.90	[0.10]	[0.20]	[0.10]	1.60
Home improvements - contracted out	23.20	20.00	18.30	15.30	18.40	15.00	18.10
Bathroom fittings	0.40	[0.60]	0.40	[0.20]	[1.00]	[0.10]	0.50
Purchase of materials for Capital Improvements	[0.10]	[0.00]	0.90	[1.10]	[0.00]	[1.30]	0.80
Household insurances	**5.30**	**5.00**	**5.10**	**5.10**	**4.90**	**4.30**	**5.00**
Structure	2.70	2.40	2.50	2.80	2.10	2.10	2.50
Contents	2.60	2.50	2.50	2.30	2.60	2.30	2.50
Household appliances	[0.00]	[0.10]	0.10	[0.00]	[0.10]	[0.00]	0.10
Housing expenditure	**172.30**	**142.90**	**149.70**	**106.30**	**119.50**	**101.80**	**143.40**
Total expenditure[2]	**756.50**	**684.40**	**686.50**	**570.10**	**620.60**	**673.80**	**674.10**

Note: Please see page xiii for symbols and conventions used in this report.

1   The figure included in total expenditure is net rent as opposed to gross rent.

2   This total includes all categories recorded in the LCF, including those outside the 'COICOP' total expenditure.

Table 2.6

Housing expenditure by socio-economic classification of household reference person, 2008

	Large employers & higher managerial	Higher professional	Lower managerial & professional	Intermediate	Small employers	Lower supervisory
Weighted number of households (thousands)	1,190	1,940	4,590	1,310	1,510	1,790
Total number of households in sample	260	430	1,040	290	360	390
Total number of persons in sample	780	1,120	2,750	680	1,050	1,090
Total number of adults in sample	540	820	2,010	510	760	810
Weighted average number of persons per household	2.9	2.5	2.6	2.4	2.9	2.8

Commodity or service	Average weekly household expenditure (£)					
Primary dwelling						
Rent	**[23.80]**	**21.80**	**17.50**	**31.10**	**22.00**	**27.90**
Gross rent	[23.80]	21.80	17.50	31.10	22.00	27.90
less housing benefit, rebates and allowances received	[0.10]	[0.90]	0.80	3.80	2.90	4.10
Net rent[3]	[23.80]	20.90	16.70	27.20	19.20	23.70
Mortgage	**145.10**	**124.90**	**109.80**	**67.10**	**83.20**	**70.20**
Mortgage interest payments	95.20	87.40	71.90	44.80	55.40	45.60
Mortgage protection premiums	3.10	3.50	3.80	2.20	2.90	2.90
Capital repayment of mortgage	46.90	33.90	34.10	20.20	24.90	21.70
Outright purchase, including deposits	**[0.20]**	**[0.10]**	**[0.20]**	**[0.70]**	**–**	**[0.10]**
Secondary dwelling	**[32.30]**	**29.10**	**3.90**	**[1.10]**	**[0.50]**	**[0.80]**
Rent	–	[0.00]	[0.40]	–	–	–
Council tax, mortgage, insurance (secondary dwelling)	[1.40]	[3.00]	[0.80]	[0.70]	[0.20]	[0.20]
Purchase of second dwelling	[30.80]	[26.00]	[2.70]	[0.50]	[0.30]	[0.60]
Charges	**35.90**	**33.40**	**30.40**	**26.40**	**29.80**	**27.10**
Council tax, domestic rates	27.20	25.10	22.80	19.50	22.60	20.20
Water charges	7.40	6.60	6.60	6.20	6.70	6.40
Other regular housing payments including service charge for rent	1.20	1.60	0.90	0.70	0.50	0.50
Refuse collection, including skip hire	[0.20]	[0.10]	[0.10]	–	–	–
Moving house	**[3.50]**	**4.10**	**3.30**	**[2.20]**	**[2.40]**	**[1.20]**
Property transaction - purchase and sale	[1.70]	[0.80]	2.20	[1.90]	[0.80]	[0.60]
Property transaction - sale only	[0.60]	[1.50]	[0.50]	[0.10]	[0.70]	[0.10]
Property transaction - purchase only	[0.40]	[1.10]	0.50	[0.10]	[0.60]	[0.50]
Property transaction - other payments	[0.80]	[0.70]	[0.10]	[0.20]	[0.30]	[0.10]
Household maintenance and repair	**13.50**	**11.50**	**9.40**	**6.90**	**11.90**	**5.00**
Central heating repairs	2.00	2.20	1.80	1.70	1.40	1.10
House maintenance etc.	6.50	6.70	5.20	3.10	8.70	2.40
Paint, wallpaper, timber	2.00	1.80	1.20	1.40	0.90	0.50
Equipment hire, small materials	3.00	0.90	1.20	0.80	0.80	1.00
Household alterations and improvements	**47.10**	**49.90**	**34.70**	**28.90**	**23.00**	**13.80**
Central heating installation	[2.00]	[1.20]	1.00	[0.90]	[0.80]	[1.20]
DIY improvements: double glazing, kitchen units, sheds etc.	[3.10]	[7.70]	[0.60]	[0.50]	[5.30]	[0.90]
Home improvements - contracted out	41.40	38.30	29.80	25.70	16.30	10.90
Bathroom fittings	[0.10]	[1.00]	1.00	[0.10]	[0.20]	[0.60]
Purchase of materials for capital improvements	[0.60]	[1.70]	[2.40]	[1.70]	[0.30]	[0.10]
Household insurances	**7.60**	**6.90**	**6.60**	**5.10**	**6.50**	**4.90**
Structure	3.80	3.40	3.30	2.60	3.40	2.30
Contents	3.70	3.40	3.20	2.50	3.10	2.50
Household appliances	[0.10]	[0.10]	[0.10]	[0.00]	[0.00]	[0.10]
Housing expenditure	**309.00**	**280.70**	**215.10**	**165.80**	**176.50**	**146.80**
Total expenditure[4]	**1,597.70**	**1,222.00**	**987.70**	**684.60**	**725.00**	**726.70**

Note: Please see page xiii for symbols and conventions used in this report.

1 Includes those who have never worked.

2 Includes those who are economically inactive.

3 The figure included in total expenditure is net rent as opposed to gross rent.

4 This total includes all categories recorded in the LCF, including those outside the 'COICOP' total expenditure.

Table 2.6

Housing expenditure by socio-economic classification of household reference person, 2008 (cont.)

	Semi-routine	Routine	Long-term unemployed[1]	Students	Occupation not stated[2] & not classifiable	All groups
Weighted number of households (thousands)	1,930	1,700	520	320	8,900	25,690
Total number of households in sample	420	380	120	60	2,080	5,850
Total number of persons in sample	1,150	1,010	350	160	3,680	13,830
Total number of adults in sample	820	740	190	120	3,320	10,640
Weighted average number of persons per household	2.8	2.7	2.9	2.9	1.7	2.4

Commodity or service	Average weekly household expenditure (£)					
Primary dwelling						
Rent	**43.90**	**47.50**	**98.70**	**119.80**	**31.50**	**31.50**
Gross rent	43.90	47.50	98.70	119.80	31.50	31.50
less housing benefit, rebates and allowances received	11.10	10.00	78.70	29.90	22.50	12.10
Net rent[3]	32.80	37.40	20.00	89.80	9.00	19.40
Mortgage	**40.30**	**42.70**	**11.50**	**33.20**	**4.90**	**57.20**
Mortgage interest payments	23.80	24.70	[8.90]	[23.90]	2.90	37.50
Mortgage protection premiums	1.60	2.00	[0.10]	[1.10]	0.10	1.90
Capital repayment of mortgage	14.90	16.00	[2.50]	[8.20]	1.90	17.80
Outright purchase, including deposits	–	–	–	–	–	[0.10]
Secondary dwelling	[0.10]	[0.50]	–	–	[0.40]	4.70
Rent	[0.00]	[0.10]	–	–	–	[0.10]
Council tax, mortgage, insurance (secondary dwelling)	[0.00]	–	–	–	[0.10]	0.50
Purchase of second dwelling	[0.00]	[0.40]	–	–	[0.30]	4.10
Charges	**24.50**	**24.10**	**11.50**	**12.40**	**21.70**	**25.90**
Council tax, domestic rates	17.30	16.90	5.20	6.20	14.30	18.50
Water charges	6.30	6.40	5.90	5.60	5.80	6.30
Other regular housing payments including service charge for rent	0.80	0.60	[0.40]	[0.60]	1.40	1.10
Refuse collection, including skip hire	–	[0.20]	–	–	[0.10]	[0.10]
Moving house	**[1.20]**	**[0.90]**	–	**[2.60]**	**0.70**	**1.80**
Property transaction - purchase and sale	[0.60]	[0.60]	–	[1.40]	[0.40]	0.90
Property transaction - sale only	[0.20]	[0.00]	–	–	[0.20]	0.40
Property transaction - purchase only	[0.10]	[0.00]	–	[1.20]	[0.00]	0.30
Property transaction - other payments	[0.20]	[0.20]	–	–	[0.10]	0.20
Household maintenance and repair	**4.60**	**5.70**	**3.90**	**[1.60]**	**5.20**	**7.20**
Central heating repairs	0.80	0.80	[1.20]	[0.30]	1.50	1.50
House maintenance etc.	2.30	3.00	[1.50]	[0.80]	2.70	3.90
Paint, wallpaper, timber	0.90	0.60	[0.20]	[0.40]	0.60	0.90
Equipment hire, small materials	0.60	1.30	[1.00]	[0.10]	0.50	0.90
Household alterations and improvements	**11.90**	**14.80**	**2.00**	**9.40**	**11.90**	**22.10**
Central heating installation	[0.80]	[1.00]	–	[1.60]	1.30	1.20
DIY improvements: double glazing, kitchen units, sheds etc.	[0.60]	[1.80]	–	–	[0.50]	1.60
Home improvements - contracted out	10.10	11.50	[1.90]	[7.70]	9.40	18.10
Bathroom fittings	[0.50]	[0.10]	[0.00]	–	0.30	0.50
Purchase of materials for capital improvements	-	[0.30]	[0.00]	–	[0.40]	0.80
Household insurances	**4.00**	**3.80**	**1.20**	**2.30**	**4.00**	**5.00**
Structure	1.80	1.80	[0.60]	[1.10]	1.90	2.50
Contents	2.10	1.90	0.50	1.30	2.00	2.50
Household appliances	[0.00]	[0.10]	–	–	0.10	0.10
Housing expenditure	**119.30**	**129.80**	**50.20**	**151.40**	**57.80**	**143.40**
Total expenditure[4]	**535.70**	**521.90**	**286.70**	**543.20**	**335.10**	**674.10**

Note: Please see page xiii for symbols and conventions used in this report.

1   Includes those who have never worked.

2   Includes those who are economically inactive.

3   The figure included in total expenditure is net rent as opposed to gross rent.

4   This total includes all categories recorded in the LCF, including those outside the 'COICOP' total expenditure.

Table 2.7

Housing expenditure by household composition, 2008

	Retired households		Non-retired		Retired and non-retired households			
	One person	One man and one woman	One person	One man and one woman	One adult with children	Two adults with children	Three or more adults without children	with children
Weighted number of households (thousands)	3,630	2,610	3,860	5,550	1,490	4,950	2,480	1,110
Total number of households in sample	770	700	850	1,260	380	1,180	460	240
Total number of persons in sample	770	1,410	850	2,530	1,010	4,580	1,560	1,140
Total number of adults in sample	770	1,410	850	2,530	380	2,370	1,560	780
Weighted average number of persons per household	1.0	2.0	1.0	2.0	2.6	3.8	3.4	4.9
Commodity or service	Average weekly household expenditure (£)							
Primary dwelling								
Rent	**29.10**	**12.80**	**40.20**	**23.20**	**80.70**	**31.40**	**32.60**	**27.00**
Gross rent	29.10	12.80	40.20	23.20	80.70	31.40	32.60	27.00
less housing benefit, rebates & allowances received	19.70	7.10	17.90	2.90	53.50	7.80	4.40	6.50
Net rent[1]	9.40	5.70	22.20	20.30	27.30	23.60	28.20	20.50
Mortgage	**1.00**	**4.00**	**48.20**	**76.40**	**33.60**	**112.70**	**55.20**	**89.30**
Mortgage interest payments[1]	0.50	2.40	33.20	52.20	21.10	76.40	29.40	48.80
Mortgage protection premiums	[0.00]	[0.10]	1.60	2.40	1.20	3.80	1.70	3.20
Capital repayment of mortgage[2]	[0.50]	1.50	13.50	21.70	11.40	32.50	24.00	37.30
Outright purchase, including deposits	–	–	[0.00]	[0.10]	[0.50]	[0.30]	–	–
Secondary dwelling	**0.30**	**0.50**	**0.80**	**16.90**	**0.40**	**3.00**	**1.40**	**2.30**
Rent	–	–	–	–	–	[0.40]	[0.10]	–
Council tax, mortgage, insurance (secondary dwelling)	[0.20]	–	[0.30]	[0.60]	–	[1.10]	[0.50]	[1.50]
Purchase of second dwelling	[0.10]	[0.50]	[0.50]	16.30	[0.40]	[1.50]	[0.80]	[0.70]
Charges	**18.70**	**28.30**	**19.40**	**30.10**	**16.10**	**30.40**	**30.50**	**29.10**
Council tax, domestic rates	11.30	21.00	13.00	22.60	9.40	22.50	22.40	21.00
Water charges	4.80	6.50	5.00	6.40	6.30	7.30	7.20	7.70
Other regular housing payments including service charge for rent	2.60	0.90	1.50	1.00	0.20	0.40	0.60	[0.40]
Refuse collection, including skip hire	[0.00]	[0.00]	[0.00]	[0.10]	[0.20]	[0.20]	[0.20]	–
Moving house	**0.50**	**1.30**	**2.20**	**3.00**	**0.70**	**2.20**	**1.20**	**1.10**
Property transaction - purchase and sale	[0.20]	[0.90]	[1.10]	1.50	[0.50]	1.30	[0.50]	[0.70]
Property transaction - sale only	[0.30]	[0.30]	[0.30]	[0.60]	–	[0.50]	[0.20]	–
Property transaction - purchase only	[0.00]	[0.00]	[0.60]	0.60	[0.10]	[0.20]	[0.10]	[0.30]
Property transaction - other payments	[0.10]	[0.00]	[0.20]	0.30	[0.10]	[0.10]	[0.30]	[0.10]
Household maintenance and repair	**4.10**	**7.70**	**4.30**	**8.50**	**4.30**	**9.00**	**9.50**	**10.50**
Central heating repairs	1.20	2.60	0.80	1.50	1.10	1.60	1.70	1.40
House maintenance etc.	2.40	3.70	2.30	4.60	2.10	4.50	6.00	6.50
Paint, wallpaper, timber	[0.30]	0.60	0.40	1.10	0.70	1.80	0.70	1.40
Equipment hire, small materials	[0.20]	0.80	0.80	1.20	[0.40]	1.20	1.10	1.30
Household alterations and improvements	**8.00**	**17.60**	**8.50**	**22.70**	**4.80**	**41.00**	**33.20**	**36.70**
Central heating installation	[2.10]	[1.10]	[0.50]	1.00	[0.60]	1.00	[1.30]	[2.00]
DIY improvements: double glazing, kitchen units, sheds etc.	[0.00]	[1.50]	[0.80]	1.00	[0.00]	0.80	[8.70]	[1.90]
Home improvements - contracted out	5.30	14.40	6.60	18.80	4.20	36.60	21.80	32.10
Bathroom fittings	[0.30]	[0.60]	[0.50]	0.70	[0.10]	0.60	[0.30]	[0.30]
Purchase of materials for capital improvements	[0.30]	[0.10]	[0.20]	[1.30]	–	[1.90]	[0.90]	[0.30]
Household insurances	**3.40**	**5.40**	**3.70**	**5.70**	**2.70**	**6.00**	**6.70**	**5.90**
Structure	1.60	2.70	1.70	2.90	1.20	3.00	3.30	3.10
Contents	1.80	2.50	2.00	2.70	1.50	3.00	3.30	2.70
Household appliances	[0.00]	[0.30]	[0.00]	[0.00]	[0.00]	0.10	[0.10]	[0.10]
Housing expenditure	**45.30**	**70.60**	**109.50**	**183.60**	**90.40**	**228.20**	**165.80**	**195.30**
Total expenditure[2]	**207.10**	**428.80**	**433.90**	**840.10**	**381.00**	**1014.20**	**985.20**	**963.60**

Note: Please see page xiii for symbols and conventions used in this report.

1 The figure included in total expenditure is net rent as opposed to gross rent.

2 This total includes all categories recorded in the LCF, including those outside the 'COICOP' total expenditure.

Table 2.8

Expenditure on rent[1] by renters, 2006 to 2008

	2006		2007		2008	
	£[2]	% of total expenditure	£[2]	% of total expenditure	£[2]	% of total expenditure
Weighted number of households (thousands)	7,230		7,660		7,520	
Total number of households in sample	1,790		1,780		1,610	
Total number of persons in sample	4,040		4,050		3,610	
Total number of adults in sample	2,870		2,920		2,570	
Weighted average number of persons per household	2.2		2.3		2.3	
Total expenditure for renters	**374.30**		**396.50**		**420.90**	
Rent	**99.30**	**26.5**	**103.80**	**26.2**	**107.70**	**25.6**
Gross rent	99.30	26.5	103.80	26.2	107.70	25.6
less housing benefit, rebates and allowances received	40.20	10.7	38.90	9.8	41.50	9.9
Net rent[3]	59.10	15.8	64.90	16.4	66.30	15.7

Note: Please see page xiii for symbols and conventions used in this report.
1   Primary dwelling.
2   Average weekly household expenditure (£).
3   The figure included in total expenditure is net rent as opposed to gross rent.

Table 2.9

Expenditure on mortgages[1] by mortgage holders, 2006 to 2008

	2006		2007		2008	
	£[2]	% of total expenditure	£[2]	% of total expenditure	£[2]	% of total expenditure
Weighted number of households (thousands)	9,960		9,680		9,830	
Total number of households in sample	2,610		2,330		2,210	
Total number of persons in sample	7,430		6,680		6,330	
Total number of adults in sample	5,090		4,670		4,450	
Weighted average number of persons per household	2.8		2.8		2.8	
Total expenditure for mortgage payers	**926.30**		**971.60**		**985.30**	
Mortgage	**120.90**	**13.1**	**138.80**	**14.3**	**148.50**	**15.1**
Mortgage interest payments[3]	77.60	8.4	92.80	9.5	97.40	9.9
Mortgage protection premiums	4.50	0.5	4.80	0.5	4.80	0.5
Capital repayment of mortgage[4]	38.80	4.2	41.20	4.2	46.30	4.7

Note: Please see page xiii for symbols and conventions used in this report.
1   Primary dwelling.
2   Average weekly household expenditure (£).
3   An improvement to the imputation of mortgage interest payments has been implemented for 2006 and 2007 data which should lead to more accurate figures. This will lead to a slight discontinuity.
4   An error was discovered in the derivation of mortgage capital repayments which was leading to double counting. This has been amended for the 2006 and 2007 data.

Table 2.10

Expenditure on rent and mortgages[1] by renters and mortgage holders by gross income decile group, 2008

| | Gross income decile group | | | | | | | | | | |
	1	2	3	4	5	6	7	8	9	10	All
Weighted number of households (thousands)	1,650	1,210	1,120	840	700	660	500	430	250	150	7,520
Total number of households in sample	360	270	260	190	150	140	100	90	50	30	1,610
Total number of persons in sample	480	520	550	470	400	390	300	240	140	110	3,610
Total number of adults in sample	400	350	370	300	280	270	220	190	120	80	2,570
Weighted average number of persons per household	1.4	1.9	2.1	2.5	2.7	2.8	3.0	2.7	3.2	4.1	2.3
Commodity or service	Average weekly household expenditure (£)										
Rent for renters	**98.90**	**101.90**	**96.40**	**99.10**	**100.10**	**94.00**	**116.30**	**142.90**	**132.10**	**306.40**	**107.70**
Gross rent	98.90	101.90	96.40	99.10	100.10	94.00	116.30	142.90	132.10	306.40	107.70
less housing benefit, rebates and allowances received	74.80	70.50	48.50	33.10	16.70	4.30	4.50	[6.80]	[1.10]	[4.80]	41.50
Net rent[2]	24.00	31.40	47.90	65.90	83.30	89.70	111.80	136.10	131.00	301.50	66.30
Weighted number of households (thousands)	100	130	300	630	860	1,170	1,430	1,610	1,760	1,830	9,830
Total number of households in sample	20	30	80	150	200	270	320	370	370	410	2,210
Total number of persons in sample	40	70	140	300	500	700	950	1,090	1,180	1,360	6,330
Total number of adults in sample	30	50	110	220	340	490	640	770	840	970	4,450
Weighted average number of persons per household	1.8	2.4	1.8	2.1	2.5	2.5	2.9	2.9	3.1	3.3	2.8
Commodity or service	Average weekly household expenditure (£)										
Mortgage for mortgage holders	**109.50**	**74.60**	**88.40**	**95.00**	**102.00**	**116.20**	**135.20**	**146.40**	**165.20**	**223.10**	**148.50**
Mortgage interest payments	70.40	44.20	51.00	61.30	63.90	72.50	88.90	97.20	111.00	148.10	97.40
Mortgage protection premiums	[2.70]	[2.60]	3.40	3.90	4.40	4.20	5.10	4.90	5.80	5.20	4.80
Capital repayment of mortgage	[36.40]	27.80	34.00	29.80	33.70	39.60	41.20	44.20	48.40	69.80	46.30

Note: Please see page xiii for symbols and conventions used in this report.

1 Primary dwelling.

2 The figure included in total expenditure is net rent as opposed to gross rent.

Table 2.11

Expenditure on rent and mortgages[1] by renters and mortgage holders by UK Countries and Government Office Region, 2008

	North East	North West	Yorkshire and the Humber	East Midlands	West Midlands	East	London
Weighted number of households (thousands)	400	840	610	550	610	550	1,270
Total number of households in sample	70	160	130	110	130	130	200
Total number of persons in sample	150	380	300	230	290	310	470
Total number of adults in sample	120	240	200	170	200	210	330
Weighted average number of persons per household	2.2	2.4	2.2	2.2	2.3	2.3	2.5
Commodity or service	Average weekly household expenditure (£)						
Rent by renters	**87.40**	**90.10**	**83.00**	**92.10**	**92.70**	**111.70**	**161.90**
Gross rent	87.40	90.10	83.00	92.10	92.70	111.70	161.90
less housing benefit, rebates and allowances							
received	42.30	43.40	29.70	38.10	43.30	34.80	56.80
Net rent[2]	45.10	46.70	53.30	54.00	49.40	76.90	105.10
Weighted number of households (thousands)	480	1,200	860	830	870	790	1,060
Total number of households in sample	90	220	200	170	190	200	160
Total number of persons in sample	270	620	580	480	540	570	450
Total number of adults in sample	180	430	410	340	390	390	330
Weighted average number of persons per household	3.1	2.9	2.7	2.9	2.9	2.7	2.8
Commodity or service	Average weekly household expenditure (£)						
Mortgage by mortgage holders	**126.10**	**139.60**	**114.80**	**120.90**	**147.30**	**165.20**	**216.10**
Mortgage interest payments	80.70	86.20	74.30	77.90	87.70	111.50	153.30
Mortgage protection premiums	4.10	5.50	4.30	4.10	6.20	4.80	4.80
Capital repayment of mortgage	41.20	48.00	36.20	39.00	53.40	49.00	58.00

	South East	South West	England	Wales	Scotland	Northern Ireland	United Kingdom
Weighted number of households (thousands)	860	640	6,320	310	700	190	7,520
Total number of households in sample	210	130	1,250	60	140	160	1,610
Total number of persons in sample	480	270	2,870	120	260	350	3,610
Total number of adults in sample	360	200	2,020	100	200	250	2,570
Weighted average number of persons per household	2.3	2.2	2.3	1.9	1.9	2.2	2.3
Commodity or service	Average weekly household expenditure (£)						
Rent by renters	**120.50**	**106.20**	**111.70**	**89.60**	**86.20**	**83.60**	**107.70**
Gross rent	120.50	106.20	111.70	89.60	86.20	83.60	107.70
less housing benefit, rebates and allowances							
received	36.50	41.20	42.30	38.20	36.60	35.50	41.50
Net rent[2]	84.00	65.00	69.40	51.50	49.60	48.10	66.30
Weighted number of households (thousands)	1,140	980	8,220	460	900	250	9,830
Total number of households in sample	330	190	1,740	90	180	210	2,210
Total number of persons in sample	930	520	4,940	280	460	650	6,330
Total number of adults in sample	660	370	3,490	190	350	430	4,450
Weighted average number of persons per household	2.7	2.9	2.8	3.0	2.5	3.2	2.8
Commodity or service	Average weekly household expenditure (£)						
Mortgage by mortgage holders	**186.20**	**143.80**	**154.40**	**110.00**	**120.70**	**126.70**	**148.50**
Mortgage interest payments	129.70	93.50	101.90	63.80	78.70	78.10	97.40
Mortgage protection premiums	4.80	5.70	5.00	2.80	3.80	7.60	4.80
Capital repayment of mortgage	51.80	44.60	47.50	43.30	38.20	41.10	46.30

Note: Please see page xiii for symbols and conventions used in this report.

1   Primary dwelling.

2   The figure included in total expenditure is net rent as opposed to gross rent.

Equivalised income

Background

Equivalisation is a standard methodology that adjusts the total annual income of a household to account for differing demands on resources, by considering the household size and composition. The purpose of this chapter is to show the impact of implementing this methodology on LCF data. The chapter describes the methodology used and presents the LCF data by both equivalised and gross income groups. This is the only chapter of the current edition of Family Spending that presents equivalised income data; all other tables and figures in the publication use non-equivalised income data. This chapter presents a selection of tables and charts using equivalised income data; other tables included within Family Spending are available on an equivalised income basis on request from ONS (see page xvi Introduction).

Equivalisation methodology

An adjustment often made when seeking to compare household incomes, particularly as a measure of economic well-being or standard of living, is to equivalise them by adjusting for household size and composition.

The process reflects the common sense notion that a household of five will need a higher income than a single person living alone to enjoy a comparable standard of living. It takes into account both the greater income needs of larger households and the economies of scale achieved when people live together, because household resources can be shared. By adjusting income in this way it is possible to make comparisons between households of different sizes and compositions.

There are several equivalisation scales, the most widely used in the UK being the McClements (1977) and the Modified OECD. Following consultation with a group of the main users of the survey, it was decided to use the McClements (Before Housing Costs) Scale for this report. Tables using the Modified OECD scales are also available on request.

The process of equivalisation utilises a scale which weights each household member, and compares the total income of that household against that of a childless cohabiting/married couple. The scale takes childless couple households as standard (that is, they are weighted by 1), scales up the income of households with fewer people and scales down the income of households with more people. The weight applied to each additional adult has a decreasing value, children's weights are also applied on a sliding scale according to age. The logic behind this is that the additional cost of adding another adult to the household decreases and that children have lower costs than adults dependent upon their age.

McClements Equivalence Scale (Before Housing Costs)	
Position of household member	**Equivalence value**
Cohabiting head of household	0.61
Partner/Spouse	0.39
1st additional adult	0.42
Subsequent adults	0.36
Single head of household	0.61
1st additional adult	0.46
2nd additional adult	0.42
Subsequent adults	0.36
Child aged: 16–18	0.36
13–15	0.27
11–12	0.25
8–10	0.23
5–7	0.21
2–4	0.18
Under 2	0.09

Equivalised income is calculated by firstly assigning an equivalence value from the McClements Equivalence Scale to each household member. These individual values are then summed to give a total equivalence number for the household. The household income is then divided by this total equivalence number to produce the equivalised income.

Equivalisation reduces relatively the incomes of households with three or more adults (since their incomes are divided by values greater than 1) and increases the incomes of single person households (since their incomes are divided by values less than 1).

For example, if a household consisting of a married couple and two children (aged twelve and sixteen) has an income of £30,000, their equivalised household size is 0.61 + 0.39 + 0.36 + 0.25 = 1.61. This implies they need 61 per cent more income than a couple with no children to have the same standard of living. Their equivalised income would therefore be £30,000/1.61 = £18,634.

A household consisting of one person with an income of £30,000 has an equivalised household size of 0.61 and an equivalised income of £30,000/0.61=£49,180. Single person households generally need less money than couples, hence when their income is equivalised it increases in relation to a couple with the same income.

Results

Equivalised household incomes were calculated for each LCF household in 2008 using the McClements Equivalence Scale. Household equivalised incomes were then ranked in ascending order and divided into decile groups, with households having the lowest equivalised income in the first decile group. All individuals in the household were then allocated to the equivalised income decile group to which their household belonged. For the purposes of analysis, some tables (3.2E, 3.3E and 3.2, 3.3) show ten income groups (deciles) and some (3.4E to 3.11E and 3.4 to 3.11) show five income groups (quintiles), all have a comparable number of households in each group.

In 2008 the income decile groups shown in Table 3.2E and 3.2 (household expenditure by gross equivalised income and gross income decile group in £ per week) were as follows:

Income decile	Gross weekly equivalised income	Gross weekly income
1	Up to £196	Up to £145
2	£197 to £259	£146 to £223
3	£260 to £333	£224 to £304
4	£334 to £411	£305 to £407
5	£412 to £496	£408 to £521
6	£497 to £599	£522 to £663
7	£600 to £730	£664 to £816
8	£731 to £897	£817 to £1,026
9	£898 to £1,195	£1,026 to £1,355
10	£1,196 and over	£1,356 and over

Household composition by income groups

To assess the impact that the scale has on the distribution of households in the lowest and highest income groups, Table 3.1 shows the household composition in each income decile group by equivalised and gross (recorded, that is, non-equivalised) income. Equivalisation changed the distribution of income among some household types.

Equivalisation of income had a large impact on one-person retired households. As Table 3.1 shows, this group accounted for more than two-fifths of all households in the lowest income decile group (45 per cent). When their income was equivalised the proportion of such households in the lowest income decile group fell to 15 per cent. It can be seen that these households moved up the income distribution by the process of equivalisation; one-person retired households accounted for 11 per cent of the fourth gross income decile group but 21 per

cent of the fourth decile group after income was equivalised. This trend continues in the other decile groups.

As with one-person retired households, one-person non-retired households made up a larger proportion of the decile groups in the bottom half of the gross income distribution (i.e. in the five lowest decile groups) than after equivalisation. In the upper half of the distribution, the proportion of one-person non-retired households increased after equivalisation. For example, the percentage of one-person non-retired households fell from 34 per cent of the lowest gross income decile group to 27 per cent of the lowest equivalised income decile group, while in the ninth decile group they increased from 6 per cent to 20 per cent after equivalisation.

Equivalisation also had an effect on households with two adults and one or more children. The proportion of such households in the lower decile groups increased with equivalisation while the proportion in the higher decile groups fell. As discussed above, equivalisation increases relatively the incomes of single person households and reduces incomes of households with three or more persons and so these changes were expected.

Figures 3.1 and 3.1E show the distribution of households before and after income equivalisation by whether or not they have children. It can be seen that as gross income increased, the proportion of households with children increased; from 15 per cent of households in the bottom gross income decile group to 41 per cent of those in the top gross income decile group (Figure 3.1). The pattern was somewhat different after equivalisation: the decile group with the highest proportion of households with children was the first (40 per cent), the proportion fell to 21 per cent in the second decile group and slowly increased to 34 per cent in the seventh decile group. After the seventh decile group, as equivalised income increased, the proportion of each decile group made up of households with children fell (Figure 3.1E).

Figures 3.2 and 3.2E show the distribution before and after income equivalisation by retired and non-retired households. It can be seen that equivalisation has a large effect on the proportion of retired households in the lowest income decile group. When their income was equivalised the proportion of retired households in the lowest income decile group fell from 46 per cent to 23 per cent in the lowest gross income decile group.

For each income group the average number of persons per household is also shown in Table 3.1. As gross income increased the average number of people in each household also increased, the average household size for the highest income group was almost two and a half times that of the lowest income group (3.2 people compared with 1.3 people). After income was equivalised the average number of people in each household was very similar over the income decile groups.

Figure 3.1

Percentage of households with children in each gross income decile group, 2008

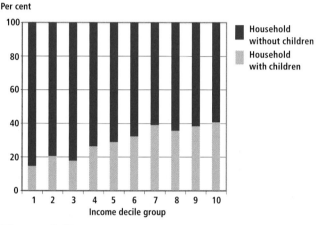

Figure 3.1E

Percentage of retired and non-retired households by gross income decile group, 2008

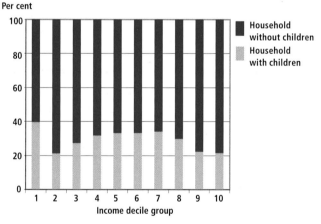

Figure 3.2

Percentage of retired and non-retired households by gross income decile group, 2008

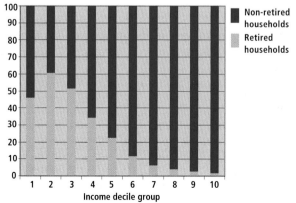

Figure 3.2E

Percentage of retired and non-retired households by equivalised income decile group, 2008

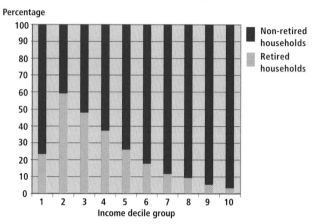

Household expenditure by income

Tables 3.2E, 3.2, 3.3E and 3.3 show household expenditure on commodities and services. Differences in spending may be the result of other factors as well as income, for example household size, and so the tables show both gross income decile groups and equivalised income decile groups.

Generally, although expenditure on different commodities and services increased as income increased using both of the measures of income, the effect was slightly less marked when equivalised income was used. In the lowest gross income decile group, households spent £153.70 on average per week, rising to £1,044.90 in the highest decile group (Table 3.2). In comparison, households in the lowest equivalised income decile group spent £206.50 on average per week, rising to £906.10 in the highest equivalised income decile group (Table 3.2E).

This pattern is particularly evident for spending on food and non-alcoholic drinks, and clothing and footwear (see Figures 3.3 and 3.4). In the lowest gross income decile group, households spent £26.40 on average per week on food and non-alcoholic drinks, rising to £79.40 in the highest decile group. In comparison, households in the lowest equivalised income decile group spent £35.20 on average per week, rising to £61.60 in the highest decile group. In terms of spending on clothing and footwear, households in the lowest gross income decile group spent £6.40 on average per week, increasing to £48.80 in the highest decile group. The corresponding results for the lowest and highest equivalised income decile groups were £10.80 and £38.70.

Table 3.3E shows the percentage of total expenditure spent on different commodities and services by equivalised income decile group. Households in the lowest equivalised income decile group spent a considerably higher proportion of their total expenditure on housing, fuel and power than households in the highest income decile group (21 per cent compared with 8 per cent). Conversely, households with the highest equivalised incomes spent a greater proportion of their income on transport than those with lower equivalised incomes: 14 per cent of the expenditure of the highest decile group of equivalised income distribution was on transport, compared with 9 per cent of the expenditure of those households in the first decile group (see Figure 3.5).

Figure 3.3

Expenditure on food and non-alcoholic drinks by gross and equivalised income decile group, 2008

£ per week

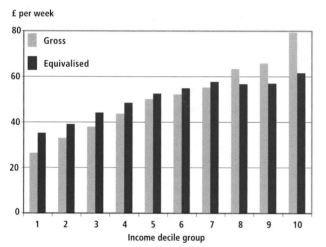

Figure 3.4

Expenditure on clothing and footwear by gross and equivalised income decile group, 2008

£ per week

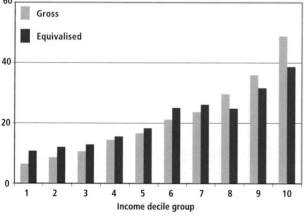

Figure 3.5

Percentage of total expenditure on selected items by equivalised income decile group, 2008

Per cent

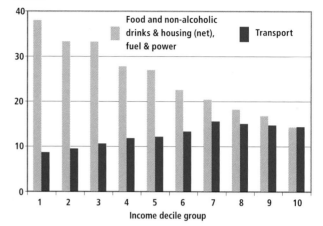

Household expenditure by household composition and income

This section looks at the effect that equivalisation has when looking at the expenditure in the income decile groups of different household types. Tables 3.4E to 3.11E and 3.4 to 3.11 show the expenditure of different household composition groups by equivalised income and gross income. The analysis focuses on one and two adult households, with and without children. It is worth noting that some groups contain a small number of households in the sample and should therefore be treated with caution, in particular one-person retired households mainly dependent on the state pension (200 households); and one-man-one-woman retired households mainly dependent on the state pension (150 households). Information on standard errors and estimates of precision can be found in Appendix B.

As discussed earlier, equivalisation increases relatively the incomes of single-person households and reduces the incomes of households with three or more adults. We would therefore expect equivalisation to have the greatest effect on these types of households.

As anticipated, equivalisation had a large effect among one-person non-retired and retired (not mainly dependent on the state pension) households, and two adult households with children. For example, the average amount spent each week on all expenditure items by one-person non-retired households in the top fifth of the gross income distribution was £638.10 compared with an average £463.60 in the top fifth of the equivalised income distribution (see Tables 3.4 and 3.4E). Equivalisation increased spending among richer two adult households with children: the average amount spent each week on all expenditure items was £1,039.60 in the top fifth of the gross income distribution compared with £1,176.10 in the top fifth of the equivalised income distribution (see Tables 3.6 and 3.6E).

Sources of income

Households receive income from a variety of sources, the main ones being: earnings and self-employment; Social Security Benefits/Tax Credits; interest on investments; and occupational pensions.

Tables 3.12E and 3.12 and Figures 3.6 and 3.6E show the distribution of gross income sources for each income quintile, by gross household income and equivalised household income. The various sources of income are shown as a percentage of the total gross income of the quintile.

Social security benefits were the principal source of income (80 per cent) of the lowest gross income quintile; this did not change markedly when income was equivalised (74 per cent). However, the proportion of income made up from wages and salaries was smaller in the lowest gross income quintile than for the lowest equivalised income quintile: 6 per cent compared with 15 per cent. The reverse was true for annuities and pensions, the proportion almost halved when income was equivalised: among households in the lowest gross income quintle, 9 per cent of income consisted of annuities and pensions, compared with 4 per cent for households in the lowest gross equivalised income quintile. These differences largely reflect the fact that, after equivalising income, the lowest quintile group contained fewer pensioner households.

Figure 3.6

Source of income by gross income quintile group, 2008

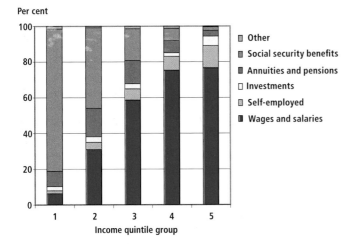

Figure 3.6E

Sources of income by gross equivalised income quintile group, 2008

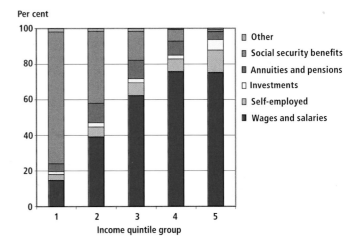

Table 3.1

Percentage of households by composition in each gross, and equivalised income decile group, 2008

Percentages

| | Income decile group | | | | | | | | | |
| | Lowest ten per cent | | Second | | Third | | Fourth | | Fifth | |
	Gross	Equivalised	Gross	Equivalised	Gross	Equivalised	Gross	Equivalised	Gross	Equivalised
Lower boundary of group (£ per week)			146	197	224	260	305	334	408	412
Average size of household	**1.3**	**2.2**	**1.7**	**2.0**	**1.8**	**2.2**	**2.1**	**2.4**	**2.3**	**2.5**
One adult retired mainly dependent on state pensions[1]	20	9	12	15	5	7	[0]	5	–	[2]
One adult, other retired	25	6	33	26	22	19	11	16	8	13
One adult, non-retired	34	27	13	9	17	7	20	10	19	10
One adult, one child	8	10	5	[3]	6	4	6	4	[2]	4
One adult, two or more children	[2]	11	7	4	5	4	5	[2]	3	[2]
One man one woman, retired mainly dependent on state pensions[1]	[0]	4	8	9	9	5	3	[1]	[1]	[1]
One man and one woman, other retired	[1]	4	7	9	15	16	20	15	14	11
One man and one woman, non-retired	[3]	6	5	6	10	10	14	11	20	16
One man and one woman, one child	[2]	7	4	[3]	[2]	4	5	6	8	7
One man and one woman, two children	[1]	4	[2]	3	[1]	6	5	9	7	11
One man and one woman, three children	[0]	[2]	[0]	[3]	[1]	[3]	[2]	[3]	[3]	3
Two adults, four or more children	–	[2]	[0]	[1]	[1]	[1]	[1]	[1]	[0]	[0]
Three adults	[0]	[2]	[0]	[2]	[1]	4	[3]	6	5	8
Three adults, one or more children	[0]	[2]	[1]	[2]	[1]	4	[1]	5	[3]	3
All other households without children	[2]	[3]	[1]	[2]	[2]	[3]	[2]	5	5	6
All other households with children	[0]	[2]	[1]	[3]	[1]	[1]	[2]	[2]	[2]	[3]

| | Income decile group | | | | | | | | | |
| | Sixth | | Seventh | | Eighth | | Ninth | | Highest ten per cent | |
	Gross	Equivalised	Gross	Equivalised	Gross	Equivalised	Gross	Equivalised	Gross	Equivalised
Lower boundary of group (£ per week)	522	497	664	600	817	731	1,026	898	1,356	1,196
Average size of household	**2.5**	**2.7**	**2.8**	**2.6**	**2.8**	**2.5**	**3.1**	**2.3**	**3.2**	**2.2**
One adult retired mainly dependent on state pensions[1]	–	[1]	–	–	–	–	–	–	–	–
One adult, other retired	[2]	9	[2]	6	[0]	5	–	[3]	–	[1]
One adult, non-retired	18	14	13	12	7	17	6	20	[3]	24
One adult, one child	[3]	[1]	[1]	[3]	[1]	[2]	[0]	[1]	[0]	[1]
One adult, two or more children	[1]	[1]	[1]	[1]	[1]	[1]	[0]	[0]	[0]	[0]
One man one woman, retired mainly dependent on state pensions[1]	–	[0]	–	–	–	–	–	–	–	–
One man and one woman, other retired	9	8	5	5	4	5	[2]	[3]	[2]	[2]
One man and one woman, non-retired	25	18	26	24	33	27	29	37	31	42
One man and one woman, one child	8	8	11	11	12	10	10	8	10	9
One man and one woman, two children	10	13	16	10	11	11	14	9	16	8
One man and one woman, three children	[3]	4	[3]	[2]	4	[2]	3	[2]	5	[2]
Two adults, four or more children	[1]	[0]	[1]	[1]	[0]	[0]	[1]	[0]	[1]	[0]
Three adults	8	7	8	12	12	9	13	9	11	5
Three adults, one or more children	5	4	5	5	4	[4]	7	[2]	6	[2]
All other households without children	5	10	7	6	8	8	11	6	13	[4]
All other households with children	[1]	[2]	[1]	[2]	[2]	[1]	4	[0]	[2]	–

Note: Please see page xiii for symbols and conventions used in this report.

1 Mainly dependent on state pension and not economically active – see Appendix B.

Table 3.2E

Household expenditure by gross equivalised income decile group, 2008
based on weighted data and including children's expenditure

	Lowest ten per cent	Second decile group	Third decile group	Fourth decile group	Fifth decile group	Sixth decile group
Lower boundary of group (£ per week)		197	260	334	412	497
Weighted number of households (thousands)	2,570	2,570	2,570	2,570	2,570	2,570
Total number of households in sample	570	580	610	590	580	590
Total number of persons in sample	1,250	1,160	1,370	1,440	1,430	1,570
Total number of adults in sample	820	890	1,050	1,090	1,090	1,200
Weighted average number of persons per household	2.2	2.0	2.2	2.4	2.5	2.7
Commodity or service	Average weekly household expenditure (£)					
1 Food & non-alcoholic drinks	35.20	39.00	44.10	48.40	52.50	54.80
2 Alcoholic drinks, tobacco & narcotics	8.70	7.60	8.50	10.00	10.20	11.50
3 Clothing & footwear	10.80	12.00	12.90	15.50	18.30	25.00
4 Housing (net)[1], fuel & power	43.40	39.00	51.20	51.10	58.40	57.60
5 Household goods & services	13.30	19.10	16.50	23.10	22.70	27.90
6 Health	1.10	3.00	3.00	4.90	4.90	6.00
7 Transport	17.90	22.20	30.50	42.40	50.00	66.50
8 Communication	7.70	7.60	9.00	11.80	11.40	13.10
9 Recreation & culture	22.20	28.10	34.20	46.40	51.70	75.40
10 Education	1.80	0.80	1.10	2.20	3.00	4.60
11 Restaurants & hotels	13.70	16.00	19.60	26.40	28.50	38.30
12 Miscellaneous goods & services	13.20	15.90	20.30	26.20	31.80	37.00
1-12 All expenditure groups	188.90	210.30	251.10	308.50	343.60	417.60
13 Other expenditure items	17.60	23.60	35.60	49.60	67.70	80.40
Total expenditure	206.50	234.00	286.70	358.10	411.30	498.10
Average weekly expenditure per person (£)						
Total expenditure	94.50	119.70	129.90	147.40	163.40	187.00

Note: The commodity and service categories are not comparable to those in publications before 2001-02.
Please see page xiii for symbols and conventions used in this report

1 Excluding mortgage interest payments, council tax and Northern Ireland rates.

Table 3.2E

Household expenditure by gross equivalised income decile group, 2008 (cont.)

based on weighted data and including children's expenditure

	Seventh decile group	Eighth decile group	Ninth decile group	Highest ten per cent	All house-holds
Lower boundary of group (£ per week)	600	731	898	1,196	
Weighted number of households (thousands)	2,570	2,570	2,570	2,560	25,690
Total number of households in sample	600	580	560	580	5,850
Total number of persons in sample	1,560	1,430	1,310	1,300	13,830
Total number of adults in sample	1,210	1,130	1,090	1,070	10,640
Weighted average number of persons per household	2.6	2.5	2.3	2.2	2.4
Commodity or service	Average weekly household expenditure (£)				
1 Food & non-alcoholic drinks	57.70	56.70	56.90	61.60	50.70
2 Alcoholic drinks, tobacco & narcotics	11.30	12.90	13.00	14.20	10.80
3 Clothing & footwear	26.10	24.80	31.60	38.70	21.60
4 Housing (net)[1], fuel & power	52.50	52.70	56.30	68.10	53.00
5 Household goods & services	34.20	37.20	51.50	56.00	30.10
6 Health	4.40	8.50	6.20	9.30	5.10
7 Transport	84.20	90.40	99.40	130.30	63.40
8 Communication	14.10	14.40	14.60	15.80	12.00
9 Recreation & culture	68.20	74.50	81.90	118.10	60.10
10 Education	4.00	5.20	9.60	29.70	6.20
11 Restaurants & hotels	39.30	53.80	62.70	79.10	37.70
12 Miscellaneous goods & services	41.70	50.20	52.60	67.40	35.60
1-12 All expenditure groups	437.90	481.20	536.60	688.30	386.30
13 Other expenditure items	100.70	117.40	136.20	217.70	84.60
Total expenditure	538.60	598.60	672.80	906.10	471.00
Average weekly expenditure per person (£) Total expenditure	204.10	242.40	291.30	411.80	199.80

Note: The commodity and service categories are not comparable to those in publications before 2001-02.
Please see page xiii for symbols and conventions used in this report

1   Excluding mortgage interest payments, council tax and Northern Ireland Rates.

Table 3.2

Household expenditure by gross income decile group, 2008

based on weighted data and including children's expenditure

	Lowest ten per cent	Second decile group	Third decile group	Fourth decile group	Fifth decile group	Sixth decile group
Lower boundary of group (£ per week)		146	224	305	408	522
Weighted number of households (thousands)	2,570	2,570	2,570	2,570	2,570	2,570
Total number of households in sample	550	580	610	630	590	600
Total number of persons in sample	710	970	1,130	1,320	1,380	1,520
Total number of adults in sample	600	770	920	1,040	1,070	1,160
Weighted average number of persons per household	1.3	1.7	1.8	2.1	2.3	2.5
Commodity or service	Average weekly household expenditure (£)					
1 Food & non-alcoholic drinks	26.40	33.00	37.90	43.70	50.10	52.10
2 Alcoholic drinks, tobacco & narcotics	6.70	6.10	7.60	9.90	10.30	11.80
3 Clothing & footwear	6.40	8.60	10.60	14.40	16.60	21.10
4 Housing (net)[1], fuel & power	36.30	38.40	47.90	51.30	53.80	55.90
5 Household goods & services	9.10	15.20	19.30	21.60	24.10	25.20
6 Health	1.20	3.20	3.10	3.90	5.20	5.10
7 Transport	12.10	17.10	24.10	38.90	51.90	61.00
8 Communication	5.80	7.10	7.90	9.10	12.20	13.10
9 Recreation & culture	15.30	23.90	31.70	39.30	50.70	69.30
10 Education	[1.40]	[0.50]	0.50	0.80	2.60	2.40
11 Restaurants & hotels	9.00	12.00	14.80	23.80	28.20	34.10
12 Miscellaneous goods & services	10.40	15.40	19.10	21.30	28.10	33.90
1-12 All expenditure groups	140.10	180.50	224.50	278.00	333.90	385.10
13 Other expenditure items	13.70	19.50	32.60	52.10	59.10	74.10
Total expenditure	153.70	200.00	257.10	330.10	393.00	459.20
Average weekly expenditure per person (£)						
Total expenditure	117.70	119.20	142.20	157.00	169.50	184.60

Note: The commodity and service categories are not comparable to those in publications before 2001-02.
Please see page xiii for symbols and conventions used in this report

1 Excluding mortgage interest payments, council tax and Northern Ireland rates.

Table 3.2

Household expenditure by gross income decile group, 2008 (cont.)

based on weighted data and including children's expenditure

	Seventh decile group	Eighth decile group	Ninth decile group	Highest ten per cent	All house-holds
Lower boundary of group (£ per week)	664	817	1,026	1,356	
Weighted number of households (thousands)	2,570	2,560	2,570	2,560	25,690
Total number of households in sample	590	570	550	580	5,850
Total number of persons in sample	1,620	1,640	1,680	1,860	13,830
Total number of adults in sample	1,190	1,240	1,280	1,380	10,640
Weighted average number of persons per household	2.8	2.8	3.1	3.2	2.4
Commodity or service	Average weekly household expenditure (£)				
1 Food & non-alcoholic drinks	55.20	63.40	65.90	79.40	50.70
2 Alcoholic drinks, tobacco & narcotics	12.10	14.60	13.30	15.50	10.80
3 Clothing & footwear	23.70	29.60	36.00	48.80	21.60
4 Housing (net)[1], fuel & power	57.10	63.00	54.80	72.00	53.00
5 Household goods & services	34.60	37.70	46.50	68.10	30.10
6 Health	4.50	7.00	7.10	10.90	5.10
7 Transport	73.60	81.90	112.20	161.10	63.40
8 Communication	14.10	14.90	16.70	18.70	12.00
9 Recreation & culture	69.00	75.80	86.50	139.30	60.10
10 Education	4.80	7.30	7.10	34.60	6.20
11 Restaurants & hotels	45.50	53.20	60.50	96.30	37.70
12 Miscellaneous goods & services	38.00	53.50	57.10	79.60	35.60
1-12 All expenditure groups	432.30	501.90	563.60	824.40	386.30
13 Other expenditure items	104.50	123.80	146.80	220.50	84.60
Total expenditure	**536.70**	**625.70**	**710.40**	**1044.90**	**471.00**
Average weekly expenditure per person (£)					
Total expenditure	**192.80**	**223.10**	**232.70**	**323.20**	**199.80**

Note: The commodity and service categories are not comparable to those in publications before 2001-02.
Please see page xiii for symbols and conventions used in this report

1 Excluding mortgage interest payments, council tax and Northern Ireland rates.

Table 3.3E

Household expenditure as a percentage of total expenditure by gross equivalised income decile group, 2008

based on weighted data and including children's expenditure

	Lowest ten per cent	Second decile group	Third decile group	Fourth decile group	Fifth decile group	Sixth decile group
Lower boundary of group (£ per week)		197	260	334	412	497
Weighted number of households (thousands)	2,570	2,570	2,570	2,570	2,570	2,570
Total number of households in sample	570	580	610	590	580	590
Total number of persons in sample	1,250	1,160	1,370	1,440	1,430	1,570
Total number of adults in sample	820	890	1,050	1,090	1,090	1,200
Weighted average number of persons per household	2.2	2.0	2.2	2.4	2.5	2.7
Commodity or service	Percentage of total expenditure					
1 Food & non-alcoholic drinks	17	17	15	14	13	11
2 Alcoholic drinks, tobacco & narcotics	4	3	3	3	2	2
3 Clothing & footwear	5	5	5	4	4	5
4 Housing (net)[1], fuel & power	21	17	18	14	14	12
5 Household goods & services	6	8	6	6	6	6
6 Health	1	1	1	1	1	1
7 Transport	9	10	11	12	12	13
8 Communication	4	3	3	3	3	3
9 Recreation & culture	11	12	12	13	13	15
10 Education	1	0	0	1	1	1
11 Restaurants & hotels	7	7	7	7	7	8
12 Miscellaneous goods & services	6	7	7	7	8	7
1-12 All expenditure groups	91	90	88	86	84	84
13 Other expenditure items	9	10	12	14	16	16
Total expenditure	100	100	100	100	100	100

Note: The commodity and service categories are not comparable to those in publications before 2001-02.
Please see page xiii for symbols and conventions used in this report

1 Excluding mortgage interest payments, council tax and Northern Ireland rates.

Table 3.3E

Household expenditure as a percentage of total expenditure by gross equivalised income decile group, 2008 (cont.)

based on weighted data and including children's expenditure

	Seventh decile group	Eighth decile group	Ninth decile group	Highest ten per cent	All house-holds
Lower boundary of group (£ per week)	600	731	898	1,196	
Weighted number of households (thousands)	2,570	2,570	2,570	2,560	25,690
Total number of households in sample	600	580	560	580	5,850
Total number of persons in sample	1,560	1,430	1,310	1,300	13,830
Total number of adults in sample	1,210	1,130	1,090	1,070	10,640
Weighted average number of persons per household	2.6	2.5	2.3	2.2	2.4
Commodity or service	Percentage of total expenditure				
1 Food & non-alcoholic drinks	11	9	8	7	11
2 Alcoholic drinks, tobacco & narcotics	2	2	2	2	2
3 Clothing & footwear	5	4	5	4	5
4 Housing (net)1, fuel & power	10	9	8	8	11
5 Household goods & services	6	6	8	6	6
6 Health	1	1	1	1	1
7 Transport	16	15	15	14	13
8 Communication	3	2	2	2	3
9 Recreation & culture	13	12	12	13	13
10 Education	1	1	1	3	1
11 Restaurants & hotels	7	9	9	9	8
12 Miscellaneous goods & services	8	8	8	7	8
1-12 All expenditure groups	*81*	*80*	*80*	*76*	*82*
13 Other expenditure items	*19*	*20*	*20*	*24*	*18*
Total expenditure	*100*	*100*	*100*	*100*	*100*

Note: The commodity and service categories are not comparable to those in publications before 2001-02.
         Please see page xiii for symbols and conventions used in this report

1 Excluding mortgage interest payments, council tax and Northern Ireland rates.

Table 3.3

Household expenditure as a percentage of total expenditure by gross income decile group, 2008

based on weighted data and including children's expenditure

	Lowest ten per cent	Second decile group	Third decile group	Fourth decile group	Fifth decile group	Sixth decile group
Lower boundary of group (£ per week)		146	224	305	408	522
Weighted number of households (thousands)	2,570	2,570	2,570	2,570	2,570	2,570
Total number of households in sample	550	580	610	630	590	600
Total number of persons in sample	710	970	1,130	1,320	1,380	1,520
Total number of adults in sample	600	770	920	1,040	1,070	1,160
Weighted average number of persons per household	1.3	1.7	1.8	2.1	2.3	2.5
Commodity or service	Percentage of total expenditure					
1 Food & non-alcoholic drinks	17	16	15	13	13	11
2 Alcoholic drinks, tobacco & narcotics	4	3	3	3	3	3
3 Clothing & footwear	4	4	4	4	4	5
4 Housing (net)[1], fuel & power	24	19	19	16	14	12
5 Household goods & services	6	8	8	7	6	5
6 Health	1	2	1	1	1	1
7 Transport	8	9	9	12	13	13
8 Communication	4	4	3	3	3	3
9 Recreation & culture	10	12	12	12	13	15
10 Education	[1]	[0]	0	0	1	1
11 Restaurants & hotels	6	6	6	7	7	7
12 Miscellaneous goods & services	7	8	7	6	7	7
1-12 All expenditure groups	91	90	87	84	85	84
13 Other expenditure items	9	10	13	16	15	16
Total expenditure	100	100	100	100	100	100

Note: The commodity and service categories are not comparable to those in publications before 2001-02.
Please see page xiii for symbols and conventions used in this report

1 Excluding mortgage interest payments, council tax and Northern Ireland rates.

Table 3.3

Household expenditure as a percentage of total expenditure by gross income decile group, 2008 (cont.)

based on weighted data and including children's expenditure

	Seventh decile group	Eighth decile group	Ninth decile group	Highest ten per cent	All house- holds
Lower boundary of group (£ per week)	664	817	1026	1,356	
Weighted number of households (thousands)	2,570	2,560	2,570	2,560	25,690
Total number of households in sample	590	570	550	580	5,850
Total number of persons in sample	1,620	1,640	1,680	1,860	13,830
Total number of adults in sample	1,190	1,240	1,280	1,380	10,640
Weighted average number of persons per household	2.8	2.8	3.1	3.2	2.4
Commodity or service	Percentage of total expenditure				
1 Food & non-alcoholic drinks	10	10	9	8	11
2 Alcoholic drinks, tobacco & narcotics	2	2	2	1	2
3 Clothing & footwear	4	5	5	5	5
4 Housing (net)[1], fuel & power	11	10	8	7	11
5 Household goods & services	6	6	7	7	6
6 Health	1	1	1	1	1
7 Transport	14	13	16	15	13
8 Communication	3	2	2	2	3
9 Recreation & culture	13	12	12	13	13
10 Education	1	1	1	3	1
11 Restaurants & hotels	8	8	9	9	8
12 Miscellaneous goods & services	7	9	8	8	8
1-12 All expenditure groups	81	80	79	79	82
13 Other expenditure items	19	20	21	21	18
Total expenditure	100	100	100	100	100

Note: The commodity and service categories are not comparable to those in publications before 2001-02.
            Please see page xiii for symbols and conventions used in this report

1 Excluding mortgage interest payments, council tax and Northern Ireland rates.

Table 3.4E

Expenditure of one adult non-retired households by gross equivalised income quintile group, 2008

based on weighted data

	Lowest twenty per cent	Second quintile group	Third quintile group	Fourth quintile group	Highest twenty per cent	All house-holds
Lower boundary of group (£ per week)		260	412	600	898	
Weighted number of households (thousands)	930	430	610	750	1,120	3,860
Total number of households in sample	210	100	140	170	240	850
Total number of persons in sample	210	100	140	170	240	850
Total number of adults in sample	210	100	140	170	240	850
Weighted average number of persons per household	1.0	1.0	1.0	1.0	1.0	1.0
Commodity or service	Average weekly household expenditure (£)					
1 Food & non-alcoholic drinks	20.10	25.30	23.00	25.90	29.40	25.00
2 Alcoholic drinks, tobacco & narcotics	9.50	7.90	8.50	7.40	9.80	8.80
3 Clothing & footwear	4.80	6.40	6.40	9.80	14.70	9.10
4 Housing (net)[1], fuel & power	33.70	42.70	55.70	44.10	53.70	46.10
5 Household goods & services	7.50	10.00	13.60	16.60	27.60	16.40
6 Health	1.10	2.20	3.10	2.90	6.00	3.30
7 Transport	15.20	23.20	36.20	50.30	64.90	40.80
8 Communication	6.10	9.10	8.10	9.50	10.50	8.70
9 Recreation & culture	14.30	22.90	23.90	32.00	38.80	27.40
10 Education	[2.10]	[1.40]	[0.40]	[1.60]	[6.70]	3.00
11 Restaurants & hotels	7.70	11.90	18.40	24.50	37.60	21.80
12 Miscellaneous goods & services	9.10	17.90	16.00	19.50	29.00	19.00
1-12 All expenditure groups	131.20	180.90	213.20	244.20	328.70	229.40
13 Other expenditure items	14.80	34.00	49.20	77.00	134.90	69.50
Total expenditure	146.00	214.90	262.40	321.20	463.60	298.90
Average weekly expenditure per person (£)						
Total expenditure	146.00	214.90	262.40	321.20	463.60	298.90

Note: The commodity and service categories are not comparable to those in publications before 2001-02.
Please see page xiii for symbols and conventions used in this report

1 Excluding mortgage interest payments, council tax and Northern Ireland rates.

Table 3.4

Expenditure of one adult non-retired households by gross income quintile group, 2008

based on weighted data

	Lowest twenty per cent	Second quintile group	Third quintile group	Fourth quintile group	Highest twenty per cent	All house-holds
Lower boundary of group (£ per week)		223	408	664	1,026	
Weighted number of households (thousands)	1,200	950	930	520	240	3,860
Total number of households in sample	270	220	200	110	50	850
Total number of persons in sample	270	220	200	110	50	850
Total number of adults in sample	270	220	200	110	50	850
Weighted average number of persons per household	1.0	1.0	1.0	1.0	1.0	1.0
Commodity or service	Average weekly household expenditure (£)					
1 Food & non-alcoholic drinks	21.30	24.60	25.20	30.50	32.30	25.00
2 Alcoholic drinks, tobacco & narcotics	8.80	8.40	8.30	10.30	9.70	8.80
3 Clothing & footwear	5.30	6.60	9.10	15.10	24.80	9.10
4 Housing (net)[1], fuel & power	34.30	53.80	44.70	56.80	56.10	46.10
5 Household goods & services	8.00	13.40	19.60	27.90	32.80	16.40
6 Health	1.60	2.70	2.60	10.50	1.50	3.30
7 Transport	17.10	39.20	47.90	55.30	105.60	40.80
8 Communication	6.60	8.50	10.20	9.40	12.60	8.70
9 Recreation & culture	16.10	25.00	33.00	41.30	41.10	27.40
10 Education	[2.10]	[0.30]	[1.40]	[10.80]	[7.40]	3.00
11 Restaurants & hotels	8.40	17.20	29.60	33.10	52.90	21.80
12 Miscellaneous goods & services	11.20	16.90	19.50	31.90	36.40	19.00
1-12 All expenditure groups	140.60	216.70	251.10	332.90	413.20	229.40
13 Other expenditure items	17.20	56.40	82.60	118.50	224.90	69.50
Total expenditure	**157.80**	**273.00**	**333.70**	**451.50**	**638.10**	**298.90**
Average weekly expenditure per person (£)						
Total expenditure	**157.80**	**273.00**	**333.70**	**451.50**	**638.10**	**298.90**

Note: The commodity and service categories are not comparable to those in publications before 2001-02.
         Please see page xiii for symbols and conventions used in this report

1 Excluding mortgage interest payments, council tax and Northern Ireland rates.

Table 3.5E

Expenditure of one person retired households not mainly dependent on state pensions[1] by gross equivalised income quintile group, 2008
based on weighted data

	Lowest twenty per cent	Second quintile group	Third quintile group	Fourth quintile group	Highest twenty per cent	All house-holds
Lower boundary of group (£ per week)		260	412	600	898	
Weighted number of households (thousands)	830	900	550	290	100	2,660
Total number of households in sample	170	190	130	70	20	570
Total number of persons in sample	170	190	130	70	20	570
Total number of adults in sample	170	190	130	70	20	570
Weighted average number of persons per household	1.0	1.0	1.0	1.0	1.0	1.0
Commodity or service			Average weekly household expenditure (£)			
1 Food & non-alcoholic drinks	25.10	25.70	30.20	32.90	32.40	27.50
2 Alcoholic drinks, tobacco & narcotics	3.40	2.80	5.70	6.10	[12.00]	4.30
3 Clothing & footwear	4.90	7.50	9.20	7.60	[12.50]	7.20
4 Housing (net)[2], fuel & power	32.50	33.50	36.30	40.70	62.90	35.60
5 Household goods & services	9.60	11.40	14.30	26.90	[41.90]	14.20
6 Health	2.70	5.30	4.30	5.20	[11.80]	4.50
7 Transport	8.40	12.30	20.30	25.80	37.80	15.10
8 Communication	5.00	5.20	6.20	8.90	9.00	5.90
9 Recreation & culture	13.10	21.30	29.50	55.30	41.90	24.80
10 Education	[0.00]	[0.00]	[0.10]	[3.50]	[2.70]	[0.50]
11 Restaurants & hotels	6.20	7.90	12.50	15.40	[24.70]	9.70
12 Miscellaneous goods & services	9.60	13.90	21.20	23.20	37.20	15.90
1-12 All expenditure groups	120.40	146.80	189.80	251.60	326.80	165.30
13 Other expenditure items	9.90	17.40	45.90	52.90	173.70	30.50
Total expenditure	130.30	164.20	235.70	304.50	500.40	195.80
Average weekly expenditure per person (£)						
Total expenditure	130.30	164.20	235.70	304.50	500.40	195.80

Note: The commodity and service categories are not comparable to those in publications before 2001-02.
Please see page xiii for symbols and conventions used in this report

1   Mainly dependent on state pension and not economically active - see appendix B.

2   Excluding mortgage interest payments, council tax and Northern Ireland rates.

Table 3.5

Expenditure of one person retired households not mainly dependent on state pensions[1] by gross income quintile group, 2008

based on weighted data

	Lowest twenty per cent	Second quintile group	Third quintile group	Fourth quintile group	Highest twenty per cent	All house-holds
Lower boundary of group (£ per week)		223	408	664	1,026	
Weighted number of households (thousands)	1,500	850	260	50	0	2,660
Total number of households in sample	310	190	60	10	0	570
Total number of persons in sample	310	190	60	10	0	570
Total number of adults in sample	310	190	60	10	0	570
Weighted average number of persons per household	1.0	1.0	1.0	1.0	0	1.0
Commodity or service	Average weekly household expenditure (£)					
1 Food & non-alcoholic drinks	25.20	29.30	33.00	[35.20]	–	27.50
2 Alcoholic drinks, tobacco & narcotics	2.90	4.90	8.60	[11.70]	–	4.30
3 Clothing & footwear	6.30	8.70	5.00	[22.30]	–	7.20
4 Housing (net)[2], fuel & power	32.70	36.00	45.40	[61.30]	–	35.60
5 Household goods & services	10.00	15.50	27.30	[48.00]	–	14.20
6 Health	3.90	4.60	6.70	[11.40]	–	4.50
7 Transport	10.00	17.40	36.70	[16.80]	–	15.10
8 Communication	5.10	5.90	9.50	[10.30]	–	5.90
9 Recreation & culture	14.60	30.80	57.90	[55.80]	–	24.80
10 Education	–	0.10	4.10	[3.80]	–	0.50
11 Restaurants & hotels	6.60	12.70	14.00	[30.30]	–	9.70
12 Miscellaneous goods & services	10.50	20.00	28.70	[38.80]	–	15.90
1-12 All expenditure groups	127.70	186.00	276.90	[345.70]	–	165.30
13 Other expenditure items	13.60	36.90	54.00	[282.70]	–	30.50
Total expenditure	**141.30**	**222.90**	**330.90**	**[628.40]**	**–**	**195.80**
Average weekly expenditure per person (£)						
Total expenditure	**141.30**	**222.90**	**330.90**	**[628.40]**	**–**	**195.80**

Note: The commodity and service categories are not comparable to those in publications before 2001-02.
        Please see page xiii for symbols and conventions used in this report

1   Mainly dependent on state pension and not economically active – see Appendix B.
2   Excluding mortgage interest payments, council tax and Northern Ireland rates.

Table 3.6E

Expenditure of two adult households with children by gross equivalised income quintile group, 2008

based on weighted data and including children's expenditure

	Lowest twenty per cent	Second quintile group	Third quintile group	Fourth quintile group	Highest twenty per cent	All house-holds
Lower boundary of group (£ per week)		260	412	600	898	
Weighted number of households (thousands)	670	870	1,200	1,220	990	4,950
Total number of households in sample	140	210	290	300	250	1,180
Total number of persons in sample	570	830	1,130	1,120	910	4,580
Total number of adults in sample	280	410	580	600	490	2,370
Weighted average number of persons per household	4.0	4.0	3.9	3.7	3.7	3.8
Commodity or service	Average weekly household expenditure (£)					
1 Food & non-alcoholic drinks	54.40	63.90	63.80	75.30	89.30	70.50
2 Alcoholic drinks, tobacco & narcotics	14.10	12.40	11.10	13.50	16.90	13.50
3 Clothing & footwear	23.50	21.50	28.80	32.50	46.20	31.20
4 Housing (net)[1], fuel & power	61.20	67.60	59.90	53.00	79.90	63.70
5 Household goods & services	29.90	20.50	30.80	44.50	84.90	43.10
6 Health	1.60	2.90	4.80	4.70	5.10	4.10
7 Transport	33.90	55.70	67.90	104.10	154.60	87.40
8 Communication	11.10	14.70	13.60	14.50	17.60	14.50
9 Recreation & culture	38.90	53.00	72.30	82.80	137.80	80.10
10 Education	[3.10]	3.00	3.80	5.60	64.10	16.00
11 Restaurants & hotels	29.00	31.70	43.20	53.10	90.10	51.10
12 Miscellaneous goods & services	21.20	29.90	50.30	65.30	107.00	57.80
1-12 All expenditure groups	321.90	376.80	450.30	548.90	893.40	532.90
13 Other expenditure items	38.30	69.50	115.00	153.90	282.60	139.80
Total expenditure	360.20	446.30	565.30	702.80	1176.10	672.70
Average weekly expenditure per person (£)						
Total expenditure	90.20	111.50	146.80	190.40	321.30	176.10

Note: The commodity and service categories are not comparable to those in publications before 2001-02.
Please see page xiii for symbols and conventions used in this report

1   Excluding mortgage interest payments, council tax and Northern Ireland rates.

Table 3.6

Expenditure of two adult households with children by gross income quintile group, 2008

based on weighted data and including children's expenditure

	Lowest twenty per cent	Second quintile group	Third quintile group	Fourth quintile group	Highest twenty per cent	All house-holds
Lower boundary of group (£ per week)		223	408	664	1,026	
Weighted number of households (thousands)	290	530	1,100	1,500	1,530	4,950
Total number of households in sample	60	120	260	370	380	1,180
Total number of persons in sample	200	460	1,010	1,420	1,490	4,580
Total number of adults in sample	110	230	520	740	760	2,370
Weighted average number of persons per household	3.6	4.0	3.8	3.8	3.9	3.8
Commodity or service	Average weekly household expenditure (£)					
1 Food & non-alcoholic drinks	49.30	52.90	64.70	68.30	86.90	70.50
2 Alcoholic drinks, tobacco & narcotics	15.00	13.40	11.10	12.50	15.90	13.50
3 Clothing & footwear	15.50	25.20	22.30	30.50	43.40	31.20
4 Housing (net)[1], fuel & power	54.50	71.60	65.90	56.00	68.70	63.70
5 Household goods & services	19.00	31.40	20.40	37.90	73.00	43.10
6 Health	1.60	1.20	3.50	4.70	5.30	4.10
7 Transport	23.60	43.00	56.50	82.60	142.00	87.40
8 Communication	9.60	12.10	14.40	13.70	16.90	14.50
9 Recreation & culture	33.60	41.50	49.70	81.80	122.50	80.10
10 Education	[5.10]	[1.10]	3.00	4.80	43.70	16.00
11 Restaurants & hotels	30.90	28.70	31.00	49.70	78.50	51.10
12 Miscellaneous goods & services	16.80	24.20	41.20	51.70	95.30	57.80
1-12 All expenditure groups	274.50	346.30	383.80	494.20	792.10	532.90
13 Other expenditure items	31.30	47.80	75.50	130.70	247.50	139.80
Total expenditure	**305.70**	**394.10**	**459.20**	**624.90**	**1039.60**	**672.70**
Average weekly expenditure per person (£)						
Total expenditure	**85.90**	**99.70**	**120.20**	**165.60**	**268.90**	**176.10**

Note: The commodity and service categories are not comparable to those in publications before 2001-02.
        Please see page xiii for symbols and conventions used in this report

1   Excluding mortgage interest payments, council tax and Northern Ireland rates.

Table 3.7E

Expenditure of one adult households with children by gross equivalised income quintile group, 2008

based on weighted data and including children's expenditure

	Lowest twenty per cent	Second quintile group	Third quintile group	Fourth quintile group	Highest twenty per cent	All house-holds
Lower boundary of group (£ per week)		260	412	600	898	
Weighted number of households (thousands)	710	360	200	160	50	1,490
Total number of households in sample	180	90	50	40	10	380
Total number of persons in sample	520	240	120	100	30	1,010
Total number of adults in sample	180	90	50	40	10	380
Weighted average number of persons per household	2.8	2.5	2.3	2.4	2.1	2.6
Commodity or service			Average weekly household expenditure (£)			
1 Food & non-alcoholic drinks	39.70	44.10	43.80	49.20	[52.10]	42.80
2 Alcoholic drinks, tobacco & narcotics	8.10	8.60	5.00	13.50	[14.30]	8.60
3 Clothing & footwear	14.60	21.50	24.70	25.40	[30.80]	19.40
4 Housing (net)[1], fuel & power	41.40	68.40	71.00	42.60	[98.60]	54.10
5 Household goods & services	15.00	22.30	23.10	34.30	[39.70]	20.80
6 Health	0.60	1.60	1.70	13.60	[5.00]	2.60
7 Transport	13.90	33.00	35.20	47.60	[81.80]	27.40
8 Communication	7.50	11.80	12.50	14.80	[15.90]	10.30
9 Recreation & culture	26.10	44.60	39.00	53.60	[88.40]	37.50
10 Education	[0.80]	[3.70]	[2.20]	[5.70]	[43.10]	3.70
11 Restaurants & hotels	16.40	20.30	22.40	39.90	[35.50]	21.40
12 Miscellaneous goods & services	11.30	24.40	29.90	56.20	[72.90]	24.00
1-12 All expenditure groups	195.60	304.30	310.50	396.30	[578.10]	272.40
13 Other expenditure items	12.90	52.30	61.50	123.30	[146.10]	45.50
Total expenditure	**208.40**	**356.60**	**372.00**	**519.60**	**[724.20]**	**317.90**
Average weekly expenditure per person (£)						
Total expenditure	**73.20**	**141.10**	**160.10**	**218.00**	**[342.80]**	**121.10**

Note: The commodity and service categories are not comparable to those in publications before 2001-02.
Please see page xiii for symbols and conventions used in this report

1 Excluding mortgage interest payments, council tax and Northern Ireland rates.

Table 3.7

Expenditure of one adult households with children by gross income quintile group, 2008

based on weighted data and including children's expenditure

	Lowest twenty per cent	Second quintile group	Third quintile group	Fourth quintile group	Highest twenty per cent	All house-holds
Lower boundary of group (£ per week)		223	408	664	1,026	
Weighted number of households (thousands)	580	550	220	110	30	1,490
Total number of households in sample	140	140	60	30	–	380
Total number of persons in sample	350	400	170	70	20	1,010
Total number of adults in sample	140	140	60	30	–	380
Weighted average number of persons per household	2.5	2.8	2.6	2.4	2.6	2.6
Commodity or service			Average weekly household expenditure (£)			
1 Food & non-alcoholic drinks	35.10	46.10	45.90	54.10	[64.80]	42.80
2 Alcoholic drinks, tobacco & narcotics	7.40	8.70	8.90	14.30	[7.10]	8.60
3 Clothing & footwear	10.90	22.80	29.30	20.40	[42.60]	19.40
4 Housing (net)[1], fuel & power	43.80	60.10	57.50	61.90	[87.70]	54.10
5 Household goods & services	10.70	24.70	22.50	43.30	[47.70]	20.80
6 Health	0.60	1.20	1.60	[16.00]	[21.40]	2.60
7 Transport	13.70	24.50	47.30	54.30	[96.50]	27.40
8 Communication	7.10	9.50	17.00	14.90	[19.70]	10.30
9 Recreation & culture	23.70	37.70	51.20	60.80	[109.60]	37.50
10 Education	[0.70]	2.70	[3.50]	[9.70]	[59.40]	3.70
11 Restaurants & hotels	14.90	18.30	30.90	46.40	[38.10]	21.40
12 Miscellaneous goods & services	11.20	19.40	48.60	49.80	[74.50]	24.00
1-12 All expenditure groups	179.80	275.80	364.10	445.90	[669.00]	272.40
13 Other expenditure items	11.50	37.40	101.80	117.90	[161.30]	45.50
Total expenditure	**191.30**	**313.20**	**465.90**	**563.80**	**[830.30]**	**317.90**
Average weekly expenditure per person (£)						
Total expenditure	**75.60**	**112.60**	**181.60**	**230.30**	**[314.60]**	**121.10**

Note: The commodity and service categories are not comparable to those in publications before 2001-02.
        Please see page xiii for symbols and conventions used in this report

1   Excluding mortgage interest payments, council tax and Northern Ireland rates.

Table 3.8E

Expenditure of one man one woman non-retired households by gross equivalised income quintile group, 2008

based on weighted data

	Lowest twenty per cent	Second quintile group	Third quintile group	Fourth quintile group	Highest twenty per cent	All house-holds
Lower boundary of group (£ per week)		260	412	600	898	
Weighted number of households (thousands)	310	530	890	1,310	2,020	5,050
Total number of households in sample	70	130	210	310	450	1,170
Total number of persons in sample	140	260	420	610	900	2,340
Total number of adults in sample	140	260	420	610	900	2,340
Weighted average number of persons per household	2.0	2.0	2.0	2.0	2.0	2.0
Commodity or service	Average weekly household expenditure (£)					
1 Food & non-alcoholic drinks	43.40	48.10	53.10	49.50	55.60	52.00
2 Alcoholic drinks, tobacco & narcotics	9.60	11.40	13.40	12.60	12.00	12.20
3 Clothing & footwear	16.40	11.80	18.70	21.00	36.60	25.60
4 Housing (net)[1], fuel & power	50.60	54.60	52.80	54.40	53.60	53.60
5 Household goods & services	29.20	24.60	26.90	36.60	52.90	39.70
6 Health	3.80	3.90	7.40	4.60	8.90	6.70
7 Transport	33.20	40.90	64.90	84.00	115.50	85.60
8 Communication	8.40	9.70	12.80	13.90	15.50	13.50
9 Recreation & culture	33.20	39.60	53.80	62.40	107.80	74.80
10 Education	[1.20]	[0.30]	[1.30]	[2.90]	8.90	4.60
11 Restaurants & hotels	21.40	24.80	26.90	46.00	70.00	48.50
12 Miscellaneous goods & services	20.10	26.90	28.80	37.40	51.10	39.20
1-12 All expenditure groups	270.50	296.40	360.80	425.10	588.40	456.00
13 Other expenditure items	27.80	51.30	55.00	96.80	164.90	107.60
Total expenditure	**298.30**	**347.70**	**415.70**	**521.90**	**753.30**	**563.70**
Average weekly expenditure per person (£)						
Total expenditure	**149.20**	**173.90**	**207.90**	**261.00**	**376.60**	**281.80**

Note: The commodity and service categories are not comparable to those in publications before 2001-02.
Please see page xiii for symbols and conventions used in this report

1 Excluding mortgage interest payments, council tax and Northern Ireland rates.

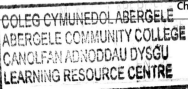

Table 3.8

Expenditure of one man one woman non-retired households by gross income quintile group, 2008

based on weighted data

Commodity or service	Lowest twenty per cent	Second quintile group	Third quintile group	Fourth quintile group	Highest twenty per cent	All house-holds
Lower boundary of group (£ per week)		223	408	664	1,026	
Weighted number of households (thousands)	200	640	1,170	1,520	1,530	5,050
Total number of households in sample	50	150	280	350	340	1,170
Total number of persons in sample	90	310	560	690	690	2,340
Total number of adults in sample	90	310	560	690	690	2,340
Weighted average number of persons per household	2.0	2.0	2.0	2.0	2.0	2.0
Commodity or service			Average weekly household expenditure (£)			
1 Food & non-alcoholic drinks	42.20	47.40	50.70	51.60	56.70	52.00
2 Alcoholic drinks, tobacco & narcotics	9.30	11.30	12.50	13.30	11.50	12.20
3 Clothing & footwear	10.50	14.30	19.90	24.40	37.70	25.60
4 Housing (net)[1], fuel & power	45.10	55.90	50.90	56.50	52.90	53.60
5 Household goods & services	33.40	24.40	29.40	36.70	57.60	39.70
6 Health	3.40	4.00	6.80	5.20	9.70	6.70
7 Transport	26.70	40.80	66.60	83.20	128.70	85.60
8 Communication	7.60	9.70	12.70	14.50	15.60	13.50
9 Recreation & culture	27.60	40.10	54.50	70.60	115.10	74.80
10 Education	[1.90]	[0.20]	[1.70]	2.90	10.80	4.60
11 Restaurants & hotels	11.60	27.20	27.40	54.20	72.40	48.50
12 Miscellaneous goods & services	22.20	25.20	28.50	44.20	50.40	39.20
1-12 All expenditure groups	241.40	300.50	361.50	457.40	619.20	456.00
13 Other expenditure items	23.00	48.60	60.80	109.70	176.80	107.60
Total expenditure	**264.30**	**349.10**	**422.30**	**567.10**	**796.10**	**563.70**
Average weekly expenditure per person (£) **Total expenditure**	**132.20**	**174.60**	**211.10**	**283.50**	**398.00**	**281.80**

Note: The commodity and service categories are not comparable to those in publications before 2001-02.
Please see page xiii for symbols and conventions used in this report

1   Excluding mortgage interest payments, council tax and Northern Ireland rates.

Table 3.9E

Expenditure of one person retired households mainly dependent on state pensions[1] by gross equivalised income quintile group, 2008

based on weighted data

	Lowest twenty per cent	Second quintile group	Third quintile group	Fourth quintile group	Highest twenty per cent	All house-holds
Lower boundary of group (£ per week)		260	412	600	898	
Weighted number of households (thousands)	600	320	60	0	0	970
Total number of households in sample	120	70	10	0	0	200
Total number of persons in sample	120	70	10	0	0	200
Total number of adults in sample	120	70	10	0	0	200
Weighted average number of persons per household	1.0	1.0	1.0	0	0	1.0
Commodity or service	Average weekly household expenditure (£)					
1 Food & non-alcoholic drinks	24.90	23.20	[22.10]	–	–	24.20
2 Alcoholic drinks, tobacco & narcotics	3.70	3.10	[0.40]	–	–	3.30
3 Clothing & footwear	4.40	5.00	[0.80]	–	–	4.40
4 Housing (net)[2], fuel & power	29.90	35.40	[52.00]	–	–	33.00
5 Household goods & services	10.50	16.70	[13.50]	–	–	12.70
6 Health	1.20	1.60	[16.70]	–	–	2.20
7 Transport	6.30	4.90	[10.60]	–	–	6.10
8 Communication	5.30	6.10	[4.00]	–	–	5.50
9 Recreation & culture	14.70	14.60	[24.70]	–	–	15.20
10 Education	–	–	–	–	–	–
11 Restaurants & hotels	6.60	7.40	[9.90]	–	–	7.10
12 Miscellaneous goods & services	13.10	13.80	[15.10]	–	–	13.40
1-12 All expenditure groups	120.70	131.80	169.80	–	–	127.10
13 Other expenditure items	15.50	16.60	[61.80]	–	–	18.60
Total expenditure	**136.20**	**148.40**	**[231.50]**	**–**	**–**	**145.70**
Average weekly expenditure per person (£)						
Total expenditure	**136.20**	**148.40**	**[231.50]**	**–**	**–**	**145.70**

Note: The commodity and service categories are not comparable to those in publications before 2001-02.
Please see page xiii for symbols and conventions used in this report

1 Mainly dependent on state pension and not economically active - see appendix B.

2 Excluding mortgage interest payments, council tax and Northern Ireland rates.

Table 3.9

Expenditure of one person retired households mainly dependent on state pensions[1] by gross income quintile group, 2008

based on weighted data

	Lowest twenty per cent	Second quintile group	Third quintile group	Fourth quintile group	Highest twenty per cent	All house-holds
Lower boundary of group (£ per week)		223	408	664	1,026	
Weighted number of households (thousands)	830	150	0	0	0	970
Total number of households in sample	170	30	0	0	0	200
Total number of persons in sample	170	30	0	0	0	200
Total number of adults in sample	170	30	0	0	0	200
Weighted average number of persons per household	1.0	1.0	0	0	0	1.0
Commodity or service	Average weekly household expenditure (£)					
1 Food & non-alcoholic drinks	24.70	21.00	–	–	–	24.20
2 Alcoholic drinks, tobacco & narcotics	3.80	[0.20]	–	–	–	3.30
3 Clothing & footwear	4.50	[4.10]	–	–	–	4.40
4 Housing (net)[2], fuel & power	31.70	40.30	–	–	–	33.00
5 Household goods & services	11.00	22.20	–	–	–	12.70
6 Health	1.30	[7.60]	–	–	–	2.20
7 Transport	6.30	[4.80]	–	–	–	6.10
8 Communication	5.60	5.10	–	–	–	5.50
9 Recreation & culture	15.40	14.20	–	–	–	15.20
10 Education	–	–	–	–	–	–
11 Restaurants & hotels	6.90	[7.80]	–	–	–	7.10
12 Miscellaneous goods & services	13.10	15.00	–	–	–	13.40
1-12 All expenditure groups	124.40	142.20	–	–	–	127.10
13 Other expenditure items	17.10	[26.90]	–	–	–	18.60
Total expenditure	141.50	169.10	–	–	–	145.70
Average weekly expenditure per person (£) Total expenditure	141.50	169.10	–	–	–	145.70

Note: The commodity and service categories are not comparable to those in publications before 2001-02.
Please see page xiii for symbols and conventions used in this report

1 Mainly dependent on state pension and not economically active - see appendix B.
2 Excluding mortgage interest payments, council tax and Northern Ireland rates.

Table 3.10E

Expenditure of one man one woman retired households mainly dependent on state pensions[1] by gross equivalised income quintile group, 2008

based on weighted data

Commodity or service	Lowest twenty per cent	Second quintile group	Third quintile group	Fourth quintile group	Highest twenty per cent	All house-holds
Lower boundary of group (£ per week)		260	412	600	898	
Weighted number of households (thousands)	350	170	20	0	0	540
Total number of households in sample	100	50	-	0	0	150
Total number of persons in sample	190	100	10	0	0	300
Total number of adults in sample	190	100	10	0	0	300
Weighted average number of persons per household	2.0	2.0	2.0	0	0	2.0
			Average weekly household expenditure (£)			
1 Food & non-alcoholic drinks	47.80	46.00	[49.40]	–	–	47.30
2 Alcoholic drinks, tobacco & narcotics	6.70	12.00	[6.50]	–	–	8.30
3 Clothing & footwear	9.50	7.80	[13.70]	–	–	9.10
4 Housing (net)[2], fuel & power	35.20	35.50	[71.40]	–	–	36.60
5 Household goods & services	15.70	24.80	[15.60]	–	–	18.50
6 Health	3.70	6.30	[8.50]	–	–	4.70
7 Transport	23.10	28.80	[47.70]	–	–	25.80
8 Communication	6.10	7.10	[4.90]	–	–	6.40
9 Recreation & culture	43.90	37.40	[46.00]	–	–	42.00
10 Education	[0.70]	–	–	–	–	[0.50]
11 Restaurants & hotels	13.30	14.90	[23.20]	–	–	14.20
12 Miscellaneous goods & services	18.90	18.90	[19.50]	–	–	18.90
1-12 All expenditure groups	224.60	239.50	[306.20]	–	–	232.20
13 Other expenditure items	25.60	27.70	[9.80]	–	–	25.70
Total expenditure	250.20	267.20	[316.00]	–	–	257.90
Average weekly expenditure per person (£) **Total expenditure**	125.10	133.60	[158.00]	–	–	128.90

Note: The commodity and service categories are not comparable to those in publications before 2001-02.
Please see page xiii for symbols and conventions used in this report

1   Mainly dependent on state pension and not economically active - see appendix B.

2   Excluding mortgage interest payments, council tax and Northern Ireland rates.

Table 3.10

Expenditure of one man one woman retired households mainly dependent on state pensions[1] by gross income quintile group, 2008

based on weighted data

Commodity or service	Lowest twenty per cent	Second quintile group	Third quintile group	Fourth quintile group	Highest twenty per cent	All house-holds
Lower boundary of group (£ per week)		223	408	664	1,026	
Weighted number of households (thousands)	210	310	20	0	0	540
Total number of households in sample	60	90	–	0	0	150
Total number of persons in sample	120	180	10	0	0	300
Total number of adults in sample	120	180	10	0	0	300
Weighted average number of persons per household	2.0	2.0	2.0	0	0	2.0
Commodity or service	Average weekly household expenditure (£)					
1 Food & non-alcoholic drinks	47.30	47.20	[49.40]	–	–	47.30
2 Alcoholic drinks, tobacco & narcotics	6.50	9.60	[6.50]	–	–	8.30
3 Clothing & footwear	8.30	9.30	[13.70]	–	–	9.10
4 Housing (net)[2], fuel & power	33.00	36.90	[71.40]	–	–	36.60
5 Household goods & services	12.50	22.80	[15.60]	–	–	18.50
6 Health	2.80	5.70	[8.50]	–	–	4.70
7 Transport	25.30	24.70	[47.70]	–	–	25.80
8 Communication	6.50	6.40	[4.90]	–	–	6.40
9 Recreation & culture	29.40	50.30	[46.00]	–	–	42.00
10 Education	–	[0.80]	–	–	–	0.50
11 Restaurants & hotels	13.40	14.10	[23.20]	–	–	14.20
12 Miscellaneous goods & services	19.40	18.60	[19.50]	–	–	18.90
1-12 All expenditure groups	204.40	246.40	[306.20]	–	–	232.20
13 Other expenditure items	21.90	29.30	[9.80]	–	–	25.70
Total expenditure	**226.20**	**275.70**	**[316.00]**	**–**	**–**	**257.90**
Average weekly expenditure per person (£)						
Total expenditure	**113.10**	**137.80**	**[158.00]**	**–**	**–**	**128.90**

Note: The commodity and service categories are not comparable to those in publications before 2001-02.
        Please see page xiii for symbols and conventions used in this report

1   Mainly dependent on state pension and not economically active - see appendix B.
2   Excluding mortgage interest payments, council tax and Northern Ireland rates.

Table 3.11E

Expenditure of one man one woman retired households not mainly dependent on state pensions[1] by gross equivalised income quintile group, 2008

based on weighted data

	Lowest twenty per cent	Second quintile group	Third quintile group	Fourth quintile group	Highest twenty per cent	All house-holds
Lower boundary of group (£ per week)		260	412	600	898	
Weighted number of households (thousands)	330	800	490	260	120	2,000
Total number of households in sample	80	220	130	70	30	530
Total number of persons in sample	160	440	250	140	70	1,070
Total number of adults in sample	160	440	250	140	70	1,070
Weighted average number of persons per household	2.0	2.0	2.0	2.0	2.0	2.0
Commodity or service	Average weekly household expenditure (£)					
1 Food & non-alcoholic drinks	46.20	50.60	56.70	65.10	60.40	53.80
2 Alcoholic drinks, tobacco & narcotics	5.90	7.90	7.80	12.20	17.70	8.70
3 Clothing & footwear	6.30	9.20	16.60	21.60	31.90	13.60
4 Housing (net)[2], fuel & power	36.30	40.10	38.30	43.30	75.20	41.60
5 Household goods & services	20.40	25.60	33.00	48.20	83.10	33.10
6 Health	2.30	4.70	5.70	4.80	[9.90]	4.90
7 Transport	22.60	36.30	50.80	68.20	71.10	43.90
8 Communication	7.50	7.20	7.20	9.20	12.10	7.80
9 Recreation & culture	32.50	44.30	145.20	114.80	133.00	81.70
10 Education	[0.80]	–	[0.80]	[1.50]	[2.30]	[0.70]
11 Restaurants & hotels	12.60	18.90	29.30	45.40	73.90	27.30
12 Miscellaneous goods & services	17.30	22.00	26.80	65.50	72.80	31.20
1-12 All expenditure groups	210.80	266.90	418.00	499.80	643.40	348.20
13 Other expenditure items	23.20	35.30	48.70	89.30	102.00	47.70
Total expenditure	**234.00**	**302.20**	**466.70**	**589.10**	**745.50**	**395.90**
Average weekly expenditure per person (£)						
Total expenditure	**117.00**	**151.10**	**233.30**	**294.50**	**372.70**	**197.90**

Note: The commodity and service categories are not comparable to those in publications before 2001-02.
Please see page xiii for symbols and conventions used in this report.
1 Mainly dependent on state pension and not economically active – see Appendix B.
2 Excluding mortgage interest payments, council tax and Northern Ireland rates.

Table 3.11

Expenditure of one man one woman retired households not mainly dependent on state pensions[1] by gross income quintile group, 2008

based on weighted data

Commodity or service	Lowest twenty per cent	Second quintile group	Third quintile group	Fourth quintile group	Highest twenty per cent	All house-holds
Lower boundary of group (£ per week)		223	408	664	1,026	
Weighted number of households (thousands)	200	890	600	210	100	2,000
Total number of households in sample	50	250	160	60	30	530
Total number of persons in sample	90	500	310	110	60	1,070
Total number of adults in sample	90	500	310	110	60	1,070
Weighted average number of persons per household	2.0	2.0	2.0	2.0	2.0	2.0
Commodity or service			Average weekly household expenditure (£)			
1 Food & non-alcoholic drinks	46.60	50.00	56.20	67.20	60.90	53.80
2 Alcoholic drinks, tobacco & narcotics	6.50	7.60	8.00	12.80	18.80	8.70
3 Clothing & footwear	7.30	8.70	15.80	23.60	34.10	13.60
4 Housing (net)[2], fuel & power	35.80	40.20	37.90	46.80	76.30	41.60
5 Household goods & services	18.80	21.10	38.70	58.40	80.30	33.10
6 Health	1.40	4.70	5.30	4.60	[11.30]	4.90
7 Transport	19.90	34.40	55.30	59.00	75.80	43.90
8 Communication	8.20	7.00	7.60	9.40	12.30	7.80
9 Recreation & culture	37.30	39.80	133.40	124.70	143.50	81.70
10 Education	–	[0.30]	[0.60]	[1.80]	[2.80]	[0.70]
11 Restaurants & hotels	11.30	18.50	29.50	52.00	70.90	27.30
12 Miscellaneous goods & services	19.70	20.50	27.10	73.90	82.20	31.20
1-12 All expenditure groups	212.70	252.80	415.30	534.40	669.10	348.20
13 Other expenditure items	17.30	34.90	47.40	102.10	108.70	47.70
Total expenditure	**230.00**	**287.70**	**462.70**	**636.40**	**777.70**	**395.90**
Average weekly expenditure per person (£)						
Total expenditure	**115.00**	**143.80**	**231.40**	**318.20**	**388.90**	**197.90**

Note: The commodity and service categories are not comparable to those in publications before 2001-02.
         Please see page xiii for symbols and conventions used in this report.
1   Mainly dependent on state pension and not economically active – see Appendix B.
2   Excluding mortgage interest payments, council tax and Northern Ireland rates.

Table 3.12E

Income and source of income by gross equivalised income quintile group, 2008

based on weighted data

| | Weighted number of house-holds | Number of house-holds in the sample | Weekly household income | | Source of income | | | | | |
			Dispo-sable	Gross	Wages and salaries	Self employ-ment	Invest-ments	Annuities and pensions[1]	Social security benefits[2]	Other sources
Gross Equivalised income quintile group	(000s)	Number	£	£	Percentage of gross weekly household income					
Lowest twenty per cent	5,140	1,150	166	173	15	3	2	4	74	2
Second quintile group	5,140	1,210	322	353	39	6	2	11	40	2
Third quintile group	5,140	1,170	490	574	62	7	2	10	16	2
Fourth quintile group	5,140	1,170	679	838	76	7	2	8	7	1
Highest twenty per cent	5,130	1,140	1,251	1,629	75	13	6	4	2	0

Note: Please see page xiii for symbols and conventions used in this report.
1 Other than social security benefits.
2 Excluding housing benefit and council tax benefit (rates rebate in Northern Ireland) – see Appendix B.

Table 3.12

Income and source of income by gross income quintile group, 2008

based on weighted data

| | Weighted number of house-holds | Number of house-holds in the sample | Weekly household income | | Source of income | | | | | |
			Dispo-sable	Gross	Wages and salaries	Self employ-ment	Invest-ments	Annuities and pensions[1]	Social security benefits[2]	Other sources
Gross income quintile group	(000s)	Number	£	£	Percentage of gross weekly household income					
Lowest twenty per cent	5,140	1,120	141	146	6	2	2	9	80	1
Second quintile group	5,130	1,240	285	310	31	4	3	16	45	1
Third quintile group	5,140	1,190	450	528	59	6	3	13	18	1
Fourth quintile group	5,140	1,160	673	826	75	8	2	7	7	1
Highest twenty per cent	5,140	1,130	1,359	1,757	77	12	5	3	2	0

Note: Please see page xiii for symbols and conventions used in this report.
1 Other than social security benefits.
2 Excluding housing benefit and council tax benefit (rates rebate in Northern Ireland) – see Appendix B.

Trends in household expenditure over time

Background

This chapter presents household expenditure data over time using both the Family Expenditure Survey (FES) and the Classification Of Individual COnsumption by Purpose (COICOP) classifications. In 2001/02 the decision was made to move from the FES method of classification to COICOP as it is the internationally agreed standard classification for reporting household consumption expenditure. COICOP data are presented in Tables 4.3 – 4.5, but commentary in the chapter refers only to Tables 4.3 and 4.4 as these use figures that have been deflated using the All Items RPI Index. This allows a comparison of expenditure in real terms to be made between the survey years.

Interpreting EFS/LCF time series data

Prior to the introduction of the Expenditure and Food Survey (EFS) in 2001/02, expenditure data were collected via the Family Expenditure Survey (FES) and classified using the FES method of classification. These data have been retained and published alongside the COICOP time series and are presented in Tables 4.1 and 4.2.

Time series data based on the FES classification from 2001/02 (Tables 4.1 and 4.2) have been constructed by mapping COICOP data onto the FES classification. As such the 'all expenditure groups' totals in Table 4.1 may not equal the sum of the component commodities or services as the mapping process is not exact. Due to the differences in the definitions of the classification headings it is not possible to directly compare the FES data with the COICOP data (for example 'Motoring' in the FES classification includes vehicle insurance, whereas the 'Transport' heading under COICOP excludes this expenditure).

As mentioned above, tables 4.1 and 4.3 contain data that have been deflated to 2008 prices. To produce these data, each year's expenditure figures have been adjusted using the "All items" RPI Index to account for price inflation that has occurred since that year. This results in a table of figures displayed in "real terms" (i.e. at prices relative to 2008 prices), which allows comparisons to be made between different survey years. (The All items RPI Index can be downloaded from the National

Statistics website at: www.statistics.gov.uk/cci/nugget. asp?ID=21). Data in Table 4.5 have not been deflated to 2008 prices and therefore show the actual expenditure figures for each survey year.

Each year the Living Costs and Food Survey (LCF), previously the EFS, is reviewed and changes are made to keep it up to date. As such, year-on-year changes should be interpreted with caution. A detailed explanation of the items that feed into each COICOP heading can be found in Appendix A, while details of definition changes can be found in Appendix B.

Trends for the categories with lower levels of spending need to be treated with a degree of caution as the standard errors for these categories tend to be higher (standard errors are discussed in more detail in Appendix B). It should also be noted that there may be underreporting on certain items (notably tobacco and alcohol).

COICOP time series data in this publication are not directly comparable with UK National Accounts household expenditure data, which are published in Consumer Trends. (The Consumer Trends publication can be downloaded from the National Statistics website at www.statistics.gov.uk/statbase/Product. asp?vlnk=242). National Accounts figures draw on a number of sources in addition to the LCF (please refer to Appendix B of Consumer Trends for details) and may be more appropriate for deriving long term trends on expenditure.

Household expenditure over time

Prior to the introduction of the Expenditure and Food Survey (EFS) in 2001/02, expenditure data were collected via the Family Expenditure Survey (FES) and classified using the FES method of classification. These data have been retained and published alongside the COICOP time series and are presented in Tables 4.1 and 4.2.

Figure 4.1 and Table 4.3 show total household expenditure at 2008 prices, broken down by COICOP, over the period 2002/03 to 2008. In 2002/03 the total average weekly expenditure was £491.50, which grew to a peak of £496.00 in 2004/05 before declining to its lowest value of £471.00 in 2008.

Figure 4.1

Total household expenditure based on COICOP classification, 2002-03 to 2008, at 2008 prices.[1]

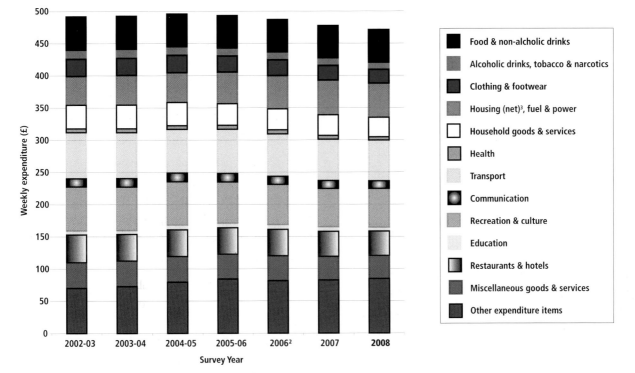

1. Figures have been deflated to 2008 prices using the RPI all items index.
2. Figures shown from 2006 onwards are based on weighted data using updated weights, with non-response weights and population figs based on 2001 census.
3. Excluding mortgage interest payments, council tax and Northern Ireland rates.

Figure 4.2

Household expenditure based on COICOP classification, 2002-03 to 2008, at 2008 prices[1]

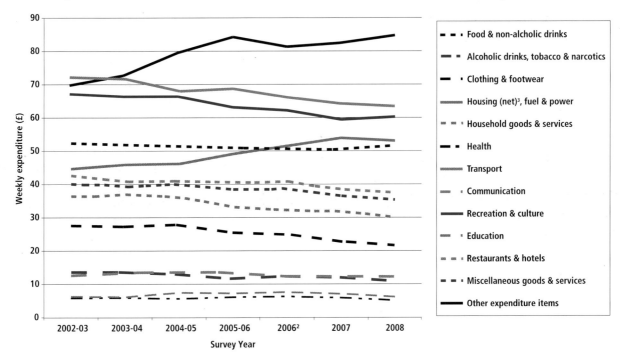

1. Figures have been deflated to 2008 prices using the RPI all items index.
2. Figures shown from 2006 onwards are based on weighted data using updated weights, with non-response weights and population figs based on 2001 census.
3. Excluding mortgage interest payments, council tax and Northern Ireland rates.

Figure 4.2, Table 4.3 and Table 4.4 show trends in household expenditure based on COICOP classification, from 2002/03 to 2008. Spending levels for most of the headline groups followed a similar trend, with peak levels of spending in 2002/03 which dropped gradually to a lowest amount in 2008. The only exception to this was housing, fuel and power, which increased steadily over this time period.

Excluding the other items category, transport consistently had the highest average weekly spend throughout the time series. Spending levels were greatest at the start of the time series, with households spending £71.70 per week in 2002/03; subsequently this fell every year to a lowest level of £63.40 in 2008. Expenditure was next highest on recreation and culture, which followed a similar trend to expenditure on transport; with a weekly spending level of £68.20 in 2002/03 before steadily declining to its lowest amount of £59.70 in 2007. Recreation and culture, and transport each accounted for between 12 and 15 per cent of overall spending throughout the time series.

Among the twelve COICOP headings, food and non–alcoholic drink had the most consistent expenditure over the time series, varying between £50.00 and £51.70 per week. This represents between 10 and 11 per cent of total expenditure for each year. Food and non–alcoholic drink was the only headline group

apart from housing, fuel and power that did not experience a noticeable decline in expenditure between 2002/03 and 2008.

Of the twelve main categories, housing, fuel and power was the only one to have higher levels of spending in 2008 than it did in 2002/03. It had the fourth highest level of spending in 2002/03 (£44.60 per week; 9 per cent of total expenditure), but increased progressively to become the third highest category in 2006 (£51.50 per week; 11 per cent of total expenditure).

As a proportion of total weekly expenditure, spending on each of the following categories remained relatively stable across the time series: restaurants and hotels (between 8 and 9 per cent of total expenditure), household goods and services (between 6 and 7 per cent) and clothing and footwear (5 per cent). Out of these three categories, clothing and footwear experienced the greatest variation in average weekly spending throughout the time series, from a highest level of £27.20 per week in 2004/05 to a lowest of £21.60 per week in 2008. Household goods and services experienced a similar decline in average weekly expenditure, from £36.60 in 2002/03 to £30.10 in 2008. Expenditure on restaurants and hotels was relatively stable over the time series, with spending varying between £42.90 per week in 2002/03 and £37.70 in 2008.

Table 4.1

Household expenditure based on the FES classification, 1992 to 2008 at 2008 prices[1]

Commodity or service	1992	1994 -95	1995[2] -96	1995[3] -96	1996 -97	1997 -98	1998 -1999	1999 -2000	2000 -2001
Weighted number of households (thousands)				24130	24,310	24,560	24,660	25,330	25,030
Total number of households in sample	7,420	6,850	6,800	6,800	6,420	6,410	6,630	7,100	6,640
Total number of persons	18,170	16,620	16,590	16,590	15,730	15,430	16,220	16,790	15,930
Average number of persons per household	2.5	2.4	2.4	2.4	2.5	2.4	2.4	2.3	2.4
Commodity or service				Average weekly household expenditure (£)					
1 Housing (Net)[7]	73.50	68.60	69.00	69.60	68.40	69.60	75.00	73.70	80.10
2 Fuel and power	20.20	19.10	18.50	18.40	18.50	17.00	15.30	14.60	14.90
3 Food and non-alcoholic drinks	73.90	74.50	75.70	77.40	78.40	77.20	77.30	77.00	77.60
4 Alcoholic drink	17.20	18.20	16.30	17.50	18.30	19.20	18.30	19.80	18.80
5 Tobacco	8.30	8.30	8.30	8.40	8.70	8.50	7.60	7.70	7.60
6 Clothing and footwear	25.40	25.30	24.50	25.40	26.20	27.50	28.50	27.10	27.60
7 Household goods	34.00	33.50	33.60	34.10	37.20	36.50	38.90	39.70	40.90
8 Household services	20.80	22.30	21.70	21.70	22.60	23.90	24.80	24.40	27.50
9 Personal goods and services	15.80	15.90	16.50	16.80	16.50	17.10	17.50	17.90	18.40
10 Motoring	55.30	53.50	52.90	54.70	58.90	63.90	67.90	67.90	69.10
11 Fares and other travel costs	11.20	9.80	8.80	9.50	10.80	11.60	10.90	11.80	11.90
12 Leisure goods	20.70	20.50	19.60	20.70	22.10	23.50	23.40	23.90	24.80
13 Leisure services	42.70	46.10	45.90	46.90	48.90	53.40	55.00	56.70	63.50
14 Miscellaneous	2.70	3.40	3.40	1.70	1.40	1.40	1.60	1.80	0.90
1-14 All expenditure groups	421.60	419.10	414.80	422.90	436.90	450.40	462.00	464.10	483.60
Average weekly expenditure per person (£) Total expenditure	168.60	174.60	172.80	176.70	174.80	187.70	192.50	201.80	205.50
				Average weekly household expenditure (£)[8]					
Gross income (£)	532	546	545	558	564	581	599	620	630
Disposable income (£)	434	441	439	448	461	473	486	505	513

Note: The commodity and service categories are not comparable to the COICOP categories used in Tables 4.3 and 4.4.
Figures are based on FES data between 1984 and 2000-01 and EFS data thereafter.

1   Figures have been deflated to 2008 prices using the RPI all items index. 1994-95 to 2005-06 figures have been adjusted using financial year index numbers downloaded at http://nswebcopy/StatBase/tsdataset.asp?vlnk=7173. 1992 and 2006 to 2007 figures have been adjusted using calendar year index numbers downloaded at http://nswebcopy/StatBase/tsdataset.asp?vlnk=7172

2   From 1992 to this version of 1995-96, figures shown are based on unweighted, adult only data.

3   From this version of 1995-96, figures are shown based on weighted data, including children's expenditure. Weighting is based on the population figures from the 1991 and 2001 Censuses

4   From 2001-02 onwards, commodities and services are based on COICOP codes broadly mapped to FES.

5   From 1995-96 to this version of 2006, figures shown are based on weighted data using non-response weights based on the 1991 Census and population figures from the 1991 and 2001 Censuses.

6   From this version of 2006, figures shown are based on weighted data using updated weights, with non-response weights and population figures based on the 2001 Census.

7   An improvement to the imputation of mortgage interest payments has been implemented for 2006 and 2007 data which should lead to more accurate figures. This will lead to a slight discontinuity. An error was discovered in the derivation of mortgage capital repayments which was leading to double counting. This has been amended for the 2006 and 2007 data.

8   Does not include imputed income from owner-occupied and rent-free households.

Table 4.1

Household expenditure based on the FES classification, 1992 to 2008 at 2008 prices[1] (cont.)

	2001 –02	2002 –03	2003 –04	2004 –05	2005 –06	2006[5]	2006[6]	2007	2008
Weighted number of households (thousands)	24,450	24,350	24,670	24,430	24,800	24,790	25,440	25,350	25,690
Total number of households in sample	7,470	6,930	7,050	6,800	6,790	6,650	6,650	6,140	5,850
Total number of persons	18,120	16,590	16,970	16,260	16,090	15,850	15,850	14,650	13,830
Weighted average number of persons per household	2.4	2.4	2.4	2.4	2.4	2.4	2.3	2.4	2.4

Commodity or service	Average weekly household expenditure (£)								
1 Housing (Net)[7]	81.40	80.70	82.30	87.60	89.90	90.50	90.20	95.70	94.00
2 Fuel and power	14.50	14.10	14.10	14.30	15.40	17.20	17.10	17.80	18.90
3 Food and non-alcoholic drinks	76.50	77.90	76.40	76.90	75.60	76.30	75.50	74.20	74.50
4 Alcoholic drink	17.70	17.90	17.40	16.90	16.40	16.10	16.00	15.20	13.40
5 Tobacco	6.80	6.60	6.40	5.70	5.10	5.00	5.10	4.70	4.60
6 Clothing and footwear	27.60	26.60	26.40	26.80	24.90	24.80	24.50	22.50	21.20
7 Household goods	40.80	40.90	41.30	40.70	37.30	37.40	36.90	36.00	34.00
8 Household services	29.10	28.30	29.30	30.00	30.20	28.80	28.60	27.50	27.30
9 Personal goods and services	18.50	18.40	19.00	18.30	18.80	19.10	19.00	18.50	17.20
10 Motoring	71.50	74.60	73.40	71.50	71.00	67.60	66.30	64.50	63.60
11 Fares and other travel costs	11.50	11.80	11.40	10.80	12.30	12.00	11.90	11.30	14.20
12 Leisure goods	24.30	24.80	25.20	24.50	21.60	21.30	21.00	20.90	19.00
13 Leisure services	64.10	64.90	64.80	68.00	70.10	71.90	70.80	64.10	65.90
14 Miscellaneous	2.30	2.40	2.30	2.30	2.40	2.30	2.20	2.00	2.00
1-14 All expenditure groups	486.50	489.80	489.50	494.20	491.00	490.40	485.10	474.90	469.70
Average weekly expenditure per person (£) **Total expenditure**	205.70	205.60	207.70	207.10	207.10	207.40	207.50	201.50	199.20

	Average weekly household expenditure (£)[8]								
Gross income (£)	668	668	671	686	685	696	688	686	713
Disposable income (£)	546	549	546	558	557	565	559	555	582

Note: The commodity and service categories are not comparable to the COICOP categories used in Tables 4.3 and 4.4.
Figures are based on FES data between 1984 and 2000-01 and EFS data thereafter.

1   Figures have been deflated to 2008 prices using the RPI all items index. 1994-95 to 2005-06 figures have been adjusted using financial year index numbers downloaded at http://nswebcopy/StatBase/tsdataset.asp?vlnk=7173. 1992 and 2006 to 2007 figures have been adjusted using calendar year index numbers downloaded at http://nswebcopy/StatBase/tsdataset.asp?vlnk=7172.

2   From 1992 to this version of 1995-96, figures shown are based on unweighted, adult only data.

3   From this version of 1995-96, figures are shown based on weighted data, including children's expenditure. Weighting is based on the population figures from the 1991 and 2001 Censuses.

4   From 2001-02 onwards, commodities and services are based on COICOP codes broadly mapped to FES.

5   From 1995-96 to this version of 2006, figures shown are based on weighted data using non-response weights based on the 1991 Census and population figures from the 1991 and 2001 Censuses.

6   From this version of 2006, figures shown are based on weighted data using updated weights, with non-response weights and population figures based on the 2001 Census.

7   An improvement to the imputation of mortgage interest payments has been implemented for 2006 and 2007 data which should lead to more accurate figures. This will lead to a slight discontinuity. An error was discovered in the derivation of mortgage capital repayments which was leading to double counting. This has been amended for the 2006 and 2007 data.

8   Does not include imputed income from owner-occupied and rent-free households.

Table 4.2

Household expenditure as a percentage of total expenditure, 1992 to 2008 based on the FES classification at 2008 prices[1]

Commodity or service	1992	1994 –95	1995[2] –96	1995[3] –96	1996 –97	1997 –98	1998 –99	1999 –2000	2000 –01
Weighted number of households (thousands)				24,130	24,310	24,560	24,660	25,330	25,030
Total number of households in sample	7,420	6,850	6,800	6,800	6,420	6,410	6,630	7,100	6,640
Total number of persons	18,170	16,620	16,590	16,590	15,730	15,430	16,220	16,790	15,930
Average number of persons per household	2.5	2.4	2.4	2.4	2.5	2.4	2.4	2.3	2.4
Commodity or service				Percentage of total expenditure					
1 Housing (Net)[7]	17	16	17	16	16	15	16	16	17
2 Fuel and power	5	5	4	4	4	4	3	3	3
3 Food and non-alcoholic drinks	18	18	18	18	18	17	17	17	16
4 Alcoholic drink	4	4	4	4	4	4	4	4	4
5 Tobacco	2	2	2	2	2	2	2	2	2
6 Clothing and footwear	6	6	6	6	6	6	6	6	6
7 Household goods	8	8	8	8	9	8	8	9	8
8 Household services	5	5	5	5	5	5	5	5	6
9 Personal goods and services	4	4	4	4	4	4	4	4	4
10 Motoring	13	13	13	13	13	14	15	15	14
11 Fares and other travel costs	3	2	2	2	2	3	2	3	2
12 Leisure goods	5	5	5	5	5	5	5	5	5
13 Leisure services	10	11	11	11	11	12	12	12	13
14 Miscellaneous	1	1	1	0	0	0	0	0	0
1-14 All expenditure groups	100	100	100	100	100	100	100	100	100

1   Figures have been deflated to 2008 prices using the RPI all items index. 1994-95 to 2005-06 figures have been adjusted using financial year index numbers downloaded at http://nswebcopy/StatBase/tsdataset.asp?vlnk=7173. 1992 and 2006 to 2007 figures have been adjusted using calendar year index numbers downloaded at http://nswebcopy/StatBase/tsdataset.asp?vlnk=7172.

2   From 1992 to this version of 1995-96, figures shown are based on unweighted, adult only data.

3   From this version of 1995-96, figures are shown based on weighted data, including children's expenditure. Weighting is based on the population figures from the 1991 and 2001 Censuses

4   From 2001-02 onwards, commodities and services are based on COICOP codes broadly mapped to FES.

5   From 1995-96 to this version of 2006, figures shown are based on weighted data using non-response weights based on the 1991 Census and population figures from the 1991 and 2001 Censuses.

6   From this version of 2006, figures shown are based on weighted data using updated weights, with non-response weights and population figures based on the 2001 Census.

7   An improvement to the imputation of mortgage interest payments has been implemented for 2006 and 2007 data which should lead to more accurate figures. This will lead to a slight discontinuity. An error was discovered in the derivation of mortgage capital repayments which was leading to double counting. This has been amended for the 2006 and 2007 data.

Table 4.2

Household expenditure as a percentage of total expenditure, 1992 to 2008 based on the FES classification at 2008 prices[1] (cont.)

	2001[4] –02	2002 –03	2003 –04	2004 –05	2005 –06	2006[5]	2006[7]	2007	2008
Weighted number of households (thousands)	24,450	24,350	24,670	24,430	24,800	24,790	25,440	25,350	25,690
Total number of households in sample	7,470	6,930	7,050	6,800	6,790	6,650	6,650	6,140	5,850
Total number of persons	18,120	16,590	16,970	16,260	16,090	15,850	15,850	14,650	13,830
Weighted average number of persons per household	2.4	2.4	2.4	2.4	2.4	2.4	2.3	2.4	2.4

Commodity or service	Percentage of total expenditure								
1 Housing (Net)[7]	17	16	17	18	18	18	19	20	20
2 Fuel and power	3	3	3	3	3	4	4	4	4
3 Food and non-alcoholic drinks	16	16	16	16	15	16	16	16	16
4 Alcoholic drink	4	4	4	3	3	3	3	3	3
5 Tobacco	1	1	1	1	1	1	1	1	1
6 Clothing and footwear	6	5	5	5	5	5	5	5	5
7 Household goods	8	8	8	8	8	8	8	8	7
8 Household services	6	6	6	6	6	6	6	6	6
9 Personal goods and services	4	4	4	4	4	4	4	4	4
10 Motoring	15	15	15	14	14	14	14	14	14
11 Fares and other travel costs	2	2	2	2	3	2	2	2	3
12 Leisure goods	5	5	5	5	4	4	4	4	4
13 Leisure services	13	13	13	14	14	15	15	13	14
14 Miscellaneous	0	0	0	0	0	0	0	0	0
1-14 All expenditure groups	100	100	100	100	100	100	100	100	100

1 Figures have been deflated to 2008 prices using the RPI all items index. 1994-95 to 2005-06 figures have been adjusted using financial year index numbers downloaded at http://nswebcopy/StatBase/tsdataset.asp?vlnk=7173. 1992 and 2006 to 2007 figures have been adjusted using calendar year index numbers downloaded at http://nswebcopy/StatBase/tsdataset.asp?vlnk=7172.

2 From 1992 to this version of 1995-96, figures shown are based on unweighted, adult only data.

3 From this version of 1995-96, figures are shown based on weighted data, including children's expenditure. Weighting is based on the population figures from the 1991 and 2001 Censuses

4 From 2001-02 onwards, commodities and services are based on COICOP codes broadly mapped to FES.

5 From 1995-96 to this version of 2006, figures shown are based on weighted data using non-response weights based on the 1991 Census and population figures from the 1991 and 2001 Censuses.

6 From this version of 2006, figures shown are based on weighted data using updated weights, with non-response weights and population figures based on the 2001 Census.

7 An improvement to the imputation of mortgage interest payments has been implemented for 2006 and 2007 data which should lead to more accurate figures. This will lead to a slight discontinuity. An error was discovered in the derivation of mortgage capital repayments which was leading to double counting. This has been amended for the 2006 and 2007 data.

Table 4.3

Household expenditure based on COICOP classification, 2002–03 to 2008 at 2008 prices[1]
based on weighted data and including children's expenditure

	2002–03	2003–04	2004–05	2005–06	2006[2]	2006[3]	2007	2008
Weighted number of households (thousands)	24,350	24,670	24,430	24,799	24,786	25,441	25,350	25,690
Total number of households in sample	6,930	7,050	6,800	6,790	6,650	6,650	6,140	5,850
Total number of persons in sample	16,590	16,970	16,260	16,090	15,850	15,850	14,650	13,830
Total number of adults in sample	12,450	12,620	12,260	12,170	12,000	12,000	11,220	10,640
Weighted average number of persons per household	2.4	2.4	2.4	2.4	2.4	2.3	2.4	2.4

Commodity or service	Average weekly household expenditure (£)							
1 Food & non-alcoholic drinks	51.70	51.20	51.10	50.40	50.80	50.20	50.00	50.70
2 Alcoholic drinks, tobacco & narcotics	13.80	13.80	12.90	12.00	12.10	12.00	11.60	10.80
3 Clothing & footwear	27.00	26.80	27.20	25.30	25.20	24.90	22.90	21.60
4 Housing(net)[4], fuel & power	44.60	45.90	46.20	49.10	51.60	51.50	53.80	53.00
5 Household goods & services	36.60	36.80	36.00	33.40	32.80	32.50	31.90	30.10
6 Health	5.80	5.90	5.70	6.10	6.40	6.30	5.90	5.10
7 Transport	71.70	71.50	68.00	68.70	67.30	66.00	64.10	63.40
8 Communication	12.80	13.20	13.40	13.20	12.70	12.60	12.40	12.00
9 Recreation & culture	68.20	67.40	67.40	64.00	63.40	62.40	59.70	60.10
10 Education	6.30	6.20	7.40	7.30	7.80	7.60	7.10	6.20
11 Restaurants & hotels	42.90	41.10	41.20	40.80	41.10	40.70	38.70	37.70
12 Miscellaneous goods & services	40.00	39.60	39.80	38.50	39.00	38.70	36.70	35.60
1-12 All expenditure groups	421.50	419.40	416.30	408.90	410.10	405.30	394.90	386.30
13 Other expenditure items[5]	70.10	72.90	79.60	84.30	82.00	81.40	82.50	84.60
Total expenditure	491.50	492.30	496.00	493.20	492.10	486.70	477.40	471.00

Average weekly expenditure per person (£) Total expenditure	206.40	208.80	207.80	209.20	208.10	208.20	202.60	199.80

	Average weekly household expenditure (£)							
Gross income (£)	668	671	686	685	696	688	686	713
Disposable income (£)	549	546	558	557	565	559	555	582

Note: The commodity and service categories are not comparable to the FES categories used in Tables 4.2 and 4.3.
1 Figures have been deflated to 2008 prices using the RPI all items index. 2002-03 to 2005-06 figures have been adjusted using financial year index numbers downloaded at http://nswebcopy/StatBase/tsdataset.asp?vlnk=7173. 2006 to 2007 figures have been adjusted using calendar year index numbers downloaded at http://nswebcopy/StatBase/tsdataset.asp?vlnk=7172.
2 From 2002-03 to this version of 2006, figures shown are based on weighted data using non-response weights based on the 1991 Census and population figures from the 1991 and 2001 Censuses.
3 From this version of 2006, figures shown are based on weighted data using updated weights, with non-response weights and population figures based on the 2001 Census.
4 Excluding mortgage interest payments, council tax and Northern Ireland rates.
5 An error was discovered in the derivation of mortgage capital repayments which was leading to double counting. This has been amended for the 2006 and 2007 data.

Table 4.4

Household expenditure as a percentage of total expenditure based on COICOP classification, 2002–03 to 2008 at 2008 prices[1]

based on weighted data and including children's expenditure

	2002–03	2003–04	2004–05	2005–06	2006[2]	2006[3]	2007	200
Weighted number of households (thousands)	24,350	24,670	24,430	24,800	24,790	25,440	25,350	25,690
Total number of households in sample	6,930	7,050	6,800	6,790	6,650	6,650	6,140	5,850
Total number of persons in sample	16,590	16,970	16,260	16,090	15,850	15,850	14,650	13,830
Total number of adults in sample	12,450	12,620	12,260	12,170	12,000	12,000	11,220	10,640
Weighted average number of persons per household	2.4	2.4	2.4	2.4	2.4	2.3	2.4	2.4

Commodity or service		Percentage of total expenditure						
1	Food & non-alcoholic drinks	11	10	10	10	10	10	10	11
2	Alcoholic drinks, tobacco & narcotics	3	3	3	2	2	2	2	2
3	Clothing & footwear	5	5	5	5	5	5	5	5
4	Housing(net)[4], fuel & power	9	9	9	10	10	11	11	11
5	Household goods & services	7	7	7	7	7	7	7	6
6	Health	1	1	1	1	1	1	1	1
7	Transport	15	15	14	14	14	14	13	13
8	Communication	3	3	3	3	3	3	3	3
9	Recreation & culture	14	14	14	13	13	13	12	13
10	Education	1	1	1	1	2	2	1	1
11	Restaurants & hotels	9	8	8	8	8	8	8	8
12	Miscellaneous goods & services	8	8	8	8	8	8	8	8
1-12	All expenditure groups	86	85	84	83	83	83	83	82
13	Other expenditure items[5]	14	15	16	17	17	17	17	18
	Total expenditure	100	100	100	100	100	100	100	100

Note: The commodity and service categories are not comparable to the FES categories used in Tables 4.2 and 4.3.

1 Figures have been deflated to 2008 prices using the RPI all items index. 2002-03 to 2005-06 figures have been adjusted using financial year index numbers downloaded at http://nswebcopy/StatBase/tsdataset.asp?vlnk=7173. 2006 to 2007 figures have been adjusted using calendar year index numbers downloaded at http://nswebcopy/StatBase/tsdataset.asp?vlnk=7172.

2 From 1995-96 to this version of 2006, figures shown are based on weighted data using non-response weights based on the 1991 Census and population figures from the 1991 and 2001 Censuses.

3 From this version of 2006, figures shown are based on weighted data using updated weights, with non-response weights and population figures based on the 2001 Census.

4 Excluding mortgage interest payments, council tax and Northern Ireland rates.

5 An error was discovered in the derivation of mortgage capital repayments which was leading to double counting. This has been amended for the 2006 and 2007 data.

Table 4.5

Household expenditure 2002-03 to 2008 COICOP based current prices

based on weighted data and including children's expenditure

	2002–03	2003–04	2004–05	2005–06	2006[2]	2006[3]	2007	2008
Weighted number of households (thousands)	24,350	24,670	24,430	24,800	24,790	25,440	25,350	25690
Total number of households in sample	6,930	7,050	6,800	6,790	6,650	6,650	6,140	5,850
Total number of persons in sample	16,590	16,970	16,260	16,090	15,850	15,850	14,650	13,830
Total number of adults in sample	12,450	12,620	12,260	12,170	12,000	12,000	11,220	10,640
Weighted average number of persons per household	2.4	2.4	2.4	2.4	2.4	2.3	2.4	2.4

Commodity or service	Average weekly household expenditure (£)							
1 Food & non-alcoholic drinks	42.70	43.50	44.70	45.30	46.90	46.30	48.10	50.70
2 Alcoholic drinks, tobacco & narcotics	11.40	11.70	11.30	10.80	11.10	11.10	11.20	10.79
3 Clothing & footwear	22.30	22.70	23.90	22.70	23.20	23.00	22.00	21.58
4 Housing(net)[4], fuel & power	36.90	39.00	40.40	44.20	47.60	47.50	51.80	53.04
5 Household goods & services	30.20	31.30	31.60	30.00	30.30	29.90	30.70	30.14
6 Health	4.80	5.00	4.90	5.50	5.90	5.80	5.70	5.13
7 Transport	59.20	60.70	59.60	61.70	62.00	60.80	61.70	63.38
8 Communication	10.60	11.20	11.70	11.90	11.70	11.60	11.90	11.95
9 Recreation & culture	56.40	57.30	59.00	57.50	58.50	57.60	57.40	60.06
10 Education	5.20	5.20	6.50	6.60	7.20	7.00	6.80	6.19
11 Restaurants & hotels	35.40	34.90	36.10	36.70	37.90	37.60	37.20	37.73
12 Miscellaneous goods & services	33.10	33.60	34.90	34.60	36.00	35.70	35.30	35.64
1-12 All expenditure groups	348.30	356.20	364.70	367.60	378.30	373.80	379.80	386.35
13 Other expenditure items[5]	57.90	61.90	69.70	75.80	75.60	75.10	79.30	84.65
Total expenditure[5]	406.20	418.10	434.40	443.40	453.90	449.00	459.20	470.99

Average weekly expenditure per person (£)								
Total expenditure	170.50	177.40	182.00	188.00	192.00	192.00	194.80	199.78

	Average weekly household expenditure (£)							
Gross income (£)	552	570	601	616	642	635	659	713.09
Disposable income (£)	453	464	489	500	521	515	534	581.64

Note: The commodity and service categories are not comparable to those in publications before 2001-02

1 Data in Table 4.5 have not been deflated to 2008 prices and therefore show the actual expenditure for the year they were collected. Because inflation is not taken into account, comparisons between the years should be made with caution.

2 From 2002-03 to this version of 2006, figures shown are based on weighted data using non-response weights based on the 1991 Census and population figures from the 1991 and 2001 Censuses.

3 From this version of 2006, figures shown are based on weighted data using updated weights, with non-response weights and population figures based on the 2001 Census.

4 Excluding mortgage interest payments, council tax and Northern Ireland rates.

5 An error was discovered in the derivation of mortgage capital repayments which was leading to double counting. This has been amended for the 2006 and 2007 data.

Regression analysis of household expenditure and income

Background

The purpose of this chapter is to demonstrate a multivariate analysis based on the Living Costs and Food survey (LCF). The aim of the analysis is to identify key characteristics of households affecting both household income and household expenditure, using regression techniques. The analysis uses the complete LCF 2008 sample containing 5,850 responding households across Great Britain and Northern Ireland.

This chapter outlines the techniques used for the quality assurance of the modelling, as well as the methodology used. It then presents the main findings of the analysis. Tables 5.3 and 5.4 summarise the regression analyses and provide more detailed results.

This chapter uses technical language to explain the regression techniques used. Therefore this chapter, unlike the others in Family Spending, may be less suitable for readers without a statistical background.

Explanatory variables for household expenditure and income

A number of potential explanatory variables were identified within the LCF dataset for modelling household expenditure and household income. These are variables that are likely to be associated with income and expenditure and are easy to define. Table 5.1 presents these variables and distinguishes between individual characteristics of the Household Reference Person (HRP) and household characteristics.

Table 5.1

Potential key variables to explain household expenditure and income

Individual characteristics
Gender of HRP
Age of HRP
Economic activity status of HRP
Socio-economic status of HRP
Household characteristics
Number of workers in the household
Household composition
Household tenure
Government Office Region
Urban/rural location of household
Gross normal weekly household income[1]

1 Please note that the gross normal weekly household income was considered as a potential predictor for household expenditure only.

Testing the Standard Assumptions

In order to apply a valid regression model, the analysis relies on certain assumptions being met. Firstly, there must be a linear relationship between the dependent and independent variables and secondly the independent variables must be linearly independent. Thirdly, multicollinearity tests can be used to check that the variables are not highly correlated with one another. In addition, the assumption of homoscedasticity requires the errors to have a constant variance, which can otherwise distort the precision of the β coefficient. Finally, the error distribution should also be normal.

The distributions for both dependent variables were found to be positively skewed; they did not follow a normal distribution. Consequently, these variables needed to be transformed, for which a log-transformation was chosen. Figures 5.1 and 5.2 illustrate the skewed distributions of the raw data. Figures 5.3 and 5.4 present the distribution after log-transformation which shows an approximately normal distribution.

Figure 5.1

Histogram of Total Household Expenditure

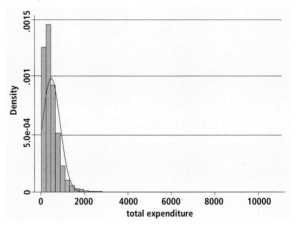

Figure 5.2

Histogram of Gross Normal Household Income

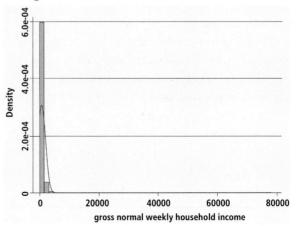

Figure 5.3

Histogram of Log-transformed Total Household Expenditure

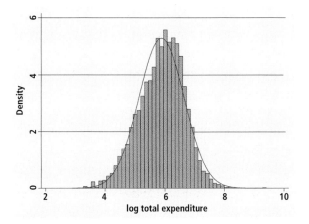

Figure 5.4

Histogram of Log-transformed Gross Normal Household Income

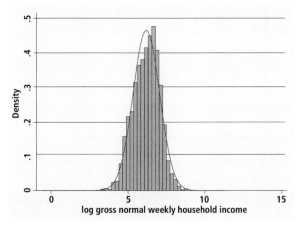

In order to test the linear relationship assumption, plots of the residuals versus predicted values of the model were run. These plots showed that the points were distributed around the diagonal which meant that the second assumption was held.

A multicollinearity test on the LCF dataset revealed that economic status of the HRP and socio-economic status were highly correlated. Also, the number of workers in the household was correlated with household composition and the government office regions were correlated with the urban/rural identifier. Different models were investigated using combinations of these variables and it was found that socio-economic status, household composition and the urban/ rural indicator produced the best fit. Therefore, economic activity status, number of workers and government office regions were excluded from the model.

The LCF sample is likely to include a marginal proportion of households reporting household expenditure and/or income figures that are large enough to be considered outliers. Outliers

can have an effect on the assumption of normality and also on the regression slope if the data point is influential. Outliers were detected by using standardised z-scores, which represent the relative position of an individual score compared to the mean and variation of the values in a distribution. In a normally distributed sample, z-scores of cases should not exceed a value of 3.29. The observation of standardised z-scores of the total household expenditure revealed that eight outliers had a z-score higher than six which were dropped for the household expenditure regression model; three cases were dropped for the regression model for household income. These outliers were dropped in order to produce a more robust estimate of the coefficients.

Finally, the assumption of homogeneity of variance was assessed using scatter plots of standardized residuals against standardised predicted values. Additionally, the Breusch-Pegan test for hetereoscedasticity was used to explore whether the estimated variance of residuals in the analysed models were constant. The expected result was a homoscedastic variance of residuals in the sample. However, the observed result of this test revealed that the data for both analysis models were heteroscedastic. Referring first to the analysis for household income, six outliers were excluded to try to solve this data issue. This resulted in an improvement of the test results, as the data appeared to be homoscedastic. Conversely, the heteroscedasticity discovered in the analysis of household expenditure could not be improved by removing outliers from the data model. Therefore care had to be taken in the choice of mode of analysis and interpretation of results.

Multivariate Regression Modelling

Sampling Design

The sampling methodology for the LCF sample differs between Great Britain, conducted by ONS, and Northern Ireland, conducted by the Central Survey Unit of Northern Ireland Social Research Association (NISRA). A representative sample for Great Britain is drawn as a two-stage stratified random sample with clustering from the 'small user' Postal Address File. Postcode sectors are used as the Primary Sampling Units (PSUs), with 18 addresses selected from each PSU to form the monthly interviewer quota. For Northern Ireland a simple random sample of private addresses is drawn from the Valuation and Lands Agency List. (For further information on the LCF sampling methodology, please refer to the LCF Technical Report 2008).

To consider the sampling methodology in the analysis a special multivariate regression model was chosen, which takes the structure of PSUs and geographical strata into account.

Northern Ireland cases were sampled in a different way but included in the same model and therefore Northern Ireland as a whole was considered as one stratum, while each Northern Ireland case represented one PSU. Using the program STATA to analyse the data, the sampling method for the multiple linear regression could be specified through the 'svy' prefix. This method enables the calculation of robust standard errors in the regression model, which removes the bias introduced to the model through the heteroscedastic data. (For further information on this type of regression, please refer to: www.stata.com/help.cgi?=svy))

Statistical Modelling

Multiple linear regression models were chosen as the mode of analysis to identify the effects of individual and household characteristics on household income and expenditure. The dependent variable chosen for the expenditure model was the total household expenditure, which included the total consumption expenditure of the twelve, Classification Of Individual COnsumption by Purpose (COICOP), categories, as well as other expenditure items (e.g. mortgage interest payments, tax payments, holiday spending, cash gifts and charitable donations). For the income model the gross normal weekly household income was chosen as the dependent variable, which was derived from the income of all household members, taking into account not only earnings but also any incomings from self-employment, social security benefits, investments, pensions and annuities, as well as any other sources specified by respondents.

As previously mentioned, the multicollinearity test revealed collinearity between some variables in the original list. Table 5.2 presents the explanatory variables that were included in the final regression models for expenditure and income. The list also indicates the type of variable.

Table 5.2

Regression models used for analysis

Regression model for total household expenditure	Regression model for gross weekly household income
Gender for HRP (categorical)	Age of HRP (continuous)
Socio-economic status of HRP (categorical)	Socio-economic status of HRP (categorical)
Gross weekly household income (continuous)	Household composition (categorical)
Household composition (categorical)	Household tenure (categorical)
Household tenure (categorical)	Urban/rural identifier of household (categorical)
Urban/rural identifier of household (categorical)	

As a result of the test for normal distribution, evidence was found for highly skewed data. In order to conduct analysis based on normally distributed data, the dependent variables for the models were transformed using a natural logarithm. The regression analyses were modelled using the following formula:

$$\ln(Y_i) = \beta_0 + \beta_1 X_i + \beta_2 Z_i + e_i$$

The natural logarithm of household expenditure or household income, $\ln(Y)$, was modelled as a function of individual characteristics of the HRP (X_i) and household characteristics (Z_i), and e_i represents the random error term. The model predicting household income included six cases with zero income. Since log-transformation cannot be applied to zero values, and recoding these values to 0.01 increased the homogeneity of variance of residuals, these six cases were excluded from the final model.

Results

To enable interpretation of the results, the regression coefficients need to be back-transformed by using the inverse of the natural logarithm function. It should be noted, when interpreting the results, that the coefficients can be back-transformed in this way however the model becomes multiplicative.

Total Household Expenditure Model

The results show that the explanatory variables in this model accounted for 64 per cent of the variance in total household expenditure ($R^2 = 0.64$). The full regression model is shown in Table 5.3. Examination of individual explanatory variables are summarised below. Unless otherwise stated the results are significant at the 95 per cent level.

- Gender was not significant in the original model and was therefore excluded from the analysis.

- The final analysis shows that the age of the HRP had an effect on the total household expenditure after controlling for all other characteristics in the model. The model shows less than one per cent decrease per unit increase of age.

- The socio-economic status of the HRP had an effect on household expenditure when all other characteristics in the model were kept constant (Table 5.3). In comparison to the reference group (households where the HRP had never worked or was in long-term unemployment), the model shows that households with a HRP employed by a large employer or in a higher management position had 59.5 per cent higher expenditure. This was followed by households with a HRP employed in a high professional occupation with

53.9 per cent higher spending than the reference group. This was closely followed by households with a HRP employed in a lower managerial or professional occupation.

- The household composition also had an effect on total household expenditure within the model (Table 5.3). When controlling for other characteristics, all other household combinations reported significantly higher household expenditure than the reference category of one adult (retired on state pension) households. Households with three or more adults with children had the highest expenditure, closely followed by other large household compositions such as households with three or more adults without children, and households with two adults and three or more children (155.3 per cent, 146.4 per cent and 145.2 per cent respectively).

- Relative to households that rent from local authorities, households owning a property by rental purchase had 64.2 per cent higher spending. This was also the case for households owning a property with a mortgage with 52.0 per cent higher expenditure when all other characteristics in the model were kept constant (Table 5.3).

- The model shows that the expenditure of households located in urban areas was 7.0 per cent lower than spending of rural households, when keeping all other characteristics constant.

Gross Weekly Household Income Model

The analysis shows that 64 per cent of the variance in total household expenditure was explained by the model ($R^2 = 0.64$). The full regression model is shown in Table 5.4. All regression coefficients proved to be significant at the 95 per cent level unless stated otherwise.

- After keeping all other explanatory variables constant, gender proved to be significant, indicating that households with a male HRP had 8.3 per cent higher gross weekly incomes than households with a female HRP. The age coefficient did not result in a significant value and was therefore excluded from the final model.

- The analysis shows that socio-economic status of the HRP had an effect on the gross weekly household income, after controlling for all other characteristics in the model. Results show that compared to the reference group (households where the HRP worked in routine occupations), households with a HRP employed by a large employer or in a higher management position had the largest incomes being 114.4 per cent above the income of reference households. This

was followed by households where the HRP was employed in a high professional occupation, indicating a 102.0 per cent higher income. Unsurprisingly, those which were likely to have the lowest household incomes were households where the HRP has never worked or were long-term unemployed.

- Similar to the analysis on household expenditure, the household composition had an effect on gross weekly household income. Compared to the reference category (households with one adult retired on state pension), households with three or more adults without children had the highest income. This was followed by households with three or more adults with children, followed by households with two adults and 3 or more children.

- By observing the tenure type it can be seen that compared to households that rent from local authorities, households that own a property either with a mortgage, by rental purchase or outright, are more likely to have a higher gross weekly income.

- When comparing income in urban and rural households, the analysis showed that the gross weekly household income of urban households was less than 7.0 per cent lower than those of rural households.

Conclusion

The regression models produced for household income and household expenditure differ slightly in terms of the final variables. For the household expenditure model, the age of the HRP coefficient was found to be significant where it was not significant within the income model. Household income was included as an explanatory variable for the expenditure model but as it cannot be used as both a dependent and independent variable was therefore excluded from the income model. The age of the HRP was not found to be significant when modelling household income and was therefore excluded. However, the sex of the HRP coefficient was significant within the household income model but was not for household expenditure. It was therefore excluded from the final expenditure regression model. Apart from those exceptions the variables for both models were the same. This is to be expected because a higher income would generally lead to higher expenditure, so those variables which are significant in the income model would also be likely to have an effect on expenditure.

The section below describes ways in which the model could be improved and also a way to test the model coefficients further.

Further research

Through the test of the homogeneity of variance assumption it was discovered that the data model for household expenditure was biased due to heteroscedasticity of residuals. A possible reason for this could be that the fitted model could not explain cases with higher expenditure. Further analysis is necessary to explore this assumption.

A possible avenue for further investigation may be to explore whether adding an age squared variable to the regression analyses could help to explain more of the variance in the model. Income and expenditure generally increase as the age of the HRP increases before decreasing again. The age squared variable may be more appropriate to model this distribution within the regression analysis.

The inclusion of interaction terms could help improve the fit of the model. The investigation of interaction terms would also reveal how certain individual and household characteristics moderate each other. For example, there may be different linear models for male and female HRP gross income.

To further test the model an investigation could be carried out to identify the extent to which the explanatory variables predict household income and expenditure. One way to do this would be to use the model to predict household income and expenditure. These predicted values could then be compared to the actual values in an alternate dataset.

Table 5.3

Outcome variable: Total household expenditure

Explanatory variables:	Back-transformed coefficient	Significance[1]	Back-transformed 95% confidence interval	
Age of HRP	0.998	0.004	0.997	0.999
Socio-economic status:				
Never worked/long term unemployed		reference		
Large employer/higher management	1.595	0.000	1.398	1.820
High professional occupations	1.539	0.000	1.355	1.748
Lower managerial and professional occupations	1.518	0.000	1.346	1.712
Students	1.476	0.000	1.257	1.732
Small employers and own account workers	1.459	0.000	1.286	1.655
Intermediate occupations	1.449	0.000	1.276	1.646
Lower supervisory and technical occupations	1.388	0.000	1.230	1.568
Semi-routine occupations	1.251	0.000	1.103	1.419
Routine occupations	1.199	0.006	1.054	1.363
Not classified for other reasons	1.139	0.035	1.009	1.285
Gross weekly household income	1.000	0.000	1.000	1.000
Household composition:				
1 adult retired mainly dependent on state pension		reference		
3 or more adults with children	2.553	0.000	2.292	2.844
3 or more adults without children	2.464	0.000	2.235	2.717
2 adults and 3 or more children	2.452	0.000	2.188	2.747
2 adults and 2 children	2.221	0.000	2.006	2.459
2 adults and 1 child	2.129	0.000	1.915	2.366
1 man and 1 woman - other retired household	2.112	0.000	1.929	2.312
1 man and 1 woman - non-retired household	1.997	0.000	1.817	2.196
2 men or 2 women	1.826	0.000	1.620	2.058
1 adult and 2 or more children	1.784	0.000	1.569	2.029
1 man and 1 woman retired mainly dependent on state pension	1.694	0.000	1.524	1.882
1 adult and 1 child	1.560	0.000	1.384	1.758
1 adult - non-retired household	1.323	0.000	1.201	1.457
1 adult - other retired household	1.244	0.000	1.133	1.366
Household tenure:				
Local authority		reference		
Own by rental purchase	1.642	0.000	1.334	2.020
Own with mortgage	1.520	0.000	1.436	1.609
Private rented - unfurnished	1.433	0.000	1.344	1.529
Private rented furnished	1.413	0.000	1.267	1.577
Own outright	1.394	0.000	1.308	1.485
Housing association	1.161	0.000	1.084	1.244
Rentfree	1.128	0.054	0.998	1.274
Urban-rural classification:				
Rural household		reference		
Urban household	0.929	0.000	0.901	0.957
Constant	96.658	0.000	81.871	114.116
	R-squared = 0.6388			

1 Significance relates to log tranformed coefficient

Table 5.4

Outcome variable: Gross weekly household income

Explanatory variables:	Back-transformed coefficient	Significance[1]	Back-transformed 95% confidence interval	
Sex of HRP:				
Female	reference			
Male	1.083	0.000	1.047	1.120
Socio-economic status:				
Routine occupations	reference			
Large employer/higher management	2.144	0.000	1.963	2.341
High professional occupations	2.020	0.000	1.852	2.202
Lower managerial and professional occupations	1.701	0.000	1.593	1.816
Lower supervisory and technical occupations	1.274	0.000	1.185	1.370
Intermediate occupations	1.229	0.000	1.132	1.333
Small employers and own account workers	1.126	0.007	1.034	1.227
Semi-routine occupations	1.054	0.170	0.978	1.136
Students	0.902	0.279	0.749	1.087
Never worked and long term unemployed	0.708	0.000	0.616	0.814
Not classified for other reasons	0.768	0.000	0.710	0.831
Household composition:				
1 adult retired mainly dependent on state pension	reference			
3 or more adults without children	3.613	0.000	3.284	3.974
3 or more adults with children	3.204	0.000	2.817	3.645
2 adults and 3 or more children	2.594	0.000	2.289	2.940
2 adults and 2 children	2.545	0.000	2.302	2.814
1 man and 1 woman non-retired household	2.510	0.000	2.287	2.754
1 man and 1 woman other retired household	2.509	0.000	2.321	2.712
2 adults and 1 child	2.336	0.000	2.107	2.591
2 men or 2 women	2.251	0.000	1.948	2.601
1 adult and 2 or more children	1.608	0.000	1.435	1.801
1 adult - other retired household	1.525	0.000	1.422	1.635
1 man and 1 woman retired mainly dependent on state pension	1.459	0.000	1.355	1.572
1 adult and 1 child	1.408	0.000	1.262	1.571
1 adult non-retired household	1.323	0.000	1.204	1.453
Household tenure:				
Local authority	reference			
Own with mortgage	1.731	0.000	1.628	1.842
Own by rental purchase	1.662	0.000	1.435	1.923
Own outright	1.529	0.000	1.442	1.622
Housing association	1.182	0.000	1.100	1.271
Rentfree	1.169	0.029	1.016	1.346
Private rented - unfurnished	1.293	0.000	1.205	1.388
Private rented furnished	1.154	0.085	0.980	1.358
Urban-rural classification:				
Rural household	reference			
Urban household	0.935	0.000	0.905	0.966
Constant	141.330	0.000	125.000	159.793
	R-squared = 0.6438			

1 Significance relates to log tranformed coefficient

Appendix A

Table A1

Components of household expenditure, 2008

based on weighted data and including children's expenditure

Commodity or service	Average weekly expenditure all house-holds (£)	Total weekly expenditure (£ million)	Recording house-holds in sample	Percentage standard error (full method)
Total number of households			5,850	
1 Food & non-alcoholic drinks	**50.70**	**1,302**	**5,800**	*0.8*
1.1 Food	46.70	1,198	5,800	*0.8*
1.1.1 Bread, rice and cereals	4.90	125	5,680	*1.0*
1.1.1.1 Rice	0.40	9	1,400	*6.3*
1.1.1.2 Bread	2.60	67	5,530	*1.0*
1.1.1.3 Other breads and cereals	1.90	49	4,620	*1.4*
1.1.2 Pasta products	0.40	10	2,400	*2.7*
1.1.3 Buns, cakes, biscuits etc.	3.20	82	5,150	*1.4*
1.1.3.1 Buns, crispbread and biscuits	1.80	46	4,740	*1.5*
1.1.3.2 Cakes and puddings	1.40	36	3,810	*2.1*
1.1.4 Pastry (savoury)	0.70	17	2,000	*2.5*
1.1.5 Beef (fresh, chilled or frozen)	1.60	41	2,700	*2.4*
1.1.6 Pork (fresh, chilled or frozen)	0.60	17	1,460	*3.3*
1.1.7 Lamb (fresh, chilled or frozen)	0.60	17	1,120	*3.6*
1.1.8 Poultry (fresh, chilled or frozen)	1.90	49	3,030	*2.0*
1.1.9 Bacon and ham	0.90	24	2,730	*2.1*
1.1.10 Other meats and meat preparations	5.20	133	5,200	*1.4*
1.1.10.1 Sausages	0.70	18	2,600	*2.4*
1.1.10.2 Offal, pate etc.	0.10	3	790	*5.0*
1.1.10.3 Other preserved or processed meat and meat preparations	4.30	112	5,010	*1.4*
1.1.10.4 Other fresh, chilled or frozen edible meat	0.00	1	40	*41.7*
1.1.11 Fish and fish products	2.30	59	3,850	*2.2*
1.1.11.1 Fish (fresh, chilled or frozen)	0.80	20	1,520	*3.8*
1.1.11.2 Seafood, dried, smoked or salted fish	0.50	14	1,290	*4.2*
1.1.11.3 Other preserved or processed fish and seafood	1.00	26	3,010	*2.6*
1.1.12 Milk	2.60	68	5,360	*1.4*
1.1.12.1 Whole milk	0.70	17	1,720	*3.6*
1.1.12.2 Low fat milk	1.80	46	4,430	*1.7*
1.1.12.3 Preserved milk	0.20	4	440	*7.6*
1.1.13 Cheese and curd	1.70	43	4,180	*1.6*
1.1.14 Eggs	0.60	16	3,350	*1.7*
1.1.15 Other milk products	1.90	48	4,380	*1.7*
1.1.15.1 Other milk products	0.90	22	3,330	*2.1*
1.1.15.2 Yoghurt	1.00	26	3,200	*2.2*
1.1.16 Butter	0.40	10	1,880	*2.7*
1.1.17 Margarine, other vegetable fats and peanut butter	0.50	13	2,860	*2.0*
1.1.18 Cooking oils and fats	0.30	8	1,380	*3.7*
1.1.18.1 Olive oil	0.10	3	490	*6.2*
1.1.18.2 Edible oils and other edible animal fats	0.20	4	990	*4.6*
1.1.19 Fresh fruit	3.00	76	4,920	*1.6*
1.1.19.1 Citrus fruits (fresh)	0.50	12	2,590	*2.6*
1.1.19.2 Bananas (fresh)	0.50	13	3,710	*1.6*
1.1.19.3 Apples (fresh)	0.50	14	2,920	*2.0*
1.1.19.4 Pears (fresh)	0.10	4	1,180	*3.5*
1.1.19.5 Stone fruits (fresh)	0.40	10	1,620	*3.5*
1.1.19.6 Berries (fresh)	0.90	24	2,710	*2.3*
1.1.20 Other fresh, chilled or frozen fruits	0.40	9	1,690	*3.5*
1.1.21 Dried fruit and nuts	0.50	12	1,860	*3.4*
1.1.22 Preserved fruit and fruit based products	0.10	3	1,080	*4.1*
1.1.23 Fresh vegetables	3.70	96	5,220	*1.4*
1.1.23.1 Leaf and stem vegetables (fresh or chilled)	0.70	19	3,440	*2.0*
1.1.23.2 Cabbages (fresh or chilled)	0.40	10	2,900	*2.1*
1.1.23.3 Vegetables grown for their fruit (fresh, chilled or frozen)	1.30	33	4,300	*1.8*
1.1.23.4 Root crops, non-starchy bulbs and mushrooms (fresh, chilled or frozen)	1.30	33	4,660	*1.6*

Note: The commodity and service categories are not comparable with those in publications before 2001-02.

The numbering is sequential, it does not use actual COICOP codes.

Please see page xiii for symbols and conventions used in this report.

Table A1

Components of household expenditure, 2008 (cont.)

based on weighted data and including children's expenditure

Commodity or service			Average weekly expenditure all house-holds (£)	Total weekly expenditure (£ million)	Recording house-holds in sample	Percentage standard error (full method)
1	**Food & non-alcoholic drinks (continued)**					
	1.1.24	Dried vegetables	0.00	1	250	56.6
	1.1.25	Other preserved or processed vegetables	1.20	30	4,260	0.0
	1.1.26	Potatoes	0.90	23	4,020	1.5
	1.1.27	Other tubers and products of tuber vegetables	1.30	32	3,950	1.6
	1.1.28	Sugar and sugar products	0.30	8	2,180	2.6
		1.1.28.1 Sugar	0.20	6	1,930	2.7
		1.1.28.2 Other sugar products	0.10	2	510	5.6
	1.1.29	Jams, marmalades	0.30	7	1,720	3.7
	1.1.30	Chocolate	1.50	38	3,470	2.5
	1.1.31	Confectionery products	0.60	15	2,700	2.5
	1.1.32	Edible ices and ice cream	0.50	13	1,790	2.7
	1.1.33	Other food products	2.30	58	4,850	2.2
		1.1.33.1 Sauces, condiments	1.10	28	3,730	1.9
		1.1.33.2 Baker's yeast, dessert preparations, soups	0.80	21	3,270	3.4
		1.1.33.3 Salt, spices, culinary herbs and other food products	0.40	10	1,580	10.0
	1.2	Non-alcoholic drinks	4.00	104	5,260	1.3
	1.2.1	Coffee	0.60	15	1,770	3.1
	1.2.2	Tea	0.40	11	2,050	2.3
	1.2.3	Cocoa and powdered chocolate	0.10	2	520	6.3
	1.2.4	Fruit and vegetable juices	1.10	29	3,450	1.9
	1.2.5	Mineral or spring waters	0.20	6	1,200	4.7
	1.2.6	Soft drinks (inc. fizzy and ready to drink fruit drinks)	1.60	41	3,770	2.1
2	**Alcoholic drink, tobacco & narcotics**		**10.80**	**277**	**3,600**	**2.0**
	2.1	Alcoholic drinks	6.20	160	2,970	2.5
	2.1.1	Spirits and liqueurs (brought home)	1.20	30	820	4.1
	2.1.2	Wines, fortified wines (brought home)	3.30	84	2,030	3.5
		2.1.2.1 Wine from grape or other fruit (brought home)	2.90	75	1,870	3.7
		2.1.2.2 Fortified wine (brought home)	0.20	4	210	8.9
		2.1.2.3 Champagne and sparkling wines (brought home)	0.20	4	170	12.1
	2.1.3	Beer, lager, ciders and perry (brought home)	1.70	44	1,510	3.4
		2.1.3.1 Beer and lager (brought home)	1.50	38	1,320	3.6
		2.1.3.2 Ciders and perry (brought home)	0.30	7	390	8.0
	2.1.4	Alcopops (brought home)	0.10	2	110	16.0
	2.2	Tobacco and narcotics	4.60	117	1,390	3.2
	2.2.1	Cigarettes	3.90	100	1,270	3.5
	2.2.2	Cigars, other tobacco products and narcotics	0.70	17	360	7.5
		2.2.2.1 Cigars	0.10	3	40	20.8
		2.2.2.2 Other tobacco	0.50	13	330	6.9
		2.2.2.3 Narcotics	[0.10]	[1]	–	47.0
3	**Clothing & footwear**		**21.60**	**554**	**3,940**	**2.2**
	3.1	Clothing	17.50	449	3,720	2.5
	3.1.1	Men's outer garments	4.50	116	1,200	5.7
	3.1.2	Men's under garments	0.30	9	440	8.1
	3.1.3	Women's outer garments	7.60	196	2,170	2.9
	3.1.4	Women's under garments	1.10	27	1,110	4.9
	3.1.5	Boys' outer garments (5-15)	0.80	20	430	7.7
	3.1.6	Girls' outer garments (5-15)	1.00	25	540	6.1
	3.1.7	Infants' outer garments (under 5)	0.60	16	450	7.0
	3.1.8	Children's under garments (under 16)	0.30	8	500	6.1

Note: The commodity and service categories are not comparable with those in publications before 2001-02.

The numbering is sequential, it does not use actual COICOP codes.

Please see page xiii for symbols and conventions used in this report.

Table A1

Components of household expenditure, 2008 (cont.)
based on weighted data and including children's expenditure

Commodity or service			Average weekly expenditure all house-holds (£)	Total weekly expenditure (£ million)	Recording house-holds in sample	Percentage standard error (full method)
3	**Clothing & footwear (continued)**		0.70	18	900	5.5
	3.1.9	Accessories	0.20	6	300	8.7
		3.1.9.1 Men's accessories	0.30	8	460	6.7
		3.1.9.2 Women's accessories	0.10	3	230	10.6
		3.1.9.3 Children's accessories	[0.00]	[1]	20	35.2
		3.1.9.4 Protective head gear (crash helmets)				
	3.1.10	Haberdashery, clothing materials and clothing hire	0.30	7	270	19.9
	3.1.11	Dry cleaners, laundry and dyeing	0.30	7	200	10.4
		3.1.11.1 Dry cleaners and dyeing	0.20	6	160	11.3
		3.1.11.2 Laundry, launderettes	0.00	1	40	20.2
	3.2	Footwear	4.10	106	1,620	3.2
	3.2.1	Footwear for men	1.20	31	420	6.2
	3.2.2	Footwear for women	2.10	53	950	4.4
	3.2.3	Footwear for children (5 to 15 years) and infants (under 5)	0.80	21	470	6.6
	3.2.4	Repair and hire of footwear	0.10	1	60	19.2
4	**Housing(net)[1], fuel & power**		**53.00**	**1,362**	**5,820**	**1.9**
	4.1	Actual rentals for housing	31.60	812	1,610	3.5
	4.1.1	Gross rent	31.50	810	1,610	3.5
	4.1.2	*less* housing benefit, rebates and allowances received	12.10	312	1,080	3.6
	4.1.3	Net rent[2]	19.40	498	1,220	5.1
	4.1.4	Second dwelling - rent	[0.10]	[2]	–	87.2
	4.2	Maintenance and repair of dwelling	7.20	185	2,590	5.0
	4.2.1	Central heating repairs	1.50	38	1,520	6.3
	4.2.2	House maintenance etc.	3.90	100	1,150	7.0
	4.2.3	Paint, wallpaper, timber	0.90	23	440	7.6
	4.2.4	Equipment hire, small materials	0.90	23	420	17.0
	4.3	Water supply and miscellaneous services relating to the dwelling	7.40	191	4,900	1.3
	4.3.1	Water charges	6.30	161	4,710	0.8
	4.3.2	Other regular housing payments including service charge for rent	1.10	27	640	8.0
	4.3.3	Refuse collection, including skip hire	[0.10]	[2]	20	34.4
	4.4	Electricity, gas and other fuels	18.90	487	5,540	1.0
	4.4.1	Electricity	9.00	232	5,410	1.1
	4.4.2	Gas	8.20	210	4,270	1.4
	4.4.3	Other fuels	1.70	44	590	7.5
		4.4.3.1 Coal and coke	0.20	6	120	20.1
		4.4.3.2 Oil for central heating	1.40	37	480	8.0
		4.4.3.3 Paraffin, wood, peat, hot water etc.	0.10	2	50	24.9
5	**Household goods & services**		**30.10**	**774**	**5,350**	**3.2**
	5.1	Furniture and furnishings, carpets and other floor coverings	16.60	427	2,200	4.8
	5.1.1	Furniture and furnishings	13.00	333	1,820	5.4
		5.1.1.1 Furniture	11.90	304	1,250	5.7
		5.1.1.2 Fancy, decorative goods	0.90	23	740	11.1
		5.1.1.3 Garden furniture	0.20	6	40	29.7
	5.1.2	Floor coverings	3.70	94	800	6.5
		5.1.2.1 Soft floor coverings	3.20	82	750	6.6
		5.1.2.2 Hard floor coverings	0.50	12	60	27.2
	5.2	Household textiles	1.50	40	1,100	5.9
	5.2.1	Bedroom textiles, including duvets and pillows	0.70	18	450	7.3
	5.2.2	Other household textiles, including cushions, towels, curtains	0.80	21	780	8.3

Note: The commodity and service categories are not comparable with those in publications before 2001-02.

The numbering is sequential, it does not use actual COICOP codes.

Please see page xiii for symbols and conventions used in this report.

1 Excluding mortgage interest payments, council tax and NI rates.

2 The figure included in total expenditure is net rent as opposed to gross rent

Table A1

Components of household expenditure, 2008 (cont.)

based on weighted data and including children's expenditure

Commodity or service	Average weekly expenditure all house-holds (£)	Total weekly expenditure (£ million)	Recording house-holds in sample	Percentage standard error (full method)
5 Household goods & services (continued)				
5.3 Household appliances	3.50	90	490	11.9
5.3.1 Gas cookers	[0.20]	[4]	–	41.7
5.3.2 Electric cookers, combined gas/electric cookers	0.20	6	40	47.0
5.3.3 Clothes washing machines and drying machines	0.70	19	90	19.6
5.3.4 Refrigerators, freezers and fridge-freezers	0.60	14	60	29.0
5.3.5 Other major electrical appliances, dishwashers, micro-waves vacuum cleaners, heaters etc.	1.10	27	150	19.4
5.3.6 Fire extinguisher, water softener, safes etc	[0.10]	[4]	–	78.1
5.3.7 Small electric household appliances, excluding hairdryers	0.40	10	190	13.9
5.3.8 Repairs to gas and electrical appliances and spare parts	0.20	4	50	23.3
5.3.9 Rental/hire of major household appliances	[0.00]	[0]	–	43.2
5.4 Glassware, tableware and household utensils	1.30	34	1,660	4.5
5.4.1 Glassware, china, pottery, cutlery and silverware	0.40	11	640	7.5
5.4.2 Kitchen and domestic utensils	0.50	14	950	5.9
5.4.3 Repair of glassware, tableware and household utensils	-	-	0	-
5.4.4 Storage and other durable household articles	0.40	9	540	6.7
5.5 Tools and equipment for house and garden	2.10	54	1,880	5.7
5.5.1 Electrical tools	0.30	9	70	25.4
5.5.2 Garden tools, equipment and accessories e.g. lawn mowers etc.	0.30	6	280	10.7
5.5.3 Small tools	0.40	9	380	10.7
5.5.4 Door, electrical and other fittings	0.60	15	450	12.1
5.5.5 Electrical consumables	0.60	15	1,210	4.9
5.6 Goods and services for routine household maintenance	5.10	130	4,890	2.8
5.6.1 Cleaning materials	2.20	55	4,090	1.7
5.6.1.1 Detergents, washing-up liquid, washing powder	1.00	26	2,840	2.2
5.6.1.2 Disinfectants, polishes, other cleaning materials etc.	1.10	29	3,330	2.1
5.6.2 Household goods and hardware	1.10	28	3,600	2.3
5.6.2.1 Kitchen disposables	0.70	17	3,050	2.6
5.6.2.2 Household hardware and appliances, matches	0.20	5	680	6.2
5.6.2.3 Kitchen gloves, cloths etc.	0.10	3	950	4.7
5.6.2.4 Pins, needles, tape measures, nails, nuts and bolts etc.	0.10	3	370	7.2
5.6.3 Domestic services, carpet cleaning, hire/repair of furniture/furnishings	1.80	47	910	7.1
5.6.3.1 Domestic services, including cleaners, gardeners, au pairs	1.30	34	360	9.1
5.6.3.2 Carpet cleaning, ironing service, window cleaner	0.50	13	640	8.3
5.6.3.3 Hire/repair of household furniture and furnishings	[0.00]	[0]	–	58.1
6 Health	**5.10**	**132**	**2,940**	**6.5**
6.1 Medical products, appliances and equipment	3.10	80	2,790	5.8
6.1.1 Medicines, prescriptions and healthcare products	1.70	43	2,680	4.1
6.1.1.1 NHS prescription charges and payments	0.30	7	260	9.8
6.1.1.2 Medicines and medical goods (not NHS)	1.20	31	2,460	3.7
6.1.1.3 Other medical products (e.g. plasters, condoms, hot water bottle etc.)	0.10	3	300	9.0
6.1.1.4 Non-optical appliances and equipment (e.g. wheelchairs, batteries for hearing aids, shoe build-up)	0.10	2	30	50.6
6.1.2 Spectacles, lenses, accessories and repairs	1.40	37	300	11.3
6.1.2.1 Purchase of spectacles, lenses, prescription sunglasses	1.40	36	260	11.5
6.1.2.2 Accessories/repairs to spectacles/lenses	0.00	1	60	19.9
6.2 Hospital services	2.00	52	400	13.4
6.2.1 Out patient services	2.00	52	400	13.5
6.2.1.1 NHS medical, optical, dental and medical auxiliary services	0.90	23	230	10.4
6.2.1.2 Private medical, optical, dental and medical auxiliary services	1.10	29	170	21.3
6.2.1.3 Other services	[0.00]	[0]	–	81.2
6.2.2 In-patient hospital services	[0.00]	[0]	–	66.5

Note: The commodity and service categories are not comparable with those in publications before 2001-02.

The numbering is sequential, it does not use actual COICOP codes.

Please see page xiii for symbols and conventions used in this report.

Table A1

Components of household expenditure, 2008 (cont.)

based on weighted data and including children's expenditure

Commodity or service			Average weekly expenditure all house- holds (£)	Total weekly expenditure (£ million)	Recording house- holds in sample	Percentage standard error (full method)
7	**Transport**		**63.40**	**1,628**	**5,000**	*2.0*
7.1	Purchase of vehicles		21.10	543	1,420	*4.2*
	7.1.1	Purchase of new cars and vans	6.60	171	350	*7.5*
		7.1.1.1 Outright purchases	4.20	109	130	*10.1*
		7.1.1.2 Loan/Hire Purchase of new car/van	2.40	62	230	*9.5*
	7.1.2	Purchase of second hand cars or vans	13.60	350	1,080	*5.1*
		7.1.2.1 Outright purchases	9.80	253	640	*6.7*
		7.1.2.2 Loan/Hire Purchase of second hand car/van	3.80	97	500	*5.7*
	7.1.3	Purchase of motorcycles	0.90	23	80	*20.5*
		7.1.3.1 Outright purchases of new or second hand motorcycles	0.40	9	30	*23.6*
		7.1.3.2 Loan/Hire Purchase of new or second hand motorcycles	0.20	4	20	*29.5*
		7.1.3.3 Purchase of bicycles and other vehicles	0.40	10	30	*40.5*
7.2	Operation of personal transport		31.80	816	4,300	*1.8*
	7.2.1	Spares and accessories	2.40	61	480	*11.3*
		7.2.1.1 Car/van accessories and fittings	0.60	15	130	*33.8*
		7.2.1.2 Car/van spare parts	1.50	39	270	*10.9*
		7.2.1.3 Motorcycle accessories and spare parts	[0.00]	[1]	20	*49.0*
		7.2.1.4 Bicycle accessories, repairs and other costs	0.20	5	100	*17.2*
	7.2.2	Petrol, diesel and other motor oils	21.00	540	3,810	*1.7*
		7.2.2.1 Petrol	15.70	404	3,200	*1.9*
		7.2.2.2 Diesel oil	5.30	135	1,070	*3.9*
		7.2.2.3 Other motor oils	0.10	2	70	*16.1*
	7.2.3	Repairs and servicing	6.20	160	1,800	*3.6*
		7.2.3.1 Car or van repairs, servicing and other work	6.20	159	1,800	*3.6*
		7.2.3.2 Motorcycle repairs and servicing	0.00	1	20	*30.2*
	7.2.4	Other motoring costs	2.10	55	2,170	*4.2*
		7.2.4.1 Motoring organisation subscription (e.g. AA and RAC)	0.40	9	910	*5.8*
		7.2.4.2 Garage rent, other costs (excluding fines), car washing etc.	0.60	14	310	*8.5*
		7.2.4.3 Parking fees, tolls, and permits (excluding motoring fines)	0.80	21	1,260	*6.4*
		7.2.4.4 Driving lessons	0.30	8	60	*15.9*
		7.2.4.5 Anti-freeze, battery water, cleaning materials	0.10	3	290	*9.7*
7.3	Transport services		10.50	269	2,390	*4.1*
	7.3.1	Rail and tube fares	2.40	62	730	*5.8*
		7.3.1.1 Season tickets	1.00	25	150	*10.4*
		7.3.1.2 Other than season tickets	1.50	37	630	*6.1*
	7.3.2	Bus and coach fares	1.40	35	1,000	*5.0*
		7.3.2.1 Season tickets	0.50	12	200	*8.0*
		7.3.2.2 Other than season tickets	0.90	23	900	*5.5*
	7.3.3	Combined fares	1.20	31	230	*9.3*
		7.3.3.1 Combined fares other than season tickets	0.30	8	130	*13.0*
		7.3.3.2 Combined fares season tickets	0.90	23	120	*11.9*
	7.3.4	Other travel and transport	5.40	140	1,350	*7.0*
		7.3.4.1 Air fares (within UK)	0.30	9	20	*37.1*
		7.3.4.2 Air fares (international)	1.50	39	50	*19.7*
		7.3.4.3 School travel	0.10	2	40	*48.8*
		7.3.4.4 Taxis and hired cars with drivers	1.10	29	800	*5.2*
		7.3.4.5 Other personal travel and transport services	0.20	6	290	*11.7*
		7.3.4.6 Hire of self-drive cars, vans, bicycles	0.20	6	30	*27.3*
		7.3.4.7 Car leasing	1.80	46	220	*8.1*
		7.3.4.8 Water travel, ferries and season tickets	0.10	3	60	*28.3*

Note: The commodity and service categories are not comparable with those in publications before 2001-02.

The numbering is sequential, it does not use actual COICOP codes.

Please see page xiii for symbols and conventions used in this report.

Table A1

Components of household expenditure, 2008 (cont.)

based on weighted data and including children's expenditure

Commodity or service	Average weekly expenditure all house-holds (£)	Total weekly expenditure (£ million)	Recording house-holds in sample	Percentage standard error (full method)
8 Communication	**12.00**	**307**	**5,570**	*1.2*
8.1 Postal services	0.50	12	1,050	*5.9*
8.2 Telephone and telefax equipment	0.50	13	160	*11.4*
8.2.1 Telephone purchase	0.10	2	30	*25.8*
8.2.2 Mobile phone purchase	0.40	10	130	*12.7*
8.2.3 Answering machine, fax machine, modem purchase	[0.00]	[0]	–	*66.9*
8.3 Telephone and telefax services	11.00	282	5,530	*1.1*
8.3.1 Telephone account	5.70	146	5,150	*1.1*
8.3.2 Telephone coin and other payments	0.00	1	70	*18.3*
8.3.3 Mobile phone account	4.00	104	2,120	*2.5*
8.3.4 Mobile phone - other payments	1.20	31	920	*3.9*
9 Recreation & culture	**60.10**	**1,543**	**5,790**	*3.6*
9.1 Audio-visual, photographic and information processing equipment	7.20	184	1,720	*7.2*
9.1.1 Audio equipment and accessories, CD players	1.30	33	750	*7.8*
9.1.1.1 Audio equipment, CD players including in car	0.50	13	130	*16.7*
9.1.1.2 Audio accessories e.g. tapes, headphones etc.	0.80	20	650	*6.9*
9.1.2 TV, video and computers	4.80	123	1,210	*8.7*
9.1.2.1 Purchase of TV and digital decoder	1.70	43	140	*18.4*
9.1.2.2 Satellite dish purchase and installation	[0.00]	[0]	–	*81.7*
9.1.2.3 Cable TV connection	[0.00]	[0]	–	*78.0*
9.1.2.4 Video recorder	[0.00]	[0]	–	*78.0*
9.1.2.5 DVD player/recorder	0.20	5	30	*26.2*
9.1.2.6 Blank, pre-recorded video cassettes, DVDs	1.00	26	770	*6.0*
9.1.2.7 Personal computers, printers and calculators	1.70	43	370	*13.5*
9.1.2.8 Spare parts for TV, video, audio	0.20	4	70	*25.5*
9.1.2.9 Repair of audio-visual, photographic and information processing	0.10	2	30	*23.6*
9.1.3 Photographic, cine and optical equipment	1.10	27	150	*25.0*
9.1.3.1 Photographic and cine equipment	1.00	26	100	*26.1*
9.1.3.2 Camera films	0.00	1	30	*24.4*
9.1.3.3 Optical instruments, binoculars, telescopes, microscopes	[0.00]	[1]	10	*44.7*
9.2 Other major durables for recreation and culture	4.10	106	130	*40.1*
9.2.1 Purchase of boats, trailers and horses	[2.50]	[65]	10	*62.1*
9.2.2 Purchase of caravans, mobile homes (including decoration)	0.50	13	20	*47.0*
9.2.3 Accessories for boats, horses, caravans and motor caravans	0.20	6	20	*44.5*
9.2.4 Musical instruments (purchase and hire)	0.10	3	40	*37.8*
9.2.5 Major durables for indoor recreation	[0.00]	[0]	–	*118.5*
9.2.6 Maintenance and repair of other major durables	0.40	10	40	*34.0*
9.2.7 Purchase of motor caravan (new and second-hand) - outright purchase	[0.30]	[9]	–	*45.4*
9.2.8 Purchase of motor caravan (new and second-hand) - loan/HP	[0.00]	[1]	–	*67.4*
9.3 Other recreational items and equipment, gardens and pets	10.70	276	3,970	*2.9*
9.3.1 Games, toys and hobbies	1.80	47	1,450	*4.5*
9.3.2 Computer software and games	2.00	51	410	*8.1*
9.3.2.1 Computer software and game cartridges	1.10	28	350	*7.2*
9.3.2.2 Computer games consoles	0.90	23	100	*15.1*
9.3.3 Equipment for sport, camping and open-air recreation	0.90	23	460	*11.1*
9.3.4 Horticultural goods, garden equipment and plants etc.	2.60	67	2,080	*4.8*
9.3.4.1 BBQ and swings	0.00	1	30	*39.4*
9.3.4.2 Plants, flowers, seeds, fertilisers, insecticides	2.50	64	2,020	*5.0*
9.3.4.3 Garden decorative	0.10	2	80	*18.4*
9.3.4.4 Artificial flowers, pot pourri	0.00	1	80	*21.3*
9.3.5 Pets and pet food	3.40	87	2,120	*4.9*
9.3.5.1 Pet food	1.80	47	1,990	*3.3*
9.3.5.2 Pet purchase and accessories	0.60	15	570	*12.0*
9.3.5.3 Veterinary and other services for pets identified separately	1.00	25	190	*11.7*

Note: The commodity and service categories are not comparable with those in publications before 2001-02.

       The numbering is sequential, it does not use actual COICOP codes.

       Please see page xiii for symbols and conventions used in this report.

Table A1

Components of household expenditure, 2008 (cont.)

based on weighted data and including children's expenditure

Commodity or service		Average weekly expenditure all house- holds (£)	Total weekly expenditure (£ million)	Recording house- holds in sample	Percentage standard error (full method)
9	**Recreation & culture (continued)**				
9.4	Recreational and cultural services	17.30	443	5,510	2.0
9.4.1	Sports admissions, subscriptions, leisure class fees and equipment hire	4.80	123	2,080	3.9
9.4.1.1	Spectator sports: admission charges	0.50	12	180	14.9
9.4.1.2	Participant sports (excluding subscriptions)	1.20	30	940	6.2
9.4.1.3	Subscriptions to sports and social clubs	1.50	39	860	6.8
9.4.1.4	Leisure class fees	1.60	41	860	5.7
9.4.1.5	Hire of equipment for sport and open air recreation	0.00	1	20	44.6
9.4.2	Cinema, theatre and museums etc.	1.90	50	960	5.6
9.4.2.1	Cinemas	0.50	14	520	5.1
9.4.2.2	Live entertainment: theatre, concerts, shows	1.10	28	330	9.2
9.4.2.3	Museums, zoological gardens, theme parks, houses and gardens	0.30	8	210	9.2
9.4.3	TV, video, satellite rental, cable subscriptions, TV licences and Internet	5.80	150	5,150	1.3
9.4.3.1	TV licences	2.20	57	4,930	0.4
9.4.3.2	Satellite subscriptions	2.40	63	1,760	2.6
9.4.3.3	Rent for TV/Satellite/VCR	0.20	6	190	10.1
9.4.3.4	Cable subscriptions	0.50	14	620	6.0
9.4.3.5	TV slot meter payments	[0.00]	[1]	10	37.4
9.4.3.6	Video, cassette and CD hire	0.10	2	140	11.0
9.4.3.7	Internet subscription fees	0.30	8	310	10.0
9.4.4	Miscellaneous entertainments	1.20	31	1,110	7.6
9.4.4.1	Admissions to clubs, dances, discos, bingo	0.60	14	500	8.5
9.4.4.2	Social events and gatherings	0.40	10	270	19.2
9.4.4.3	Subscriptions for leisure activities and other subscriptions	0.30	7	520	8.6
9.4.5	Development of film, deposit for film development, passport photos, holiday and school photos	0.30	8	250	18.2
9.4.6	Gambling payments	3.20	81	2,770	5.9
9.4.6.1	Football pools stakes	0.10	2	50	26.5
9.4.6.2	Bingo stakes excluding admission	0.30	8	160	12.1
9.4.6.3	Lottery	1.90	49	2,480	3.0
9.4.6.4	Bookmaker, tote, other betting stakes	0.90	23	630	18.3
9.5	Newspapers, books and stationery	6.00	155	5,090	1.9
9.5.1	Books	1.40	35	1,250	4.5
9.5.2	Stationery, diaries, address books, art materials	0.70	18	1,480	6.6
9.5.3	Cards, calendars, posters and other printed matter	1.20	31	2,670	2.9
9.5.4	Newspapers	1.90	48	3,670	2.2
9.5.5	Magazines and periodicals	0.90	23	2,670	2.8
9.6	Package holidays	14.70	378	880	5.5
9.6.1	Package holidays - UK	1.10	28	180	9.4
9.6.2	Package holidays - abroad	13.60	350	730	5.9
10	**Education**	**6.20**	**159**	**470**	**12.8**
10.1	Education fees	5.90	151	340	13.4
10.1.1	Nursery and primary education	1.00	25	60	17.6
10.1.2	Secondary education	1.30	35	50	27.6
10.1.3	Sixth form college/college education	0.40	11	40	41.5
10.1.4	University education	2.00	52	130	13.4
10.1.5	Other education	1.10	29	90	41.9
10.2	Payments for school trips, other ad-hoc expenditure	0.30	8	140	16.0
10.2.1	Nursery and primary education	0.10	2	80	18.1
10.2.2	Secondary education	0.10	3	50	28.6
10.2.3	Sixth form college/college education	[0.00]	[0]	–	75.3
10.2.4	University education	[0.00]	[1]	–	49.3
10.2.5	Other education	[0.00]	[1]	10	33.7

Note: The commodity and service categories are not comparable with those in publications before 2001-02.

The numbering is sequential, it does not use actual COICOP codes.

Please see page xiii for symbols and conventions used in this report.

Table A1

Components of household expenditure, 2008 (cont.)

based on weighted data and including children's expenditure

Commodity or service	Average weekly expenditure all house-holds (£)	Total weekly expenditure (£ million)	Recording house-holds in sample	Percentage standard error (full method)
11 Restaurants & hotels	**37.70**	**969**	**5,090**	*2.1*
11.1 Catering services	31.00	796	5,050	*2.0*
11.1.1 Restaurant and café meals	13.20	340	4,100	*2.4*
11.1.2 Alcoholic drinks (away from home)	7.20	185	2,550	*3.0*
11.1.3 Take away meals eaten at home	3.90	99	2,510	*2.7*
11.1.4 Other take-away and snack food	4.20	107	3,340	*2.2*
11.1.4.1 Hot and cold food	2.90	75	2,900	*2.5*
11.1.4.2 Confectionery	0.30	9	1,720	*3.3*
11.1.4.3 Ice cream	0.10	3	540	*6.6*
11.1.4.4 Soft drinks	0.80	21	2,220	*2.5*
11.1.5 Contract catering (food)	0.60	16	30	*30.0*
11.1.6 Canteens	1.90	49	1,740	*3.5*
11.1.6.1 School meals	0.60	15	610	*6.1*
11.1.6.2 Meals bought and eaten at the workplace	1.30	34	1,360	*4.1*
11.2 Accommodation services	6.80	173	1,020	*5.3*
11.2.1 Holiday in the UK	2.80	71	650	*6.1*
11.2.2 Holiday abroad	4.00	102	440	*7.7*
11.2.3 Room hire	[0.00]	[1]	–	*37.8*
12 Miscellaneous goods and services	**35.60**	**915**	**5,710**	*2.5*
12.1 Personal care	9.90	254	5,030	*1.9*
12.1.1 Hairdressing, beauty treatment	3.10	79	1,430	*3.7*
12.1.2 Toilet paper	0.80	20	2,720	*2.2*
12.1.3 Toiletries and soap	2.00	52	3,980	*1.9*
12.1.3.1 Toiletries (disposable including tampons, lipsyl, toothpaste etc.)	1.20	30	3,350	*2.2*
12.1.3.2 Bar of soap, liquid soap, shower gel etc.	0.40	9	1,690	*3.7*
12.1.3.3 Toilet requisites (durable including razors, hairbrushes, toothbrushes etc.)	0.50	13	1,370	*4.3*
12.1.4 Baby toiletries and accessories (disposable)	0.60	16	920	*5.0*
12.1.5 Hair products, cosmetics and electrical appliances for personal care	3.40	87	3,140	*3.1*
12.1.5.1 Hair products	0.80	19	1,850	*3.4*
12.1.5.2 Cosmetics and related accessories	2.40	62	2,320	*3.7*
12.1.5.3 Electrical appliances for personal care, including hairdryers, shavers etc.	0.20	6	110	*14.4*
12.2 Personal effects	3.30	85	1,500	*13.7*
12.2.1 Jewellery, clocks and watches and other personal effects	2.10	54	1,040	*20.3*
12.2.2 Leather and travel goods (excluding baby items)	0.80	21	550	*8.1*
12.2.3 Sunglasses (non-prescription)	0.10	2	90	*16.9*
12.2.4 Baby equipment (excluding prams and pushchairs)	0.10	4	60	*21.9*
12.2.5 Prams, pram accessories and pushchairs	0.10	3	20	*39.3*
12.2.6 Repairs to personal goods	0.00	1	30	*25.2*
12.3 Social protection	3.60	93	280	*12.1*
12.3.1 Residential homes	[0.20]	[5]	–	*63.8*
12.3.2 Home help	0.30	7	40	*33.2*
12.3.3 Nursery, crèche, playschools	0.90	23	90	*19.7*
12.3.4 Child care payments	2.30	58	170	*15.2*

Note: The commodity and service categories are not comparable with those in publications before 2001-02.

The numbering is sequential, it does not use actual COICOP codes.

Please see page xiii for symbols and conventions used in this report.

Table A1

Components of household expenditure, 2008 (cont.)

based on weighted data and including children's expenditure

Commodity or service			Average weekly expenditure all house-holds (£)	Total weekly expenditure (£ million)	Recording house-holds in sample	Percentage standard error (full method)
12	**Miscellaneous goods and services (continued)**					
12.4	Insurance		14.60	374	5,210	1.5
	12.4.1	Household insurances	5.00	129	4,690	1.4
		12.4.1.1 Structure insurance	2.50	63	3,770	1.8
		12.4.1.2 Contents insurance	2.50	64	4,520	1.6
		12.4.1.3 Insurance for household appliances	0.10	2	90	23.2
	12.4.2	Medical insurance premiums	1.40	36	650	6.4
	12.4.3	Vehicle insurance including boat insurance	7.90	204	4,350	1.8
		12.4.3.1 Vehicle insurance	7.90	203	4,350	1.8
		12.4.3.2 Boat insurance (not home)	[0.00]	[1]	–	84.5
	12.4.4	Non-package holiday, other travel insurance	0.20	4	50	25.7
12.5	Other services		4.20	109	1,890	7.9
	12.5.1	Moving house	2.10	53	350	8.3
		12.5.1.1 Moving and storage of furniture	0.30	7	150	18.5
		12.5.1.2 Property transaction - purchase and sale	0.90	24	100	13.8
		12.5.1.3 Property transaction - sale only	0.40	10	50	18.9
		12.5.1.4 Property transaction - purchase only	0.30	8	80	14.9
		12.5.1.5 Property transaction - other payments	0.20	5	80	19.6
	12.5.2	Bank, building society, post office, credit card charges	0.40	11	890	6.1
		12.5.2.1 Bank and building society charges	0.40	10	760	6.4
		12.5.2.2 Bank and Post Office counter charges	[0.00]	[0]	20	38.1
		12.5.2.3 Annual standing charge for credit cards	0.00	1	150	16.1
		12.5.2.4 Commission travellers' cheques and currency	[0.00]	[0]	–	60.2
	12.5.3	Other services and professional fees	1.70	45	1,010	16.4
		12.5.3.1 Other professional fees including court fines	0.60	15	60	23.9
		12.5.3.2 Legal fees	[0.10]	[3]	20	41.7
		12.5.3.3 Funeral expenses	[0.30]	[8]	–	75.6
		12.5.3.4 TU and professional organisations	0.60	15	810	11.7
		12.5.3.5 Other payments for services e.g. photocopying	0.10	4	180	17.7
1-12	**All expenditure groups**		**386.30**	**9,924**	**5,850**	**1.2**
13	**Other expenditure items**		**84.60**	**2,174**	**5,470**	**2.6**
	13.1	Housing: mortgage interest payments, council tax etc.	58.40	1,500	5,060	1.7
		13.1.1 Mortgage interest payments	37.50	963	2,230	2.3
		13.1.2 Mortgage protection premiums	1.90	48	1,110	4.2
		13.1.3 Council tax, domestic rates	18.50	475	5,020	0.8
		13.1.5 Council tax, mortgage (second dwelling)	0.50	14	30	29.5
	13.2	Licences, fines and transfers	3.20	83	4,260	2.4
		13.2.1 Stamp duty, licences and fines (excluding motoring fines)	0.30	9	90	18.4
		13.2.2 Motoring fines	[0.10]	[2]	20	27.8
		13.2.3 Motor vehicle road taxation payments *less* refunds	2.80	72	4,250	1.3
	13.3	Holiday spending	11.50	295	330	15.6
		13.3.1 Money spent abroad	11.50	294	330	15.6
		13.3.2 Duty free goods bought in UK	[0.00]	[0]	–	65.1

Note: The commodity and service categories are not comparable with those in publications before 2001-02.

The numbering is sequential, it does not use actual COICOP codes.

Please see page xiii for symbols and conventions used in this report.

Table A1

Components of household expenditure, 2008 (cont.)
based on weighted data and including children's expenditure

Commodity or service	Average weekly expenditure all house-holds (£)	Total weekly expenditure (£ million)	Recording house-holds in sample	Percentage standard error (full method)
13 **Other expenditure items (continued)**				
13.4 Money transfers and credit	11.50	297	3,070	6.0
13.4.1 Money, cash gifts given to children	0.10	2	110	14.2
13.4.1.1 Money given to children for specific purposes	0.10	2	110	14.2
13.4.1.2 Cash gifts to children (no specific purpose)	[0.00]	[0]	–	82.8
13.4.2 Cash gifts and donations	9.80	251	2,570	6.9
13.4.2.1 Money/presents given to those outside the household	3.40	88	1,040	9.4
13.4.2.2 Charitable donations and subscriptions	2.30	60	1,710	7.6
13.4.2.3 Money sent abroad	2.00	51	350	23.5
13.4.2.4 Maintenance allowance expenditure	2.00	53	150	14.5
13.4.3 Club instalment payments (child) and interest on credit cards	1.70	43	980	5.8
13.4.3.1 Club instalment payment	[0.00]	[0]	–	-
13.4.3.2 Interest on credit cards	1.70	43	980	5.8
Total expenditure	**471.00**	**12,098**	**5,850**	**1.3**
14 **Other items recorded**				
14.1 Life assurance, contributions to pension funds	20.30	522	3,040	3.3
14.1.1 Life assurance premiums eg mortgage endowment policies	4.60	118	1,970	6.2
14.1.2 Contributions to pension and superannuation funds etc.	11.20	288	1,750	2.9
14.1.3 Personal pensions	4.50	116	730	9.5
14.2 Other insurance including friendly societies	1.20	31	1,230	5.2
14.3 Income tax, payments *less* refunds	98.60	2,532	4,630	6.5
14.3.1 Income tax paid by employees under PAYE	72.30	1,858	3,180	2.2
14.3.2 Income tax paid direct eg by retired or unoccupied persons	2.10	53	170	24.1
14.3.3 Income tax paid direct by self-employed	6.70	172	300	11.3
14.3.4 Income tax deducted at source from income under covenant from investments or from annuities and pensions	11.60	297	2,760	15.9
14.3.5 Income tax on bonus earnings	6.90	176	900	59.1
14.3.6 Income tax refunds under PAYE	0.30	7	50	30.7
14.3.7 Income tax refunds other than PAYE	0.70	18	300	14.5
14.4 National insurance contribution	28.50	731	3,100	1.5
14.4.1 NI contributions paid by employees	28.40	730	3,080	1.5
14.4.2 NI contributions paid by non-employees	0.10	1	40	25.8
14.5 Purchase or alteration of dwellings (contracted out), mortgages	44.10	1,132	2,490	5.9
14.5.1 Outright purchase of houses, flats etc. including deposits	[0.10]	[3]	–	44.7
14.5.2 Capital repayment of mortgage	17.80	457	1,830	2.5
14.5.3 Central heating installation	1.20	30	130	20.9
14.5.4 DIY improvements: Double glazing, kitchen units, sheds etc.	1.60	40	90	33.7
14.5.5 Home improvements - contracted out	18.10	464	940	8.5
14.5.6 Bathroom fittings	0.50	12	100	25.6
14.5.7 Purchase of materials for Capital Improvements	0.80	22	50	38.2
14.5.8 Purchase of second dwelling	4.10	105	50	40.7
14.6 Savings and investments	6.50	168	910	7.5
14.6.1 Savings, investments (excluding AVCs)	5.70	146	680	8.3
14.6.2 Additional Voluntary Contributions	0.70	17	110	14.9
14.6.3 Food stamps, other food related expenditure	0.20	4	190	12.5
14.7 Pay off loan to clear other debt	2.20	56	280	7.4
14.8 Windfall receipts from gambling etc.[3]	1.70	43	560	13.5

Note: The commodity and service categories are not comparable with those in publications before 2001-02.

         The numbering is sequential, it does not use actual COICOP codes.

         Please see page xiii for symbols and conventions used in this report.

3 Expressed as an income figure as opposed to an expenditure figure.

Table A2

Expenditure on alcoholic drink by place of purchase, 2008

based on weighted data and including children's expenditure

			Average weekly expenditure all households (£)	Total weekly expenditure (£ million)	Recording households in sample
By type of premises					
11	**Bought and consumed on licenced premises:**				
	11.1.2	Alcoholic drinks (away from home)	7.20	185	2,550
	11.1.2.1	Spirits and liqueurs (away from home)	0.80	22	700
	11.1.2.2	Wine from grape or other fruit (away from home)	1.30	33	1,040
	11.1.2.3	Fortified wine (away from home)	0.00	1	60
	11.1.2.4	Champagne and sparkling wines (away from home)	0.10	3	100
	11.1.2.5	Ciders and perry (away from home)	0.30	6	280
	11.1.2.6	Beer and lager (away from home)	3.90	100	1,960
	11.1.2.7	Alcopops (away from home)	0.10	3	120
	11.1.2.8	Round of drinks (away from home)	0.70	18	250
2	**Bought at off-licences (including large supermarket chains):**				
	2.1	Alcoholic drinks	6.20	160	2,970
	2.1.1	Spirits and liqueurs (brought home)	1.20	30	820
	2.1.2	Wines, fortified wines (brought home)	3.30	84	2,030
	2.1.2.1	Wine from grape or other fruit (brought home)	2.90	75	1,870
	2.1.2.2	Fortified wine (brought home)	0.20	4	210
	2.1.2.3	Champagne and sparkling wines (brought home)	0.20	4	170
	2.1.3	Beer, lager, ciders and perry (brought home)	1.70	44	1,510
	2.1.3.1	Beer and lager (brought home)	1.50	38	1,320
	2.1.3.2	Ciders and perry (brought home)	0.30	7	390
	2.1.4	Alcopops (brought home)	0.10	2	110
2A	**Bought from large supermarket chains:**				
	2.1A	Alcoholic drinks	4.30	110	2,440
	2.1.1A	Spirits and liqueurs (brought home)	0.90	23	640
	2.1.2A	Wines, fortified wines (brought home)	2.20	57	1,680
	2.1.2.1A	Wine from grape or other fruit (brought home)	2.00	51	1,530
	2.1.2.2A	Fortified wine (brought home)	0.10	3	170
	2.1.2.3A	Champagne and sparkling wines (brought home)	0.10	3	150
	2.1.3A	Beer, lager, ciders and perry (brought home)	1.10	29	1,120
	2.1.3.1A	Beer and lager (brought home)	0.90	24	970
	2.1.3.2A	Ciders and perry (brought home)	0.20	4	290
	2.1.4A	Alcopops (brought home)	0.00	1	80
2B	**Bought from other off-licence outlets:**				
	2.1B	Alcoholic drinks	1.90	50	1,230
	2.1.1B	Spirits and liqueurs (brought home)	0.30	7	230
	2.1.2B	Wines, fortified wines (brought home)	1.00	26	710
	2.1.2.1B	Wine from grape or other fruit (brought home)	1.00	25	660
	2.1.2.2B	Fortified wine (brought home)	0.00	1	50
	2.1.2.3B	Champagne and sparkling wines (brought home)	0.00	1	30
	2.1.3B	Beer, lager, ciders and perry (brought home)	0.60	16	600
	2.1.3.1B	Beer and lager (brought home)	0.50	13	530
	2.1.3.2B	Ciders and perry (brought home)	0.10	2	110
	2.1.4B	Alcopops (brought home)	0.00	1	40

Note: The commodity and service categories are not comparable with those in publications before 2001-02.

The numbering is sequential, it does not use actual COICOP codes.

Please see page xiii for symbols and conventions used in this report.

Table A3

Expenditure on food and non-alcoholic drinks by place of purchase, 2008
based on weighted data and including children's expenditure

			Large supermarket chains			Other outlets		
			Average weekly expenditure all house-holds (£)	Total weekly expenditure (£ million)	Recording house-holds in sample	Average weekly expenditure all house-holds (£)	Total weekly expenditure (£ million)	Recording house-holds in sample
1	Food and non-alcoholic drinks		36.50	937	5,400	14.20	365	5,330
1.1	Food		33.50	861	5,400	13.10	337	5,300
1.1.1	Bread, rice and cereals		3.50	89	5,090	1.40	36	3,370
	1.1.1.1	Rice	0.20	6	1,130	0.10	4	320
	1.1.1.2	Bread	1.80	46	4,800	0.80	21	3,000
	1.1.1.3	Other breads and cereals	1.50	37	4,000	0.40	11	1,540
1.1.2	Pasta products		0.30	8	2,050	0.10	2	520
1.1.3	Buns, cakes, biscuits etc.		2.40	61	4,540	0.80	21	2,440
	1.1.3.1	Buns, crispbread and biscuits	1.40	35	4,060	0.40	11	1,960
	1.1.3.2	Cakes and puddings	1.00	26	3,170	0.40	10	1,410
1.1.4	Pastry (savoury)		0.50	14	1,640	0.10	3	490
1.1.5	Beef (fresh, chilled or frozen)		1.00	26	1,940	0.60	15	1,030
1.1.6	Pork (fresh, chilled or frozen)		0.40	11	1,050	0.20	6	480
1.1.7	Lamb (fresh, chilled or frozen)		0.40	9	740	0.30	7	410
1.1.8	Poultry (fresh, chilled or frozen)		1.40	35	2,360	0.50	14	950
1.1.9	Bacon and ham		0.70	17	2,120	0.30	7	880
1.1.10	Other meats and meat preparations		3.90	99	4,520	1.30	34	2,440
	1.1.10.1	Sausages	0.50	13	1,930	0.20	6	900
	1.1.10.2	Offal, pate etc.	0.10	2	610	0.00	1	220
	1.1.10.3	Other preserved or processed meat and meat preparations	3.30	85	4,340	1.00	27	2,160
	1.1.10.4	Other fresh, chilled or frozen meat	[0.00]	0	20	0.00	1	20
1.1.11	Fish and fish products		1.70	43	3,230	0.60	16	1,130
	1.1.11.1	Fish (fresh, chilled or frozen)	0.50	13	1,190	0.30	7	420
	1.1.11.2	Seafood, dried, smoked or salted fish	0.40	10	1,060	0.10	4	290
	1.1.11.3	Other preserved or processed fish and seafood	0.80	20	2,510	0.20	6	730
1.1.12	Milk		1.50	39	4,250	1.10	29	3,070
	1.1.12.1	Whole milk	0.30	8	1,220	0.30	8	950
	1.1.12.2	Low fat milk	1.10	27	3,470	0.80	19	2,420
	1.1.12.3	Preserved milk	0.10	3	360	0.00	1	100
1.1.13	Cheese and curd		1.30	34	3,570	0.30	8	1,160
1.1.14	Eggs		0.40	11	2,380	0.20	5	1,220
1.1.15	Other milk products		1.50	39	3,870	0.30	9	1,260
	1.1.15.1	Other milk products	0.70	18	2,860	0.20	4	870
	1.1.15.2	Yoghurt	0.80	22	2,790	0.20	4	700
1.1.16	Butter		0.30	8	1,540	0.10	2	460
1.1.17	Margarine, other vegetable fats and peanut butter		0.40	10	2,360	0.10	3	680
1.1.18	Cooking oils and fats		0.20	6	1,160	0.10	2	270
	1.1.18.1	Olive oil	0.10	3	430	0.00	1	70
	1.1.18.2	Edible oils and other edible animal fats	0.10	3	810	0.00	1	210
1.1.19	Fresh fruit		2.30	60	4,320	0.60	16	1,820
	1.1.19.1	Citrus fruits (fresh)	0.40	10	2,160	0.10	2	660
	1.1.19.2	Bananas (fresh)	0.40	10	3,120	0.10	3	1,030
	1.1.19.3	Apples (fresh)	0.40	11	2,370	0.10	3	800
	1.1.19.4	Pears (fresh)	0.10	3	980	0.00	1	240
	1.1.19.5	Stone fruits (fresh)	0.30	8	1,330	0.10	2	410
	1.1.19.6	Berries (fresh)	0.70	19	2,280	0.20	5	710

Note: The commodity and service categories are not comparable with those in publications before 2001-02.

The numbering is sequential, it does not use actual COICOP codes.

Please see page xiii for symbols and conventions used in this report.

Table A3

Expenditure on food and non-alcoholic drinks by place of purchase, 2008 (cont.)

based on weighted data and including children's expenditure

			Large supermarket chains			Other outlets		
			Average weekly expenditure all house- holds (£)	Total weekly expenditure (£ million)	Recording house- holds in sample	Average weekly expenditure all house- holds (£)	Total weekly expenditure (£ million)	Recording house- holds in sample
1	**Food and non-alcoholic drinks (continued)**							
	1.1.20	Other fresh, chilled or frozen fruits	0.30	7	1,400	0.10	2	380
	1.1.21	Dried fruit and nuts	0.30	9	1,510	0.20	4	510
	1.1.22	Preserved fruit and fruit based products	0.10	3	910	0.00	1	200
	1.1.23	Fresh vegetables	2.90	74	4,630	0.80	21	2,200
		1.1.23.1 Leaf and stem vegetables (fresh or chilled)	0.60	15	2,990	0.10	3	870
		1.1.23.2 Cabbages (fresh or chilled)	0.30	8	2,380	0.10	3	800
		1.1.23.3 Vegetables grown for their fruit (fresh, chilled or frozen)	1.00	27	3,710	0.30	7	0 1,290
		1.1.23.4 Root crops, non-starchy bulbs and mushrooms (fresh, chilled or frozen)	1.00	25	4,010	0.30	9	1,650
	1.1.24	Dried vegetables and other preserved and processed vegetables	0.60	14	3,130	0.60	17	2,850
	1.1.25	Potatoes	0.70	17	3,180	0.20	6	1,350
	1.1.26	Other tubers and products of tuber vegetables	0.90	24	3,290	0.30	8	1,470
	1.1.27	Sugar and sugar products	0.20	6	1,710	0.10	2	600
		1.1.28.1 Sugar	0.20	4	1,500	0.10	2	540
		1.1.28.2 Other sugar products	0.10	1	420	0.00	0	100
	1.1.28	Jams, marmalades	0.20	5	1,390	0.10	2	410
	1.1.29	Chocolate	0.90	23	2,610	0.60	15	1,810
	1.1.30	Confectionery products	0.30	8	1,840	0.30	7	1,490
	1.1.31	Edible ices and ice cream	0.40	9	1,350	0.10	3	580
	1.1.32	Other food products	1.60	42	4,200	0.60	16	1,710
		1.1.32.1 Sauces, condiments	0.90	23	3,240	0.20	5	960
		1.1.32.2 Baker's yeast, dessert preparations, soups	0.60	15	2,730	0.20	5	910
		1.1.32.3 Salt, spices, culinary herbs and other food products	0.20	4	1,210	0.20	6	470
1.2	Non-alcoholic drinks		3.00	76	4,560	1.10	28	2,700
	1.2.1	Coffee	0.40	11	1,400	0.10	3	460
	1.2.2	Tea	0.30	8	1,530	0.10	3	620
	1.2.3	Cocoa and powdered chocolate	0.10	2	410	0.00	1	120
	1.2.4	Fruit and vegetable juices (inc. fruit squash)	0.90	24	2,980	0.20	6	930
	1.2.5	Mineral or spring waters	0.20	4	940	0.10	1	360
	1.2.6	Soft drinks	1.10	28	3,000	0.50	14	1,820

Note: The commodity and service categories are not comparable with those in publications before 2001-02.

The numbering is sequential, it does not use actual COICOP codes.

Please see page xiii for symbols and conventions used in this report.

Table A4

Expenditure on selected items by place of purchase, 2008
based on weighted data and including children's expenditure

		Large supermarket chains			Other outlets		
		Average weekly expenditure all house-holds (£)	Total weekly expenditure (£ million)	Recording house-holds in sample	Average weekly expenditure all house-holds (£)	Total weekly expenditure (£ million)	Recording house-holds in sample
2	**Alcoholic drink and tobacco**						
2.2	Tobacco	1.20	32	660	3.30	84	1,210
2.2.1	Cigarettes	1.00	27	580	2.90	73	1,110
2.2.2	Cigars and other tobacco products	0.20	5	140	0.40	11	280
2.2.2.1	Cigars	0.10	1	20	0.00	1	20
2.2.2.2	Other tobacco	0.10	3	130	0.40	10	260
5	**Household goods and services**						
5.5.5	Electrical consumable	0.20	4	520	0.40	11	790
5.6.1	Cleaning materials	1.50	39	3,290	0.60	17	1,630
7	**Transport**						
7.2.2	Petrol, diesel & other motor oils	8.60	221	2,110	12.40	319	2,640
7.2.2.1	Petrol	6.50	167	1,750	9.20	237	2,160
7.2.2.2	Diesel oil	2.10	54	480	3.10	81	730
7.2.2.3	Other motor oils	[0.00]	0	20	0.10	1	60
8	**Communication**						
8.1	Postal services	-	-	0	0.50	12	1,050
9	**Recreation and culture**						
9.3.5.1	Pet food	0.80	22	1,360	1.00	25	1,090
9.5.2 &	Stationery, diaries, address books, art materials						
9.5.3	Cards, calendars, posters and other printed matter	0.50	12	1,410	1.40	37	2,560
9.5.4	Newspapers	0.30	7	1,710	1.60	40	3,260
9.5.5	Magazines and periodicals	0.30	7	1,280	0.60	16	1,930
12	**Miscellaneous goods and services**						
12.1.2	Toilet paper	0.60	15	2,060	0.20	5	800
12.1.3.1 & 12.1.3.3	Toiletries and other toilet requisites - toothpaste, deodorant, tampons, razors, hairbrushes, toothbrushes	0.90	24	2,620	0.80	19	1,860
12.1.3.2	Bar of soap, liquid soap, shower gel etc	0.20	5	1,190	0.10	4	620
12.1.5.2	Cosmetics and related accessories	0.50	13	1,210	1.90	50	1,500

Note: The commodity and service categories are not comparable with those in publications before 2001-02.

The numbering is sequential, it does not use actual COICOP codes.

Please see page xiii for symbols and conventions used in this report.

Table A5

Expenditure on clothing and footwear by place of purchase, 2008
based on weighted data and including children's expenditure

			Large supermarket chains			Clothing chains			Other outlets		
			Average weekly expenditure all house-holds (£)	Total weekly expenditure (£ million)	Recording house-holds in sample	Average weekly expenditure all house-holds (£)	Total weekly expenditure (£ million)	Recording house-holds in sample	Average weekly expenditure all house-holds (£)	Total weekly expenditure (£ million)	Recording house-holds in sample
3	Clothing and footwear		1.50	39	1,330	8.00	206	2,040	11.70	300	2,840
3.1	Clothing		1.40	36	1,290	7.20	185	1,960	8.60	220	2,460
	3.1.1	Men's outer garments	0.20	6	220	1.80	45	510	2.50	65	670
	3.1.2	Men's under garments	0.10	2	130	0.20	5	180	0.10	2	160
	3.1.3	Women's outer garments	0.50	13	460	3.70	95	1,200	3.40	88	1,140
	3.1.4	Women's under garments	0.10	4	370	0.50	14	530	0.40	10	370
	3.1.5	Boys' outer garments	0.10	2	120	0.20	5	120	0.50	13	270
	3.1.6	Girls' outer garments	0.10	3	150	0.30	7	190	0.60	14	330
	3.1.7	Infants' outer garments	0.10	3	140	0.20	5	160	0.30	8	210
	3.1.8	Children's under garments	0.10	2	180	0.10	3	170	0.10	3	230
	3.1.9	Accessories	0.00	1	160	0.20	6	290	0.40	9	530
	3.1.9.1	Men's accessories	0.00	0	50	0.10	3	100	0.10	3	170
	3.1.9.2	Women's accessories	0.00	1	70	0.10	3	170	0.20	4	250
	3.1.9.3	Children's accessories	0.00	0	40	0.00	0	40	0.10	2	160
	3.1.10	Haberdashery and clothing hire	[0.00]	0	40	0.00	0	10	0.30	7	230
3.2	Footwear		0.10	3	160	0.80	21	440	3.10	80	1,190
	3.2.1	Men's	0.00	1	30	0.20	4	70	1.00	26	340
	3.2.2	Women's	0.10	2	90	0.60	15	320	1.40	36	620
	3.2.3	Children's	0.00	1	40	0.10	2	70	0.70	18	390

Note: The commodity and service categories are not comparable with those in publications before 2001-02.

The numbering is sequential, it does not use actual COICOP codes.

Please see page xiii for symbols and conventions used in this report.

Table A6

Household expenditure by gross income decile group, 2008
based on weighted data and including children's expenditure

Commodity or service	Lowest ten per cent	Second decile group	Third decile group	Fourth decile group	Fifth decile group	Sixth decile group
Lower boundary of group (£ per week)		146	224	305	408	522
Weighted number of households (thousands)	2,570	2,570	2,570	2,570	2,570	2,570
Total number of households in sample	550	580	610	630	590	600
Total number of persons in sample	710	970	1,130	1,320	1,380	1,520
Total number of adults in sample	600	770	920	1,040	1,070	1,160
Weighted average number of persons per household	1.3	1.7	1.8	2.1	2.3	2.5
Commodity or service	Average weekly household expenditure (£)					
1 Food & non-alcoholic drinks	26.40	33.00	37.90	43.70	50.10	52.10
2 Alcoholic drinks, tobacco & narcotics	6.70	6.10	7.60	9.90	10.30	11.80
3 Clothing & footwear	6.40	8.60	10.60	14.40	16.60	21.10
4 Housing(net)[1], fuel & power	36.30	38.40	47.90	51.30	53.80	55.90
5 Household goods & services	9.10	15.20	19.30	21.60	24.10	25.20
6 Health	1.20	3.20	3.10	3.90	5.20	5.10
7 Transport	12.10	17.10	24.10	38.90	51.90	61.00
8 Communication	5.80	7.10	7.90	9.10	12.20	13.10
9 Recreation & culture	15.30	23.90	31.70	39.30	50.70	69.30
10 Education	[1.40]	[0.50]	0.50	0.80	2.60	2.40
11 Restaurants & hotels	9.00	12.00	14.80	23.80	28.20	34.10
12 Miscellaneous goods & services	10.40	15.40	19.10	21.30	28.10	33.90
1–12 All expenditure groups	140.10	180.50	224.50	278.00	333.90	385.10
13 Other expenditure items	13.70	19.50	32.60	52.10	59.10	74.10
Total expenditure	**153.70**	**200.00**	**257.10**	**330.10**	**393.00**	**459.20**
Average weekly expenditure per person (£) **Total expenditure**	**117.70**	**119.20**	**142.20**	**157.00**	**169.50**	**184.60**

Note: The commodity and service categories are not comparable to those in publications before 2001-02.
              Please see page xiii for symbols and conventions used in this report.
1   Excluding mortgage interest payments, council tax and Northern Ireland rates.

Table A6

Household expenditure by gross income decile group, 2008 (cont.)
based on weighted data and including children's expenditure

		Seventh decile group	Eighth decile group	Ninth decile group	Highest ten per cent	All house-holds
Lower boundary of group (£ per week)		664	817	1026	1,356	
Weighted number of households (thousands)		2,570	2,560	2,570	2,560	25,690
Total number of households in sample		590	570	550	580	5,850
Total number of persons in sample		1,620	1,640	1,680	1,860	13,830
Total number of adults in sample		1,190	1,240	1,280	1,380	10,640
Weighted average number of persons per household		2.8	2.8	3.1	3.2	2.4
Commodity or service		Average weekly household expenditure (£)				
1	Food & non-alcoholic drinks	55.20	63.40	65.90	79.40	50.70
2	Alcoholic drinks, tobacco & narcotics	12.10	14.60	13.30	15.50	10.80
3	Clothing & footwear	23.70	29.60	36.00	48.80	21.60
4	Housing(net)[1], fuel & power	57.10	63.00	54.80	72.00	53.00
5	Household goods & services	34.60	37.70	46.50	68.10	30.10
6	Health	4.50	7.00	7.10	10.90	5.10
7	Transport	73.60	81.90	112.20	161.10	63.40
8	Communication	14.10	14.90	16.70	18.70	12.00
9	Recreation & culture	69.00	75.80	86.50	139.30	60.10
10	Education	4.80	7.30	7.10	34.60	6.20
11	Restaurants & hotels	45.50	53.20	60.50	96.30	37.70
12	Miscellaneous goods & services	38.00	53.50	57.10	79.60	35.60
1-12	All expenditure groups	432.30	501.90	563.60	824.40	386.30
13	Other expenditure items	104.50	123.80	146.80	220.50	84.60
Total expenditure		**536.70**	**625.70**	**710.40**	**1044.90**	**471.00**
Average weekly expenditure per person (£) **Total expenditure**		**192.80**	**223.10**	**232.70**	**323.20**	**199.80**

Note: The commodity and service categories are not comparable to those in publications before 2001-02.
Please see page xiii for symbols and conventions used in this report.
1 Excluding mortgage interest payments, council tax and Northern Ireland rates.

Table A7

Household expenditure as a percentage of total expenditure by gross income decile group, 2008

based on weighted data and including children's expenditure

	Lowest ten per cent	Second decile group	Third decile group	Fourth decile group	Fifth decile group	Sixth decile group
Lower boundary of group (£ per week)		146	224	305	408	522
Weighted number of households (thousands)	2,570	2,570	2,570	2,570	2,570	2,570
Total number of households in sample	550	580	610	630	590	600
Total number of persons in sample	710	970	1,130	1,320	1,380	1,520
Total number of adults in sample	600	770	920	1,040	1,070	1,160
Weighted average number of persons per household	1.3	1.7	1.8	2.1	2.3	2.5
Commodity or service	Percentage of total expenditure					
1 Food & non-alcoholic drinks	17	16	15	13	13	11
2 Alcoholic drinks, tobacco & narcotics	4	3	3	3	3	3
3 Clothing & footwear	4	4	4	4	4	5
4 Housing(net)[1], fuel & power	24	19	19	16	14	12
5 Household goods & services	6	8	8	7	6	5
6 Health	1	2	1	1	1	1
7 Transport	8	9	9	12	13	13
8 Communication	4	4	3	3	3	3
9 Recreation & culture	10	12	12	12	13	15
10 Education	[1]	[0]	0	0	1	1
11 Restaurants & hotels	6	6	6	7	7	7
12 Miscellaneous goods & services	7	8	7	6	7	7
1-12 All expenditure groups	91	90	87	84	85	84
13 Other expenditure items	9	10	13	16	15	16
Total expenditure	100	100	100	100	100	100

Note: The commodity and service categories are not comparable to those in publications before 2001-02.
Please see page xiii for symbols and conventions used in this report.
1   Excluding mortgage interest payments, council tax and Northern Ireland rates.

Table A7

Household expenditure as a percentage of total expenditure by gross income decile group, 2008 (cont.)

based on weighted data and including children's expenditure

	Seventh decile group	Eighth decile group	Ninth decile group	Highest ten per cent	All house- holds
Lower boundary of group (£ per week)	664	817	1026	1,356	
Weighted number of households (thousands)	2,570	2,560	2,570	2,560	25,690
Total number of households in sample	590	570	550	580	5,850
Total number of persons in sample	1,620	1,640	1,680	1,860	13,830
Total number of adults in sample	1,190	1,240	1,280	1,380	10,640
Weighted average number of persons per household	2.8	2.8	3.1	3.2	2.4
Commodity or service	Percentage of total expenditure				
1 Food & non-alcoholic drinks	10	10	9	8	11
2 Alcoholic drinks, tobacco & narcotics	2	2	2	1	2
3 Clothing & footwear	4	5	5	5	5
4 Housing(net)[1], fuel & power	11	10	8	7	11
5 Household goods & services	6	6	7	7	6
6 Health	1	1	1	1	1
7 Transport	14	13	16	15	13
8 Communication	3	2	2	2	3
9 Recreation & culture	13	12	12	13	13
10 Education	1	1	1	3	1
11 Restaurants & hotels	8	8	9	9	8
12 Miscellaneous goods & services	7	9	8	8	8
1-12 All expenditure groups	81	80	79	79	82
13 Other expenditure items	19	20	21	21	18
Total expenditure	100	100	100	100	100

Note: The commodity and service categories are not comparable to those in publications before 2001-02.
            Please see page xiii for symbols and conventions used in this report.
1   Excluding mortgage interest payments, council tax and Northern Ireland rates.

Table A8

Detailed household expenditure by gross income decile group, 2008

based on weighted data and including children's expenditure

	Lowest ten per cent	Second decile group	Third decile group	Fourth decile group	Fifth decile group	Sixth decile group
Lower boundary of group (£ per week)		146	224	305	408	522
Weighted number of households (thousands)	2,570	2,570	2,570	2,570	2,570	2,570
Total number of households in sample	550	580	610	630	590	600
Total number of persons in sample	710	970	1,130	1,320	1,380	1,520
Total number of adults in sample	600	770	920	1,040	1,070	1,160
Weighted average number of persons per household	1.3	1.7	1.8	2.1	2.3	2.5

Commodity or service	Average weekly household expenditure (£)					
1 Food & non-alcoholic drinks	**26.40**	**33.00**	**37.90**	**43.70**	**50.10**	**52.10**
1.1 Food	24.30	30.60	35.30	40.00	46.20	47.80
1.1.1 Bread, rice and cereals	2.70	3.40	3.50	4.20	4.80	5.10
1.1.2 Pasta products	0.20	0.20	0.20	0.30	0.40	0.30
1.1.3 Buns, cakes, biscuits etc.	1.80	2.30	2.50	3.00	3.20	3.30
1.1.4 Pastry (savoury)	0.30	0.40	0.40	0.40	0.70	0.70
1.1.5 Beef (fresh, chilled or frozen)	0.60	0.80	1.10	1.30	1.80	1.60
1.1.6 Pork (fresh, chilled or frozen)	0.40	0.40	0.50	0.50	0.80	0.70
1.1.7 Lamb (fresh, chilled or frozen)	0.40	0.50	0.50	0.50	0.70	0.70
1.1.8 Poultry (fresh, chilled or frozen)	0.90	1.10	1.30	1.50	1.90	1.90
1.1.9 Bacon and ham	0.50	0.70	0.70	0.90	1.00	1.00
1.1.10 Other meat and meat preparations	3.00	3.50	4.10	4.40	5.00	5.30
1.1.11 Fish and fish products	1.10	1.40	2.00	1.90	2.20	2.20
1.1.12 Milk	1.60	2.10	2.30	2.50	2.70	2.70
1.1.13 Cheese and curd	0.90	0.90	1.00	1.30	1.60	1.70
1.1.14 Eggs	0.40	0.40	0.50	0.60	0.70	0.60
1.1.15 Other milk products	0.90	1.10	1.30	1.60	1.80	2.00
1.1.16 Butter	0.20	0.30	0.40	0.30	0.30	0.40
1.1.17 Margarine, other vegetable fats and peanut butter	0.30	0.40	0.40	0.50	0.50	0.50
1.1.18 Cooking oils and fats	0.20	0.20	0.20	0.20	0.30	0.30
1.1.19 Fresh fruit	1.40	1.90	2.30	2.40	2.80	2.80
1.1.20 Other fresh, chilled or frozen fruits	0.20	0.20	0.20	0.20	0.30	0.30
1.1.21 Dried fruit and nuts	0.20	0.30	0.40	0.40	0.40	0.40
1.1.22 Preserved fruit and fruit based products	0.10	0.10	0.10	0.10	0.10	0.10
1.1.23 Fresh vegetables	1.60	2.20	2.50	2.90	3.50	3.60
1.1.24 Dried vegetables	[0.00]	[0.00]	0.00	0.00	0.00	0.00
1.1.25 Other preserved or processed vegetables	0.60	0.60	0.80	0.80	1.10	1.30
1.1.26 Potatoes	0.50	0.70	0.80	0.90	0.90	0.90
1.1.27 Other tubers and products of tuber vegetables	0.70	0.80	0.90	1.10	1.30	1.40
1.1.28 Sugar and sugar products	0.20	0.30	0.30	0.30	0.30	0.30
1.1.29 Jams, marmalades	0.20	0.20	0.30	0.20	0.30	0.30
1.1.30 Chocolate	0.80	1.00	1.00	1.30	1.40	1.70
1.1.31 Confectionery products	0.30	0.40	0.50	0.60	0.60	0.60
1.1.32 Edible ices and ice cream	0.20	0.30	0.40	0.50	0.50	0.50
1.1.33 Other food products	1.10	1.40	1.80	1.70	2.30	2.50
1.2 Non-alcoholic drinks	2.10	2.40	2.70	3.60	3.90	4.30
1.2.1 Coffee	0.30	0.40	0.40	0.60	0.60	0.70
1.2.2 Tea	0.40	0.40	0.40	0.40	0.40	0.40
1.2.3 Cocoa and powdered chocolate	0.10	0.10	0.10	0.10	0.10	0.10
1.2.4 Fruit and vegetable juices (inc. fruit squash)	0.50	0.60	0.60	0.80	0.90	1.10
1.2.5 Mineral or spring waters	0.10	0.10	0.10	0.20	0.20	0.20
1.2.6 Soft drinks (inc. fizzy and ready to drink fruit drinks)	0.70	0.90	1.10	1.60	1.60	1.80

Note: The commodity and service categories are not comparable to those in publications before 2001-02.
The numbering system is sequential, it does not use actual COICOP codes.
Please see page xiii for symbols and conventions used in this report.

Table A8

Detailed household expenditure by gross income decile group, 2008 (cont.)

based on weighted data and including children's expenditure

		Seventh decile group	Eighth decile group	Ninth decile group	Highest ten per cent	All house- holds
Lower boundary of group (£ per week)		664	817	1026	1,356	
Weighted number of households (thousands)		2,570	2,560	2,570	2,560	25,690
Total number of households in sample		590	570	550	580	5,850
Total number of persons in sample		1,620	1,640	1,680	1,860	13,830
Total number of adults in sample		1,190	1,240	1,280	1,380	10,640
Weighted average number of persons per household		2.8	2.8	3.1	3.2	2.4
Commodity or service		Average weekly household expenditure (£)				
1	**Food & non-alcoholic drinks**	**55.20**	**63.40**	**65.90**	**79.40**	**50.70**
1.1	Food	50.70	58.10	60.50	73.10	46.70
1.1.1	Bread, rice and cereals	5.40	6.10	6.20	7.20	4.90
1.1.2	Pasta products	0.40	0.50	0.50	0.60	0.40
1.1.3	Buns, cakes, biscuits etc.	3.60	3.70	4.00	4.50	3.20
1.1.4	Pastry (savoury)	0.70	0.90	1.10	1.20	0.70
1.1.5	Beef (fresh, chilled or frozen)	1.80	2.00	2.20	2.80	1.60
1.1.6	Pork (fresh, chilled or frozen)	0.70	0.80	0.70	0.90	0.60
1.1.7	Lamb (fresh, chilled or frozen)	0.60	0.80	0.70	1.10	0.60
1.1.8	Poultry (fresh, chilled or frozen)	2.00	2.50	2.60	3.30	1.90
1.1.9	Bacon and ham	1.00	1.10	1.10	1.40	0.90
1.1.10	Other meat and meat preparations	5.60	6.30	6.80	7.70	5.20
1.1.11	Fish and fish products	2.20	3.20	2.80	4.00	2.30
1.1.12	Milk	3.00	3.10	3.10	3.10	2.60
1.1.13	Cheese and curd	1.90	2.20	2.30	2.80	1.70
1.1.14	Eggs	0.70	0.70	0.80	0.90	0.60
1.1.15	Other milk products	2.10	2.50	2.50	2.90	1.90
1.1.16	Butter	0.40	0.40	0.40	0.60	0.40
1.1.17	Margarine, other vegetable fats and peanut butter	0.50	0.50	0.50	0.60	0.50
1.1.18	Cooking oils and fats	0.30	0.30	0.30	0.50	0.30
1.1.19	Fresh fruit	3.30	3.60	3.90	5.30	3.00
1.1.20	Other fresh, chilled or frozen fruits	0.40	0.50	0.60	0.80	0.40
1.1.21	Dried fruit and nuts	0.50	0.70	0.70	0.80	0.50
1.1.22	Preserved fruit and fruit based products	0.10	0.10	0.10	0.20	0.10
1.1.23	Fresh vegetables	3.90	5.00	5.20	6.90	3.70
1.1.24	Dried vegetables	0.10	0.10	0.00	0.10	0.00
1.1.25	Other preserved or processed vegetables	1.20	1.50	1.70	2.00	1.20
1.1.26	Potatoes	0.90	1.00	1.10	1.20	0.90
1.1.27	Other tubers and products of tuber vegetables	1.50	1.50	1.60	1.70	1.30
1.1.28	Sugar and sugar products	0.30	0.40	0.30	0.40	0.30
1.1.29	Jams, marmalades	0.20	0.30	0.30	0.40	0.30
1.1.30	Chocolate	1.70	1.70	2.00	2.10	1.50
1.1.31	Confectionery products	0.60	0.70	0.60	0.70	0.60
1.1.32	Edible ices and ice cream	0.60	0.50	0.70	0.70	0.50
1.1.33	Other food products	2.30	2.80	2.80	3.80	2.30
1.2	Non-alcoholic drinks	4.50	5.20	5.40	6.30	4.00
1.2.1	Coffee	0.60	0.60	0.70	0.80	0.60
1.2.2	Tea	0.40	0.50	0.50	0.50	0.40
1.2.3	Cocoa and powdered chocolate	0.10	0.10	0.10	0.10	0.10
1.2.4	Fruit and vegetable juices, mineral waters	1.30	1.50	1.80	2.20	1.10
1.2.5	Mineral or spring waters	0.20	0.30	0.30	0.50	0.20
1.2.6	Soft drinks (inc. fizzy and ready to drink fruit drinks)	1.80	2.10	2.10	2.20	1.60

Note: The commodity and service categories are not comparable to those in publications before 2001-02.

The numbering system is sequential, it does not use actual COICOP codes.

Please see page xiii for symbols and conventions used in this report.

Table A8

Detailed household expenditure by gross income decile group, 2008 (cont.)

based on weighted data and including children's expenditure

Commodity or service	Lowest ten per cent	Second decile group	Third decile group	Fourth decile group	Fifth decile group	Sixth decile group
	Average weekly household expenditure (£)					
2 Alcoholic drink, tobacco & narcotics	**6.70**	**6.10**	**7.60**	**9.90**	**10.30**	**11.80**
2.1 Alcoholic drinks	2.40	3.10	3.60	4.90	5.20	6.00
2.1.1 Spirits and liqueurs (brought home)	0.50	0.90	1.00	1.20	1.40	1.30
2.1.2 Wines, fortified wines (brought home)	0.90	1.10	1.60	2.40	2.20	2.70
2.1.3 Beer, lager, ciders and perry (brought home)	1.00	1.00	1.00	1.20	1.50	1.90
2.1.4 Alcopops (brought home)	[0.00]	[0.00]	[0.00]	[0.10]	[0.10]	[0.10]
2.2 Tobacco and narcotics	4.30	3.10	4.00	4.90	5.10	5.80
2.2.1 Cigarettes	3.40	2.20	3.40	4.30	4.30	4.80
2.2.2 Cigars, other tobacco products and narcotics	0.90	0.80	0.60	0.60	0.80	1.00
3 Clothing & footwear	**6.40**	**8.60**	**10.60**	**14.40**	**16.60**	**21.10**
3.1 Clothing	5.10	6.90	8.70	11.30	13.00	16.70
3.1.1 Men's outer garments	1.30	1.10	1.60	1.90	2.50	4.10
3.1.2 Men's under garments	0.10	0.20	0.10	0.30	0.20	0.30
3.1.3 Women's outer garments	2.40	3.20	4.40	4.60	6.00	7.30
3.1.4 Women's under garments	0.40	0.50	0.50	0.80	0.90	1.30
3.1.5 Boys' outer garments (5-15)	[0.20]	0.20	0.60	0.80	0.60	0.60
3.1.6 Girls' outer garments (5-15)	[0.10]	0.50	0.30	1.10	1.20	0.90
3.1.7 Infants' outer garments (under 5)	0.20	0.40	0.40	0.50	0.50	0.60
3.1.8 Children's under garments (under 16)	[0.10]	0.10	0.20	0.30	0.30	0.30
3.1.9 Accessories	0.10	0.40	0.20	0.70	0.60	0.50
3.1.10 Haberdashery and clothing hire	[0.10]	0.10	0.10	0.10	0.20	0.70
3.1.11 Dry cleaners, laundry and dyeing	[0.10]	[0.00]	[0.20]	[0.10]	[0.10]	[0.10]
3.2 Footwear	1.30	1.70	1.90	3.10	3.70	4.40
4 Housing (net)[1], fuel & power	**36.30**	**38.40**	**47.90**	**51.30**	**53.80**	**55.90**
4.1 Actual rentals for housing	63.40	47.90	42.00	32.50	27.40	24.10
4.1.1 Gross rent	63.40	47.90	42.00	32.50	27.40	24.10
4.1.2 *less* housing benefit, rebates & allowances rec'd	48.00	33.20	21.20	10.90	4.60	1.10
4.1.3 Net rent[2]	15.40	14.70	20.90	21.60	22.80	23.00
4.1.4 Second dwelling rent	–	–	–	–	–	–
4.2 Maintenance and repair of dwelling	2.10	2.50	3.90	5.20	6.00	6.60
4.3 Water supply and miscellaneous services relating to the dwelling	5.80	6.40	7.50	7.30	7.40	7.50
4.4 Electricity, gas and other fuels	12.90	14.70	15.60	17.20	17.60	18.80
4.4.1 Electricity	6.30	7.10	7.80	8.20	8.60	9.20
4.4.2 Gas	5.50	6.30	6.60	7.40	7.60	8.00
4.4.3 Other fuels	1.10	1.30	1.20	1.60	1.40	1.60

Note: The commodity and service categories are not comparable to those in publications before 2001-02.
         The numbering system is sequential, it does not use actual COICOP codes.
         Please see page xiii for symbols and conventions used in this report.
1   Excluding mortgage interest payments, council tax and Northern Ireland rates.
2   The figure included in total expenditure is net rent as opposed to gross rent.

Table A8

Detailed household expenditure by gross income decile group, 2008 (cont.)
based on weighted data and including children's expenditure

Commodity or service	Seventh decile group	Eighth decile group	Ninth decile group	Highest ten per cent	All house-holds
	Average weekly household expenditure (£)				
2 Alcoholic drink, tobacco & narcotics	**12.10**	**14.60**	**13.30**	**15.50**	**10.80**
2.1 Alcoholic drinks	7.20	9.50	8.90	11.40	6.20
2.1.1 Spirits and liqueurs (brought home)	1.40	1.50	1.50	1.20	1.20
2.1.2 Wines, fortified wines (brought home)	3.40	5.60	4.80	7.80	3.30
2.1.3 Beer, lager, ciders and perry (brought home)	2.40	2.40	2.50	2.30	1.70
2.1.4 Alcopops (brought home)	[0.10]	[0.10]	[0.10]	[0.10]	0.10
2.2 Tobacco and narcotics	4.90	5.10	4.50	4.00	4.60
2.2.1 Cigarettes	4.20	4.50	4.10	3.70	3.90
2.2.2 Cigars, other tobacco products and narcotics	0.70	0.60	0.40	[0.30]	0.70
3 Clothing & footwear	**23.70**	**29.60**	**36.00**	**48.80**	**21.60**
3.1 Clothing	19.70	23.90	29.70	39.70	17.50
3.1.1 Men's outer garments	5.00	6.20	10.40	11.30	4.50
3.1.2 Men's under garments	0.40	0.50	0.70	0.60	0.30
3.1.3 Women's outer garments	7.70	10.60	12.00	18.20	7.60
3.1.4 Women's under garments	1.00	1.30	1.40	2.50	1.10
3.1.5 Boys' outer garments (5-15)	1.20	1.00	1.10	1.40	0.80
3.1.6 Girls' outer garments (5-15)	1.60	0.90	1.20	1.70	1.00
3.1.7 Infants' outer garments (under 5)	1.00	1.00	0.60	1.00	0.60
3.1.8 Children's under garments (under 16)	0.40	0.40	0.40	0.40	0.30
3.1.9 Accessories	0.90	1.00	1.10	1.50	0.70
3.1.10 Haberdashery and clothing hire	0.30	0.60	0.20	0.30	0.30
3.1.11 Dry cleaners, laundry and dyeing	[0.20]	0.40	0.50	1.00	0.30
3.2 Footwear	4.00	5.80	6.20	9.10	4.10
4 Housing (net)[1], fuel & power	**57.10**	**63.00**	**54.80**	**72.00**	**53.00**
4.1 Actual rentals for housing	22.70	24.30	12.70	19.00	31.60
4.1.1 Gross rent	22.70	24.20	12.70	18.30	31.50
4.1.2 less housing benefit, rebates & allowances rec'd	0.90	1.10	0.10	0.30	12.10
4.1.3 Net rent[2]	21.80	23.10	12.60	18.00	19.40
4.1.4 Second dwelling rent	[0.00]	[0.10]	–	[0.70]	[0.10]
4.2 Maintenance and repair of dwelling	7.90	11.20	11.00	15.60	7.20
4.3 Water supply and miscellaneous services relating to the dwelling	7.40	7.70	8.30	8.90	7.40
4.4 Electricity, gas and other fuels	19.90	21.00	23.00	28.70	18.90
4.4.1 Electricity	9.50	9.90	11.10	12.60	9.00
4.4.2 Gas	8.90	9.00	10.00	12.60	8.20
4.4.3 Other fuels	1.50	2.20	1.90	3.50	1.70

Note: The commodity and service categories are not comparable to those in publications before 2001-02.
The numbering system is sequential, it does not use actual COICOP codes.
Please see page xiii for symbols and conventions used in this report.
1 Excluding mortgage interest payments, council tax and Northern Ireland rates.
2 The figure included in total expenditure is net rent as opposed to gross rent.

Table A8

Detailed household expenditure by gross income decile group, 2008 (cont.)

based on weighted data and including children's expenditure

Commodity or service	Lowest ten per cent	Second decile group	Third decile group	Fourth decile group	Fifth decile group	Sixth decile group
	Average weekly household expenditure (£)					
5 Household goods & services	**9.10**	**15.20**	**19.30**	**21.60**	**24.10**	**25.20**
5.1 Furniture and furnishings, carpets and other floor coverings	4.00	8.10	9.80	12.20	10.30	14.40
5.1.1 Furniture and furnishings	3.20	6.30	6.90	9.10	8.10	11.70
5.1.2 Floor coverings	0.90	1.80	2.90	3.20	2.20	2.70
5.2 Household textiles	0.50	0.70	1.10	1.10	1.40	1.30
5.3 Household appliances	0.70	0.80	2.90	2.20	5.10	1.60
5.4 Glassware, tableware and household utensils	0.60	0.40	0.70	0.90	1.40	1.20
5.5 Tools and equipment for house and garden	0.50	1.50	1.30	1.30	1.80	1.90
5.6 Goods and services for routine household maintenance	2.70	3.60	3.60	3.90	4.10	4.70
5.6.1 Cleaning materials	1.00	1.50	1.70	2.00	2.00	2.10
5.6.2 Household goods and hardware	0.40	0.70	0.70	0.90	1.00	1.00
5.6.3 Domestic services, carpet cleaning, hire of furniture/furnishings	1.20	1.40	1.20	0.90	1.00	1.60
6 Health	**1.20**	**3.20**	**3.10**	**3.90**	**5.20**	**5.10**
6.1 Medical products, appliances and equipment	0.80	2.50	2.10	2.60	3.50	3.60
6.1.1 Medicines, prescriptions, healthcare products etc.	0.70	0.90	1.00	1.30	1.70	2.10
6.1.2 Spectacles, lenses, accessories and repairs	[0.10]	[1.60]	[1.00]	1.30	1.80	1.50
6.2 Hospital services	[0.40]	0.70	1.00	1.20	1.70	1.50
7 Transport	**12.10**	**17.10**	**24.10**	**38.90**	**51.90**	**61.00**
7.1 Purchase of vehicles	3.40	4.70	4.90	12.20	16.60	20.10
7.1.1 Purchase of new cars and vans	[0.40]	[1.20]	[0.90]	5.30	5.30	7.00
7.1.2 Purchase of second hand cars or vans	2.90	3.50	3.90	6.70	10.80	12.40
7.1.3 Purchase of motorcycles and other vehicles	[0.10]	[0.10]	[0.10]	[0.10]	[0.40]	[0.60]
7.2 Operation of personal transport	6.00	8.90	14.50	20.00	29.60	32.20
7.2.1 Spares and accessories	[0.30]	[0.20]	1.20	1.50	3.20	1.90
7.2.2 Petrol, diesel and other motor oils	4.00	5.70	9.30	14.10	18.60	21.30
7.2.3 Repairs and servicing	1.40	2.40	3.10	3.50	5.20	6.80
7.2.4 Other motoring costs	0.30	0.60	1.00	0.90	2.50	2.20
7.3 Transport services	2.70	3.60	4.60	6.80	5.80	8.70
7.3.1 Rail and tube fares	0.50	0.70	0.60	0.80	1.00	1.70
7.3.2 Bus and coach fares	1.20	0.80	0.80	1.70	1.20	1.80
7.3.3 Combined fares	[0.20]	[0.30]	[0.30]	[0.20]	[0.60]	1.20
7.3.4 Other travel and transport	0.80	1.90	3.00	4.00	3.00	4.00
8 Communication	**5.80**	**7.10**	**7.90**	**9.10**	**12.20**	**13.10**
8.1 Postal services	0.20	0.30	0.20	0.40	0.50	0.50
8.2 Telephone and telefax equipment	[0.10]	[0.30]	[0.20]	[0.30]	0.60	0.90
8.3 Telephone and telefax services	5.50	6.50	7.40	8.30	11.10	11.70

Note: The commodity and service categories are not comparable to those in publications before 2001-02.
The numbering system is sequential, it does not use actual COICOP codes.
Please see page xiii for symbols and conventions used in this report.

Table A8

Detailed household expenditure by gross income decile group, 2008 (cont.)

based on weighted data and including children's expenditure

Commodity or service	Seventh decile group	Eighth decile group	Ninth decile group	Highest ten per cent	All house-holds
	Average weekly household expenditure (£)				
5 Household goods & services	**34.60**	**37.70**	**46.50**	**68.10**	**30.10**
5.1 Furniture and furnishings, carpets and other floor coverings	19.10	23.10	26.60	38.60	16.60
5.1.1 Furniture and furnishings	14.80	18.50	20.10	31.00	13.00
5.1.2 Floor coverings	4.30	4.60	6.50	7.60	3.70
5.2 Household textiles	2.10	1.50	2.50	3.20	1.50
5.3 Household appliances	4.00	3.50	6.40	7.70	3.50
5.4 Glassware, tableware and household utensils	1.50	1.90	2.00	2.50	1.30
5.5 Tools and equipment for house and garden	2.90	2.70	3.00	4.20	2.10
5.6 Goods and services for routine household maintenance	5.20	5.00	6.00	11.80	5.10
5.6.1 Cleaning materials	2.40	2.50	2.80	3.40	2.20
5.6.2 Household goods and hardware	1.20	1.40	1.50	1.90	1.10
5.6.3 Domestic services, carpet cleaning, hire/repair of furniture/furnishings	1.60	1.20	1.70	6.50	1.80
6 Health	**4.50**	**7.00**	**7.10**	**10.90**	**5.10**
6.1 Medical products, appliances and equipment	2.60	4.10	4.10	5.10	3.10
6.1.1 Medicines, prescriptions, healthcare products etc.	1.70	2.10	2.10	3.00	1.70
6.1.2 Spectacles, lenses, accessories and repairs	0.90	2.00	2.00	2.10	1.40
6.2 Hospital services	2.00	3.00	3.00	5.80	2.00
7 Transport	**73.60**	**81.90**	**112.20**	**161.10**	**63.40**
7.1 Purchase of vehicles	26.30	24.70	38.00	60.60	21.10
7.1.1 Purchase of new cars and vans	8.80	6.80	8.30	22.50	6.60
7.1.2 Purchase of second hand cars or vans	16.70	16.80	28.30	34.20	13.60
7.1.3 Purchase of motorcycles and other vehicles	[0.80]	[1.10]	[1.50]	[3.90]	0.90
7.2 Operation of personal transport	37.10	43.60	55.90	70.00	31.80
7.2.1 Spares and accessories	2.10	2.40	5.40	5.40	2.40
7.2.2 Petrol, diesel and other motor oils	25.80	30.10	36.50	44.90	21.00
7.2.3 Repairs and servicing	6.90	8.20	10.30	14.70	6.20
7.2.4 Other motoring costs	2.40	2.90	3.70	5.00	2.10
7.3 Transport services	10.20	13.60	18.30	30.50	10.50
7.3.1 Rail and tube fares	2.10	4.10	3.90	9.00	2.40
7.3.2 Bus and coach fares	1.60	1.70	1.30	1.60	1.40
7.3.3 Combined fares	1.90	1.50	2.30	3.80	1.20
7.3.4 Other travel and transport	4.70	6.30	10.70	16.20	5.40
8 Communication	**14.10**	**14.90**	**16.70**	**18.70**	**12.00**
8.1 Postal services	0.70	0.50	0.60	0.70	0.50
8.2 Telephone and telefax equipment	0.60	[0.60]	[0.60]	[0.60]	0.50
8.3 Telephone and telefax services	12.80	13.80	15.40	17.40	11.00

Note: The commodity and service categories are not comparable to those in publications before 2001-02.
The numbering system is sequential, it does not use actual COICOP codes.
Please see page xiii for symbols and conventions used in this report.

Table A8

Detailed household expenditure by gross income decile group, 2008 (cont.)

based on weighted data and including children's expenditure

Commodity or service	Lowest ten per cent	Second decile group	Third decile group	Fourth decile group	Fifth decile group	Sixth decile group
	Average weekly household expenditure (£)					
9 Recreation & culture	**15.30**	**23.90**	**31.70**	**39.30**	**50.70**	**69.30**
9.1 Audio-visual, photographic and information processing equipment	2.20	2.20	5.10	3.70	6.40	5.20
9.1.1 Audio equipment and accessories, CD players	0.50	0.30	0.70	0.80	0.80	1.00
9.1.2 TV, video and computers	1.50	1.70	4.20	2.30	5.10	3.90
9.1.3 Photographic, cine and optical equipment	[0.20]	[0.20]	[0.10]	[0.60]	[0.40]	[0.20]
9.2 Other major durables for recreation and culture	[0.10]	[0.30]	[1.80]	[0.80]	[0.40]	[15.30]
9.3 Other recreational items and equipment, gardens and pets	3.00	5.00	5.30	8.60	8.30	12.70
9.3.1 Games, toys and hobbies	0.50	0.90	1.10	1.70	1.60	2.10
9.3.2 Computer software and games	[0.40]	[0.60]	[0.60]	1.30	1.60	3.20
9.3.3 Equipment for sport, camping and open-air recreation	[0.10]	[0.20]	0.20	0.30	0.40	1.20
9.3.4 Horticultural goods, garden equipment and plants	0.80	1.40	1.50	2.50	1.80	2.60
9.3.5 Pets and pet food	1.20	1.90	1.80	2.70	2.80	3.50
9.4 Recreational and cultural services	6.10	7.90	8.40	12.20	16.50	16.90
9.4.1 Sports admissions, subscriptions, leisure class fees and equipment hire	1.00	1.40	0.90	2.00	3.00	4.40
9.4.2 Cinema, theatre and museums etc.	0.30	0.60	0.70	1.00	1.60	1.60
9.4.3 TV, video, satellite rental, cable subscriptions, TV licences and the Internet	3.00	3.40	3.70	4.90	5.80	6.50
9.4.4 Miscellaneous entertainments	0.20	0.50	0.40	0.80	0.90	1.00
9.4.5 Development of film, deposit for film development, passport photos, holiday and school photos	[0.10]	[0.10]	0.10	[0.10]	0.30	0.30
9.4.6 Gambling payments	1.50	2.00	2.70	3.30	5.00	3.20
9.5 Newspapers, books and stationery	2.60	3.80	4.40	5.00	5.50	6.30
9.5.1 Books	0.30	0.60	0.80	0.80	0.90	1.40
9.5.2 Diaries, address books, cards etc.	0.70	1.10	1.00	1.40	1.50	2.10
9.5.3 Newspapers	1.10	1.50	1.90	2.10	2.20	1.90
9.5.4 Magazines and periodicals	0.40	0.60	0.60	0.70	0.90	0.90
9.6 Package holidays	1.20	4.70	6.70	9.10	13.60	12.90
9.6.1 Package holidays - UK	[0.30]	1.20	2.00	0.70	1.60	[1.30]
9.6.2 Package holidays - abroad	[0.90]	3.50	4.70	8.50	12.00	11.60
10 Education	**[1.40]**	**[0.50]**	**0.50**	**0.80**	**2.60**	**2.40**
10.1 Education fees	[1.40]	[0.40]	[0.50]	[0.60]	2.50	2.10
10.2 Payments for school trips, other ad-hoc expenditure	[0.00]	[0.00]	[0.10]	[0.20]	[0.10]	[0.30]
11 Restaurants & hotels	**9.00**	**12.00**	**14.80**	**23.80**	**28.20**	**34.10**
11.1 Catering services	8.30	9.90	12.60	20.80	24.80	29.40
11.1.1 Restaurant and café meals	3.60	4.50	6.10	9.60	10.30	11.90
11.1.2 Alcoholic drinks (away from home)	1.70	1.70	2.90	4.30	6.30	6.90
11.1.3 Take away meals eaten at home	1.60	1.90	1.80	2.90	3.50	4.40
11.1.4 Other take-away and snack food	1.00	1.50	1.40	2.80	3.40	4.20
11.1.5 Contract catering (food) and canteens	0.40	0.30	0.50	1.10	1.40	2.10
11.2 Accommodation services	0.70	2.00	2.20	3.00	3.40	4.70
11.2.1 Holiday in the UK	[0.60]	0.70	1.00	1.50	2.30	2.50
11.2.2 Holiday abroad	[0.20]	[1.30]	[1.30]	1.40	1.10	2.10
11.2.3 Room hire	–	–	–	[0.10]	[0.00]	[0.00]

Note: The commodity and service categories are not comparable to those in publications before 2001-02.
The numbering system is sequential, it does not use actual COICOP codes.
Please see page xiii for symbols and conventions used in this report.

Table A8

Detailed household expenditure by gross income decile group, 2008 (cont.)

based on weighted data and including children's expenditure

Commodity or service	Seventh decile group	Eighth decile group	Ninth decile group	Highest ten per cent	All house-holds
	Average weekly household expenditure (£)				
9 Recreation & culture	**69.00**	**75.80**	**86.50**	**139.30**	**60.10**
9.1 Audio-visual, photographic and information processing equipment	8.80	10.70	12.70	14.80	7.20
9.1.1 Audio equipment and accessories, CD players	2.00	1.40	2.00	3.20	1.30
9.1.2 TV, video and computers	5.70	7.00	7.10	9.50	4.80
9.1.3 Photographic, cine and optical equipment	[1.10]	[2.20]	[3.50]	2.00	1.10
9.2 Other major durables for recreation and culture	[5.00]	[1.50]	1.80	14.40	4.10
9.3 Other recreational items and equipment, gardens and pets	12.00	15.60	15.60	21.20	10.70
9.3.1 Games, toys and hobbies	2.30	2.40	2.70	2.90	1.80
9.3.2 Computer software and games	2.30	2.80	3.20	3.90	2.00
9.3.3 Equipment for sport, camping and open-air recreation	1.00	1.60	1.60	2.30	0.90
9.3.4 Horticultural goods, garden equipment and plants	2.60	4.00	3.60	5.40	2.60
9.3.5 Pets and pet food	3.90	4.90	4.50	6.80	3.40
9.4 Recreational and cultural services	19.30	23.70	26.40	35.20	17.30
9.4.1 Sports admissions, subscriptions, leisure class fees and equipment hire	5.00	7.10	8.60	14.70	4.80
9.4.2 Cinema, theatre and museums etc.	2.30	3.00	3.70	4.60	1.90
9.4.3 TV, video, satellite rental, cable subscriptions, TV licences and the Internet	7.10	7.40	8.20	8.60	5.80
9.4.4 Miscellaneous entertainments	1.20	1.80	1.60	3.60	1.20
9.4.5 Development of film, deposit for film development, passport photos, holiday and school photos	0.30	0.20	1.00	0.60	0.30
9.4.6 Gambling payments	3.40	4.20	3.30	3.10	3.20
9.5 Newspapers, books and stationery	6.50	7.20	7.90	11.30	6.00
9.5.1 Books	1.50	1.60	2.20	3.70	1.40
9.5.2 Diaries, address books, cards etc.	2.20	2.80	2.60	3.60	1.90
9.5.3 Newspapers	1.80	1.70	1.80	2.40	1.90
9.5.4 Magazines and periodicals	1.10	1.10	1.20	1.60	0.90
9.6 Package holidays	17.50	17.10	22.10	42.40	14.70
9.6.1 Package holidays - UK	[1.20]	[0.50]	[1.20]	[0.90]	1.10
9.6.2 Package holidays - abroad	16.30	[16.70]	20.90	41.50	13.60
10 Education	**4.80**	**7.30**	**7.10**	**34.60**	**6.20**
10.1 Education fees	4.50	7.00	6.40	33.60	5.90
10.2 Payments for school trips, other ad-hoc expenditure	0.30	[0.30]	0.70	1.00	0.30
11 Restaurants & hotels	**45.50**	**53.20**	**60.50**	**96.30**	**37.70**
11.1 Catering services	38.00	46.10	51.00	68.70	31.00
11.1.1 Restaurant and café meals	14.10	18.90	21.20	32.30	13.20
11.1.2 Alcoholic drinks (away from home)	8.90	10.50	12.60	16.10	7.20
11.1.3 Take away meals eaten at home	5.00	4.90	6.00	6.60	3.90
11.1.4 Other take-away and snack food	5.60	5.50	7.50	8.90	4.20
11.1.5 Contract catering (food) and canteens	4.40	6.30	3.80	4.80	2.50
11.2 Accommodation services	7.40	7.10	9.40	27.60	6.80
11.2.1 Holiday in the UK	4.00	3.20	4.10	7.70	2.80
11.2.2 Holiday abroad	3.40	3.80	5.30	19.70	4.00
11.2.3 Room hire	[0.10]	[0.00]	[0.00]	[0.10]	[0.00]

Note: The commodity and service categories are not comparable to those in publications before 2001-02.
         The numbering system is sequential, it does not use actual COICOP codes.
         Please see page xiii for symbols and conventions used in this report.

Table A8

Detailed household expenditure by gross income decile group, 2008 (cont.)
based on weighted data and including children's expenditure

Commodity or service	Lowest ten per cent	Second decile group	Third decile group	Fourth decile group	Fifth decile group	Sixth decile group
	Average weekly household expenditure (£)					
12 Miscellaneous goods & services	**10.40**	**15.40**	**19.10**	**21.30**	**28.10**	**33.90**
12.1 Personal care	3.70	5.50	6.00	6.80	8.80	9.30
12.1.1 Hairdressing, beauty treatment	1.20	1.70	1.80	2.00	2.60	2.70
12.1.2 Toilet paper	0.40	0.60	0.60	0.70	0.70	0.80
12.1.3 Toiletries and soap	0.70	1.10	1.30	1.50	1.80	2.10
12.1.4 Baby toiletries and accessories (disposable)	0.30	0.40	0.50	0.60	0.60	0.50
12.1.5 Hair products, cosmetics and related electrical appliances	1.10	1.70	1.80	1.90	3.00	3.20
12.2 Personal effects	0.60	0.90	1.10	1.60	1.80	2.60
12.3 Social protection	[0.60]	[0.70]	2.20	[0.50]	1.80	4.00
12.4 Insurance	4.70	6.30	7.60	10.00	13.40	14.70
12.4.1 Household insurances - structural, contents and appliances	2.10	2.80	3.40	4.00	4.90	5.30
12.4.2 Medical insurance premiums	[0.30]	[0.40]	0.30	0.70	1.20	1.20
12.4.3 Vehicle insurance including boat insurance	2.30	3.10	3.80	5.30	7.20	8.20
12.4.4 Non-package holiday, other travel insurance	–	–	[0.10]	[0.00]	[0.20]	[0.00]
12.5 Other services n.e.c	0.80	2.00	2.20	2.50	2.40	3.20
12.5.1 Moving house	[0.40]	1.40	1.40	1.20	1.20	1.60
12.5.2 Bank, building society, post office, credit card charges	0.10	0.20	0.10	0.30	0.50	0.40
12.5.3 Other services and professional fees	[0.30]	0.40	0.60	0.90	0.80	1.30
1-12 All expenditure groups	**140.10**	**180.50**	**224.50**	**278.00**	**333.90**	**385.10**
13 Other expenditure items	**13.70**	**19.50**	**32.60**	**52.10**	**59.10**	**74.10**
13.1 Housing: mortgage interest payments, council tax etc.	9.10	12.20	20.10	33.50	41.90	56.00
13.2 Licences, fines and transfers	0.80	1.30	1.60	2.30	2.80	3.40
13.3 Holiday spending	[0.60]	[1.60]	5.10	6.20	[3.80]	[5.50]
13.4 Money transfers and credit	3.20	4.30	5.90	10.10	10.70	9.30
13.4.1 Money, cash gifts given to children	[0.10]	[0.00]	[0.00]	[0.00]	[0.10]	[0.10]
13.4.2 Cash gifts and donations	2.80	3.90	5.20	9.50	8.90	6.90
13.4.3 Club instalment payments (child) and interest on credit cards	0.30	0.40	0.70	0.60	1.70	2.30
Total expenditure	**153.70**	**200.00**	**257.10**	**330.10**	**393.00**	**459.20**
14 Other items recorded						
14.1 Life assurance and contributions to pension funds	0.80	1.10	2.70	4.90	9.20	14.30
14.2 Other insurance inc. friendly societies	0.10	0.30	0.40	0.50	0.90	0.90
14.3 Income tax, payments *less* refunds	0.90	7.90	11.50	24.90	43.50	64.30
14.4 National insurance contributions	[0.10]	0.50	2.40	7.60	14.20	24.70
14.5 Purchase or alteration of dwellings, mortgages	3.60	6.70	14.40	16.70	24.30	36.50
14.6 Savings and investments	0.40	0.40	1.00	1.40	2.50	3.00
14.7 Pay off loan to clear other debt	[0.40]	[0.40]	[0.80]	1.30	1.80	3.30
14.8 Windfall receipts from gambling etc[3]	0.90	2.40	1.50	0.80	2.10	2.70

Note: The commodity and service categories are not comparable to those in publications before 2001-02.
The numbering system is sequential, it does not use actual COICOP codes.
Please see page xiii for symbols and conventions used in this report.
3 Expressed as an income figure as opposed to an expenditure figure.

Table A8

Detailed household expenditure by gross income decile group, 2008 (cont.)
based on weighted data and including children's expenditure

		Seventh decile group	Eighth decile group	Ninth decile group	Highest ten per cent	All house-holds
Commodity or service				Average weekly household expenditure (£)		
12	**Miscellaneous goods & services**	**38.00**	**53.50**	**57.10**	**79.60**	**35.60**
12.1	Personal care	10.70	13.10	14.50	20.90	9.90
12.1.1	Hairdressing, beauty treatment	3.50	4.50	4.20	6.80	3.10
12.1.2	Toilet paper	0.80	0.90	1.00	1.20	0.80
12.1.3	Toiletries and soap	2.30	2.60	3.10	3.90	2.00
12.1.4	Baby toiletries and accessories (disposable)	0.80	0.70	0.80	1.00	0.60
12.1.5	Hair products, cosmetics and related electrical appliances	3.40	4.30	5.50	8.00	3.40
12.2	Personal effects	2.90	6.70	5.30	9.80	3.30
12.3	Social protection	3.00	3.20	7.30	12.60	3.60
12.4	Insurance	16.60	19.50	24.10	28.80	14.60
12.4.1	Household insurances - structural, contents and appliances	5.50	6.00	7.40	9.10	5.00
12.4.2	Medical insurance premiums	1.70	1.60	2.50	4.30	1.40
12.4.3	Vehicle insurance including boat insurance	9.30	11.90	13.60	14.90	7.90
12.4.4	Non-package holiday, other travel insurance	[0.10]	[0.10]	[0.70]	[0.50]	0.20
12.5	Other services n.e.c	4.80	11.00	5.90	7.50	4.20
12.5.1	Moving house	2.00	4.70	3.00	3.80	2.10
12.5.2	Bank, building society, post office, credit card charges	0.60	0.70	0.60	0.70	0.40
12.5.3	Other services and professional fees	2.10	5.60	2.40	3.00	1.70
1-12	**All expenditure groups**	**432.30**	**501.90**	**563.60**	**824.40**	**386.30**
13	**Other expenditure items**	**104.50**	**123.80**	**146.80**	**220.50**	**84.60**
13.1	Housing: mortgage interest payments, council tax etc.	74.40	88.30	106.00	142.70	58.40
13.2	Licences, fines and transfers	4.10	4.50	5.50	6.10	3.20
13.3	Holiday spending	13.70	15.10	18.60	44.70	11.50
13.4	Money transfers and credit	12.30	15.90	16.70	27.10	11.50
13.4.1	Money, cash gifts given to children	0.10	[0.20]	[0.10]	0.20	0.10
13.4.2	Cash gifts and donations	10.20	13.10	13.10	24.20	9.80
13.4.3	Club instalment payments (child) & interest on credit cards	2.00	2.60	3.40	2.70	1.70
Total expenditure		**536.70**	**625.70**	**710.40**	**1044.90**	**471.00**
14	**Other items recorded**					
14.1	Contributions to pension funds	20.10	30.00	42.70	77.60	20.30
14.2	Other insurance inc. friendly societies	1.20	1.80	2.30	3.50	1.20
14.3	Income tax, payments *less* refunds	89.90	119.00	166.70	457.70	98.60
14.4	National insurance contributions	35.50	49.10	65.30	85.30	28.50
14.5	Purchase or alteration of dwellings, mortgages	45.90	68.40	95.10	129.40	44.10
14.6	Savings and investments	6.80	8.00	15.50	26.30	6.50
14.7	Pay off loan to clear other debt	3.60	4.50	3.80	2.10	2.20
14.8	Windfall receipts from gambling etc[3]	1.30	2.30	1.20	1.60	1.70

Note: The commodity and service categories are not comparable to those in publications before 2001-02.
The numbering system is sequential, it does not use actual COICOP codes.
Please see page xiii for symbols and conventions used in this report.

3 Expressed as an income figure as opposed to an expenditure figure.

Table A9

Household expenditure by disposable income decile group, 2008

based on weighted data and including children's expenditure

	Lowest ten per cent	Second decile group	Third decile group	Fourth decile group	Fifth decile group	Sixth decile group
Lower boundary of group (£ per week)		146	224	305	408	522
Weighted number of households (thousands)	2,570	2,570	2,570	2,570	2,570	2,570
Total number of households in sample	550	580	600	630	590	600
Total number of persons in sample	710	950	1,090	1,310	1,320	1,560
Total number of adults in sample	600	770	880	1,030	1,030	1,170
Weighted average number of persons per household	1.3	1.6	1.8	2.1	2.2	2.5
Commodity or service	Average weekly household expenditure (£)					
1 Food & non-alcoholic drinks	26.50	32.40	36.90	41.90	49.20	52.80
2 Alcoholic drinks, tobacco & narcotics	6.80	6.00	8.20	8.80	10.40	12.10
3 Clothing & footwear	6.90	8.20	10.50	13.30	17.30	19.20
4 Housing(net)[1], fuel & power	38.70	38.80	45.80	51.70	53.70	53.10
5 Household goods & services	10.20	14.30	18.60	21.10	25.20	25.60
6 Health	1.30	3.00	3.30	3.80	4.60	4.80
7 Transport	13.40	18.00	24.90	37.70	52.60	60.00
8 Communication	6.30	7.00	7.50	9.10	11.90	12.60
9 Recreation & culture	16.20	23.10	30.90	38.50	48.10	68.70
10 Education	[1.70]	[0.30]	0.50	0.70	2.70	2.80
11 Restaurants & hotels	9.70	12.30	15.40	22.10	27.00	35.00
12 Miscellaneous goods & services	11.50	15.00	18.50	21.00	28.40	34.70
1-12 All expenditure groups	149.30	178.40	221.10	269.80	331.10	381.50
13 Other expenditure items	16.40	22.20	32.90	49.80	57.40	73.00
Total expenditure	165.70	200.60	254.00	319.60	388.50	454.40
Average weekly expenditure per person (£) Total expenditure	125.80	124.90	143.20	154.80	173.00	178.70

Note: The commodity and service categories are not comparable to those in publications before 2001-02.
        Please see page xiii for symbols and conventions used in this report.
1   Excluding mortgage interest payments, council tax and Northern Ireland rates.

Table A9

Household expenditure by disposable income decile group 2008, (cont.)
based on weighted data and including children's expenditure

		Seventh decile group	Eighth decile group	Ninth decile group	Highest ten per cent	All house-holds
Lower boundary of group (£ per week)		664	817	1026	1,356	
Weighted number of households (thousands)		2,570	2,570	2,570	2,570	25,690
Total number of households in sample		590	580	550	580	5,850
Total number of persons in sample		1,630	1,690	1,720	1,860	13,830
Total number of adults in sample		1,190	1,270	1,300	1,400	10,640
Weighted average number of persons per household		2.8	2.9	3.1	3.2	2.4
Commodity or service		Average weekly household expenditure (£)				
1	Food & non-alcoholic drinks	55.90	63.10	69.10	79.20	50.70
2	Alcoholic drinks, tobacco & narcotics	11.70	14.30	13.50	16.10	10.80
3	Clothing & footwear	25.40	30.00	36.50	48.60	21.60
4	Housing(net)[1], fuel & power	57.80	60.50	58.40	71.80	53.00
5	Household goods & services	34.20	43.00	43.10	66.00	30.10
6	Health	5.90	6.60	6.90	11.10	5.10
7	Transport	71.30	82.90	114.20	159.10	63.40
8	Communication	14.00	14.80	17.00	19.30	12.00
9	Recreation & culture	69.00	75.90	89.80	140.40	60.10
10	Education	4.60	5.10	10.80	32.60	6.20
11	Restaurants & hotels	42.40	54.60	61.80	97.00	37.70
12	Miscellaneous goods & services	38.10	51.50	57.10	80.50	35.60
1-12	All expenditure groups	430.50	502.30	578.10	821.70	386.30
13	Other expenditure items	106.60	125.20	142.40	220.60	84.60
Total expenditure		**537.00**	**627.60**	**720.50**	**1042.30**	**471.00**
Average weekly expenditure per person (£)						
Total expenditure		**192.50**	**219.30**	**230.20**	**321.50**	**199.80**

Note: The commodity and service categories are not comparable to those in publications before 2001-02.
    Please see page xiii for symbols and conventions used in this report.

1   Excluding mortgage interest payments, council tax and Northern Ireland rates.

Table A10

Household expenditure as a percentage of total expenditure by disposable income decile group, 2008

based on weighted data and including children's expenditure

	Lowest ten per cent	Second decile group	Third decile group	Fourth decile group	Fifth decile group	Sixth decile group
Lower boundary of group (£ per week)		146	224	305	408	522
Weighted number of households (thousands)	2,570	2,570	2,570	2,570	2,570	2,570
Total number of households in sample	550	580	600	630	590	600
Total number of persons in sample	710	950	1,090	1,310	1,320	1,560
Total number of adults in sample	600	770	880	1,030	1,030	1,170
Weighted average number of persons per household	1.3	1.6	1.8	2.1	2.2	2.5
Commodity or service	Percentage of total expenditure					
1 Food & non-alcoholic drinks	16	16	15	13	13	12
2 Alcoholic drinks, tobacco & narcotics	4	3	3	3	3	3
3 Clothing & footwear	4	4	4	4	4	4
4 Housing(net)[1], fuel & power	23	19	18	16	14	12
5 Household goods & services	6	7	7	7	6	6
6 Health	1	1	1	1	1	1
7 Transport	8	9	10	12	14	13
8 Communication	4	4	3	3	3	3
9 Recreation & culture	10	12	12	12	12	15
10 Education	[1]	[0]	0	0	1	1
11 Restaurants & hotels	6	6	6	7	7	8
12 Miscellaneous goods & services	7	7	7	7	7	8
1-12 All expenditure groups	90	89	87	84	85	84
13 Other expenditure items	10	11	13	16	15	16
Total expenditure	100	100	100	100	100	100

Note: The commodity and service categories are not comparable to those in publications before 2001-02.
Please see page xiii for symbols and conventions used in this report.

1   Excluding mortgage interest payments, council tax and Northern Ireland rates.

Table A10

Household expenditure as a percentage of total expenditure by disposable income decile group, 2008 (cont.)

based on weighted data and including children's expenditure

		Seventh decile group	Eighth decile group	Ninth decile group	Highest ten per cent	All house-holds
Lower boundary of group (£ per week)		664	817	1026	1,356	
Weighted number of households (thousands)		2,570	2,570	2,570	2,570	25,690
Total number of households in sample		590	580	550	580	5,850
Total number of persons in sample		1,630	1,690	1,720	1,860	13,830
Total number of adults in sample		1,190	1,270	1,300	1,400	10,640
Weighted average number of persons per household		2.8	2.9	3.1	3.2	2.4
Commodity or service		Percentage of total expenditure				
1	Food & non-alcoholic drinks	10	10	10	8	11
2	Alcoholic drinks, tobacco & narcotics	2	2	2	2	2
3	Clothing & footwear	5	5	5	5	5
4	Housing(net)[1], fuel & power	11	10	8	7	11
5	Household goods & services	6	7	6	6	6
6	Health	1	1	1	1	1
7	Transport	13	13	16	15	13
8	Communication	3	2	2	2	3
9	Recreation & culture	13	12	12	13	13
10	Education	1	1	1	3	1
11	Restaurants & hotels	8	9	9	9	8
12	Miscellaneous goods & services	7	8	8	8	8
1-12	All expenditure groups	80	80	80	79	82
13	Other expenditure items	20	20	20	21	18
Total expenditure		100	100	100	100	100

Note: The commodity and service categories are not comparable to those in publications before 2001-02.
Please see page xiii for symbols and conventions used in this report.

1 Excluding mortgage interest payments, council tax and Northern Ireland rates.

Table A11

Household expenditure by age of household reference person, 2008

based on weighted data and including children's expenditure

		Less than 30	30 to 49	50 to 64	65 to 74	75 or over	All house-holds
Weighted number of households (thousands)		2,530	9,740	6,750	3,140	3,520	25,690
Total number of households in sample		460	2,230	1,590	810	760	5,850
Total number of persons in sample		1,120	6,710	3,480	1,410	1,120	13,830
Total number of adults in sample		800	4,170	3,160	1,390	1,110	10,640
Weighted average number of persons per household		2.4	3.0	2.3	1.8	1.4	2.4
Commodity or service		Average weekly household expenditure (£)					
1	Food & non-alcoholic drinks	38.70	57.00	55.50	48.20	34.90	50.70
2	Alcoholic drinks, tobacco & narcotics	10.50	12.30	12.80	9.30	4.30	10.80
3	Clothing & footwear	23.20	27.50	23.70	12.70	7.70	21.60
4	Housing(net)[1], fuel & power	76.20	59.50	49.10	42.00	36.10	53.00
5	Household goods & services	23.90	35.60	32.90	26.20	17.60	30.10
6	Health	2.80	4.20	7.70	4.50	4.90	5.10
7	Transport	55.80	77.90	80.30	41.20	16.00	63.40
8	Communication	13.20	14.10	13.20	8.20	5.90	12.00
9	Recreation & culture	41.40	67.20	70.90	63.70	29.60	60.10
10	Education	3.00	8.90	8.80	[1.30]	[0.40]	6.20
11	Restaurants & hotels	38.20	46.40	44.00	25.10	12.60	37.70
12	Miscellaneous goods & services	31.30	45.40	36.60	24.00	20.10	35.60
1-12	All expenditure groups	358.20	456.20	435.60	306.50	190.10	386.30
13	Other expenditure items	83.00	125.70	73.60	47.20	26.80	84.60
Total expenditure		**441.20**	**581.90**	**509.20**	**353.60**	**216.80**	**471.00**
Average weekly expenditure per person (£)							
Total expenditure		**183.00**	**197.20**	**226.00**	**200.30**	**154.20**	**199.80**

Note: The commodity and service categories are not comparable to those in publications before 2001-02.
        Please see page xiii for symbols and conventions used in this report.
1   Excluding mortgage interest payments, council tax and Northern Ireland rates.

Table A12

Household expenditure as a percentage of total expenditure by age of household reference person, 2008

based on weighted data and including children's expenditure

	Less than 30	30 to 49	50 to 64	65 to 74	75 or over	All house-holds
Weighted number of households (thousands)	2,530	9,740	6,750	3,140	3,520	25,690
Total number of households in sample	460	2,230	1,590	810	760	5,850
Total number of persons in sample	1,120	6,710	3,480	1,410	1,120	13,830
Total number of adults in sample	800	4,170	3,160	1,390	1,110	10,640
Weighted average number of persons per household	2.4	3.0	2.3	1.8	1.4	2.4

Commodity or service			Percentage of total expenditure			
1	Food & non-alcoholic drinks	9	10	11	14	16	11
2	Alcoholic drinks, tobacco & narcotics	2	2	3	3	2	2
3	Clothing & footwear	5	5	5	4	4	5
4	Housing(net)[1], fuel & power	17	10	10	12	17	11
5	Household goods & services	5	6	6	7	8	6
6	Health	1	1	2	1	2	1
7	Transport	13	13	16	12	7	13
8	Communication	3	2	3	2	3	3
9	Recreation & culture	9	12	14	18	14	13
10	Education	1	2	2	[0]	[0]	1
11	Restaurants & hotels	9	8	9	7	6	8
12	Miscellaneous goods & services	7	8	7	7	9	8
1-12	All expenditure groups	81	78	86	87	88	82
13	Other expenditure items	19	22	14	13	12	18
Total expenditure		100	100	100	100	100	100

Note: The commodity and service categories are not comparable to those in publications before 2001-02.
        Please see page xiii for symbols and conventions used in this report.

1   Excluding mortgage interest payments, council tax and Northern Ireland rates.

Table A13

Detailed household expenditure by age of household reference person, 2008
based on weighted data and including children's expenditure

	Less than 30	30 to 49	50 to 64	65 to 74	75 or over	All house-holds
Weighted number of households (thousands)	2,530	9,740	6,750	3,140	3,520	25,690
Total number of households in sample	460	2,230	1,590	810	760	5,850
Total number of persons in sample	1,120	6,700	3,480	1,410	1,120	13,830
Total number of adults in sample	810	4,170	3,160	1,390	1,110	10,640
Weighted average number of persons per household	2.4	3.0	2.3	1.8	1.4	2.4

Commodity or service	Average weekly household expenditure (£)					
1 Food & non-alcoholic drinks	**38.70**	**57.00**	**55.50**	**48.20**	**34.90**	**50.70**
1.1 Food	35.00	52.00	51.30	45.00	32.60	46.70
1.1.1 Bread, rice and cereals	4.10	5.80	5.00	4.10	3.10	4.90
1.1.2 Pasta products	0.50	0.60	0.30	0.20	0.10	0.40
1.1.3 Buns, cakes, biscuits etc.	2.20	3.40	3.40	3.30	2.80	3.20
1.1.4 Pastry (savoury)	0.80	0.90	0.60	0.40	0.20	0.70
1.1.5 Beef (fresh, chilled or frozen)	0.90	1.70	2.00	1.50	1.00	1.60
1.1.6 Pork (fresh, chilled or frozen)	0.40	0.60	0.90	0.70	0.40	0.60
1.1.7 Lamb (fresh, chilled or frozen)	0.30	0.60	0.80	0.80	0.60	0.60
1.1.8 Poultry (fresh, chilled or frozen)	1.30	2.20	2.10	1.90	0.90	1.90
1.1.9 Bacon and ham	0.50	0.90	1.10	1.10	0.80	0.90
1.1.10 Other meat and meat preparations	4.00	5.70	5.80	4.70	3.70	5.20
1.1.11 Fish and fish products	1.30	2.20	2.60	2.60	2.20	2.30
1.1.12 Milk	2.10	3.00	2.70	2.50	2.10	2.60
1.1.13 Cheese and curd	1.40	1.90	1.90	1.60	0.90	1.70
1.1.14 Eggs	0.50	0.70	0.70	0.60	0.50	0.60
1.1.15 Other milk products	1.40	2.10	2.10	1.70	1.30	1.90
1.1.16 Butter	0.20	0.30	0.40	0.50	0.40	0.40
1.1.17 Margarine, other vegetable fats and peanut butter	0.30	0.50	0.60	0.60	0.50	0.50
1.1.18 Cooking oils and fats	0.20	0.30	0.30	0.40	0.20	0.30
1.1.19 Fresh fruit	1.80	3.10	3.30	3.40	2.40	3.00
1.1.20 Other fresh, chilled or frozen fruits	0.20	0.40	0.40	0.30	0.20	0.40
1.1.21 Dried fruit and nuts	0.20	0.50	0.60	0.70	0.40	0.50
1.1.22 Preserved fruit and fruit based products	0.10	0.10	0.10	0.20	0.20	0.10
1.1.23 Fresh vegetables	2.60	4.10	4.30	3.70	2.40	3.70
1.1.24 Dried vegetables	[0.00]	0.10	0.00	0.10	0.00	0.00
1.1.25 Other preserved or processed vegetables	1.00	1.40	1.30	0.90	0.50	1.20
1.1.26 Potatoes	0.60	0.90	1.00	1.00	0.70	0.90
1.1.27 Other tubers and products of tuber vegetables	1.20	1.60	1.30	0.90	0.60	1.30
1.1.28 Sugar and sugar products	0.20	0.40	0.30	0.30	0.30	0.30
1.1.29 Jams, marmalades	0.10	0.20	0.20	0.40	0.40	0.30
1.1.30 Chocolate	1.10	1.70	1.60	1.20	1.10	1.50
1.1.31 Confectionery products	0.40	0.70	0.60	0.50	0.40	0.60
1.1.32 Edible ices and ice cream	0.40	0.60	0.50	0.40	0.30	0.50
1.1.33 Other food products	2.40	2.70	2.30	1.80	1.20	2.30
1.2 Non-alcoholic drinks	3.60	5.00	4.20	3.20	2.20	4.00
1.2.1 Coffee	0.30	0.60	0.70	0.60	0.40	0.60
1.2.2 Tea	0.20	0.40	0.50	0.50	0.50	0.40
1.2.3 Cocoa and powdered chocolate	0.10	0.10	0.10	0.10	0.10	0.10
1.2.4 Fruit and vegetable juices (inc. fruit squash)	1.10	1.50	1.10	0.80	0.50	1.10
1.2.5 Mineral or spring waters	0.20	0.30	0.20	0.20	0.10	0.20
1.2.6 Soft drinks (inc. fizzy and ready to drink fruit drinks)	1.80	2.20	1.50	1.00	0.60	1.60

Note: The commodity and service categories are not comparable to those in publications before 2001-02.
The numbering system is sequential, it does not use actual COICOP codes.
Please see page xiii for symbols and conventions used in this report.

Table A13

Detailed household expenditure by age of household reference person, 2008 (cont.)
based on weighted data and including children's expenditure

Commodity or service	Less than 30	30 to 49	50 to 64	65 to 74	75 or over	All house-holds
	Average weekly household expenditure (£)					
2 Alcoholic drink, tobacco & narcotics	**10.50**	**12.30**	**12.80**	**9.30**	**4.30**	**10.80**
2.1 Alcoholic drinks	4.90	7.00	7.50	5.80	3.00	6.20
2.1.1 Spirits and liqueurs (brought home)	0.90	0.90	1.50	1.50	1.20	1.20
2.1.2 Wines, fortified wines (brought home)	1.90	3.70	4.10	3.30	1.40	3.30
2.1.3 Beer, lager, ciders and perry (brought home)	1.90	2.30	1.80	1.00	0.40	1.70
2.1.4 Alcopops (brought home)	0.20	0.10	0.10	[0.00]	[0.00]	0.10
2.2 Tobacco and narcotics	5.60	5.30	5.40	3.50	1.30	4.60
2.2.1 Cigarettes	4.80	4.60	4.60	2.90	1.00	3.90
2.2.2 Cigars, other tobacco products and narcotics	0.90	0.70	0.80	0.50	[0.30]	0.70
3 Clothing & footwear	**23.20**	**27.50**	**23.70**	**12.70**	**7.70**	**21.60**
3.1 Clothing	18.70	22.10	19.40	10.80	6.00	17.50
3.1.1 Men's outer garments	6.20	5.60	5.10	2.60	1.10	4.50
3.1.2 Men's under garments	0.30	0.40	0.40	0.30	0.20	0.30
3.1.3 Women's outer garments	7.10	8.80	9.80	4.80	3.30	7.60
3.1.4 Women's under garments	1.00	1.20	1.20	0.80	0.60	1.10
3.1.5 Boys' outer garments (5-15)	0.40	1.50	0.40	[0.20]	[0.10]	0.80
3.1.6 Girls' outer garments (5-15)	0.50	1.80	0.60	0.40	[0.10]	1.00
3.1.7 Infants' outer garments (under 5)	1.10	1.00	0.40	0.30	[0.10]	0.60
3.1.8 Children's under garments (under 16)	0.40	0.50	0.20	0.10	[0.00]	0.30
3.1.9 Accessories	0.80	0.80	0.80	0.50	0.30	0.70
3.1.10 Haberdashery, clothing materials and clothing hire	[0.60]	0.20	0.20	0.40	0.20	0.30
3.1.11 Dry cleaners, laundry and dyeing	[0.20]	0.20	0.40	0.30	0.20	0.30
3.2 Footwear	4.50	5.40	4.40	2.00	1.70	4.10
4 Housing (net)[1], fuel & power	**76.10**	**59.50**	**49.10**	**42.00**	**36.10**	**53.00**
4.1 Actual rentals for housing	70.80	35.50	21.20	21.50	21.70	31.60
4.1.1 Gross rent	70.80	35.50	20.90	21.50	21.70	31.50
4.1.2 less housing benefit, rebates & allowances rec'd	19.20	11.40	9.40	11.60	14.70	12.10
4.1.3 Net rent[2]	51.60	24.00	11.50	9.90	7.10	19.40
4.1.4 Second dwelling rent	–	[0.00]	[0.30]	–	–	[0.10]
4.2 Maintenance and repair of dwelling	3.10	8.10	8.80	6.70	5.00	7.20
4.3 Water supply and miscellaneous services relating to the dwelling	6.90	7.50	7.30	7.50	7.70	7.40
4.4 Electricity, gas and other fuels	14.50	19.90	21.10	17.90	16.40	18.90
4.4.1 Electricity	7.60	9.50	10.00	8.30	7.60	9.00
4.4.2 Gas	6.40	8.80	8.90	7.50	7.10	8.20
4.4.3 Other fuels	0.60	1.60	2.20	2.10	1.60	1.70

Note: The commodity and service categories are not comparable to those in publications before 2001-02.
The numbering system is sequential, it does not use actual COICOP codes.
Please see page xiii for symbols and conventions used in this report.

1 Excluding mortgage interest payments, council tax and Northern Ireland rates.

2 The figure included in total expenditure is net rent as opposed to gross rent

Table A13

Detailed household expenditure by age of household reference person, 2008 (cont.)

based on weighted data and including children's expenditure

Commodity or service	Less than 30	30 to 49	50 to 64	65 to 74	75 or over	All house-holds
	Average weekly household expenditure (£)					
5 Household goods & services	**23.90**	**35.70**	**32.90**	**26.20**	**17.60**	**30.10**
5.1 Furniture and furnishings and floor coverings	16.20	20.80	17.50	13.50	6.40	16.60
5.1.1 Furniture and furnishings	13.10	16.50	13.70	9.40	5.00	13.00
5.1.2 Floor coverings	3.20	4.40	3.80	4.20	1.40	3.70
5.2 Household textiles	1.00	1.80	1.80	1.70	0.50	1.50
5.3 Household appliances	2.00	4.30	3.80	2.00	2.90	3.50
5.4 Glassware, tableware and household utensils	1.20	1.40	1.50	1.60	0.70	1.30
5.5 Tools and equipment for house and garden	0.90	2.40	2.70	2.40	0.70	2.10
5.6 Goods and services for routine household maintenance	2.50	4.90	5.60	5.00	6.30	5.10
5.6.1 Cleaning materials	1.50	2.40	2.50	2.20	1.40	2.20
5.6.2 Household goods and hardware	0.60	1.20	1.30	1.10	0.60	1.10
5.6.3 Domestic services, carpet cleaning, hire of furniture/furnishings	0.30	1.30	1.80	1.70	4.30	1.80
6 Health	**2.80**	**4.20**	**7.70**	**4.50**	**4.90**	**5.10**
6.1 Medical products, appliances and equipment	2.20	2.60	3.90	2.80	3.70	3.10
6.1.1 Medicines, prescriptions and healthcare products	0.90	1.60	2.20	1.80	1.40	1.70
6.1.2 Spectacles, lenses, accessories and repairs	1.30	1.00	1.80	1.10	2.30	1.40
6.2 Hospital services	[0.60]	1.60	3.80	1.70	1.20	2.00
7 Transport	**55.80**	**77.90**	**80.30**	**41.20**	**16.00**	**63.40**
7.1 Purchase of vehicles	19.50	25.50	27.70	13.70	4.50	21.10
7.1.1 Purchase of new cars and vans	[3.00]	7.00	10.10	6.20	[2.00]	6.60
7.1.2 Purchase of second hand cars or vans	15.90	16.90	16.60	7.40	2.50	13.60
7.1.3 Purchase of motorcycles and other vehicles	[0.70]	1.50	[0.90]	[0.10]	–	0.90
7.2 Operation of personal transport	24.60	38.70	40.50	22.90	9.00	31.80
7.2.1 Spares and accessories	1.00	2.90	3.50	1.50	[0.40]	2.40
7.2.2 Petrol, diesel and other motor oils	17.60	25.90	26.50	14.50	5.50	21.00
7.2.3 Repairs and servicing	4.10	7.40	7.70	5.40	2.50	6.20
7.2.4 Other motoring costs	1.90	2.60	2.70	1.50	0.50	2.10
7.3 Transport services	11.70	13.70	12.20	4.60	2.50	10.50
7.3.1 Rail and tube fares	3.80	3.20	2.70	0.70	0.30	2.40
7.3.2 Bus and coach fares	2.00	1.90	1.50	0.30	0.20	1.40
7.3.4 Combined fares	2.20	1.80	1.20	[0.00]	[0.00]	1.20
7.3.5 Other travel and transport	3.70	6.80	6.80	3.50	2.00	5.40
8 Communication	**13.20**	**14.10**	**13.20**	**8.20**	**5.90**	**12.00**
8.1 Postal services	0.30	0.40	0.60	0.60	0.50	0.50
8.2 Telephone and telefax equipment	[0.50]	0.50	0.80	[0.10]	[0.10]	0.50
8.3 Telephone and telefax services	12.40	13.20	11.80	7.40	5.30	11.00

Note: The commodity and service categories are not comparable to those in publications before 2001-02.
The numbering system is sequential, it does not use actual COICOP codes.
Please see page xiii for Symbols and conventions used in this report.

Table A13

Detailed household expenditure by age of household reference person, 2008 (cont.)

based on weighted data and including children's expenditure

		Less than 30	30 to 49	50 to 64	65 to 74	75 or over	All house-holds
Commodity or service		Average weekly household expenditure (£)					
9	**Recreation & culture**	**41.40**	**67.20**	**70.90**	**63.70**	**29.60**	**60.10**
9.1	Audio-visual, photographic and information processing equipment	8.40	7.40	9.10	5.90	3.10	7.20
9.1.1	Audio equipment and accessories, CD players	1.70	1.70	1.20	0.80	0.40	1.30
9.1.2	TV, video and computers	4.50	4.90	6.10	4.30	2.60	4.80
9.1.3	Photographic, cine and optical equipment	[2.10]	0.70	1.80	[0.80]	[0.20]	1.10
9.2	Other major durables for recreation and culture	[0.20]	4.10	3.40	[13.60]	[0.10]	4.10
9.3	Other recreational items and equipment, gardens and pets	8.30	13.70	12.10	7.80	4.30	10.70
9.3.1	Games, toys and hobbies	2.40	2.50	1.70	1.00	0.50	1.80
9.3.2	Computer software and games	2.50	3.40	1.50	[0.20]	[0.20]	2.00
9.3.3	Equipment for sport, camping and open-air recreation	0.80	1.30	1.10	0.20	[0.10]	0.90
9.3.4	Horticultural goods, garden equipment and plants	0.90	2.40	3.30	3.80	2.00	2.60
9.3.5	Pets and pet food	1.60	4.10	4.50	2.60	1.50	3.40
9.4	Recreational and cultural services	14.80	21.00	20.10	14.00	6.10	17.30
9.4.1	Sports admissions, subscriptions, leisure class fees and equipment hire	3.60	6.90	5.10	3.00	0.80	4.80
9.4.2	Cinema, theatre and museums etc.	2.10	2.40	2.10	1.50	0.70	1.90
9.4.3	TV, video, satellite rental, cable subscriptions, TV licences and the Internet	6.20	7.10	6.50	5.00	1.50	5.80
9.4.4	Miscellaneous entertainments	0.70	1.50	1.50	0.80	0.40	1.20
9.4.5	Development of film, deposit for film development, passport photos, holiday and school photos	[0.70]	0.30	0.30	0.20	[0.10]	0.30
9.4.6	Gambling payments	1.50	2.70	4.60	3.60	2.60	3.20
9.5	Newspapers, books and stationery	3.60	6.20	6.90	6.60	5.30	6.00
9.5.1	Books	1.20	1.70	1.50	1.00	0.60	1.40
9.5.2	Diaries, address books, cards etc.	1.30	2.20	2.20	1.80	1.10	1.90
9.5.3	Newspapers	0.50	1.20	2.30	2.90	2.90	1.90
9.5.4	Magazines and periodicals	0.60	1.00	1.00	0.80	0.70	0.90
9.6	Package holidays	6.30	14.90	19.30	15.80	10.80	14.70
9.6.1	Package holidays - UK	[0.90]	0.60	0.70	1.80	2.80	1.10
9.6.2	Package holidays - abroad	5.40	14.30	18.60	14.00	8.00	13.60
10	**Education**	**3.00**	**8.90**	**8.80**	**[1.30]**	**[0.40]**	**6.20**
10.1	Education fees	2.80	8.30	8.60	[1.20]	[0.40]	5.90
10.2	Payments for school trips, other ad-hoc expenditure	[0.10]	0.60	0.20	[0.00]	–	0.30
11	**Restaurants & hotels**	**38.30**	**46.40**	**44.00**	**25.10**	**12.60**	**37.70**
11.1	Catering services	34.60	38.30	35.30	19.50	10.00	31.00
11.1.1	Restaurant and café meals	9.40	15.10	16.00	11.60	7.00	13.20
11.1.2	Alcoholic drinks (away from home)	7.60	8.40	9.40	4.60	1.70	7.20
11.1.3	Take away meals eaten at home	5.90	5.20	3.60	1.80	1.00	3.90
11.1.4	Other take-away and snack food	5.10	6.30	4.40	0.90	0.30	4.20
11.1.5	Contract catering (food) and canteens	6.60	3.40	2.00	0.40	[0.00]	2.50
11.2	Accommodation services	3.70	8.10	8.70	5.70	2.50	6.80
11.2.1	Holiday in the UK	0.80	2.80	3.50	3.70	1.70	2.80
11.2.2	Holiday abroad	2.80	5.20	5.20	2.00	[0.80]	4.00
11.2.3	Room hire	[0.10]	[0.00]	[0.00]	–	[0.00]	[0.00]

Note: The commodity and service categories are not comparable to those in publications before 2001-02.
The numbering system is sequential, it does not use actual COICOP codes.
Please see page xiii for Symbols and conventions used in this report.

Table A13

Detailed household expenditure by age of household reference person, 2008 (cont.)

based on weighted data and including children's expenditure

Commodity or service	Less than 30	30 to 49	50 to 64	65 to 74	75 or over	All house-holds
	Average weekly household expenditure (£)					
12 Miscellaneous goods & services	**31.30**	**45.50**	**36.60**	**24.00**	**20.10**	**35.60**
12.1 Personal care	8.80	11.30	11.50	7.70	5.90	9.90
12.1.1 Hairdressing, beauty treatment	2.00	3.10	3.80	2.70	2.80	3.10
12.1.2 Toilet paper	0.60	0.80	0.80	0.80	0.50	0.80
12.1.3 Toiletries and soap	1.50	2.40	2.30	1.60	1.10	2.00
12.1.4 Baby toiletries and accessories (disposable)	1.50	1.00	0.20	0.20	0.10	0.60
12.1.5 Hair products, cosmetics and related electrical appliances	3.10	3.90	4.30	2.50	1.40	3.40
12.2 Personal effects	2.90	5.00	3.00	1.80	1.00	3.30
12.3 Social protection	3.50	7.50	[0.50]	[0.20]	1.70	3.60
12.4 Insurance	11.30	16.10	17.70	12.40	8.60	14.60
12.4.1 Household insurances - structural, contents and appliances	2.80	5.40	5.80	4.90	4.00	5.00
12.4.2 Medical insurance premiums	0.40	1.10	2.10	2.20	1.20	1.40
12.4.3 Vehicle insurance including boat insurance	8.10	9.40	9.50	5.10	3.30	7.90
12.4.4 Non-package holiday, other travel insurance	[0.00]	0.20	[0.30]	[0.20]	–	0.20
12.5 Other services	4.90	5.50	3.90	2.00	2.80	4.20
12.5.1 Moving house	2.80	2.70	2.10	1.10	[0.50]	2.10
12.5.2 Bank, building society, post office, credit card charges	0.80	0.50	0.50	0.20	0.10	0.40
12.5.3 Other services and professional fees	1.30	2.30	1.40	0.70	2.20	1.70
1-12 All expenditure groups	**358.30**	**456.20**	**435.60**	**306.50**	**190.10**	**386.30**
13 Other expenditure items	**83.60**	**125.60**	**73.60**	**47.20**	**26.80**	**84.60**
13.1 Housing: mortgage interest payments, council tax etc.	64.10	92.00	47.30	22.00	15.00	58.40
13.2 Licences, fines and transfers	2.50	3.90	4.00	2.50	1.40	3.20
13.3 Holiday spending	10.50	16.30	11.10	6.80	[3.60]	11.50
13.4 Money transfers and credit	6.60	13.40	11.20	15.80	6.80	11.50
13.4.1 Money, cash gifts given to children	[0.00]	0.20	[0.00]	[0.00]	[0.00]	0.10
13.4.2 Cash gifts and donations	5.20	10.70	9.40	15.10	6.70	9.80
13.4.3 Club instalment payments (child) and interest on credit cards	1.40	2.50	1.80	0.80	0.20	1.70
Total expenditure	**441.90**	**581.80**	**509.20**	**353.60**	**216.80**	**471.00**
14 Other items recorded						
14.1 Life assurance & contributions to pension funds	10.40	28.10	30.30	4.20	1.30	20.30
14.2 Other insurance inc. friendly societies	0.40	1.70	1.60	0.50	0.40	1.20
14.3 Income tax, payments *less* refunds	70.00	144.30	111.90	41.90	17.80	98.60
14.4 National insurance contributions	32.70	42.90	32.30	3.40	[0.50]	28.50
14.5 Purchase or alteration of dwellings, mortgages	22.30	64.40	52.60	20.30	8.50	44.10
14.6 Savings and investments	4.30	8.80	9.20	1.90	0.70	6.50
14.7 Pay off loan to clear other debt	3.80	3.40	1.60	[0.40]	[0.40]	2.20
14.8 Windfall receipts from gambling etc[3]	0.90	2.10	1.90	1.60	0.60	1.70

Note: The commodity and service categories are not comparable to those in publications before 2001-02.
The numbering system is sequential, it does not use actual COICOP codes.
Please see page xiii for Symbols and conventions used in this report.
3 Expressed as an income figure as opposed to an expenditure figure.

Table A14

Household expenditure by gross income quintile group where the household reference person is aged under 30, 2006–2008

based on weighted data and including children's expenditure

	Lowest twenty per cent	Second quintile group	Third quintile group	Fourth quintile group	Highest twenty per cent	All house-holds
Lower boundary of group (£ per week)[1]		223	408	664	1026	
Average weighted number of households (thousands)	530	420	660	620	370	2,600
Total number of households in sample (over 3 years)	360	300	410	370	210	1,650
Total number of persons in sample (over 3 years)	790	760	1,020	930	540	4,040
Total number of adults in sample (over 3 years)	460	450	750	780	480	2,920
Weighted average number of persons per household	2.1	2.4	2.5	2.5	2.5	2.4
Commodity or service	Average weekly household expenditure (£)					
1 Food & non-alcoholic drinks	27.10	30.20	37.60	42.90	49.40	37.20
2 Alcoholic drinks, tobacco & narcotics	8.80	10.10	10.40	12.70	11.50	10.70
3 Clothing & footwear	11.20	17.30	21.30	32.50	39.10	23.70
4 Housing(net)[2], fuel & power	51.60	74.60	87.70	83.70	92.60	77.90
5 Household goods & services	14.10	15.50	22.10	34.70	43.40	25.40
6 Health	0.80	1.40	2.90	4.10	3.90	2.70
7 Transport	15.00	30.90	47.20	73.10	123.30	55.00
8 Communication	7.30	10.90	14.70	17.30	19.40	13.90
9 Recreation & culture	18.70	27.80	44.00	62.40	71.00	44.40
10 Education	[7.30]	6.20	8.10	8.40	[4.50]	7.10
11 Restaurants & hotels	15.90	23.00	36.50	53.30	72.60	39.20
12 Miscellaneous goods & services	10.30	20.50	34.50	45.10	54.20	32.60
1–12 All expenditure groups	188.10	268.40	367.10	470.30	584.90	369.70
13 Other expenditure items	8.00	37.20	69.70	107.80	166.90	74.80
Total expenditure	196.10	305.60	436.80	578.10	751.70	444.50
Average weekly expenditure per person (£) Total expenditure	91.80	128.50	175.50	235.10	295.80	185.30

Note: The commodity and service categories are not comparable to those in publications before 2001-02.
Please see page xiii for symbols and conventions used in this report.
This table is based on a three year average.
1   Lower boundary of 2008 gross income quintile groups (£ per week).
2   Excluding mortgage interest payments, council tax and Northern Ireland rates.

Table A15

Household expenditure by gross income quintile group where the household reference person is aged under 30 to 49, 2006–2008

based on weighted data and including children's expenditure

	Lowest twenty per cent	Second quintile group	Third quintile group	Fourth quintile group	Highest twenty per cent	All house-holds
Lower boundary of group (£ per week)[1]		223	408	664	1026	
Average weighted number of households (thousands)	1,030	1,260	1,990	2,590	2,910	9,770
Total number of households in sample (over 3 years)	750	960	1,510	1,890	2,020	7,130
Total number of persons in sample (over 3 years)	1,600	2,680	4,530	6,060	6,760	21,630
Total number of adults in sample (over 3 years)	940	1,450	2,700	3,840	4,440	13,370
Weighted average number of persons per household	2.1	2.7	2.9	3.1	3.2	2.9
Commodity or service	Average weekly household expenditure (£)					
1 Food & non-alcoholic drinks	32.00	41.40	49.30	57.80	68.30	54.30
2 Alcoholic drinks, tobacco & narcotics	8.30	10.50	11.60	13.00	15.40	12.60
3 Clothing & footwear	10.70	20.50	21.20	29.00	43.60	28.70
4 Housing(net)[2], fuel & power	44.00	55.20	54.10	54.10	63.00	55.80
5 Household goods & services	12.90	20.60	24.80	36.80	56.80	35.70
6 Health	1.70	2.20	3.50	4.10	7.90	4.60
7 Transport	20.30	40.70	55.80	76.00	130.20	77.60
8 Communication	8.50	11.40	13.80	14.40	17.30	14.10
9 Recreation & culture	21.80	35.70	49.70	71.60	104.20	67.00
10 Education	2.80	3.10	2.60	4.60	23.70	9.50
11 Restaurants & hotels	14.90	24.80	33.20	47.40	76.30	46.80
12 Miscellaneous goods & services	15.40	23.90	33.50	45.80	68.40	44.00
1–12 All expenditure groups	193.10	289.80	353.00	454.60	675.10	450.80
13 Other expenditure items	23.20	54.00	79.20	114.30	194.20	113.50
Total expenditure	216.30	343.80	432.20	568.80	869.40	564.30
Average weekly expenditure per person (£) Total expenditure	105.10	127.90	149.60	182.00	267.70	191.60

Note: The commodity and service categories are not comparable to those in publications before 2001-02.
          Please see page xiii for symbols and conventions used in this report.
          This table is based on a three year average.
1   Lower boundary of 2008 gross income quintile groups (£ per week).
2   Excluding mortgage interest payments, council tax and Northern Ireland rates.

Table A16

Household expenditure by gross income quintile group where the household reference person is aged 50 to 64, 2006–2008

based on weighted data and including children's expenditure

	Lowest twenty per cent	Second quintile group	Third quintile group	Fourth quintile group	Highest twenty per cent	All house-holds
Lower boundary of group (£ per week)[1]		223	408	664	1026	
Weighted number of households (thousands)	1,060	1,120	1,390	1,390	1,590	6,550
Total number of households in sample (over 3 years)	820	870	1,070	1,050	1,130	4,950
Total number of persons in sample (over 3 years)	1,150	1,550	2,270	2,560	3,270	10,790
Total number of adults in sample (over 3 years)	1,070	1,420	2,070	2,320	2,900	9,790
Weighted average number of persons per household	1.4	1.8	2.1	2.4	3.0	2.2
Commodity or service			Average weekly household expenditure (£)			
1 Food & non-alcoholic drinks	30.00	40.40	50.50	59.20	75.70	53.40
2 Alcoholic drinks, tobacco & narcotics	7.80	10.60	12.70	15.20	16.40	13.00
3 Clothing & footwear	8.10	13.40	19.00	24.00	45.00	23.60
4 Housing(net)[2], fuel & power	34.60	44.10	45.40	47.10	57.60	46.70
5 Household goods & services	13.30	24.20	28.30	36.20	55.00	33.30
6 Health	2.50	4.00	6.40	7.40	17.50	8.20
7 Transport	22.80	39.90	60.50	78.10	143.10	74.60
8 Communication	6.90	9.50	11.60	13.80	17.70	12.40
9 Recreation & culture	24.90	42.80	58.30	75.10	118.60	68.40
10 Education	[0.60]	1.00	3.20	9.70	20.20	8.00
11 Restaurants & hotels	12.00	22.40	32.80	49.70	79.30	42.50
12 Miscellaneous goods & services	13.20	23.10	29.50	41.60	66.00	37.10
1–12 All expenditure groups	176.80	275.50	358.10	457.10	712.10	421.40
13 Other expenditure items	20.50	49.30	59.10	82.50	144.70	76.90
Total expenditure	197.20	324.80	417.20	539.60	856.80	498.30
Average weekly expenditure per person (£) Total expenditure	139.40	181.90	194.80	221.40	288.10	223.70

Note: The commodity and service categories are not comparable to those in publications before 2001-02.
Please see page xiii for symbols and conventions used in this report.
This table is based on a three year average.

1   Lower boundary of 2008 gross income quintile groups (£ per week).
2   Excluding mortgage interest payments, council tax and Northern Ireland rates.

Table A17

Household expenditure by gross income quintile group where the household reference person is aged 65 to 74, 2006–2008

based on weighted data and including children's expenditure

	Lowest twenty per cent	Second quintile group	Third quintile group	Fourth quintile group	Highest twenty per cent	All house-holds
Lower boundary of group (£ per week)[1]		223	408	664	1026	
Average weighted number of households (thousands)	930	1,050	650	330	190	3,150
Total number of households in sample (over 3 years)	740	900	550	270	140	2,600
Total number of persons in sample (over 3 years)	920	1,560	1,090	580	330	4,480
Total number of adults in sample (over 3 years)	920	1,550	1,080	560	320	4,420
Weighted average number of persons per household	1.2	1.7	2.0	2.2	2.4	1.7
Commodity or service			Average weekly household expenditure (£)			
1 Food & non-alcoholic drinks	30.30	43.20	50.90	64.00	70.40	44.90
2 Alcoholic drinks, tobacco & narcotics	5.80	8.80	10.60	13.60	16.30	9.30
3 Clothing & footwear	6.70	10.30	16.70	26.00	32.40	13.60
4 Housing(net)[2], fuel & power	31.90	35.70	42.40	46.40	50.80	38.00
5 Household goods & services	11.70	21.60	31.50	43.20	54.00	25.00
6 Health	2.30	4.00	8.70	8.90	11.60	5.50
7 Transport	14.60	36.00	54.10	72.40	102.60	41.40
8 Communication	5.70	7.40	9.30	11.40	14.50	8.10
9 Recreation & culture	26.20	43.60	81.60	95.90	109.80	55.70
10 Education	[0.00]	[0.30]	[0.30]	[3.00]	[12.20]	1.30
11 Restaurants & hotels	9.60	19.30	29.40	44.60	65.20	24.00
12 Miscellaneous goods & services	12.80	20.60	28.60	38.20	70.40	24.90
1–12 All expenditure groups	157.70	250.90	363.90	467.60	610.10	291.60
13 Other expenditure items	19.40	37.30	45.30	91.80	92.80	42.60
Total expenditure	177.10	288.20	409.20	559.40	702.90	334.20
Average weekly expenditure per person (£) Total expenditure	143.20	166.50	203.30	249.80	291.00	192.20

Note: The commodity and service categories are not comparable to those in publications before 2001-02.
Please see page xiii for symbols and conventions used in this report.
This table is based on a three year average.

1   Lower boundary of 2008 gross income quintile groups (£ per week).
2   Excluding mortgage interest payments, council tax and Northern Ireland rates.

Table A18

Household expenditure by gross income quintile group where the household reference person is aged 75 or over, 2006–2008

based on weighted data and including children's expenditure

Commodity or service	Lowest twenty per cent	Second quintile group	Third quintile group	Fourth quintile group	Highest twenty per cent	All house-holds
Lower boundary of group (£ per week)[1]		223	408	664	1026	
Average weighted number of households (thousands)	1,570	1,220	400	170	50	3,410
Total number of households in sample (over 3 years)	990	860	300	120	40	2,310
Total number of persons in sample (over 3 years)	1,130	1,370	540	260	100	3,390
Total number of adults in sample (over 3 years)	1,120	1,360	540	250	100	3,370
Weighted average number of persons per household	1.1	1.5	1.8	2.1	2.7	1.4
Commodity or service			Average weekly household expenditure (£)			
1 Food & non-alcoholic drinks	24.80	35.60	45.80	57.80	68.50	33.40
2 Alcoholic drinks, tobacco & narcotics	2.80	5.00	7.70	8.40	12.50	4.60
3 Clothing & footwear	4.90	7.10	11.00	18.90	31.50	7.50
4 Housing (net)[2], fuel & power	30.10	36.70	42.60	45.20	63.10	35.10
5 Household goods & services	12.70	16.60	26.60	36.00	50.50	17.50
6 Health	2.80	6.20	10.00	11.50	8.50	5.40
7 Transport	6.50	18.50	32.90	44.50	97.20	17.20
8 Communication	4.70	5.80	8.70	10.30	11.20	5.90
9 Recreation & culture	13.90	27.10	52.60	65.60	125.70	27.50
10 Education	[0.00]	[0.20]	[2.30]	[5.10]	[2.20]	[0.60]
11 Restaurants & hotels	6.60	11.40	20.50	47.20	46.10	12.50
12 Miscellaneous goods & services	11.50	18.80	35.00	56.20	94.40	20.30
1-12 All expenditure groups	121.20	188.90	295.60	406.70	611.50	187.70
13 Other expenditure items	14.90	25.70	43.00	74.10	105.90	26.30
Total expenditure	136.10	214.70	338.60	480.80	717.40	214.00
Average weekly expenditure per person (£) Total expenditure	122.00	140.70	189.50	226.60	265.30	151.10

Note: The commodity and service categories are not comparable to those in publications before 2001-02.
        Please see page xiii for symbols and conventions used in this report.
        This table is based on a three year average.
1   Lower boundary of 2008 gross income quintile groups (£ per week).
2   Excluding mortgage interest payments, council tax and Northern Ireland rates.

Table A19

Household expenditure by economic activity status of the household reference person, 2008

based on weighted data and including children's expenditure

	Employees			Self-employed	All in employment[1]
	Full-time	Part-time	All		
Weighted number of households (thousands)	11,400	2,150	13,550	1,960	15,570
Total number of households in sample	2,510	500	3,010	470	3,490
Total number of persons in sample	6,780	1,260	8,040	1,360	9,430
Total number of adults in sample	5,000	880	5,880	990	6,880
Weighted average number of persons per household	2.7	2.5	2.7	2.8	2.7
Commodity or service	Average weekly household expenditure (£)				
1 Food & non-alcoholic drinks	56.70	50.60	55.80	64.10	56.80
2 Alcoholic drinks, tobacco & narcotics	12.70	10.50	12.40	12.40	12.40
3 Clothing & footwear	28.20	23.80	27.50	27.60	27.50
4 Housing (net)[2], fuel & power	60.90	61.40	61.00	63.30	61.20
5 Household goods & services	36.10	28.50	34.90	43.70	36.20
6 Health	6.20	4.60	6.00	4.90	5.90
7 Transport	87.90	53.80	82.50	96.30	84.20
8 Communication	14.30	12.70	14.10	17.80	14.50
9 Recreation & culture	72.30	60.20	70.40	76.80	71.10
10 Education	9.40	6.90	9.00	12.30	9.40
11 Restaurants & hotels	49.70	34.80	47.40	57.50	48.60
12 Miscellaneous goods & services	46.90	33.20	44.70	45.20	44.80
1-12 All expenditure groups	481.50	381.00	465.60	521.80	472.70
13 Other expenditure items	126.40	63.60	116.40	126.10	117.50
Total expenditure	608.00	444.60	582.00	647.90	590.20
Average weekly expenditure per person (£)					
Total expenditure	**226.70**	**175.10**	**218.90**	**227.50**	**220.00**

Note: The commodity and service categories are not comparable to those in publications before 2001-02.
Please see page xiii for symbols and conventions used in this report.
1   Includes households where household reference person was on a government supported training scheme.
2   Excluding mortgage interest payments, council tax and Northern Ireland rates.

Table A19

Household expenditure by economic activity status of the household reference person, 2008 (cont.)

based on weighted data and including children's expenditure

	Unem-ployed	All economi-cally active[1]	Economically inactive			All house-holds
			Retired	Other	All	
Weighted number of households (thousands)	500	16,070	6,660	2,960	9,620	25,690
Total number of households in sample	100	3,590	1,560	700	2,250	5,850
Total number of persons in sample	240	9,670	2,460	1,700	4,160	13,830
Total number of adults in sample	150	7,030	2,440	1,170	3,610	10,640
Weighted average number of persons per household	2.4	2.7	1.5	2.5	1.8	2.4
Commodity or service			Average weekly household expenditure (£)			
1 Food & non-alcoholic drinks	35.10	56.10	40.10	45.10	41.70	50.70
2 Alcoholic drinks, tobacco & narcotics	13.00	12.40	6.50	11.60	8.10	10.80
3 Clothing & footwear	14.50	27.10	9.60	18.40	12.30	21.60
4 Housing (net)[2], fuel & power	46.70	60.80	37.80	45.30	40.10	53.00
5 Household goods & services	18.90	35.60	21.10	20.70	21.00	30.10
6 Health	1.10	5.80	4.50	3.00	4.10	5.10
7 Transport	30.20	82.50	26.70	42.00	31.40	63.40
8 Communication	7.10	14.30	7.00	10.40	8.00	12.00
9 Recreation & culture	28.40	69.80	44.40	42.30	43.80	60.10
10 Education	[2.30]	9.20	0.70	2.40	1.20	6.20
11 Restaurants & hotels	20.90	47.80	17.50	28.80	21.00	37.70
12 Miscellaneous goods & services	18.90	44.00	21.60	22.00	21.70	35.60
1-12 All expenditure groups	237.10	465.40	237.50	292.10	254.30	386.30
13 Other expenditure items	26.40	114.70	35.10	33.20	34.50	84.60
Total expenditure	263.50	580.00	272.70	325.30	288.90	471.00
Average weekly expenditure per person (£)						
Total expenditure	108.60	216.90	176.00	132.50	158.00	199.80

Note: The commodity and service categories are not comparable to those in publications before 2001-02.
         Please see page xiii for symbols and conventions used in this report.
1   Includes households where household reference person was on a government supported training scheme.
2   Excluding mortgage interest payments, council tax and Northern Ireland rates.

Table A20

Household expenditure by gross income quintile group: the household reference person is a full-time employee, 2008

based on weighted data and including children's expenditure

	Lowest twenty per cent	Second quintile group	Third quintile group	Fourth quintile group	Highest twenty per cent	All house-holds
Lower boundary of group (£ per week)[1]		224	405	648	986	
Weighted number of households (thousands)	60	1,020	2,650	3,690	3,970	11,400
Total number of households in sample	10	230	590	810	860	2,510
Total number of persons in sample	20	380	1,400	2,290	2,690	6,780
Total number of adults in sample	20	300	1,030	1,650	1,990	5,000
Weighted average number of persons per household	1.5	1.7	2.3	2.8	3.1	2.7
Commodity or service			Average weekly household expenditure (£)			
1 Food & non-alcoholic drinks	[37.40]	32.10	45.00	56.10	71.80	56.70
2 Alcoholic drinks, tobacco & narcotics	[10.20]	9.70	10.40	13.10	14.80	12.70
3 Clothing & footwear	[9.80]	11.80	17.80	26.10	41.70	28.20
4 Housing (net)[2], fuel & power	[68.90]	62.30	59.70	58.40	63.70	60.90
5 Household goods & services	[9.50]	14.40	21.40	32.50	55.10	36.10
6 Health	[2.60]	3.60	3.60	6.10	8.80	6.20
7 Transport	[16.60]	37.90	54.00	76.70	134.80	87.90
8 Communication	[7.10]	8.90	13.10	14.00	16.90	14.30
9 Recreation & culture	[32.00]	25.90	43.00	67.90	108.50	72.30
10 Education	[0.00]	[0.70]	2.80	4.60	20.60	9.40
11 Restaurants & hotels	[7.20]	19.80	29.80	45.20	75.60	49.70
12 Miscellaneous goods & services	[16.30]	17.80	30.70	43.90	68.50	46.90
1-12 All expenditure groups	[217.60]	245.00	331.30	444.70	680.80	481.50
13 Other expenditure items	[43.00]	52.60	75.50	116.10	190.20	126.40
Total expenditure	[260.70]	297.60	406.80	560.80	871.10	608.00
Average weekly expenditure per person (£) Total expenditure	178.80	175.40	175.40	202.30	280.00	226.70

Note: The commodity and service categories are not comparable to those in publications before 2001-02.
  Please see page xiii for symbols and conventions used in this report.
1 Lower boundary of 2008 gross income quintile groups (£ per week).
2 Excluding mortgage interest payments, council tax and Northern Ireland rates.

Table A21

Household expenditure by gross income quintile group: the household reference person is self-employed, 2006-2008

based on weighted data and including children's expenditure

	Lowest twenty per cent	Second quintile group	Third quintile group	Fourth quintile group	Highest twenty per cent	All house-holds
Lower boundary of group (£ per week)[1]		223	408	664	1026	
Average weighted number of households (thousands)	180	320	450	480	600	2,040
Total number of households in sample (over 3 years)	130	250	360	360	440	1,530
Total number of persons in sample (over 3 years)	250	630	1,060	1,070	1,390	4,400
Total number of adults in sample (over 3 years)	190	430	740	770	1,020	3,160
Weighted average number of persons per household	1.9	2.5	2.9	2.9	3.1	2.8
Commodity or service			Average weekly household expenditure (£)			
1 Food & non-alcoholic drinks	36.10	46.20	59.00	64.30	73.00	60.40
2 Alcoholic drinks, tobacco & narcotics	6.10	11.20	14.40	14.80	15.10	13.50
3 Clothing & footwear	10.50	21.60	24.60	27.20	49.70	31.00
4 Housing(net)[2], fuel & power	53.40	59.50	55.10	62.80	60.70	59.00
5 Household goods & services	20.60	29.10	30.00	40.40	62.90	41.10
6 Health	2.40	3.80	6.20	4.20	9.70	6.10
7 Transport	47.60	58.30	63.40	87.50	136.40	88.40
8 Communication	10.40	13.30	15.50	18.20	20.50	16.80
9 Recreation & culture	27.90	47.60	58.40	77.40	123.30	78.20
10 Education	[5.50]	[2.30]	4.00	10.80	30.30	13.20
11 Restaurants & hotels	23.70	32.20	40.10	57.50	80.60	53.70
12 Miscellaneous goods & services	30.20	30.50	41.30	45.30	68.90	47.90
1-12 All expenditure groups	274.40	355.50	412.10	510.50	731.30	509.30
13 Other expenditure items	75.60	81.70	94.50	112.50	179.80	120.40
Total expenditure	350.00	437.10	506.60	623.00	911.10	629.70
Average weekly expenditure per person (£) Total expenditure	181.80	177.60	176.90	211.90	289.70	223.00

Note: The commodity and service categories are not comparable to those in publications before 2001-02.
        Please see page xiii for symbols and conventions used in this report.
        This table is based on a three year average.
1   Lower boundary of 2008 gross income quintile groups (£ per week).
2   Excluding mortgage interest payments, council tax and Northern Ireland rates.

Table A22

Household expenditure by number of persons working, 2008

based on weighted data and including children's expenditure

	Number of persons working					All house-holds
	None	One	Two	Three	Four or more	
Weighted number of households (thousands)	8,850	7,150	7,580	1,540	550	25,690
Total number of households in sample	2,080	1,660	1,710	300	100	5,850
Total number of persons in sample	3,530	3,670	5,060	1,130	440	13,830
Total number of adults in sample	3,030	2,660	3,630	920	390	10,640
Weighted average number of persons per household	1.7	2.2	2.9	3.7	4.7	2.4
Weighted average age of head of household	66	47	42	49	48	52
Employment status of the household reference person[1]:						
- % working full-time or self-employed	0	67	88	89	87	51
- % working part-time	0	18	10	8	9	9
- % not working	100	14	2	2	2	40

Commodity or service	Average weekly household expenditure (£)					
1 Food & non-alcoholic drinks	37.70	46.20	61.90	78.50	85.80	50.70
2 Alcoholic drinks, tobacco & narcotics	7.30	10.90	13.30	16.10	16.40	10.80
3 Clothing & footwear	10.10	20.00	29.50	42.50	58.10	21.60
4 Housing(net)[2], fuel & power	38.40	61.00	58.40	66.50	73.60	53.00
5 Household goods & services	19.60	28.00	42.70	34.10	44.50	30.10
6 Health	3.90	4.60	5.40	7.20	21.90	5.10
7 Transport	23.90	60.10	94.50	117.00	160.80	63.40
8 Communication	7.00	11.80	15.40	19.10	26.60	12.00
9 Recreation & culture	40.60	48.80	81.00	99.90	120.10	60.10
10 Education	0.80	7.00	10.90	8.20	[11.20]	6.20
11 Restaurants & hotels	16.70	33.60	55.30	72.30	90.40	37.70
12 Miscellaneous goods & services	19.30	32.60	51.10	54.70	70.30	35.60
1-12 All expenditure groups	225.40	364.50	519.30	616.30	779.70	386.30
13 Other expenditure items	29.30	90.80	135.50	112.60	116.30	84.60
Total expenditure	254.60	455.30	654.70	728.90	896.00	471.00
Average weekly expenditure per person (£) Total expenditure	153.50	209.90	226.00	194.60	190.80	199.80

Note: The commodity and service categories are not comparable to those in publications before 2001-02.
            Please see page xiii for symbols and conventions used in this report.

1   Excludes households where the household reference person was on a Government-supported training scheme.

2   Excluding mortgage interest payments, council tax and Northern Ireland rates.

Table A23

Household expenditure by age at which the household reference person completed continuous full-time education, 2008

based on weighted data and including children's expenditure

	Aged 14 and under	Aged 15	Aged 16	Aged 17 and under 19	Aged 19 and under 22	Aged 22 or over
Weighted number of households (thousands)	430	3,790	6,560	4,020	2,840	2,990
Total number of households in sample	110	910	1,490	920	640	630
Total number of persons in sample	250	1,980	4,130	2,450	1,660	1,670
Total number of adults in sample	190	1,710	2,870	1,690	1,220	1,220
Weighted average number of persons per household	2.6	2.2	2.8	2.6	2.5	2.6
Weighted average age of head of household	51	56	45	43	43	42

Commodity or service	Average weekly household expenditure (£)					
1 Food & non-alcoholic drinks	44.30	48.80	53.70	53.90	55.10	60.00
2 Alcoholic drinks, tobacco & narcotics	8.80	13.40	12.80	10.60	10.70	12.80
3 Clothing & footwear	19.30	16.30	25.60	26.50	29.00	28.10
4 Housing(net)[1], fuel & power	57.00	45.90	50.20	59.50	61.90	77.40
5 Household goods & services	23.80	23.50	28.70	34.70	44.10	42.20
6 Health	1.70	4.60	4.30	5.70	7.70	5.40
7 Transport	37.50	52.40	67.50	78.30	91.60	96.00
8 Communication	8.30	10.60	13.40	14.00	14.50	15.20
9 Recreation & culture	49.80	55.60	65.80	72.30	71.20	70.80
10 Education	[2.70]	1.90	3.30	5.80	11.90	23.20
11 Restaurants & hotels	21.70	30.10	38.50	45.50	61.10	53.30
12 Miscellaneous goods & services	21.60	24.50	34.60	45.70	47.60	55.00
1-12 All expenditure groups	296.50	327.50	398.40	452.40	506.50	539.40
13 Other expenditure items	48.50	47.80	85.90	107.30	123.30	159.50
Total expenditure	**345.00**	**375.30**	**484.30**	**559.70**	**629.90**	**698.90**
Average weekly expenditure per person (£)						
Total expenditure	**133.30**	**171.00**	**175.30**	**212.90**	**250.30**	**271.00**

Note: The commodity and service categories are not comparable to those in publications before 2001-02.
        Please see page xiii for symbols and conventions used in this report.

1   Excluding mortgage interest payments, council tax and Northern Ireland rates.

Table A24

Household expenditure by socio-economic classification of the household reference person, 2008

based on weighted data and including children's expenditure

	Large employers & higher managerial	Higher profess-ional	Lower manag-erial & professional	Inter-mediate	Small employers	Lower super-visory
Weighted number of households (thousands)	1,190	1,940	4,590	1,310	1,510	1,790
Total number of households in sample	260	430	1,040	290	360	390
Total number of persons in sample	780	1,120	2,750	680	1,050	1,090
Total number of adults in sample	540	820	2,010	510	760	810
Weighted average number of persons per household	2.9	2.5	2.6	2.4	2.9	2.8

Commodity or service	Average weekly household expenditure (£)					
1 Food & non-alcoholic drinks	66.10	63.70	57.60	50.90	59.80	57.60
2 Alcoholic drinks, tobacco & narcotics	14.60	12.40	12.60	10.90	12.10	13.70
3 Clothing & footwear	39.00	29.80	30.90	23.60	25.60	25.10
4 Housing (net)³, fuel & power	70.60	63.50	55.10	58.70	61.60	54.50
5 Household goods & services	50.30	51.10	42.60	31.20	35.90	28.30
6 Health	7.70	6.70	8.10	4.10	4.10	5.70
7 Transport	122.40	109.70	91.40	59.40	90.90	80.60
8 Communication	15.30	14.40	14.70	13.40	16.80	13.60
9 Recreation & culture	109.40	92.40	77.70	59.60	63.60	64.20
10 Education	37.00	20.30	7.70	3.20	5.80	2.00
11 Restaurants & hotels	76.30	61.00	55.70	40.70	47.70	38.70
12 Miscellaneous goods & services	70.80	54.70	52.00	37.50	42.10	35.80
1–12 All expenditure groups	679.50	579.80	506.00	393.30	466.10	419.60
13 Other expenditure items	220.80	156.70	132.60	89.20	108.20	93.30
Total expenditure	**900.30**	**736.50**	**638.60**	**482.40**	**574.30**	**512.90**
Average weekly expenditure per person (£)						
Total expenditure	**310.90**	**292.20**	**245.50**	**203.70**	**201.50**	**181.90**

Note: The commodity and service categories are not comparable to those in publications before 2001-02.
        Please see page xiii for symbols and conventions used in this report.
1   Includes those who have never worked.
2   Includes those who are economically inactive.
3   Excludes mortgage interest payments, council tax and Northern Ireland rates.

Table A24

Household expenditure by socio-economic classification of the household reference person, 2008 (cont.)

based on weighted data and including children's expenditure

	Semi-routine	Routine	Long-term unem-ployed[1]	Students	Occupation not stated[2]	All house-holds
Weighted number of households (thousands)	1,930	1,700	520	320	8,900	25,690
Total number of households in sample	420	380	120	60	2,080	5,850
Total number of persons in sample	1,150	1,010	350	160	3,680	13,830
Total number of adults in sample	820	740	190	120	3,320	10,640
Weighted average number of persons per household	2.8	2.7	2.9	2.9	1.7	2.4
Commodity or service	Average weekly household expenditure (£)					
1 Food & non-alcoholic drinks	47.10	49.20	42.90	47.60	40.90	50.70
2 Alcoholic drinks, tobacco & narcotics	10.70	12.40	9.30	10.20	8.00	10.80
3 Clothing & footwear	20.20	17.50	19.10	24.00	12.10	21.60
4 Housing (net)[3], fuel & power	61.30	66.80	44.50	115.00	38.60	53.00
5 Household goods & services	21.40	19.80	18.30	26.20	20.40	30.10
6 Health	4.40	2.60	0.80	[0.70]	4.20	5.10
7 Transport	51.30	50.90	22.40	50.10	31.30	63.40
8 Communication	13.00	12.80	9.50	15.90	7.80	12.00
9 Recreation & culture	51.20	42.10	29.30	33.80	44.10	60.10
10 Education	2.20	1.20	[0.20]	[23.90]	1.10	6.20
11 Restaurants & hotels	29.90	27.80	18.50	37.90	20.60	37.70
12 Miscellaneous goods & services	29.30	26.20	15.70	26.80	21.60	35.60
1–12 All expenditure groups	341.90	329.40	230.60	412.10	250.70	386.30
13 Other expenditure items	60.90	56.70	24.30	51.90	34.80	84.60
Total expenditure	**402.90**	**386.00**	**254.90**	**464.00**	**285.60**	**471.00**
Average weekly expenditure per person (£)						
Total expenditure	**146.10**	**142.50**	**87.20**	**159.50**	**164.20**	**199.80**

Note: The commodity and service categories are not comparable to those in publications before 2001-02.
       Please see page xiii for symbols and conventions used in this report.
1 Includes those who have never worked.
2 Includes those who are economically inactive.
3 Excludes mortgage interest payments, council tax and Northern Ireland rates.

Table A25

Expenditure by household composition, 2008

based on weighted data and including children's expenditure

	Retired households				Non-retired	
	State pension[1]		Other retired			
	One person	One man and one woman	One person	One man and one woman	One person	One man and one woman
Weighted number of households (thousands)	970	540	2,660	2,060	3,860	5,550
Total number of households in sample	200	150	570	550	850	1,260
Total number of persons in sample	200	310	570	1,100	850	2,530
Total number of adults in sample	200	310	570	1,100	850	2,530
Weighted average number of persons per household	1.0	2.0	1.0	2.0	1.0	2.0
Commodity or service	Average weekly household expenditure (£)					
1 Food & non-alcoholic drinks	24.20	47.50	27.50	53.60	25.00	51.10
2 Alcoholic drinks, tobacco & narcotics	3.30	8.30	4.30	8.80	8.80	12.10
3 Clothing & footwear	4.40	9.10	7.20	13.40	9.10	25.60
4 Housing(net)[2], fuel & power	33.00	36.70	35.60	41.60	46.10	55.70
5 Household goods & services	12.70	18.90	14.20	32.90	16.40	37.30
6 Health	2.20	4.70	4.50	4.80	3.30	6.60
7 Transport	6.10	25.70	15.10	43.40	40.80	82.70
8 Communication	5.50	6.40	5.90	7.90	8.70	13.70
9 Recreation & culture	15.20	41.90	24.80	80.80	27.40	72.70
10 Education	[0.00]	[0.50]	[0.50]	[0.60]	3.00	4.60
11 Restaurants & hotels	7.10	14.10	9.70	27.00	21.80	48.20
12 Miscellaneous goods & services	13.40	18.90	15.90	30.70	19.00	38.00
1-12 All expenditure groups	127.10	232.60	165.30	345.70	229.40	448.30
13 Other expenditure items	18.60	25.70	30.50	47.90	69.50	104.10
Total expenditure	**145.70**	**258.30**	**195.80**	**393.50**	**298.90**	**552.30**
Average weekly expenditure per person (£)						
Total expenditure	**145.70**	**129.10**	**195.80**	**196.80**	**298.90**	**276.20**

Note: The commodity and service categories are not comparable to those in publications before 2001-02.
Please see page xiii for symbols and conventions used in this report.
1   Mainly dependent on state pensions and not economically active - see definitions in Appendix B.
2   Excluding mortgage interest payments, council tax and Northern Ireland rates.

Table A25

Expenditure by household composition, 2008 (cont.)
based on weighted data and including children's expenditure

	One adult		Two adults			Three or more adults	
						Retired and non-retired households	
	with one child	with two or more children	with one child	with two children	with three or more children	without children	with children
Weighted number of households (thousands)	830	650	1,950	2,170	820	2,480	1,110
Total number of households in sample	200	180	430	540	210	460	240
Total number of persons in sample	400	610	1,300	2,170	1,110	1,560	1,140
Total number of adults in sample	200	180	860	1,080	420	1,560	780
Weighted average number of persons per household	2.0	3.4	3.0	4.0	5.3	3.4	4.9
Commodity or service	Average weekly household expenditure (£)						
1 Food & non-alcoholic drinks	37.10	50.10	62.60	72.30	84.40	73.50	84.80
2 Alcoholic drinks, tobacco & narcotics	9.00	8.10	13.90	13.80	11.50	16.70	16.10
3 Clothing & footwear	14.50	25.60	27.50	32.80	35.60	35.50	44.20
4 Housing(net)[2], fuel & power	54.20	53.80	60.90	55.60	91.60	70.60	64.90
5 Household goods & services	16.80	25.90	37.10	42.80	57.90	36.40	36.70
6 Health	2.70	2.40	3.40	4.80	3.60	11.00	4.00
7 Transport	27.10	27.80	82.80	93.20	83.10	111.70	99.80
8 Communication	9.70	11.10	14.00	14.10	16.50	18.60	21.20
9 Recreation & culture	32.60	43.60	69.30	89.20	81.80	88.60	81.40
10 Education	[3.70]	3.60	10.20	18.40	23.60	9.20	10.20
11 Restaurants & hotels	18.10	25.50	45.90	54.00	55.60	67.60	61.30
12 Miscellaneous goods & services	25.40	22.10	54.80	57.60	65.70	49.80	50.90
1-12 All expenditure groups	251.00	299.70	482.60	548.70	610.80	589.20	575.50
13 Other expenditure items	49.80	40.00	116.90	140.80	191.20	95.60	107.30
Total expenditure	**300.80**	**339.70**	**599.40**	**689.50**	**802.00**	**684.80**	**682.80**
Average weekly expenditure per person (£)							
Total expenditure	**150.40**	**99.20**	**199.80**	**172.40**	**151.80**	**199.20**	**140.70**

Note: The commodity and service categories are not comparable to those in publications before 2001-02.
Please see page xiii for symbols and conventions used in this report.
1   Mainly dependent on state pensions and not economically active - see definitions in Appendix B.
2   Excluding mortgage interest payments, council tax and Northern Ireland rates.

Table A26

Expenditure of one person retired households mainly dependent on state pensions[1] by gross income quintile group, 2006–2008

based on weighted data

	Lowest twenty per cent	Second quintile group	Third quintile group	Fourth quintile group	Highest twenty per cent	All house-holds
Lower boundary of group (£ per week)[2]		223	408	664	1026	
Average weighted number of households (thousands)	690	90	–	0	0	790
Total number of households in sample (over 3 years)	480	60	–	0	0	540
Total number of persons in sample (over 3 years)	480	60	–	0	0	540
Total number of adults in sample (over 3 years)	480	60	–	0	0	540
Weighted average number of persons per household	1.0	1.0	1.0	0	0	1.0
Commodity or service			Average weekly household expenditure (£)			
1 Food & non-alcoholic drinks	23.50	21.70	[18.10]	–	–	23.30
2 Alcoholic drinks, tobacco & narcotics	3.10	[2.70]	[1.60]	–	–	3.00
3 Clothing & footwear	4.70	6.70	[3.00]	–	–	4.80
4 Housing(net)[3], fuel & power	30.50	34.30	[33.10]	–	–	31.00
5 Household goods & services	13.30	15.10	[3.50]	–	–	13.70
6 Health	1.50	6.40	[1.50]	–	–	2.10
7 Transport	9.00	6.40	[1.90]	–	–	8.80
8 Communication	4.90	4.90	[2.20]	–	–	4.80
9 Recreation & culture	18.50	14.70	[9.70]	–	–	18.20
10 Education	–	–	–	–	–	–
11 Restaurants & hotels	6.80	7.50	[2.70]	–	–	[6.80]
12 Miscellaneous goods & services	12.70	15.60	[8.10]	–	–	13.00
1–12 All expenditure groups	128.50	136.10	[85.30]	–	–	129.60
13 Other expenditure items	17.80	33.40	[5.60]	–	–	19.10
Total expenditure	**146.30**	**169.50**	**[90.90]**	**–**	**–**	**148.70**
Average weekly expenditure per person (£)						
Total expenditure	**146.30**	**169.50**	**[90.90]**	**–**	**–**	**148.70**

Note: The commodity and service categories are not comparable to those in publications before 2001-02.
Please see page xiii for symbols and conventions used in this report.
This table is based on a three year average.
1   Mainly dependent on state pensions and not economically active - see defintions in Appendix B.
2   Lower boundary of 2008 gross income quintile groups (£ per week).
3   Excluding mortgage interest payments, council tax and Northern Ireland rates.

Table A27

Expenditure of one person retired households not mainly dependent on state pensions by gross income quintile group, 2006–2008

based on weighted data

	Lowest twenty per cent	Second quintile group	Third quintile group	Fourth quintile group	Highest twenty per cent	All house-holds
Lower boundary of group (£ per week)[1]		223	408	664	1026	
Average weighted number of households (thousands)	1,550	860	220	70	10	2,710
Total number of households in sample (over 3 years)	1,060	600	160	50	10	1,870
Total number of persons in sample (over 3 years)	1,060	600	160	50	10	1,870
Total number of adults in sample (over 3 years)	1,060	600	160	50	10	1,870
Weighted average number of persons per household	1.0	1.0	1.0	1.0	1.0	1.0
Commodity or service	Average weekly household expenditure (£)					
1　Food & non-alcoholic drinks	24.40	27.30	33.10	32.70	[17.00]	26.20
2　Alcoholic drinks, tobacco & narcotics	3.80	4.80	7.30	7.30	[3.50]	4.50
3　Clothing & footwear	5.60	7.30	10.10	16.00	[10.20]	6.70
4　Housing(net)[2] fuel & power	30.80	35.20	41.40	52.20	[19.90]	33.60
5　Household goods & services	11.30	17.60	31.90	38.70	[7.90]	15.50
6　Health	3.10	5.60	9.90	8.50	[0.30]	4.50
7　Transport	7.90	18.90	41.00	49.50	[39.40]	15.30
8　Communication	5.00	5.80	7.80	8.50	[3.30]	5.60
9　Recreation & culture	15.20	26.90	52.60	52.60	[171.80]	23.70
10　Education	[0.00]	[0.40]	[4.30]	[20.80]	–	1.00
11　Restaurants & hotels	6.70	11.70	17.00	33.90	[17.60]	9.90
12　Miscellaneous goods & services	10.20	19.60	41.40	47.40	[18.10]	16.60
1–12　All expenditure groups	123.80	181.20	297.90	368.00	[309.10]	163.10
13　Other expenditure items	13.90	30.00	51.80	165.80	[77.50]	26.00
Total expenditure	**137.70**	**211.20**	**349.70**	**533.80**	**[386.60]**	**189.10**
Average weekly expenditure per person (£)						
Total expenditure	**137.70**	**211.20**	**349.70**	**533.80**	**[579.90]**	**189.10**

Note:　The commodity and service categories are not comparable to those in publications before 2001-02.
　　　　Please see page xiii for symbols and conventions used in this report.
　　　　This table is based on a three year average.
1　Lower boundary of 2008 gross income quintile groups (£ per week).
2　Excluding mortgage interest payments, council tax and Northern Ireland rates.

Table A28

Expenditure of one adult non-retired households by gross income quintile group, 2006–2008

based on weighted data

	Lowest twenty per cent	Second quintile group	Third quintile group	Fourth quintile group	Highest twenty per cent	All house-holds
Lower boundary of group (£ per week)[1]		223	408	664	1026	
Average weighted number of households (thousands)	1,210	950	900	500	270	3,830
Total number of households in sample (over 3 years)	850	680	630	340	170	2,670
Total number of persons in sample (over 3 years)	850	680	630	340	170	2,670
Total number of adults in sample (over 3 years)	850	680	630	340	170	2,670
Weighted average number of persons per household	1.0	1.0	1.0	1.0	1.0	1.0
Commodity or service		Average weekly household expenditure (£)				
1 Food & non-alcoholic drinks	19.90	23.30	25.90	31.10	30.20	24.30
2 Alcoholic drinks, tobacco & narcotics	7.50	7.50	8.00	9.60	8.00	7.90
3 Clothing & footwear	5.50	8.50	10.80	16.00	23.70	10.20
4 Housing(net)[2], fuel & power	35.90	49.70	44.20	50.30	60.40	45.00
5 Household goods & services	9.50	14.80	18.90	34.10	43.10	18.70
6 Health	1.50	2.90	2.70	7.00	4.60	3.10
7 Transport	16.80	34.30	46.60	58.60	98.70	39.50
8 Communication	6.40	8.50	9.70	10.50	12.90	8.70
9 Recreation & culture	16.40	26.90	36.60	47.50	57.10	30.80
10 Education	1.40	[0.80]	1.00	11.70	[7.40]	2.90
11 Restaurants & hotels	10.50	17.20	29.80	36.70	56.40	23.40
12 Miscellaneous goods & services	10.50	17.60	22.70	36.10	39.80	20.60
1–12 All expenditure groups	141.70	211.80	256.90	349.10	442.20	235.00
13 Other expenditure items	18.30	52.80	78.90	110.00	194.70	65.50
Total expenditure	**160.10**	**264.60**	**335.70**	**459.10**	**636.90**	**300.50**
Average weekly expenditure per person (£)						
Total expenditure	**160.10**	**264.60**	**335.70**	**459.10**	**636.90**	**300.50**

Note: The commodity and service categories are not comparable to those in publications before 2001-02.
        Please see page xiii for symbols and conventions used in this report.
        This table is based on a three year average.
1   Lower boundary of 2008 gross income quintile groups (£ per week).
2   Excluding mortgage interest payments, council tax and Northern Ireland rates.

Table A29

Expenditure of one adult households with children by gross income quintile group, 2006–2008

based on weighted data and including children's expenditure

	Lowest twenty per cent	Second quintile group	Third quintile group	Fourth quintile group	Highest twenty per cent	All house-holds
Lower boundary of group (£ per week)[1]		223	408	664	1026	
Average weighted number of households (thousands)	600	460	250	120	30	1,460
Total number of households in sample (over 3 years)	500	410	230	90	30	1,250
Total number of persons in sample (over 3 years)	1,290	1,150	630	230	80	3,370
Total number of adults in sample (over 3 years)	500	410	230	90	30	1,250
Weighted average number of persons per household	2.5	2.7	2.7	2.5	2.7	2.6
Commodity or service	Average weekly household expenditure (£)					
1 Food & non-alcoholic drinks	35.00	42.10	44.80	48.30	60.60	40.50
2 Alcoholic drinks, tobacco & narcotics	6.80	8.60	9.40	10.10	[7.00]	8.10
3 Clothing & footwear	12.70	21.00	29.80	30.60	49.70	20.50
4 Housing(net)[2], fuel & power	42.40	55.30	56.90	58.80	100.80	51.30
5 Household goods & services	15.60	23.00	23.50	31.10	35.90	21.20
6 Health	1.50	1.40	2.40	6.90	[12.60]	2.30
7 Transport	14.10	28.30	46.20	52.20	72.40	28.30
8 Communication	7.80	11.00	15.40	14.20	17.10	10.70
9 Recreation & culture	23.70	37.90	48.50	90.40	176.60	40.70
10 Education	1.10	3.50	4.30	[6.90]	[73.00]	4.90
11 Restaurants & hotels	13.50	19.90	29.70	45.60	39.00	21.40
12 Miscellaneous goods & services	15.20	23.80	43.20	41.20	74.30	26.00
1–12 All expenditure groups	189.40	275.60	354.10	436.40	719.00	275.90
13 Other expenditure items	11.30	45.20	79.40	106.70	194.10	44.90
Total expenditure	**200.70**	**320.80**	**433.50**	**543.10**	**913.10**	**320.80**
Average weekly expenditure per person (£) **Total expenditure**	**79.10**	**117.20**	**160.60**	**219.80**	**341.10**	**122.20**

Note: The commodity and service categories are not comparable to those in publications before 2001-02.

Please see page xiii for symbols and conventions used in this report.

This table is based on a three year average.

1   Lower boundary of 2008 gross income quintile groups (£ per week).

2   Excluding mortgage interest payments, council tax and Northern Ireland rates.

Table A30

Expenditure of two adult households with children by gross income quintile group, 2006–2008

based on weighted data and including children's expenditure

	Lowest twenty per cent	Second quintile group	Third quintile group	Fourth quintile group	Highest twenty per cent	All house-holds
Lower boundary of group (£ per week)[1]		223	408	664	1026	
Average weighted number of households (thousands)	230	550	1,110	1,490	1,530	4,920
Total number of households in sample (over 3 years)	160	420	870	1,170	1,200	3,800
Total number of persons in sample (over 3 years)	560	1,690	3,390	4,460	4,630	14,730
Total number of adults in sample (over 3 years)	310	840	1,730	2,330	2,390	7,600
Weighted average number of persons per household	3.7	4.0	3.8	3.8	3.8	3.8
Commodity or service	Average weekly household expenditure (£)					
1 Food & non-alcoholic drinks	48.60	53.20	59.30	65.20	80.80	66.60
2 Alcoholic drinks, tobacco & narcotics	13.70	12.50	12.00	12.40	15.00	13.20
3 Clothing & footwear	15.10	25.80	23.40	31.60	45.70	32.70
4 Housing(net)[2], fuel & power	46.00	60.10	59.40	51.30	63.50	57.70
5 Household goods & services	18.50	26.20	27.00	38.70	62.80	41.20
6 Health	2.40	1.60	3.50	3.90	9.10	5.10
7 Transport	31.40	45.10	58.90	77.70	139.50	86.80
8 Communication	9.30	12.60	14.30	14.50	16.90	14.80
9 Recreation & culture	28.20	42.90	55.20	78.70	114.50	78.20
10 Education	[7.30]	3.30	4.20	5.80	42.30	16.60
11 Restaurants & hotels	25.20	30.60	32.40	46.10	72.90	48.70
12 Miscellaneous goods & services	18.60	27.50	38.30	51.80	83.20	54.20
1–12 All expenditure groups	264.20	341.40	387.80	477.90	746.30	515.70
13 Other expenditure items	33.30	52.00	76.70	121.40	212.00	127.60
Total expenditure	**297.50**	**393.40**	**464.50**	**599.30**	**958.30**	**643.30**
Average weekly expenditure per person (£)						
Total expenditure	**81.50**	**99.00**	**121.40**	**158.80**	**250.20**	**168.40**

Note: The commodity and service categories are not comparable to those in publications before 2001-02.
         Please see page xiii for symbols and conventions used in this report.
         This table is based on a three year average.
1   Lower boundary of 2008 gross income quintile groups (£ per week).
2   Excluding mortgage interest payments, council tax and Northern Ireland rates.

Table A31

Expenditure of one man one woman non-retired households by gross income quintile group, 2006–2008

based on weighted data

	Lowest twenty per cent	Second quintile group	Third quintile group	Fourth quintile group	Highest twenty per cent	All house- holds
Lower boundary of group (£ per week)[1]		223	408	664	1026	
Average weighted number of households (thousands)	290	600	1,230	1,550	1,610	5,280
Total number of households in sample (over 3 years)	220	460	910	1,100	1,110	3,800
Total number of persons in sample (over 3 years)	440	920	1,820	2,200	2,220	7,600
Total number of adults in sample (over 3 years)	440	920	1,820	2,200	2,220	7,600
Weighted average number of persons per household	2.0	2.0	2.0	2.0	2.0	2.0
Commodity or service	Average weekly household expenditure (£)					
1 Food & non-alcoholic drinks	41.90	45.50	47.60	49.30	55.80	50.10
2 Alcoholic drinks, tobacco & narcotics	9.80	13.50	12.90	13.60	14.30	13.40
3 Clothing & footwear	11.30	14.20	18.90	22.30	38.60	25.00
4 Housing(net)[2], fuel & power	46.10	48.40	52.90	52.50	58.30	53.60
5 Household goods & services	21.30	27.70	31.30	36.40	59.60	40.40
6 Health	3.40	4.40	6.60	6.20	11.00	7.40
7 Transport	33.10	46.60	56.90	75.80	124.40	80.60
8 Communication	7.90	9.90	11.90	13.30	15.20	12.90
9 Recreation & culture	33.90	49.20	57.20	68.40	104.00	72.50
10 Education	[3.10]	[0.80]	1.40	2.80	8.80	4.10
11 Restaurants & hotels	15.60	26.30	31.70	48.70	76.80	49.00
12 Miscellaneous goods & services	18.50	28.10	29.10	39.60	57.60	40.20
1–12 All expenditure groups	246.00	314.60	358.40	428.90	624.20	449.10
13 Other expenditure items	27.80	53.20	61.20	95.30	175.20	103.30
Total expenditure	**273.70**	**367.90**	**419.60**	**524.20**	**799.40**	**552.50**
Average weekly expenditure per person (£)						
Total expenditure	**136.90**	**183.90**	**209.80**	**262.10**	**399.70**	**276.20**

Note: The commodity and service categories are not comparable to those in publications before 2001-02

Please see page xiii for symbols and conventions used in this report.

This table is based on a three year average.

1   Lower boundary of 2008 gross income quintile groups (£ per week).

2   Excluding mortgage interest payments, council tax and Northern Ireland rates.

Table A32

Expenditure of one man one woman retired households mainly dependent on state pensions[1] by gross income quintile group, 2006–2008

based on weighted data

	Lowest twenty per cent	Second quintile group	Third quintile group	Fourth quintile group	Highest twenty per cent	All house-holds
Lower boundary of group (£ per week)[2]		223	408	664	1026	
Average weighted number of households (thousands)	200	270	10	0	0	490
Total number of households in sample (over 3 years)	170	240	10	0	0	430
Total number of persons in sample (over 3 years)	350	480	20	0	0	850
Total number of adults in sample (over 3 years)	350	480	20	0	0	850
Weighted average number of persons per household	2.0	2.0	2.0	0	0	2.0
Commodity or service	Average weekly household expenditure (£)					
1 Food & non-alcoholic drinks	43.90	45.20	[47.40]	–	–	44.70
2 Alcoholic drinks, tobacco & narcotics	5.70	8.70	[10.10]	–	–	7.50
3 Clothing & footwear	8.30	9.80	[7.70]	–	–	9.10
4 Housing(net)[3], fuel & power	33.50	35.60	[41.50]	–	–	35.10
5 Household goods & services	11.80	19.30	[8.60]	–	–	15.90
6 Health	2.40	3.90	[7.00]	–	–	3.40
7 Transport	23.80	28.90	[26.10]	–	–	26.80
8 Communication	6.10	6.30	[7.40]	–	–	6.20
9 Recreation & culture	30.10	40.00	[37.00]	–	–	35.80
10 Education	–	[0.30]	–	–	–	0.20
11 Restaurants & hotels	12.20	15.00	[19.10]	–	–	13.90
12 Miscellaneous goods & services	17.40	18.70	[15.60]	–	–	18.00
1–12 All expenditure groups	195.30	231.70	[227.50]	–	–	216.80
13 Other expenditure items	27.90	28.30	[52.20]	–	–	28.30
Total expenditure	223.20	260.10	[279.60]	–	–	245.10
Average weekly expenditure per person (£)						
Total expenditure	111.60	130.00	[139.80]	–	–	122.50

Note: The commodity and service categories are not comparable to those in publications before 2001-02.
Please see page xiii for symbols and conventions used in this report.
This table is based on a three year average
1 Mainly dependent on the state pensions and not economically active -see defintions in Appendix B.
2 Lower boundary of 2008 gross income quintile groups (£ per week).
3 Excluding mortgage interest payments, council tax and Northern Ireland rates.

Table A33

Expenditure of one man one woman retired households not mainly dependent on state pensions by gross income quintile group, 2006–2008
based on weighted data

	Lowest twenty per cent	Second quintile group	Third quintile group	Fourth quintile group	Highest twenty per cent	All house-holds
Lower boundary of group (£ per week)[1]		223	408	664	1026	
Average weighted number of households (thousands)	170	960	610	240	100	2,080
Total number of households in sample (over 3 years)	130	800	510	210	90	1,730
Total number of persons in sample (over 3 years)	250	1,600	1,020	410	170	3,450
Total number of adults in sample (over 3 years)	250	1,600	1,020	410	170	3,450
Weighted average number of persons per household	2.0	2.0	2.0	2.0	2.0	2.0
Commodity or service			Average weekly household expenditure (£)			
1 Food & non-alcoholic drinks	43.20	48.10	51.80	63.10	62.00	51.30
2 Alcoholic drinks, tobacco & narcotics	7.60	8.10	8.60	12.50	16.30	9.10
3 Clothing & footwear	7.40	9.80	15.60	23.60	26.70	13.80
4 Housing(net)[2], fuel & power	30.30	36.90	39.90	46.30	58.50	39.50
5 Household goods & services	22.40	19.90	31.20	47.70	53.20	28.20
6 Health	4.60	5.30	9.60	11.70	12.80	7.60
7 Transport	17.30	36.40	50.30	64.90	102.90	45.60
8 Communication	7.80	7.00	8.70	10.40	11.60	8.20
9 Recreation & culture	30.80	42.50	84.70	109.20	142.70	66.80
10 Education	–	[0.20]	[0.20]	[3.40]	[2.40]	0.70
11 Restaurants & hotels	10.30	17.90	28.70	52.30	61.90	26.60
12 Miscellaneous goods & services	18.80	20.70	30.20	55.80	89.50	30.70
1–12 All expenditure groups	200.40	252.90	359.60	500.80	640.50	328.00
13 Other expenditure items	22.20	31.60	45.10	92.20	97.70	44.90
Total expenditure	222.60	284.50	404.70	593.00	738.20	372.90
Average weekly expenditure per person (£)						
Total expenditure	111.30	142.30	202.40	296.50	369.10	186.50

Note: The commodity and service categories are not comparable to those in publications before 2001-02.
    Please see page xiii for symbols and conventions used in this report.
    This table is based on a three year average.
1   Lower boundary of 2008 gross income quintile groups (£ per week).
2   Excluding mortgage interest payments, council tax and Northern Ireland rates.

Table A34

Household expenditure by tenure, 2008
based on weighted data and including children's expenditure

Commodity or service	Owners			Social rented from		
	Owned outright	Buying with a mortgage[1]	All	Council[2]	Registered Social Landlord[3]	All
Weighted number of households (thousands)	8,010	9,900	17,910	2,720	2,010	4,730
Total number of households in sample	1,950	2,230	4,180	600	440	1,040
Total number of persons in sample	3,780	6,360	10,130	1,290	970	2,260
Total number of adults in sample	3,510	4,480	7,990	900	670	1,570
Weighted average number of persons per household	1.9	2.8	2.4	2.1	2.3	2.2
	Average weekly household expenditure (£)					
1 Food & non-alcoholic drinks	50.50	59.20	55.30	36.10	40.40	38.00
2 Alcoholic drinks, tobacco & narcotics	8.90	12.70	11.00	10.80	10.00	10.50
3 Clothing & footwear	17.60	28.70	23.70	11.40	18.30	14.30
4 Housing(net)[6], fuel & power	36.90	40.40	38.80	51.00	63.20	56.20
5 Household goods & services	32.20	38.70	35.80	14.10	16.30	15.00
6 Health	6.00	6.40	6.20	2.10	3.10	2.50
7 Transport	54.60	93.20	76.00	20.70	30.80	25.00
8 Communication	9.60	15.10	12.60	8.40	10.00	9.10
9 Recreation & culture	69.10	73.60	71.60	28.90	31.40	30.00
10 Education	4.30	8.60	6.70	1.00	1.60	1.20
11 Restaurants & hotels	33.20	52.80	44.00	16.90	19.00	17.80
12 Miscellaneous goods & services	32.30	49.70	41.90	12.90	16.30	14.40
1–12 All expenditure groups	355.20	479.10	423.70	214.30	260.50	234.00
13 Other expenditure items	46.10	157.80	107.90	13.70	23.50	17.90
Total expenditure	401.20	637.00	531.60	228.00	284.00	251.90
Average weekly expenditure per person (£) Total expenditure	210.20	225.90	220.30	108.30	125.50	115.90

Note: The commodity and service categories are not comparable to those in publications before 2001-02.
        Please see page xiii for symbols and conventions used in this report.
1   Including shared owners (who own part of the equity and pay mortgage, part rent).
2   "Council" includes local authorities, New Towns and Scottish Homes, but see note 3 below.
3   Formerly Housing Associations.

Table A34

Household expenditure by tenure, 2008 (cont.)
based on weighted data and including children's expenditure

	Private rented[4]				All tenures
	Rent free	Rent paid unfurn- ished[5]	Rent paid, furnished	All	
Weighted number of households (thousands)	340	2,130	580	3,040	25,690
Total number of households in sample	70	450	110	630	5,850
Total number of persons in sample	120	1,050	270	1,440	13,830
Total number of adults in sample	110	750	220	1,080	10,640
Weighted average number of persons per household	1.7	2.4	2.5	2.3	2.4
Commodity or service	Average weekly household expenditure (£)				
1 Food & non-alcoholic drinks	38.10	43.50	44.90	43.20	50.70
2 Alcoholic drinks, tobacco & narcotics	7.40	10.80	9.20	10.10	10.80
3 Clothing & footwear	13.20	19.50	27.40	20.30	21.60
4 Housing(net)[6], fuel & power	25.50	140.10	162.40	131.70	53.00
5 Household goods & services	21.90	22.50	11.30	20.30	30.10
6 Health	2.40	3.10	1.50	2.70	5.10
7 Transport	47.20	48.60	51.80	49.10	63.40
8 Communication	8.10	13.10	13.40	12.60	12.00
9 Recreation & culture	34.70	40.50	36.50	39.10	60.10
10 Education	[13.10]	10.80	[10.60]	11.00	6.20
11 Restaurants & hotels	20.80	33.20	31.90	31.60	37.70
12 Miscellaneous goods & services	23.20	34.40	26.90	31.70	35.60
1-12 All expenditure groups	255.50	420.10	427.70	403.40	386.30
13 Other expenditure items	32.20	58.60	38.40	51.80	84.60
Total expenditure	287.70	478.70	466.00	455.20	471.00
Average weekly expenditure per person (£) Total expenditure	165.10	203.00	185.70	196.30	199.80

Note: The commodity and service categories are not comparable to those in publications before 2001-02.
Please see page xiii for symbols and conventions used in this report.

4   All tenants whose accommodation goes with the job of someone in the household are allocated to "rented privately", even if the landlord is a local authority, housing association or Housing Action Trust, or if the accommodation is rent free. Squatters are also included in this category.
5   "Unfurnished" includes the answers: "partly furnished".
6   Excluding mortgage interest payments, council tax and Northern Ireland rates.

Table A35

Household expenditure by UK countries and Government Office Regions, 2006–2008

based on weighted data and including children's expenditure

	North East	North West	Yorks & the Humber	East Midlands	West Midlands	East	London
Average weighted number of households (thousands)	1,130	2,930	2,150	1,900	2,150	2,310	3,040
Total number of households in sample (over 3 years)	770	1,890	1,570	1,360	1,510	1,670	1,540
Total number of persons in sample (over 3 years)	1,820	4,490	3,700	3,240	3,730	3,950	3,700
Total number of adults in sample (over 3 years)	1,430	3,390	2,790	2,460	2,820	3,020	2,770
Weighted average number of persons per household	2.4	2.4	2.3	2.3	2.5	2.3	2.5

Commodity or service				Average weekly household expenditure (£)			
1 Food & non-alcoholic drinks	43.10	46.20	45.30	46.80	48.60	49.00	50.20
2 Alcoholic drinks, tobacco & narcotics	10.50	12.20	10.50	10.40	11.80	10.30	10.00
3 Clothing & footwear	21.60	21.50	20.10	19.40	23.80	21.90	26.10
4 Housing(net)[1], fuel & power	42.40	42.70	46.20	43.10	44.70	53.10	73.90
5 Household goods & services	29.40	26.00	30.50	27.50	29.10	34.40	31.90
6 Health	3.60	5.90	4.50	6.30	4.70	6.10	7.00
7 Transport	49.70	52.60	54.60	60.60	59.60	68.70	63.50
8 Communication	10.30	11.20	10.60	11.40	11.50	12.70	14.50
9 Recreation & culture	50.60	56.70	55.50	56.60	58.30	63.80	54.30
10 Education	4.60	4.00	4.50	4.10	4.60	6.00	14.80
11 Restaurants & hotels	33.80	35.70	37.20	35.10	36.10	37.60	45.00
12 Miscellaneous goods & services	28.40	34.10	30.30	32.10	34.60	40.60	39.40
1–12 All expenditure groups	327.90	348.70	349.80	353.20	367.30	404.20	430.60
13 Other expenditure items	58.20	72.50	64.80	69.00	69.80	89.10	114.10
Total expenditure	386.10	421.20	414.60	422.30	437.10	493.40	544.70
Average weekly expenditure per person (£)							
Total expenditure	163.60	175.40	179.90	180.80	177.90	214.10	222.20

Note: The commodity and service categories are not comparable to those in publications before 2001-02.
Please see page xiii for symbols and conventions used in this report.
This table is based on a three year average.

1 Excluding mortgage interest payments, council tax and Northern Ireland rates.

Table A35

Household expenditure by UK countries and Government Office Regions, 2006–2008 (cont.)

based on weighted data and including children's expenditure

	South East	South West	England	Wales	Scotland	Northern Ireland	United Kingdom
Average weighted number of households (thousands)	3,280	2,350	21,240	1,270	2,320	650	25,490
Total number of households in sample (over 3 years)	2,530	1,580	14,440	860	1,580	1,760	18,630
Total number of persons in sample (over 3 years)	6,080	3,540	34,260	1,970	3,530	4,570	44,330
Total number of adults in sample (over 3 years)	4,660	2,850	26,190	1,550	2,790	3,340	33,860
Weighted average number of persons per household	2.3	2.3	2.4	2.3	2.2	2.7	2.4

Commodity or service	Average weekly household expenditure (£)						
1 Food & non-alcoholic drinks	51.70	49.80	48.40	47.70	46.80	55.40	48.40
2 Alcoholic drinks, tobacco & narcotics	10.70	10.30	10.80	11.60	12.30	13.80	11.00
3 Clothing & footwear	21.10	19.90	21.90	19.40	23.30	34.50	22.20
4 Housing(net)[1], fuel & power	55.80	53.30	52.10	47.80	42.30	45.00	50.80
5 Household goods & services	32.90	31.50	30.50	25.70	30.00	32.80	30.30
6 Health	6.40	6.00	5.80	3.50	4.50	4.40	5.60
7 Transport	76.40	65.60	62.50	56.20	59.90	62.80	62.00
8 Communication	11.90	11.70	11.90	10.60	11.00	14.60	11.80
9 Recreation & culture	61.70	63.60	58.30	58.20	59.20	55.90	58.30
10 Education	7.80	8.90	7.10	5.00	4.30	4.60	6.70
11 Restaurants & hotels	39.30	36.70	37.90	30.90	35.40	44.30	37.50
12 Miscellaneous goods & services	42.00	35.20	36.10	29.70	32.50	39.20	35.50
1–12 All expenditure groups	417.50	392.50	383.20	346.30	361.70	407.30	380.00
13 Other expenditure items	94.80	76.70	82.00	60.40	71.10	72.40	79.70
Total expenditure	**512.30**	**469.20**	**465.20**	**406.70**	**432.80**	**479.70**	**459.70**
Average weekly expenditure per person (£) **Total expenditure**	**220.10**	**205.40**	**197.00**	**175.90**	**197.90**	**180.50**	**195.60**

Note: The commodity and service categories are not comparable to those in publications before 2001-02.
Please see page xiii for symbols and conventions used in this report.
This table is based on a three year average.

1   Excluding mortgage interest payments, council tax and Northern Ireland rates.

Table A36

Household expenditure as a percentage of total expenditure by UK countries and Government Office Regions, 2006–2008

based on weighted data and including children's expenditure

	North East	North West	Yorks & the Humber	East Midlands	West Midlands	East	London
Average weighted number of households (thousands)	1,130	2,930	2,150	1,900	2,150	2,310	3,040
Total number of households in sample (over 3 years)	770	1,890	1,570	1,360	1,510	1,670	1,540
Total number of persons in sample (over 3 years)	1,820	4,490	3,700	3,240	3,730	3,950	3,700
Total number of adults in sample (over 3 years)	1,430	3,390	2,790	2,460	2,820	3,020	2,770
Weighted average number of persons per household	2.4	2.4	2.3	2.3	2.5	2.3	2.5

Commodity or service	Percentage of total expenditure						
1 Food & non-alcoholic drinks	11	11	11	11	11	10	9
2 Alcoholic drinks, tobacco & narcotics	3	3	3	2	3	2	2
3 Clothing & footwear	6	5	5	5	5	4	5
4 Housing(net)[1], fuel & power	11	10	11	10	10	11	14
5 Household goods & services	8	6	7	7	7	7	6
6 Health	1	1	1	1	1	1	1
7 Transport	13	12	13	14	14	14	12
8 Communication	3	3	3	3	3	3	3
9 Recreation & culture	13	13	13	13	13	13	10
10 Education	1	1	1	1	1	1	3
11 Restaurants & hotels	9	8	9	8	8	8	8
12 Miscellaneous goods & services	7	8	7	8	8	8	7
1-12 All expenditure groups	85	83	84	84	84	82	79
13 Other expenditure items	15	17	16	16	16	18	21
Total expenditure	100	100	100	100	100	100	100

Note: The commodity and service categories are not comparable to those in publications before 2001-02.
Please see page xiii for symbols and conventions used in this report.
This table is based on a three year average.

1 Excluding mortgage interest payments, council tax and Northern Ireland rates.

Table A36

Household expenditure as a percentage of total expenditure by UK countries and Government Office Regions, 2006–2008 (cont.)
based on weighted data and including children's expenditure

	South East	South West	England	Wales	Scotland	Northern Ireland	United Kingdom
Average weighted number of households (thousands)	3,280	2,350	21,240	1,270	2,320	650	25,490
Total number of households in sample (over 3 years)	2,530	1,580	14,440	860	1,580	1,760	18,630
Total number of persons in sample (over 3 years)	6,080	3,540	34,260	1,970	3,530	4,570	44,330
Total number of adults in sample (over 3 years)	4,660	2,850	26,190	1,550	2,790	3,340	33,860
Weighted average number of persons per household	2.3	2.3	2.4	2.3	2.2	2.7	2.4

Commodity or service			Percentage of total expenditure				
1 Food & non-alcoholic drinks	10	11	10	12	11	12	11
2 Alcoholic drinks, tobacco & narcotics	2	2	2	3	3	3	2
3 Clothing & footwear	4	4	5	5	5	7	5
4 Housing(net)[1], fuel & power	11	11	11	12	10	9	11
5 Household goods & services	6	7	7	6	7	7	7
6 Health	1	1	1	1	1	1	1
7 Transport	15	14	13	14	14	13	13
8 Communication	2	2	3	3	3	3	3
9 Recreation & culture	12	14	13	14	14	12	13
10 Education	2	2	2	1	1	1	1
11 Restaurants & hotels	8	8	8	8	8	9	8
12 Miscellaneous goods & services	8	7	8	7	8	8	8
1-12 All expenditure groups	81	84	82	85	84	85	83
13 Other expenditure items	19	16	18	15	16	15	17
Total expenditure	100	100	100	100	100	100	100

Note: The commodity and service categories are not comparable to those in publications before 2001-02.
Please see page xiii for symbols and conventions used in this report.
This table is based on a three year average.
1   Excluding mortgage interest payments, council tax and Northern Ireland rates.

Table A37

Detailed household expenditure by UK countries and Government Office Regions, 2006–2008

based on weighted data and including children's expenditure

	North East	North West	Yorkshire & the Humber	East Midlands	West Midlands	East	London
Average weighted number of households (thousands)	1,130	2,930	2,150	1,900	2,150	2,310	3,040
Total number of households in sample (over 3 years)	770	1,890	1,570	1,360	1,510	1,670	1,540
Total number of persons in sample (over 3 years)	1,820	4,490	3,700	3,240	3,730	3,950	3,700
Total number of adults in sample (over 3 years)	1,430	3,390	2,790	2,460	2,820	3,020	2,770
Weighted average number of persons per household	2.4	2.4	2.3	2.3	2.5	2.3	2.5

Commodity or service		Average weekly household expenditure (£)					
1 Food & non-alcoholic drinks	**43.10**	**46.20**	**45.30**	**46.80**	**48.60**	**49.00**	**50.20**
1.1 Food	39.60	42.20	41.80	43.00	44.60	45.00	45.70
1.1.1 Bread, rice and cereals	4.30	4.40	4.30	4.50	4.70	4.40	4.60
1.1.2 Pasta products	0.30	0.30	0.30	0.30	0.30	0.30	0.40
1.1.3 Buns, cakes, biscuits etc.	2.80	2.80	2.80	3.00	2.90	3.10	2.60
1.1.4 Pastry (savoury)	0.70	0.70	0.60	0.60	0.60	0.70	0.60
1.1.5 Beef (fresh, chilled or frozen)	1.50	1.60	1.50	1.40	1.70	1.60	1.40
1.1.6 Pork (fresh, chilled or frozen)	0.40	0.50	0.60	0.60	0.70	0.70	0.60
1.1.7 Lamb (fresh, chilled or frozen)	0.30	0.70	0.50	0.50	0.90	0.70	0.90
1.1.8 Poultry (fresh, chilled or frozen)	1.50	1.70	1.60	1.60	1.90	1.80	1.90
1.1.9 Bacon and ham	0.90	1.00	1.00	0.90	0.90	0.80	0.60
1.1.10 Other meat and meat preparations	5.10	5.20	5.00	4.80	5.00	5.10	4.20
1.1.11 Fish and fish products	1.90	2.20	2.10	2.00	2.10	2.30	2.90
1.1.12 Milk	2.50	2.50	2.50	2.60	2.50	2.30	2.20
1.1.13 Cheese and curd	1.30	1.40	1.40	1.60	1.60	1.70	1.60
1.1.14 Eggs	0.50	0.50	0.50	0.50	0.50	0.50	0.60
1.1.15 Other milk products	1.50	1.60	1.60	1.70	1.60	1.90	1.70
1.1.16 Butter	0.30	0.30	0.30	0.30	0.30	0.30	0.30
1.1.17 Margarine, other vegetable fats and peanut butter	0.40	0.40	0.40	0.50	0.50	0.50	0.40
1.1.18 Cooking oils and fats	0.20	0.20	0.20	0.30	0.20	0.20	0.40
1.1.19 Fresh fruit	2.20	2.40	2.60	2.70	2.70	3.00	3.70
1.1.20 Other fresh, chilled or frozen fruits	0.20	0.30	0.30	0.30	0.30	0.30	0.50
1.1.21 Dried fruit and nuts	0.30	0.40	0.40	0.50	0.40	0.60	0.60
1.1.22 Preserved fruit and fruit based products	0.10	0.10	0.10	0.10	0.10	0.10	0.10
1.1.23 Fresh vegetables	2.90	3.10	3.20	3.60	3.60	3.90	4.60
1.1.24 Dried vegetables	0.00	0.00	0.00	0.00	0.00	0.00	0.10
1.1.25 Other preserved or processed vegetables	1.00	1.00	1.00	1.10	1.00	1.10	1.30
1.1.26 Potatoes	0.80	0.80	0.80	0.80	0.90	0.80	0.70
1.1.27 Other tubers and products of tuber vegetables	1.20	1.20	1.20	1.20	1.30	1.20	0.90
1.1.28 Sugar and sugar products	0.20	0.30	0.30	0.30	0.30	0.30	0.30
1.1.29 Jams, marmalades	0.20	0.30	0.30	0.30	0.30	0.30	0.30
1.1.30 Chocolate	1.40	1.40	1.40	1.50	1.50	1.40	1.30
1.1.31 Confectionery products	0.60	0.60	0.60	0.60	0.60	0.50	0.50
1.1.32 Edible ices and ice cream	0.40	0.50	0.40	0.50	0.40	0.50	0.50
1.1.33 Other food products	1.80	2.10	2.00	2.00	2.10	2.00	2.50
1.2 Non-alcoholic drinks	3.50	3.90	3.60	3.80	4.00	4.00	4.40
1.2.1 Coffee	0.50	0.50	0.50	0.50	0.50	0.60	0.40
1.2.2 Tea	0.40	0.40	0.40	0.50	0.50	0.40	0.40
1.2.3 Cocoa and powdered chocolate	0.10	0.10	0.10	0.10	0.10	0.10	0.10
1.2.4 Fruit and vegetable juices (inc. fruit squash)	0.90	1.10	1.00	1.10	1.10	1.20	1.40
1.2.5 Mineral or spring waters	0.20	0.20	0.20	0.20	0.20	0.20	0.50
1.2.6 Soft drinks (inc. fizzy and ready to drink fruit drinks)	1.50	1.60	1.40	1.50	1.60	1.50	1.60

Note: The commodity and service categories are not comparable to those in publications before 2001-02.
The numbering system is sequential, it does not use actual COICOP codes.
Please see page xiii for symbols and conventions used in this report.
This table is based on a three year average.

Table A37

Detailed household expenditure by UK countries and Government Office Regions, 2006–2008 (cont.)

based on weighted data and including children's expenditure

		South East	South West	England	Wales	Scotland	Northern Ireland	United Kingdom
Average weighted number of households (thousands)		3,280	2,350	21,240	1,270	2,320	650	25,490
Total number of households in sample (over 3 years)		2,530	1,580	14,440	860	1,580	1,760	18,630
Total number of persons in sample (over 3 years)		6,080	3,540	34,260	1,970	3,530	4,570	44,330
Total number of adults in sample (over 3 years)		4,660	2,850	26,190	1,550	2,790	3,340	33,860
Weighted average number of persons per household		2.3	2.3	2.4	2.3	2.2	2.7	2.4

Commodity or service		Average weekly household expenditure (£)						
1	**Food & non-alcoholic drinks**	**51.70**	**49.80**	**48.40**	**47.70**	**46.80**	**55.40**	**48.40**
1.1	Food	47.40	46.10	44.40	43.90	42.50	50.60	44.30
1.1.1	Bread, rice and cereals	4.40	4.40	4.50	4.30	4.50	5.80	4.50
1.1.2	Pasta products	0.30	0.30	0.30	0.30	0.40	0.30	0.30
1.1.3	Buns, cakes, biscuits etc.	3.20	3.20	2.90	2.90	3.00	4.10	3.00
1.1.4	Pastry (savoury)	0.70	0.70	0.70	0.70	0.70	0.60	0.70
1.1.5	Beef (fresh, chilled or frozen)	1.50	1.60	1.50	1.80	1.60	3.10	1.60
1.1.6	Pork (fresh, chilled or frozen)	0.60	0.60	0.60	0.70	0.50	0.70	0.60
1.1.7	Lamb (fresh, chilled or frozen)	0.80	0.70	0.70	0.70	0.30	0.50	0.70
1.1.8	Poultry (fresh, chilled or frozen)	1.90	1.80	1.80	1.80	1.60	2.30	1.80
1.1.9	Bacon and ham	0.90	0.90	0.90	1.00	0.90	1.30	0.90
1.1.10	Other meat and meat preparations	5.20	4.90	4.90	5.10	5.50	6.00	5.00
1.1.11	Fish and fish products	2.40	2.20	2.30	2.00	2.10	1.70	2.30
1.1.12	Milk	2.40	2.50	2.40	2.50	2.30	2.90	2.40
1.1.13	Cheese and curd	1.90	1.90	1.60	1.60	1.40	1.30	1.60
1.1.14	Eggs	0.60	0.60	0.50	0.50	0.50	0.50	0.50
1.1.15	Other milk products	2.00	2.00	1.80	1.70	1.60	1.90	1.70
1.1.16	Butter	0.40	0.30	0.30	0.30	0.40	0.40	0.30
1.1.17	Margarine, other vegetable fats and peanut butter	0.50	0.50	0.40	0.50	0.40	0.50	0.40
1.1.18	Cooking oils and fats	0.30	0.30	0.30	0.20	0.20	0.20	0.30
1.1.19	Fresh fruit	3.40	3.30	3.00	2.80	2.60	2.90	2.90
1.1.20	Other fresh, chilled or frozen fruits	0.30	0.30	0.30	0.30	0.40	0.30	0.30
1.1.21	Dried fruit and nuts	0.60	0.60	0.50	0.50	0.40	0.30	0.50
1.1.22	Preserved fruit and fruit based products	0.10	0.20	0.10	0.10	0.10	0.10	0.10
1.1.23	Fresh vegetables	4.40	4.00	3.80	3.40	2.70	3.00	3.70
1.1.24	Dried vegetables	0.00	0.00	0.00	0.00	0.00	0.00	0.00
1.1.25	Other preserved or processed vegetables	1.20	1.20	1.10	1.10	1.00	1.20	1.10
1.1.26	Potatoes	0.90	0.90	0.80	0.90	0.80	1.40	0.80
1.1.27	Other tubers and products of tuber vegetables	1.20	1.30	1.20	1.30	1.40	1.50	1.20
1.1.28	Sugar and sugar products	0.30	0.30	0.30	0.30	0.30	0.20	0.30
1.1.29	Jams, marmalades	0.30	0.30	0.20	0.20	0.30	0.30	0.20
1.1.30	Chocolate	1.40	1.40	1.40	1.50	1.50	1.50	1.40
1.1.31	Confectionery products	0.50	0.50	0.50	0.60	0.60	0.70	0.50
1.1.32	Edible ices and ice cream	0.50	0.50	0.50	0.50	0.50	0.50	0.50
1.1.33	Other food products	2.30	2.20	2.10	2.00	2.10	2.30	2.10
1.2	Non-alcoholic drinks	4.30	3.80	4.00	3.70	4.30	4.80	4.00
1.2.1	Coffee	0.60	0.50	0.50	0.50	0.50	0.40	0.50
1.2.2	Tea	0.40	0.50	0.40	0.40	0.30	0.40	0.40
1.2.3	Cocoa and powdered chocolate	0.10	0.10	0.10	0.10	0.10	0.00	0.10
1.2.4	Fruit and vegetable juices (inc. fruit squash)	1.30	1.20	1.20	1.00	1.10	1.20	1.20
1.2.5	Mineral or spring waters	0.20	0.20	0.20	0.20	0.30	0.30	0.20
1.2.6	Soft drinks (inc. fizzy and ready to drink fruit drinks)	1.60	1.30	1.50	1.50	2.10	2.40	1.60

Note: The commodity and service categories are not comparable to those in publications before 2001-02.
The numbering system is sequential, it does not use actual COICOP codes.
Please see page xiii for symbols and conventions used in this report.
This table is based on a three year average.

Table A37

Detailed household expenditure by UK countries and Government Office Regions, 2006–2008 (cont.)

based on weighted data and including children's expenditure

Commodity or service	North East	North West	Yorkshire & the Humber	East Midlands	West Midlands	East	London
			Average weekly household expenditure (£)				
2 Alcoholic drink, tobacco & narcotics	**10.50**	**12.20**	**10.50**	**10.40**	**11.80**	**10.30**	**10.00**
2.1 Alcoholic drinks	6.00	7.10	6.00	5.90	6.50	6.60	6.00
2.1.1 Spirits and liqueurs (brought home)	1.00	1.50	0.90	1.10	1.50	1.20	1.00
2.1.2 Wines, fortified wines (brought home)	2.90	3.40	2.90	2.90	3.10	3.70	3.60
2.1.3 Beer, lager, ciders and perry (brought home)	2.00	2.10	2.10	1.80	1.90	1.60	1.40
2.1.4 Alcopops (brought home)	0.10	0.10	0.10	0.10	0.10	0.10	0.00
2.2 Tobacco and narcotics	4.50	5.10	4.50	4.50	5.30	3.70	4.00
2.2.1 Cigarettes	4.10	4.60	4.00	4.00	4.60	3.20	3.60
2.2.2 Cigars, other tobacco products and narcotics	0.40	0.50	0.50	0.50	0.70	0.60	0.40
3 Clothing & footwear	**21.60**	**21.50**	**20.10**	**19.40**	**23.80**	**21.90**	**26.10**
3.1 Clothing	17.50	17.10	16.60	15.20	19.10	17.80	20.80
3.1.1 Men's outer garments	4.80	3.80	3.70	4.00	5.00	4.80	5.70
3.1.2 Men's under garments	0.40	0.30	0.40	0.30	0.30	0.30	0.50
3.1.3 Women's outer garments	7.70	7.40	7.80	6.50	8.50	8.00	9.10
3.1.4 Women's under garments	1.00	1.10	1.10	1.00	1.20	1.10	1.40
3.1.5 Boys' outer garments (5-15)	0.70	0.80	0.70	0.80	1.00	0.80	0.60
3.1.6 Girls' outer garments (5-15)	1.00	1.30	1.00	0.90	0.90	0.80	0.90
3.1.7 Infants' outer garments (under 5)	0.80	0.80	0.60	0.60	0.80	0.50	0.60
3.1.8 Children's under garments (under 16)	0.40	0.40	0.30	0.30	0.30	0.30	0.40
3.1.9 Accessories	0.60	0.70	0.70	0.50	0.70	0.70	0.90
3.1.10 Haberdashery, clothing materials and clothing hire	0.10	0.30	0.20	0.20	0.30	0.20	0.20
3.1.11 Dry cleaners, laundry and dyeing	[0.10]	0.20	0.20	0.20	0.30	0.30	0.60
3.2 Footwear	4.10	4.40	3.60	4.10	4.70	4.10	5.40
4 Housing (net)[1], fuel & power	**42.40**	**42.70**	**46.20**	**43.10**	**44.70**	**53.10**	**73.90**
4.1 Actual rentals for housing	26.60	24.50	25.70	23.90	26.20	26.90	62.60
4.1.1 Gross rent	26.40	24.30	25.70	23.70	26.20	26.90	62.60
4.1.2 *less* housing benefit, rebates & allowances rec'd	12.40	12.00	10.60	9.70	11.70	8.50	22.20
4.1.3 Net rent[2]	14.10	12.30	15.10	14.00	14.50	18.40	40.40
4.1.4 Second dwelling rent	[0.20]	[0.30]	[0.00]	[0.20]	–	[0.00]	–
4.2 Maintenance and repair of dwelling	6.00	6.30	7.50	6.40	6.10	9.50	8.60
4.3 Water supply and miscellaneous services relating to the dwelling	6.20	7.10	6.80	6.20	6.50	7.60	9.20
4.4 Electricity, gas and other fuels	15.90	16.70	16.80	16.30	17.70	17.60	15.70
4.4.1 Electricity	7.80	7.80	8.00	7.70	8.40	8.60	7.60
4.4.2 Gas	7.80	8.30	8.20	7.60	8.50	7.20	8.10
4.4.3 Other fuels	[0.30]	0.60	0.60	0.90	0.80	1.80	0.00

Note: The commodity and service categories are not comparable to those in publications before 2001-02.
The numbering system is sequential, it does not use actual COICOP codes.
Please see page xiii for symbols and conventions used in this report.
This table is based on a three year average.

1 Excluding mortgage interest payments, council tax and Northern Ireland rates.
2 The figure included in total expenditure is net rent as opposed to gross rent.

Table A37

Detailed household expenditure by UK countries and Government Office Regions, 2006–2008 (cont.)

based on weighted data and including children's expenditure

Commodity or service	South East	South West	England	Wales	Scotland	Northern Ireland	United Kingdom
			Average weekly household expenditure (£)				
2 Alcoholic drink, tobacco & narcotics	**10.70**	**10.30**	**10.80**	**11.60**	**12.30**	**13.80**	**11.00**
2.1 Alcoholic drinks	6.90	6.50	6.40	6.30	6.50	6.00	6.40
2.1.1 Spirits and liqueurs (brought home)	1.20	1.10	1.20	1.20	1.80	1.40	1.20
2.1.2 Wines, fortified wines (brought home)	3.90	3.60	3.40	3.20	2.90	2.80	3.30
2.1.3 Beer, lager, ciders and perry (brought home)	1.70	1.60	1.80	1.90	1.70	1.70	1.80
2.1.4 Alcopops (brought home)	0.00	0.10	0.10	[0.10]	0.10	0.10	0.10
2.2 Tobacco and narcotics	3.80	3.80	4.30	5.30	5.80	7.80	4.60
2.2.1 Cigarettes	3.20	3.00	3.80	4.50	5.10	7.50	4.00
2.2.2 Cigars, other tobacco products and narcotics	0.50	0.80	0.60	0.80	0.70	0.40	0.60
3 Clothing & footwear	**21.10**	**19.90**	**21.90**	**19.40**	**23.30**	**34.50**	**22.20**
3.1 Clothing	17.20	16.20	17.60	15.80	19.30	27.70	17.90
3.1.1 Men's outer garments	4.20	3.70	4.40	3.80	4.70	7.10	4.50
3.1.2 Men's under garments	0.40	0.40	0.40	0.30	0.30	0.50	0.40
3.1.3 Women's outer garments	7.70	7.50	7.80	7.50	8.70	12.80	8.00
3.1.4 Women's under garments	1.30	1.30	1.20	0.90	1.20	1.40	1.20
3.1.5 Boys' outer garments (5-15)	0.60	0.50	0.70	0.60	0.80	1.40	0.70
3.1.6 Girls' outer garments (5-15)	0.90	0.90	1.00	0.80	1.00	1.80	1.00
3.1.7 Infants' outer garments (under 5)	0.60	0.60	0.60	0.50	0.70	0.90	0.70
3.1.8 Children's under garments (under 16)	0.30	0.20	0.30	0.30	0.40	0.50	0.30
3.1.9 Accessories	0.60	0.60	0.70	0.70	0.90	0.80	0.70
3.1.10 Haberdashery, clothing materials and clothing hire	0.40	0.20	0.20	0.20	0.30	0.40	0.20
3.1.11 Dry cleaners, laundry and dyeing	0.30	0.30	0.30	0.20	0.20	0.30	0.30
3.2 Footwear	3.80	3.70	4.20	3.60	4.00	6.80	4.30
4 Housing (net)[1], fuel & power	**55.80**	**53.30**	**52.10**	**47.80**	**42.30**	**45.00**	**50.80**
4.1 Actual rentals for housing	33.00	26.10	32.10	24.20	21.70	20.80	30.40
4.1.1 Gross rent	32.90	26.10	32.00	24.20	21.70	20.80	30.40
4.1.2 less housing benefit, rebates & allowances rec'd	10.60	8.80	12.20	9.20	10.30	9.00	11.80
4.1.3 Net rent[2]	22.30	17.30	19.80	15.00	11.40	11.80	18.60
4.1.4 Second dwelling rent	[0.10]	[0.00]	[0.10]	–	–	[0.00]	[0.10]
4.2 Maintenance and repair of dwelling	8.80	10.30	7.90	6.40	6.00	8.10	7.70
4.3 Water supply and miscellaneous services relating to the dwelling	7.50	8.30	7.40	7.40	6.60	0.40	7.20
4.4 Electricity, gas and other fuels	17.10	17.40	16.80	18.90	18.40	24.70	17.30
4.4.1 Electricity	8.60	8.70	8.20	8.90	9.10	9.30	8.30
4.4.2 Gas	8.10	6.40	7.80	7.50	7.80	1.70	7.70
4.4.3 Other fuels	0.50	2.30	0.80	2.60	1.50	13.70	1.30

Note: The commodity and service categories are not comparable to those in publications before 2001-02.
The numbering system is sequential, it does not use actual COICOP codes.
Please see page xiii for symbols and conventions used in this report.
This table is based on a three year average.

1 Excluding mortgage interest payments, council tax and Northern Ireland rates.
2 The figure included in total expenditure is net rent as opposed to gross rent.

Table A37

Detailed household expenditure by UK countries and Government Office Regions, 2006–2008 (cont.)

based on weighted data and including children's expenditure

Commodity or service	North East	North West	Yorkshire & the Humber	East Midlands	West Midlands	East	London
	\multicolumn{7}{c}{Average weekly household expenditure (£)}						
5　Household goods & services	**29.40**	**26.00**	**30.50**	**27.50**	**29.10**	**34.40**	**31.90**
5.1　Furniture and furnishings, carpets and other floor coverings	19.80	14.50	17.10	13.90	16.70	19.70	17.90
5.1.1　Furniture and furnishings	15.80	11.00	12.80	10.10	12.90	15.70	14.00
5.1.2　Floor coverings	4.00	3.50	4.30	3.80	3.70	4.00	3.90
5.2　Household textiles	1.60	1.30	1.80	1.40	1.50	1.70	1.90
5.3　Household appliances	1.50	2.80	3.70	3.90	2.60	3.80	3.30
5.4　Glassware, tableware and household utensils	1.10	1.20	1.30	1.20	1.20	1.50	1.60
5.5　Tools and equipment for house and garden	1.40	1.80	2.00	2.20	2.10	2.40	1.80
5.6　Goods and services for routine household maintenance	4.00	4.30	4.60	4.70	5.00	5.20	5.50
5.6.1　Cleaning materials	2.10	1.90	2.10	2.20	2.40	2.30	2.10
5.6.2　Household goods and hardware	0.80	0.90	1.10	1.10	1.10	1.10	1.10
5.6.3　Domestic services, carpet cleaning and hire/repair of furniture/furnishings	1.10	1.50	1.40	1.40	1.60	1.80	2.20
6　Health	**3.60**	**5.90**	**4.50**	**6.30**	**4.70**	**6.10**	**7.00**
6.1　Medical products, appliances and equipment	2.50	2.80	2.90	3.10	2.60	3.70	3.50
6.1.1　Medicines, prescriptions, healthcare products and equipment	1.30	1.60	1.50	1.70	1.50	1.80	2.00
6.1.2　Spectacles, lenses, accessories and repairs	1.20	1.30	1.40	1.40	1.10	1.90	1.50
6.2　Hospital services	1.00	3.10	1.60	3.20	2.00	2.40	3.50
7　Transport	**49.70**	**52.60**	**54.60**	**60.60**	**59.60**	**68.70**	**63.50**
7.1　Purchase of vehicles	16.60	18.90	19.40	22.00	22.50	22.50	19.70
7.1.1　Purchase of new cars and vans	5.80	6.50	6.40	7.10	7.70	7.60	[6.00]
7.1.2　Purchase of second hand cars or vans	10.20	12.10	12.30	14.40	13.60	13.40	13.00
7.1.3　Purchase of motorcycles and other vehicles	[0.60]	0.40	0.70	0.50	1.20	1.50	[0.70]
7.2　Operation of personal transport	25.00	25.20	26.00	31.50	29.50	35.40	23.60
7.2.1　Spares and accessories	3.00	1.10	1.70	2.70	2.10	2.60	1.40
7.2.2　Petrol, diesel and other motor oils	16.40	17.00	17.00	20.40	20.10	21.80	14.50
7.2.3　Repairs and servicing	3.80	4.90	5.10	6.00	4.80	7.90	5.80
7.2.4　Other motoring costs	1.90	2.20	2.20	2.50	2.40	3.10	2.00
7.3　Transport services	8.20	8.50	9.10	7.00	7.60	10.90	20.20
7.3.1　Rail and tube fares	1.20	1.40	1.50	1.00	1.20	4.60	4.00
7.3.2　Bus and coach fares	1.80	1.50	1.80	1.10	1.70	0.80	1.40
7.3.3　Combined fares	[0.20]	0.10	0.40	[0.20]	0.10	0.90	7.00
7.3.4　Other travel and transport	4.90	5.50	5.40	4.80	4.60	4.50	7.70
8　Communication	**10.30**	**11.20**	**10.60**	**11.40**	**11.50**	**12.70**	**14.50**
8.1　Postal services	0.30	0.40	0.40	0.40	0.40	0.60	0.50
8.2　Telephone and telefax equipment	0.60	0.70	0.80	0.70	0.70	0.80	0.60
8.3　Telephone and telefax services	9.40	10.10	9.40	10.30	10.30	11.20	13.40

Note:　The commodity and service categories are not comparable to those in publications before 2001-02.
　　　　The numbering system is sequential, it does not use actual COICOP codes.
　　　　Please see page xiii for symbols and conventions used in this report.
　　　　This table is based on a three year average.

Table A37

Detailed household expenditure by UK countries and Government Office Regions, 2006–2008 (cont.)

based on weighted data and including children's expenditure

Commodity or service	South East	South West	England	Wales	Scotland	Northern Ireland	United Kingdom
			Average weekly household expenditure (£)				
5 Household goods & services	**32.90**	**31.50**	**30.50**	**25.70**	**30.00**	**32.80**	**30.30**
5.1 Furniture and furnishings, carpets and other floor coverings	17.40	16.20	16.90	10.90	17.50	18.50	16.70
5.1.1 Furniture and furnishings	13.10	12.70	13.00	7.80	13.00	14.10	12.80
5.1.2 Floor coverings	4.20	3.40	3.90	3.00	4.50	4.40	3.90
5.2 Household textiles	2.00	1.40	1.70	1.80	1.70	1.90	1.70
5.3 Household appliances	3.80	3.90	3.30	4.40	2.40	3.30	3.30
5.4 Glassware, tableware and household utensils	1.70	1.80	1.50	1.50	1.50	1.30	1.50
5.5 Tools and equipment for house and garden	2.30	2.50	2.10	2.60	2.10	2.40	2.10
5.6 Goods and services for routine household maintenance	5.80	5.70	5.10	4.50	4.90	5.30	5.00
5.6.1 Cleaning materials	2.40	2.30	2.20	2.10	2.00	2.50	2.20
5.6.2 Household goods and hardware	1.40	1.10	1.10	1.10	1.00	1.20	1.10
5.6.3 Domestic services, carpet cleaning and hire/repair of furniture/furnishings	1.90	2.30	1.70	1.30	1.90	1.60	1.70
6 Health	**6.40**	**6.00**	**5.80**	**3.50**	**4.50**	**4.40**	**5.60**
6.1 Medical products, appliances and equipment	3.90	3.30	3.20	2.50	2.30	3.20	3.10
6.1.1 Medicines, prescriptions, healthcare products and equipment	2.00	1.70	1.70	1.40	1.40	2.10	1.70
6.1.2 Spectacles, lenses, accessories and repairs	1.80	1.60	1.50	1.10	0.80	1.20	1.40
6.2 Hospital services	2.50	2.60	2.60	1.00	2.30	1.20	2.40
7 Transport	**76.40**	**65.60**	**62.50**	**56.20**	**59.90**	**62.80**	**62.00**
7.1 Purchase of vehicles	30.70	23.60	22.40	18.70	24.30	19.30	22.30
7.1.1 Purchase of new cars and vans	9.90	7.30	7.30	[8.20]	8.80	8.20	7.50
7.1.2 Purchase of second hand cars or vans	20.20	15.70	14.30	10.00	14.90	10.90	14.10
7.1.3 Purchase of motorcycles and other vehicles	0.60	0.60	0.70	[0.50]	0.60	[0.20]	0.70
7.2 Operation of personal transport	34.70	33.90	29.60	30.70	27.20	34.60	29.50
7.2.1 Spares and accessories	2.80	2.30	2.10	2.10	1.80	2.60	2.10
7.2.2 Petrol, diesel and other motor oils	21.00	21.10	18.80	21.70	18.40	25.10	19.10
7.2.3 Repairs and servicing	8.10	7.90	6.20	5.30	5.20	5.20	6.10
7.2.4 Other motoring costs	2.80	2.60	2.40	1.60	1.90	1.70	2.30
7.3 Transport services	10.90	8.10	10.60	6.80	8.40	8.90	10.10
7.3.1 Rail and tube fares	4.30	1.80	2.60	0.80	1.80	0.70	2.30
7.3.2 Bus and coach fares	0.80	1.10	1.30	1.00	1.70	1.00	1.30
7.3.3 Combined fares	0.90	[0.10]	1.40	[0.00]	[0.20]	[0.10]	1.20
7.3.4 Other travel and transport	4.90	5.20	5.40	4.90	4.60	7.20	5.30
8 Communication	**11.90**	**11.70**	**11.90**	**10.60**	**11.00**	**14.60**	**11.80**
8.1 Postal services	0.60	0.60	0.50	0.50	0.50	0.50	0.50
8.2 Telephone and telefax equipment	0.40	0.50	0.60	0.70	0.60	0.80	0.60
8.3 Telephone and telefax services	10.80	10.50	10.80	9.50	9.80	13.30	10.70

Note: The commodity and service categories are not comparable to those in publications before 2001-02.

The numbering system is sequential, it does not use actual COICOP codes.

Please see page xiii for symbols and conventions used in this report.

This table is based on a three year average.

Table A37

Detailed household expenditure by UK countries and Government Office Regions, 2006–2008 (cont.)

based on weighted data and including children's expenditure

Commodity or service	North East	North West	Yorkshire & the Humber	East Midlands	West Midlands	East	London
				Average weekly household expenditure (£)			
9 Recreation & culture	**50.60**	**56.70**	**55.50**	**56.60**	**58.30**	**63.80**	**54.30**
9.1 Audio-visual, photographic and information processing equipment	5.40	7.70	6.50	6.20	8.70	7.50	5.50
9.1.1 Audio equipment and accessories, CD players	1.10	1.60	1.40	1.80	1.30	2.10	1.50
9.1.2 TV, video and computers	3.80	5.30	4.70	3.50	5.60	4.50	3.30
9.1.3 Photographic, cine and optical equipment	[0.50]	0.80	0.40	0.90	1.90	0.90	0.70
9.2 Other major durables for recreation and culture	[0.30]	2.00	0.80	3.70	2.90	2.40	[4.60]
9.3 Other recreational items and equipment, gardens and pets	8.50	9.30	10.40	10.70	10.20	11.80	8.20
9.3.1 Games, toys and hobbies	2.00	1.80	1.80	2.20	2.10	2.20	1.40
9.3.2 Computer software and games	1.80	1.60	1.30	1.30	1.60	1.20	1.40
9.3.3 Equipment for sport, camping and open-air recreation	0.80	0.90	1.40	0.80	1.00	1.20	1.00
9.3.4 Horticultural goods, garden equipment and plants	1.60	2.30	2.20	2.70	2.40	2.90	2.40
9.3.5 Pets and pet food	2.30	2.80	3.70	3.60	3.20	4.30	1.90
9.4 Recreational and cultural services	17.10	16.60	17.50	18.20	16.60	19.80	17.60
9.4.1 Sports admissions, subscriptions, leisure class fees and equipment hire	4.10	4.30	5.30	5.60	4.10	6.70	6.10
9.4.2 Cinema, theatre and museums etc.	1.60	1.70	1.80	2.10	1.60	2.30	2.10
9.4.3 TV, video, satellite rental, cable subscriptions, TV licences and the Internet	5.60	6.00	5.70	5.90	5.40	6.30	5.50
9.4.4 Miscellaneous entertainments	0.90	1.10	1.10	1.20	1.00	1.10	1.20
9.4.5 Development of film, deposit for film development, passport photos, holiday and school photos	0.40	0.20	0.30	0.40	0.30	0.40	0.40
9.4.6 Gambling payments	4.50	3.40	3.20	3.00	4.20	2.90	2.30
9.5 Newspapers, books and stationery	5.50	5.90	6.00	6.00	6.40	6.20	6.20
9.5.1 Books	1.30	1.30	1.40	1.20	1.50	1.30	1.90
9.5.2 Diaries, address books, cards etc.	1.60	1.80	1.80	2.00	2.10	2.00	1.60
9.5.3 Newspapers	1.90	1.80	1.70	1.80	1.80	1.90	1.70
9.5.4 Magazines and periodicals	0.80	1.00	1.00	1.00	1.00	1.00	0.90
9.6 Package holidays	13.70	15.10	14.30	11.80	13.50	16.10	12.20
9.6.1 Package holidays - UK	0.90	1.00	1.20	0.90	1.20	1.50	[0.50]
9.6.2 Package holidays - abroad	12.80	14.20	13.10	10.90	12.30	14.60	11.70
10 Education	**4.60**	**4.00**	**4.50**	**4.10**	**4.60**	**6.00**	**14.80**
10.1 Education fees	4.30	3.70	4.00	3.80	4.40	5.70	14.40
10.2 Payments for school trips, other ad-hoc expenditure	0.30	0.40	0.40	0.30	0.30	0.40	0.40
11 Restaurants & hotels	**33.80**	**35.70**	**37.20**	**35.10**	**36.10**	**37.60**	**45.00**
11.1 Catering services	29.60	29.40	31.60	29.70	30.10	30.60	37.90
11.1.1 Restaurant and café meals	10.10	11.00	12.10	12.30	11.90	13.30	15.70
11.1.2 Alcoholic drinks (away from home)	9.00	7.90	8.80	7.90	7.30	7.30	8.90
11.1.3 Take away meals eaten at home	4.50	4.10	4.00	3.80	4.00	3.60	4.30
11.1.4 Other take-away and snack food	4.00	4.00	4.30	3.50	3.80	4.10	6.40
11.1.5 Contract catering (food) and canteens	2.00	2.50	2.40	2.20	3.00	2.30	2.70
11.2 Accommodation services	4.20	6.30	5.60	5.40	5.90	7.00	7.10
11.2.1 Holiday in the UK	1.90	2.60	2.80	2.60	3.20	3.00	2.10
11.2.2 Holiday abroad	2.30	3.60	2.80	2.70	2.70	4.00	5.10
11.2.3 Room hire	[0.00]	[0.00]	[0.00]	[0.00]	[0.00]	[0.00]	[0.00]

Note: The commodity and service categories are not comparable to those in publications before 2001-02.
The numbering system is sequential, it does not use actual COICOP codes.
Please see page xiii for symbols and conventions used in this report.
This table is based on a three year average.

Table A37

Detailed household expenditure by UK countries and Government Office Regions, 2006–2008 (cont.)

based on weighted data and including children's expenditure

Commodity or service	South East	South West	England	Wales	Scotland	Northern Ireland	United Kingdom
			Average weekly household expenditure (£)				
9 Recreation & culture	**61.70**	**63.60**	**58.30**	**58.20**	**59.20**	**55.90**	**58.30**
9.1 Audio-visual, photographic and information processing equipment	8.00	9.10	7.30	6.20	8.10	7.20	7.30
9.1.1 Audio equipment and accessories, CD players	1.70	1.60	1.60	1.40	1.40	1.40	1.60
9.1.2 TV, video and computers	5.40	6.80	4.80	4.40	6.30	5.30	4.90
9.1.3 Photographic, cine and optical equipment	0.80	0.70	0.80	0.50	0.40	0.50	0.80
9.2 Other major durables for recreation and culture	2.00	2.00	2.50	7.30	2.30	1.50	2.70
9.3 Other recreational items and equipment, gardens and pets	12.00	11.50	10.40	10.40	10.70	11.30	10.40
9.3.1 Games, toys and hobbies	2.00	1.90	1.90	1.70	1.90	2.80	1.90
9.3.2 Computer software and games	1.60	1.10	1.40	1.10	2.10	1.50	1.50
9.3.3 Equipment for sport, camping and open-air recreation	1.10	1.30	1.10	1.10	0.70	1.80	1.10
9.3.4 Horticultural goods, garden equipment and plants	3.00	3.20	2.60	2.50	3.20	2.50	2.60
9.3.5 Pets and pet food	4.40	4.00	3.40	4.10	2.90	2.70	3.40
9.4 Recreational and cultural services	18.40	17.20	17.70	15.60	18.30	17.60	17.60
9.4.1 Sports admissions, subscriptions, leisure class fees and equipment hire	5.80	5.30	5.30	4.30	4.90	4.80	5.20
9.4.2 Cinema, theatre and museums etc.	2.10	2.10	2.00	1.90	2.00	2.00	2.00
9.4.3 TV, video, satellite rental, cable subscriptions, TV licences and the Internet	5.90	5.30	5.70	5.50	6.10	5.70	5.80
9.4.4 Miscellaneous entertainments	1.00	1.50	1.10	0.80	0.80	1.30	1.10
9.4.5 Development of film, deposit for film development, passport photos, holiday and school photos	0.50	0.30	0.40	0.20	0.30	0.40	0.40
9.4.6 Gambling payments	3.00	2.60	3.10	3.00	4.10	3.50	3.20
9.5 Newspapers, books and stationery	7.20	6.80	6.30	6.00	6.70	6.80	6.30
9.5.1 Books	1.90	1.50	1.50	1.30	1.50	1.20	1.50
9.5.2 Diaries, address books, cards etc.	2.30	2.20	1.90	1.90	1.90	1.80	1.90
9.5.3 Newspapers	1.90	2.00	1.80	1.90	2.50	2.60	1.90
9.5.4 Magazines and periodicals	1.10	1.10	1.00	0.90	1.00	1.10	1.00
9.6 Package holidays	14.10	17.00	14.20	12.60	13.20	11.40	14.00
9.6.1 Package holidays - UK	1.10	1.00	1.00	1.00	0.60	0.60	1.00
9.6.2 Package holidays - abroad	12.90	16.00	13.20	11.70	12.60	10.80	13.00
10 Education	**7.80**	**8.90**	**7.10**	**5.00**	**4.30**	**4.60**	**6.70**
10.1 Education fees	7.50	8.60	6.70	4.70	4.10	4.00	6.30
10.2 Payments for school trips, other ad-hoc expenditure	0.30	0.40	0.30	0.30	0.20	0.60	0.30
11 Restaurants & hotels	**39.30**	**36.70**	**37.90**	**30.90**	**35.40**	**44.30**	**37.50**
11.1 Catering services	31.10	28.80	31.30	28.30	30.70	39.80	31.30
11.1.1 Restaurant and café meals	14.30	13.10	12.90	11.20	12.10	15.50	12.80
11.1.2 Alcoholic drinks (away from home)	7.10	7.40	7.90	8.00	7.20	8.60	7.80
11.1.3 Take away meals eaten at home	3.60	3.20	3.90	3.60	4.00	6.80	3.90
11.1.4 Other take-away and snack food	3.90	3.10	4.20	3.80	4.20	5.90	4.20
11.1.5 Contract catering (food) and canteens	2.20	2.00	2.40	1.70	3.30	3.00	2.40
11.2 Accommodation services	8.10	7.90	6.60	2.60	4.70	4.50	6.20
11.2.1 Holiday in the UK	3.30	3.30	2.80	1.10	2.10	0.90	2.60
11.2.2 Holiday abroad	4.80	4.50	3.80	1.50	2.60	3.60	3.60
11.2.3 Room hire	[0.00]	[0.00]	0.00	[0.00]	[0.00]	[0.00]	0.00

Note: The commodity and service categories are not comparable to those in publications before 2001-02.
The numbering system is sequential, it does not use actual COICOP codes.
Please see page xiii for symbols and conventions used in this report.
This table is based on a three year average.

Table A37

Detailed household expenditure by UK countries and Government Office Regions, 2006–2008 (cont.)

based on weighted data and including children's expenditure

	North East	North West	Yorkshire & the Humber	East Midlands	West Midlands	East	London
Commodity or service			Average weekly household expenditure (£)				
12 Miscellaneous goods & services	**28.40**	**34.10**	**30.30**	**32.10**	**34.60**	**40.60**	**39.40**
12.1 Personal care	8.80	9.20	9.70	8.70	9.70	10.40	10.40
12.1.1 Hairdressing, beauty treatment	2.60	3.00	3.30	2.50	3.10	3.50	2.90
12.1.2 Toilet paper	0.60	0.70	0.70	0.70	0.70	0.80	0.70
12.1.3 Toiletries and soap	1.60	1.80	2.00	1.90	2.00	2.10	2.20
12.1.4 Baby toiletries and accessories (disposable)	0.50	0.60	0.60	0.60	0.70	0.60	0.70
12.1.5 Hair products, cosmetics and electrical personal appliances	3.50	3.10	3.10	2.90	3.20	3.40	3.80
12.2 Personal effects	2.80	2.90	2.70	2.50	3.30	2.70	4.60
12.3 Social protection	2.50	3.40	2.20	2.30	3.30	3.30	3.40
12.4 Insurance	11.70	14.80	12.90	13.90	14.70	16.30	15.40
12.4.1 Household insurances - structural, contents and appliances	4.40	4.90	4.90	4.80	4.80	5.20	5.20
12.4.2 Medical insurance premiums	0.60	1.30	1.00	1.20	1.60	2.10	2.20
12.4.3 Vehicle insurance including boat insurance	6.70	8.10	6.80	7.80	8.10	8.80	7.80
12.4.4 Non-package holiday, other travel insurance	[0.10]	[0.40]	[0.20]	[0.20]	[0.20]	[0.10]	[0.20]
12.5 Other services n.e.c	2.60	3.80	2.80	4.70	3.50	7.90	5.60
12.5.1 Moving house	1.30	1.70	1.40	2.60	1.90	4.10	3.10
12.5.2 Bank, building society, post office, credit card charges	0.40	0.30	0.30	0.40	0.40	0.40	0.50
12.5.3 Other services and professional fees	0.90	1.80	1.00	1.70	1.30	3.50	1.90
1–12 All expenditure groups	**327.90**	**348.70**	**349.80**	**353.20**	**367.30**	**404.20**	**430.60**
13 Other expenditure items	**58.20**	**72.50**	**64.80**	**69.00**	**69.80**	**89.10**	**114.10**
13.1 Housing: mortgage interest payments council tax etc.	43.60	47.40	45.20	50.00	51.40	61.90	71.50
13.2 Licences, fines and transfers	2.30	2.70	3.00	3.10	2.90	3.50	2.90
13.3 Holiday spending	4.00	13.30	7.50	8.10	6.00	9.80	24.70
13.4 Money transfers and credit	8.20	9.20	9.10	7.90	9.50	13.90	14.90
13.4.1 Money, cash gifts given to children	[0.10]	0.10	0.10	0.10	0.10	0.10	[0.10]
13.4.2 Cash gifts and donations	7.10	7.90	7.60	6.10	7.80	12.00	12.60
13.4.3 Club instalment payments (child) and interest on credit cards	1.10	1.20	1.40	1.70	1.60	1.80	2.30
Total expenditure	**386.10**	**421.20**	**414.60**	**422.30**	**437.10**	**493.40**	**544.70**
14 Other items recorded							
14.1 Life assurance, contributions to pension funds	15.80	17.90	18.60	19.10	19.50	24.20	23.00
14.2 Other insurance inc. friendly societies	0.70	1.10	1.60	1.20	1.20	1.50	1.00
14.3 Income tax, payments *less* refunds	62.30	78.40	70.90	83.80	84.40	99.10	148.10
14.4 National insurance contributions	24.50	24.90	23.60	25.20	26.00	28.60	33.70
14.5 Purchase or alteration of dwellings, mortgages	41.10	51.70	51.00	35.30	44.30	50.30	42.10
14.6 Savings and investments	4.00	5.30	4.60	5.10	5.00	7.00	9.30
14.7 Pay off loan to clear other debt	1.90	2.20	2.50	2.50	3.20	2.50	2.40
14.8 Windfall receipts from gambling etc[3]	2.10	2.30	2.00	1.60	1.80	1.70	1.60

Note: The commodity and service categories are not comparable to those in publications before 2001-02.
The numbering system is sequential, it does not use actual COICOP codes.
Please see page xiii for symbols and conventions used in this report.
This table is based on a three year average.

3   Expressed as an income figure as opposed to an expenditure figure.

Table A37

Detailed household expenditure by UK countries and Government Office Regions, 2006–2008 (cont.)

based on weighted data and including children's expenditure

Commodity or service	South East	South West	England	Wales	Scotland	Northern Ireland	United Kingdom
	Average weekly household expenditure (£)						
12 Miscellaneous goods & services	**42.00**	**35.20**	**36.10**	**29.70**	**32.50**	**39.20**	**35.50**
12.1 Personal care	10.80	9.40	9.80	8.70	9.80	12.30	9.80
12.1.1 Hairdressing, beauty treatment	3.80	2.80	3.10	2.60	3.40	4.00	3.10
12.1.2 Toilet paper	0.80	0.80	0.70	0.70	0.70	0.90	0.70
12.1.3 Toiletries and soap	2.30	2.10	2.00	2.00	1.90	2.50	2.00
12.1.4 Baby toiletries and accessories (disposable)	0.70	0.50	0.60	0.50	0.50	0.70	0.60
12.1.5 Hair products, cosmetics and electrical personal appliances	3.40	3.20	3.30	2.90	3.40	4.20	3.30
12.2 Personal effects	4.30	2.90	3.30	2.30	3.70	3.00	3.30
12.3 Social protection	3.40	2.50	3.00	2.50	2.50	3.40	3.00
12.4 Insurance	17.00	15.00	15.00	13.10	12.20	15.70	14.60
12.4.1 Household insurances - structural, contents and appliances	5.50	5.10	5.00	4.70	4.90	4.40	5.00
12.4.2 Medical insurance premiums	2.60	2.00	1.70	0.80	1.10	1.00	1.60
12.4.3 Vehicle insurance including boat insurance	8.70	7.70	7.90	7.50	6.00	10.20	7.80
12.4.4 Non-package holiday, other travel insurance	0.20	[0.30]	0.20	[0.10]	[0.20]	[0.10]	0.20
12.5 Other services n.e.c	6.40	5.30	5.00	3.10	4.20	4.90	4.80
12.5.1 Moving house	4.90	3.30	2.90	1.60	2.40	1.50	2.70
12.5.2 Bank, building society, post office, credit card charges	0.50	0.50	0.40	0.30	0.40	0.50	0.40
12.5.3 Other services and professional fees	1.00	1.50	1.70	1.10	1.40	2.90	1.70
1–12 All expenditure groups	**417.50**	**392.50**	**383.20**	**346.30**	**361.70**	**407.30**	**380.00**
13 Other expenditure items	**94.80**	**76.70**	**82.00**	**60.40**	**71.10**	**72.40**	**79.70**
13.1 Housing: mortgage interest payments, council tax etc.	67.70	54.80	56.60	41.00	49.10	39.80	54.70
13.2 Licences, fines and transfers	3.50	3.60	3.10	3.00	2.60	3.30	3.10
13.3 Holiday spending	12.30	8.60	11.60	8.70	8.50	13.50	11.20
13.4 Money transfers and credit	11.30	9.80	10.80	7.80	10.80	15.80	10.70
13.4.1 Money, cash gifts given to children	0.10	0.10	0.10	[0.10]	0.10	0.20	0.10
13.4.2 Cash gifts and donations	9.20	7.70	8.90	6.30	9.10	14.70	9.00
13.4.3 Club instalment payments (child) and interest on credit cards	2.00	2.00	1.70	1.40	1.70	0.90	1.70
Total expenditure	**512.30**	**469.20**	**465.20**	**406.70**	**432.80**	**479.70**	**459.70**
14 Other items recorded							
14.1 Life assurance, contributions to pension funds	23.20	23.00	20.90	17.90	20.60	17.30	20.60
14.2 Other insurance inc. friendly societies	1.60	1.50	1.30	0.70	1.20	0.90	1.20
14.3 Income tax, payments *less* refunds	120.20	85.70	97.40	68.60	82.60	72.50	94.00
14.4 National insurance contributions	29.20	25.00	27.20	22.80	25.80	23.50	26.80
14.5 Purchase or alteration of dwellings, mortgages	53.70	41.30	46.50	34.10	49.40	33.60	45.70
14.6 Savings and investments	8.20	10.20	6.90	3.40	6.40	5.90	6.60
14.7 Pay off loan to clear other debt	3.30	2.60	2.60	1.80	2.10	0.50	2.50
14.8 Windfall receipts from gambling etc[3]	2.10	1.10	1.80	1.50	2.10	2.20	1.90

Note: The commodity and service categories are not comparable to those in publications before 2001-02.
The numbering system is sequential, it does not use actual COICOP codes.
Please see page xiii for symbols and conventions used in this report.
This table is based on a three year average.
3   Expressed as an income figure as opposed to an expenditure figure.

Table A38

Household expenditure by urban/rural areas (GB)[1], 2006–2008
based on weighted data and including children's expenditure

	Urban	Rural
Average number of weighted households (thousands)	19,540	5,300
Total number of households in sample (over 3 years)	13,070	3,810
Total number of persons in sample (over 3 years)	30,900	8,860
Total number of adults in sample (over 3 years)	23,590	6,940
Weighted average number of persons per household	2.4	2.3

Commodity or service	Average weekly household expenditure (£)	
1 Food & non-alcoholic drinks	47.20	51.80
2 Alcoholic drinks, tobacco & narcotics	10.70	11.80
3 Clothing & footwear	22.00	21.40
4 Housing (net)[2], fuel & power	51.00	50.70
5 Household goods & services	28.70	35.90
6 Health	5.20	6.90
7 Transport	58.10	76.10
8 Communication	11.80	11.50
9 Recreation & culture	56.00	67.40
10 Education	6.20	8.70
11 Restaurants & hotels	36.80	39.20
12 Miscellaneous goods & services	34.40	39.30
1-12 All expenditure groups	368.10	420.60
13 Other expenditure items	78.60	84.80
Total expenditure	**446.70**	**505.40**
Average weekly expenditure per person (£)		
Total expenditure	**189.80**	**219.40**

Note: The commodity and service categories are not comparable to those in publications before 2001-02.
        Please see page xiii for symbols and conventions used in this report.
        This table is based on a three year average.
1   Combined urban/rural classification for England & Wales and Scotland - see definitions in Appendix B.
2   Excludes mortgage interest payments and council tax.

Table A39

Government Office Regions of the United Kingdom

Table A40

Income and source of income by household composition, 2008

based on weighted data

Composition of household	Weighted number of house-holds	Number of house-holds in the sample	Weekly household income		Source of income					
			Dispo-sable	Gross	Wages and salaries	Self employ-ment	Invest-ments	Annuities and pensions[1]	Social security benefits[2]	other sources
	(000s)	Number	£	£	Percentage of gross weekly household income					
All households	25,690	5,850	582	713	67	9	4	7	12	1
Composition of household										
One adult	7,490	1,620	280	333	52	6	3	13	25	0
Retired households mainly dependent on state pensions[3]	970	200	158	159	–	–	2	3	95	[0]
Other retired households	2,660	570	226	244	–	–	7	39	54	0
Non-retired households	3,860	850	347	438	77	9	2	4	8	0
One adult, one child	830	200	297	337	56	[6]	1	[1]	32	3
One adult, two or more children	650	180	315	346	40	[3]	0	[0]	52	4
One man and one woman	7,590	1,860	607	746	62	8	4	13	13	0
Retired households mainly dependent on state pensions[3]	540	150	247	249	[0]	[0]	2	7	91	[0]
Other retired households	2,000	530	419	466	5	[1]	9	42	43	0
Non-retired households	5,050	1,170	720	910	75	10	3	7	4	0
Two men or two women	560	110	554	677	79	[5]	1	4	9	[2]
Two men or two women with children	120	30	392	434	56	[5]	[0]	[0]	36	[2]
One man one woman, one child	1,860	420	689	869	79	11	2	1	6	0
One man one woman, two children	2,150	540	884	1,098	73	18	2	[0]	6	1
One man one woman, three children	640	160	1,626	2,071	71	5	18	[0]	5	1
Two adults, four or more children	180	50	658	785	55	[14]	[2]	[0]	28	1
Three adults	1,610	320	819	1,005	73	9	3	7	8	1
Three adults, one or more children	830	180	802	978	77	10	2	1	10	1
Four or more adults	870	150	985	1,213	79	9	1	2	6	3
Four or more adults, One or more children	290	60	851	1,015	74	[6]	1	[2]	16	[1]

Note: Please see page xiii for symbols and conventions used in this report.
1   Other than social security benefits.
2   Excluding housing benefit and council tax benefit (rates rebate in Northern Ireland) - see definitions in Appendix B.
3   Mainly dependent on state pension and not economically active - see defintions in Appendix B.

Table A41

Income and source of income by age of household reference person, 2008

based on weighted data

Age of head of household	Weighted number of house-holds	Number of house-holds in the sample	Weekly household income		Source of income					
			Dispo-sable	Gross	Wages and salaries	Self employ-ment	Invest-ments	Annuities and pensions[1]	Social security benefits[2]	Other sources
	(000s)	Number	£	£	Percentage of gross weekly household income					
Less than 30	2,530	460	492	600	83	6	0	0	8	3
30 to 49	9,740	2,230	751	945	78	11	4	[0]	6	1
50 to 64	6,750	1,590	622	771	67	10	4	9	8	1
65 to 74	3,140	810	388	434	18	5	6	29	41	1
75 or over	3,520	760	272	290	3	[2]	6	32	57	0

Note: Please see page xiii for symbols and conventions used in this report.
1   Other than social security benefits.
2   Excluding housing benefit and council tax benefit (rates rebate in Northern Ireland) - see definitions in Appendix B.

Table A42

Income and source of income by gross income quintile group, 2008
based on weighted data

Gross income quintile group	Weighted number of house- holds	Number of house- holds in the sample	Weekly household income		Source of income					
			Dispo- sable	Gross	Wages and salaries	Self employ- ment	Invest- ments	Annuities and pensions[1]	Social security benefits[2]	Other sources
	(000s)	Number	£	£	Percentage of gross weekly household income					
Lowest twenty per cent	5,140	1,120	141	146	6	2	2	9	80	1
Second quintile group	5,130	1,240	285	310	31	4	3	16	45	1
Third quintile group	5,140	1,190	450	528	59	6	3	13	18	1
Fourth quintile group	5,140	1,160	673	826	75	8	2	7	7	1
Highest twenty per cent	5,140	1,130	1,359	1,757	77	12	5	3	2	0

Note: Please see page xiii for symbols and conventions used in this report.
1   Other than social security benefits.
2   Excluding housing benefit and council tax benefit (rates rebate in Northern Ireland) - see definitions in Appendix B.

Table A43

Income and source of income by household tenure, 2008
based on weighted data

Tenure of dwelling	Weighted number of house- holds	Number of house- holds in the sample	Weekly household income		Source of income					
			Dispo- sable	Gross	Wages and salaries	Self employ- ment	Invest- ments	Annuities and pensions[1]	Social security benefits[2]	Other sources
	(000s)	Number	£	£	Percentage of gross weekly household income					
Owners										
Owned outright	8,010	1,950	488	577	41	9	7	21	21	0
Buying with a mortgage[3]	9,900	2,230	788	998	80	11	2	2	4	1
All	17,910	4,180	654	810	68	10	3	8	10	1
Social rented from										
Council[4]	2,720	600	255	281	43	4	0	4	48	1
Registered social landlord[5]	2,010	440	314	354	51	[2]	0	5	41	1
All	4,730	1,040	280	312	47	3	0	4	45	1
Private rented[6]										
Rent free	340	70	356	418	65	[5]	2	[5]	21	[2]
Rent paid, unfurnished[7]	2,130	450	710	877	72	6	13	1	8	1
Rent paid, furnished	580	110	469	568	80	[5]	1	–	5	10
All	3,040	630	625	768	72	6	11	1	8	2

Note: Please see page xiii for symbols and conventions used in this report.
1   Other than social security benefits.
2   Excluding housing benefit and council tax benefit (rates rebate in Northern Ireland) - see defintions in Appendix B.
3   Including shared owners (who own part of the equity and pay mortgage, part rent).
4   "Council" includes local authorities, new towns, and Scottish homes, but see note 5 below.
5   Formerly housing association.
6   All tenants whose accomodation goes with the job of someone in the household are allocated to "rented privately", even if the landlord is a local authority, housing association, or housing action trust, or if the accomodation is rent free. Squatters are also included in this category.
7   'Unfurnished' includes the answers: 'partly furnished'.

Table A44

Income and source of income by UK countries and Government Office Regions, 2006–2008

based on weighted data

Government Office Regions	Weighted number of house-holds	Total number of house-holds	Weekly household income		Source of income					
			Dispo-sable	Gross	Wages and salaries	Self employ-ment	Invest-ments	Annuities and pensions[1]	Social security benefits[2]	Other sources
	(000s)	Number	£	£	Percentage of gross weekly household income					
United Kingdom	25,490	18,630	544	669	67	9	4	7	13	1
North East	1,130	770	449	538	68	6	2	6	17	1
North West	2,930	1,890	482	587	66	7	2	8	16	1
Yorkshire and the Humber	2,150	1,570	475	575	67	8	2	7	15	1
East Midlands	1,900	1,360	496	610	66	7	5	7	14	1
West Midlands	2,150	1,510	509	622	67	9	2	6	14	1
East	2,310	1,670	579	712	68	10	3	8	11	1
London	3,040	1,540	712	900	73	8	5	4	8	1
South East	3,280	2,530	626	783	66	12	4	7	10	1
South West	2,350	1,580	528	642	62	10	4	10	13	1
England	21,240	14,440	554	683	67	9	4	7	12	1
Wales	1,270	860	474	570	64	9	3	8	15	1
Scotland	2,320	1,580	499	611	67	8	3	8	14	1
Northern Ireland	650	1,760	512	616	66	10	2	6	15	1

Note: Please see page xiii for symbols and conventions used in this report.
This table is based on a three year average.
1 Other than social security benefits.
2 Excluding housing benefit and council tax benefit (rates rebate in Northern Ireland) - see defintions in Appendix B.

Table A45

Income and source of income by GB urban/rural area, 2006–2008

based on weighted data

GB urban rural areas	Weighted number of house-holds	Total number of house-holds	Weekly household income		Source of income					
			Dispo-sable	Gross	Wages and salaries	Self employ-ment	Invest-ments	Annuities and pensions[1]	Social security benefits[2]	Other sources
	(000s)	Number	£	£	Percentage of gross weekly household income					
Urban	19,540	13,070	532	655	69	8	3	6	13	1
Rural	5,300	3,810	591	729	61	12	5	9	11	1

Note: Please see page xiii for symbols and conventions used in this report.
This table is based on a three year average
1 Other than social security benefits.
2 Excluding housing benefit and council tax benefit (rates rebate in Northern Ireland) - see defintions in Appendix B.

Table A46
Income and source of income by socio-economic classification, 2008
based on weighted data

NS-SEC Group[3]	Weighted number of house-holds	Number of house-holds in the sample	Weekly household income Dispo-sable	Weekly household income Gross	Source of income Wages and salaries	Source of income Self employ-ment	Source of income Invest-ments	Source of income Annuities and pensions[1]	Source of income Social security benefits[2]	Source of income Other sources
	(000s)	Number	£	£	Percentage of gross weekly household income					
Large employers/higher managerial	1,190	260	1,502	1,985	85	1	11	1	1	0
Higher professional	1,940	430	1,057	1,359	73	19	3	2	2	1
Lower managerial and professional	4,590	1,040	783	1,011	86	6	2	3	3	1
Intermediate	1,310	290	533	654	82	3	2	4	8	1
Small employers	1,510	360	686	765	23	65	3	2	7	1
Lower supervisory	1,790	390	615	766	89	[2]	1	2	6	1
Semi-routine	1,930	420	464	554	81	[2]	1	3	12	1
Routine	1,700	380	451	544	83	[1]	1	3	13	0
Long-term unemployed[4]	520	120	264	285	34	[0]	1	[3]	61	[1]
Students	320	60	421	477	63	[4]	[1]	[0]	9	23
Occupation not stated[5]	8,900	2,080	309	338	12	2	7	31	49	1

Note: Please see page xiii for symbols and conventions used in this report.
1   Other than social security benefits.
2   Excluding housing benefit and council tax benefit (rates rebate in Northern Ireland) - see definitions in Appendix B.
3   National Statistics Socio-Economic Classification (NS-SEC) - see defintions in Appendix B.
4   Includes those who have never worked.
5   Includes those who are economically inactive - see defintions in Appendix B.

Table A47
Income and source of income, 1970 to 2008

	Weighted number of house-holds	Number of house-holds in the sample	Weekly household income[1] Current prices Dispo-sable	Weekly household income[1] Current prices Gross	Weekly household income[1] Constant prices Dispo-sable	Weekly household income[1] Constant prices Gross	Source of income Wages and salaries	Source of income Self employ-ment	Source of income Invest-ments	Source of income Annuities and pensions[2]	Source of income Social security benefits[3]	Source of income Other sources
	(000s)	Number	£	£	£	£	Percentage of gross weekly household income					
1970		6,390	28	34	330	398	77	7	4	3	9	1
1980		6,940	115	140	369	451	75	6	3	3	13	1
1990		7,050	258	317	439	540	67	10	6	5	11	1
1995-96		6,800	307	381	439	545	64	9	5	7	14	2
1996-97		6,420	325	397	454	555	65	9	4	7	14	1
1997-98		6,410	343	421	464	569	67	8	4	7	13	1
1998-99[4]	24,660	6,630	371	457	487	599	68	8	4	7	12	1
1999-2000	25,340	7,100	391	480	505	620	66	10	5	7	12	1
2000-01	25,030	6,640	409	503	513	630	67	9	4	7	12	1
2001-02[5]	24,450	7,470	442	541	546	668	68	8	4	7	12	1
2002-03	24,350	6,930	453	552	549	668	68	8	3	7	12	1
2003-04	24,670	7,050	464	570	546	671	67	9	3	7	13	1
2004-05	24,430	6,800	489	601	558	686	68	8	3	7	13	1
2005-06	24,800	6,790	500	616	557	685	67	8	3	7	13	1
2006[6]	24,790	6,650	521	642	565	696	67	9	3	7	12	1
2006[7]	25,440	6,650	515	635	559	688	67	9	3	7	13	1
2007	25,350	6,140	534	659	555	686	67	8	4	7	13	1
2008	25,690	5,850	582	713	582	713	67	9	4	7	12	1

Note: Please see page xiii for symbols and conventions used in this report.
1   Does not include imputed income from owner-occupied and rent-free households.
2   Other than social security benefits.
3   Excluding housing benefit and council tax benefit (rates rebate in Northern Ireland) and their predecessors in earlier years - see Appendix B.
4   Based on weighted data from 1998-99.
5   From 2001-02 onwards, weighting is based on the population estimates from the 2001 Census.
6   From 1998-99 to this version of 2006, figures shown are based on weighted data using non-response weights based on the 1991 Census and population figures from the 1991 and 2001 Censuses.
7   From this version of 2006, figures shown are based on weighted data using updated weights, with non-response weights and population figures based on the 2001 Census.

Table A48

Characteristics of households, 2008
based on weighted data

	% [1] of all house-holds	Weighted number of house-holds (000s)	House-holds in sample (number)		% [1] of all house-holds	Weighted number of house-holds (000s)	House-holds in sample (number)
Total number of households	100	25,690	5,850	**Composition of household (cont)**			
				Four adults	3	700	120
Size of household							
One person	29	7,500	1,620	Four adults, one child	1	150	30
Two persons	35	8,990	2,170	Four adults, two or more children	[0]	80	–
Three persons	16	4,010	870				
Four persons	14	3,620	840	Five adults	[0]	140	20
Five persons	4	1,150	260				
Six persons	1	280	70	Five adults, one or more children	[0]	30	–
Seven persons	[0]	80	–				
Eight persons	[0]	30	–	All other households without children	[0]	30	–
Nine or more persons	[0]	30	–	All other households with children	[0]	30	–
							0
Composition of household							
One adult	29	7,490	1,620	**Number of economically active persons in household**			
Retired households mainly dependent on state pensions[2]	4	970	200	No person	32	8,310	1,970
Other retired households	10	2,660	570	One person	27	7,060	1,640
Non-retired households	15	3,860	850	More than one person	40	10,320	2,240
One man	13	3,320	740	Two persons	31	7,940	1,780
Aged under 65	9	2,320	480	Three persons	7	1,680	330
Aged 65 and over	4	1,000	260	Four persons	2	590	110
One woman	16	4,180	880	Five persons	[0]	90	–
Aged under 60	5	1,270	310	Six or more persons	[0]	20	–
Aged 60 and over	11	2,910	570				
One adult, one child	3	830	200	Households with married women	48	12,320	2,980
One man, one child	0	110	20	Households with married women			
One woman, one child	3	730	180	economically active	27	6,940	1,630
One adult, two or more children	3	650	180	With no dependent children	15	3,750	840
One man, two or more children	[0]	50	–	With dependent children	12	3,190	790
One woman, two or more children	2	600	170	One child	5	1,300	300
				Two children	6	1,480	380
One man, one woman	29.6	7,590	1,860	Three children	1	370	100
Retired households mainly dependent on state pensions[2]	2	540	150	Four or more children	[0]	50	–
Other retired households	8	2,000	530	Households with married women			
Non-retired households	20	5,050	1,170	not economically active	21	5,380	1,350
Two men or two women	2	560	110	With no dependent children	16	4,080	1,050
				With dependent children	5	1,300	300
Two adults with children	19	4,950	1,180	One child	2	460	100
One man one woman, one child	7	1,860	420	Two children	2	510	120
Two men or two women, one child	[0]	90	–	Three children	1	210	50
One man one woman, two children	8	2,150	540	Four or more children	0	120	30
Two men or two women, two children	[0]	20	–				
One man one woman, three children	2	640	160	**Economic status of household reference person**			
Two men or two women, three children	[0]	10	–	Economically active	63	16,070	3,590
Two adults, four children	1	150	40	Employee at work	53	13,550	3,010
Two adults, five children	[0]	20	–	Full-time	44	11,400	2,510
Two adults, six or more children	[0]	10	–	Part-time	8	2,150	500
Three adults	6	1,610	320	Government-supported training	[0]	60	–
Three adults with children	3	830	180	Unemployed	2	500	100
Three adults, one child	2	580	130	Self-employed	8	1,960	470
Three adults, two children	1	180	40				
Three adults, three children	[0]	50	–	Economically inactive	37	9,620	2,250
Three adults, four or more children	[0]	20	–				

Note: Please see page xiii for symbols and conventions used in this report.
1 Based on weighted number of households.
2 Mainly dependent on state pensions and not economically active - see definitions in Appendix B.

Table A48

Characteristics of households, 2008 (cont.)
based on weighted data

	% [1] of all house-holds	Weighted number of house-holds (000s)	House-holds in sample (number)		% [1] of all house-holds	Weighted number of house-holds (000s)	House-holds in sample (number)
Age of household reference person				**GB urban/rural areas (over 3 years)**			
15 and under 20 years	[0]	80	–	GB Urban	79	19,540	4,360
20 and under 25 years	3	810	130	GB rural	21	5,300	1,270
25 and under 30 years	6	1,640	310				
30 and under 35 years	8	1,980	440				
35 and under 40 years	10	2,520	570	**Tenure of dwelling[5]**			
40 and under 45 years	10	2,660	600	Owners			
				Owned outright	31	8,010	1,950
45 and under 50 years	10	2,580	620	Buying with a mortgage	39	9,900	2,230
50 and under 55 years	10	2,450	550	All	70	17,910	4,180
55 and under 60 years	8	2,010	490	Social rented from			
				Council	11	2,720	600
60 and under 65 years	9	2,290	550	Registered social landlord	8	2,010	440
65 and under 70 years	6	1,650	420	All	18	4,730	1,040
70 and under 75 years	6	1,490	390	Private rented			
				Rent free	1	340	70
75 and under 80 years	6	1,480	340	Rent paid, unfurnished	8	2,130	450
80 and under 85 years	4	1,080	240	Rent paid, furnished	2	580	110
85 and under 90 years	3	760	150	All	12	3,040	630
90 years or more	1	210	40				
				Households with durable goods			
Government Office Regions and Countries				Car/van	74	19,140	4,500
2006-2008 (3 year average)				One	43	11,070	2,620
				Two	25	6,450	1,540
United Kingdom	100	25,490	6,210	Three or more	6	1,610	340
North East	4	1,130	260	Central heating, full or partial	95	24,410	5,580
				Fridge-freezer or deep freezer	97	24,910	5,670
North West	11	2,930	630	Washing machine	96	24,620	5,620
Yorkshire and the Humber	8	2,150	520	Tumble dryer	59	15,100	3,520
				Dishwasher	37	9,630	2,330
East Midlands	7	1,900	450	Microwave oven	92	23,650	5,400
West Midlands	8	2,150	500				
East	9	2,310	560	Telephone	90	23,150	5,300
				Mobile phone	79	20,180	4,520
London	12	3,040	510	Video recorder	70	17,980	4,160
South East	13	3,280	840	DVD Player	88	22,510	5,110
South West	9	2,350	530	Satellite receiver[6]	82	21,170	4,850
				Compact disc player	86	22,140	5,070
England	83	21,240	4,810	Home computer	72	18,520	4,190
Wales	5	1,270	290	Internet connection	66	17,000	3,840
Scotland	9	2,320	530				
Northern Ireland	3	650	590				
Socio-economic classification							
of household reference person							
Higher managerial and professional	12	3,130	700				
Large employers/higher managerial	5	1,190	260				
Higher professional	8	1,940	430				
Lower managerial and professional	18	4,590	1,040				
Intermediate	5	1,310	290				
Small employers	6	1,510	360				
Lower supervisory	7	1,790	390				
Semi-routine	7	1,930	420				
Routine	7	1,700	380				
Long-term unemployed[3]	2	520	120				
Students	1	320	60				
Occupation not stated[4]	35	8,900	2,080				

Note: Please see page xiii for symbols and conventions used in this report.
1   Based on weighted number of households.
2   Mainly dependent on state pensions and not economically active - see definitions in Appendix B.
3   Includes those who have never worked.
4   Includes those who are economically inactive - see definitions in Appendix B.
5   See footnotes in Table A34.
6   Includes digital and cable receivers.

Table A49

Characteristics of persons, 2008

based on weighted data

	Males				Females				All persons			
	Percentage[1] of		Weighted number of persons (000s)	Persons in the sample (number)	Percentage[1] of		Weighted number of persons (000s)	Persons in the sample (number)	%[1] of	Weighted number of persons (000s)	Persons in the sample (number)
	all males	all persons			all females	all persons			all persons		
All persons	100	49	29,780	6,720	100	51	30,770	7,110	100	60,560	13,830
Adults	77	38	23,020	5,090	79	40	24,460	5,550	78	47,470	10,640
Persons aged under 60	57	28	16,930	3,510	56	28	17,250	3,870	56	34,180	7,380
Persons aged 60 or under 65	6	3	1,850	450	6	3	1,980	480	6	3,830	940
Persons aged 65 or under 70	5	2	1,360	360	4	2	1,290	340	4	2,650	700
Persons aged 70 or over	10	5	2,880	770	13	6	3,930	870	11	6,810	1,630
Children	23	11	**6,770**	**1,640**	21	10	**6,320**	**1,560**	22	**13,090**	**3,200**
Children under 2 years of age	2	1	680	150	2	1	680	150	2	1,360	300
Children aged 2 or under 5	4	2	1,230	280	4	2	1,100	250	4	2,330	530
Children aged 5 or under 16	13	7	3,990	1,020	12	6	3,780	980	13	7,780	2,000
Children aged 16 or under 18	3	1	870	190	2	1	760	180	3	1,620	360
Economic activity											
Persons active (aged 16 or over)	56	28	16,660	3,520	46	24	14,250	3,180	51	30,910	6,700
Persons not active	44	22	13,120	3,200	54	27	16,520	3,930	49	29,640	7,130
Men 65 or over and women 60 or over	13	6	3,820	1,020	21	10	6,340	1,480	17	10,160	2,490
Others (Including children under 16)	31	15	9,300	2,190	33	17	10,180	2,450	32	19,480	4,640

Note: Please see page xiii for symbols and conventions used in this report.

1   Based on weighted number of households.

Table A50

Percentage of households with durable goods, 1970 to 2008

	Car/ van	Central heating[1]	Washing machine	Tumble dryer	Dish- washer	Micro- wave	Tele- phone	Mobile phone	Video recorder	DVD Player	Satellite receiver[2]	Cd player	Home computer	Internet connection
1970	52	30	65	–	–	–	35	–	–	–	–	–	–	–
1975	57	47	72	–	–	–	52	–	–	–	–	–	–	–
1980	60	59	79	–	–	–	72	–	–	–	–	–	–	–
1985	63	69	83	–	–	–	81	–	30	–	–	–	13	–
1990	67	79	86	–	–	–	87	–	61	–	–	–	17	–
1994-95	69	84	89	50	18	67	91	–	76	–	–	46	–	–
1995-96	70	85	91	50	20	70	92	–	79	–	–	51	–	–
1996-97	69	87	91	51	20	75	93	16	82	–	19	59	27	–
1997-98	70	89	91	51	22	77	94	20	84	–	26	63	29	–
1998-99	72	89	92	51	24	80	95	26	86	–	27	68	32	9
1998-99[3]	72	89	92	51	23	79	95	27	85	–	28	68	33	10
1999-2000	71	90	91	52	23	80	95	44	86	–	32	72	38	19
2000-01	72	91	92	53	25	84	93	47	87	–	40	77	44	32
2001-02,[4]	74	92	93	54	27	86	94	64	90	–	43	80	49	39
2002-03	74	93	94	56	29	87	94	70	90	31	45	83	55	45
2003-04	75	94	94	57	31	89	92	76	90	50	49	86	58	49
2004-05	75	95	95	58	33	90	93	78	88	67	58	87	62	53
2005-06	74	94	95	58	35	91	92	79	86	79	65	88	65	55
2006[5]	76	95	96	59	38	91	91	80	82	83	71	88	67	59
2006[6]	74	95	96	59	37	91	91	79	82	83	70	87	67	58
2007	75	95	96	57	37	91	89	78	75	86	77	86	70	61
2008	74	95	96	59	37	92	90	79	70	88	82	86	72	66

Note:

– Data not available.

1   Full or partial.

2   Includes digital and cable receivers.

3   From this version of 1998-99, figures shown are based on weighted data and including children's expenditure.

4   From 2001-02 onwards, weighting is based on the population figures from the 2001 census.

5   From 1998-99 to this version of 2006, figures shown are based on weighted data using non-response weights based on the 1991 Census and population figures from the 1991 and 2001 Censuses.

6   From this version of 2006, figures shown are based on weighted data using updated weights, with non-response weights and population figures based on the 2001 Census.

Table A51

Percentage[1] of households with durable goods by income group and household composition, 2008

based on weighted data

	Central heating[2]	Washing machine	Tumble dryer	Micro-wave	Dish-washer	CD player
All households	**95**	**96**	**59**	**92**	**37**	**86**
Gross income decile group						
Lowest ten per cent	93	85	37	86	11	70
Second decile group	94	92	45	90	16	73
Third decile group	93	92	49	92	18	79
Fourth decile group	93	97	57	91	27	85
Fifth decile group	94	98	58	93	33	90
Sixth decile group	95	98	63	92	39	89
Seventh decile group	96	99	65	95	42	93
Eighth decile group	97	99	69	93	50	95
Ninth decile group	97	100	70	95	61	93
Highest ten per cent	99	100	75	92	77	96
Household composition						
One adult, retired households[3]	93	86	39	85	12	57
One adult, non-retired households	91	93	45	90	22	83
One adult, one child	96	99	63	94	27	88
One adult, two or more children	96	100	66	91	26	90
One man and one woman, retired households[3]	96	97	51	91	23	81
One man and one woman, non-retired households	95	99	64	93	46	92
One man and one woman, one child	96	100	66	94	45	90
One man and one woman, two or more children	96	99	75	95	60	91
All other households without children	96	99	66	94	45	93
All other households with children	99	96	67	98	43	91

	Home computer	Internet connection	Tele-phone	Mobile phone	Satellite receiver[4]	DVD Player
All households	**72**	**66**	**90**	**79**	**82**	**88**
Gross income decile group						
Lowest ten per cent	33	26	74	61	63	66
Second decile group	41	33	87	62	73	73
Third decile group	47	40	88	66	74	78
Fourth decile group	65	54	87	77	82	87
Fifth decile group	75	68	91	83	86	91
Sixth decile group	83	76	90	86	85	93
Seventh decile group	91	85	94	87	88	95
Eighth decile group	93	88	95	86	91	97
Ninth decile group	95	94	97	89	91	97
Highest ten per cent	98	96	98	88	91	98
Household composition						
One adult, retired households[3]	15	10	96	34	53	48
One adult, non-retired households	67	58	79	82	76	85
One adult, one child	73	61	68	90	86	97
One adult, two or more children	77	65	69	82	89	95
One man and one woman, retired households[3]	35	29	97	63	81	81
One man and one woman, non-retired households	87	81	94	88	88	96
One man and one woman, one child	91	84	90	86	91	97
One man and one woman, two or more children	93	91	92	86	92	97
All other households without children	89	86	91	85	84	97
All other households with children	85	82	84	91	92	98

Note: Please see page xiii for symbols and conventions used in this report..

1   See table A52 for number of recording households.

2   Full or partial.

3   Mainly dependent on state pensions and not economically active - see Appendix B.

4   Includes digital and cable receivers.

Table A52

Percentage of households with cars by income group, tenure and household composition, 2008

based on weighted data

	One car/van	Two cars/vans	Three or more cars/vans	All with cars/vans	Weighted number of house-holds (000s)	House-holds in the sample (number)
All households	**43**	**25**	**6**	**74**	**25,690**	**5,850**
Gross income decile group						
Lowest ten per cent	26	[2]	[0]	29	2,570	550
Second decile group	38	4	[1]	44	2,570	580
Third decile group	49	5	[0]	55	2,570	610
Fourth decile group	62	11	[1]	74	2,570	630
Fifth decile group	63	18	[3]	84	2,570	590
Sixth decile group	53	28	4	85	2,570	600
Seventh decile group	48	35	8	91	2,570	590
Eighth decile group	41	43	8	93	2,560	570
Ninth decile group	31	50	14	94	2,570	550
Highest ten per cent	19	53	23	96	2,560	580
Tenure of dwelling[1]						
Owners						
Owned outright	50	21	6	77	8,010	1,950
Buying with a mortgage	41	41	9	92	9,900	2,230
All	45	32	8	85	17,910	4,180
Social rented from						
Council	30	5	[1]	35	2,720	600
Registered social landlord[2]	37	7	[4]	48	2,010	440
All	33	6	[2]	41	4,730	1,040
Private rented						
Rent free	39	[15]	[4]	59	340	70
Rent paid, unfurnished	49	16	[3]	67	2,130	450
Rent paid, furnished	40	[11]	[1]	51	580	110
All	46	15	[2]	63	3,040	630
Household composition						
One adult, retired mainly dependent on state pensions[3]	28	[0]	–	28	970	200
One adult, other retired	41	[0]	[0]	41	2,660	570
One adult, non-retired	57	6	[1]	64	3,860	850
One adult, one child	54	[2]	[0]	56	830	200
One adult, two or more children	46	[1]	–	47	650	180
One man and one woman, retired mainly dependent on state pensions[3]	71	[5]	[1]	76	540	150
One man and one woman, other retired	65	17	[2]	84	2,000	530
One man and one woman, non-retired	41	44	5	89	5,050	1,170
One man and one woman, one child	39	43	5	87	1,860	420
One man and one woman, two children	36	51	5	91	2,150	540
One man and one woman, three children	31	50	[6]	87	640	160
Two adults, four or more children	[22]	43	[7]	72	180	50
Three adults	31	34	24	89	1,610	320
Three adults, one or more children	29	35	21	86	830	180
All other households without children	27	26	27	80	1,440	260
All other households with children	33	[20]	27	80	410	80

Note: Please see page xiii for symbols and conventions used in this report.

1   See footnotes in Table A34.

2   Formerly housing association.

3   Mainly dependent on state pensions and not economically active - see Appendix B.

Table A53

Percentage of households with durable goods by UK countries and Government Office Regions, 2006–2008

based on weighted data

	North East	North West	Yorks & the Humber	East Midlands	West Midlands	East	London
Average weighted number of households (thousands)	1,130	2,930	2,150	1,900	2,150	2,310	3,040
Total number of households in sample (over 3 years)	770	1,890	1,570	1,360	1,510	1,670	1,540
Percentage of households by Government Office Region and country							
Car/van	66	71	73	79	75	83	63
One	41	42	45	45	43	45	44
Two	20	25	24	28	25	30	16
Three or more	4	5	5	7	7	8	3
Central heating full or partial	98	94	94	96	94	96	95
Fridge-freezer or deep freezer	96	96	96	97	95	96	94
Washing machine	98	97	96	97	97	97	96
Tumble dryer	55	59	59	59	63	61	45
Dishwasher	25	32	32	37	32	43	37
Microwave	92	94	94	93	93	91	87
Telephone	88	88	88	91	89	93	90
Mobile phone	73	78	81	84	84	83	79
DVD player	87	88	85	86	86	86	83
Satellite receiver[1]	79	83	77	76	75	77	71
CD player	86	87	86	88	87	89	82
Home computer	64	68	66	70	69	71	73
Internet connection	57	59	58	62	61	65	66

	South East	South West	England	Wales	Scotland	Northern Ireland	United Kingdom
Weighted number of households (thousands)	3,280	2,350	21,240	1,270	2,320	650	25,490
Total number of households in sample (over 3 years)	2,530	1,580	14,440	860	1,580	1,760	18,630
Percentage of households by Government Office Region and country							
Car/van	80	83	75	76	70	77	75
One	41	46	43	44	44	44	44
Two	30	29	25	26	22	26	25
Three or more	8	8	6	6	4	7	6
Central heating full or partial	95	94	95	94	95	98	95
Fridge-freezer or deep freezer	96	96	96	96	97	98	96
Washing machine	97	96	97	97	96	96	97
Tumble dryer	59	62	58	60	60	61	58
Dishwasher	45	41	37	34	38	47	37
Microwave	89	92	91	94	91	92	92
Telephone	92	93	90	90	91	87	90
Mobile phone	79	84	81	51	83	54	79
DVD Player	87	84	86	83	87	81	86
Satellite receiver[1]	76	76	76	77	79	78	77
CD player	88	88	87	86	87	81	87
Home computer	74	70	70	68	68	64	70
Internet connection	68	63	63	59	60	55	62

Note: This table is based on a three year average.

1 Includes digital and cable receivers.

Table A54

Percentage of households by size, composition and age in each gross income decile group, 2008

based on weighted data

	Lowest ten per cent	Second decile group	Third decile group	Fourth decile group	Fifth decile group	Sixth decile group
Lower boundary of group (£ per week)		146	224	305	408	522
Weighted number of households (thousands)	2,570	2,570	2,570	2,570	2,570	2,570
Number of households in the sample	550	580	610	630	590	600
Size of household						
One person	80	58	44	32	26	20
Two persons	13	25	42	45	40	41
Three persons	4	10	6	12	16	18
Four persons	[2]	5	4	7	12	14
Five persons	[1]	[1]	[2]	[3]	5	4
Six or more persons	–	[0]	[1]	[1]	[1]	[2]
All sizes	100	100	100	100	100	100
Household composition						
One adult, retired mainly dependent on state pensions[1]	20	12	5	[0]	–	–
One adult, other retired	25	33	22	11	8	[2]
One adult, non-retired	34	13	17	20	19	18
One adult, one child	8	5	6	6	[2]	[3]
One adult, two or more children	[2]	7	5	5	3	[1]
One man and one woman, retired mainly dependent on state pensions[1]	[0]	8	9	3	[1]	–
One man and one woman, other retired	[1]	7	15	20	14	9
One man and one woman, non-retired	[3]	5	10	14	20	25
One man and one woman, one child	[2]	4	[2]	5	8	8
One man and one woman, two children	[1]	[2]	[1]	5	7	10
One man and one woman, three children	[0]	[0]	[1]	[2]	[3]	[3]
Two adults, four or more children	–	[0]	[1]	[1]	[0]	[1]
Three adults	[0]	[0]	[1]	[1]	5	8
Three adults, one or more children	[0]	[4]	[1]	[1]	[3]	5
All other households without children	[2]	[1]	[2]	[2]	5	5
All other households with children	[0]	[1]	[1]	[2]	[2]	[1]
All compositions	100	100	100	100	100	100
Age of household reference person						
15 and under 20 years	[1]	[0]	–	[0]	[0]	[0]
20 and under 25 years	6	[3]	[3]	[3]	5	5
25 and under 30 years	5	5	4	5	8	7
30 and under 35 years	[3]	4	4	8	8	10
35 and under 40 years	6	5	4	7	7	12
40 and under 45 years	7	4	6	7	9	12
45 and under 50 years	8	3	4	9	8	9
50 and under 55 years	6	[3]	6	7	9	9
55 and under 60 years	8	5	8	7	7	9
60 and under 65 years	7	10	8	12	12	9
65 and under 70 years	8	10	10	9	8	5
70 and under 75 years	7	12	12	8	8	5
75 and under 80 years	8	16	11	9	6	[3]
80 and under 85 years	10	11	9	6	[2]	[2]
85 and under 90 years	8	7	9	[2]	[2]	[1]
90 years or more	[2]	[2]	[2]	[1]	[0]	–
All ages	100	100	100	100	100	100

Note: Please see page xiii for symbols and conventions used in this report.

1   Mainly dependent on state pensions and not economically active - see Appendix B.

Table A54

Percentage of households by size, composition and age in each gross income decile group, 2008 (cont.)

based on weighted data

	Seventh decile group	Eighth decile group	Ninth decile group	Highest ten per cent	All house-holds
Lower boundary of group (£ per week)	664	817	1026	1356	
Weighted number of households (thousands)	2,570	2,560	2,570	2,560	25,690
Number of households in the sample	590	570	550	580	5,850
Size of household					
One person	15	8	6	[3]	29
Two persons	34	40	35	34	35
Three persons	21	25	23	21	16
Four persons	23	19	24	30	14
Five persons	6	7	8	8	4
Six or more persons	[2]	[2]	[3]	4	2
All sizes	100	100	100	100	100
Household composition					
One adult, retired mainly dependent on state pensions[1]	–	–	–	–	4
One adult, other retired	[2]	[0]	–	–	10
One adult, non-retired	13	7	6	[3]	15
One adult, one child	[1]	[1]	[0]	[0]	3
One adult, two or more children	[1]	[1]	[0]	[0]	3
One man and one woman, retired mainly dependent on state pensions[1]	–	–	–	–	2
One man and one woman, other retired	5	4	[2]	[2]	8
One man and one woman, non-retired	26	33	29	31	20
One man and one woman, one child	11	12	10	10	7
One man and one woman, two children	16	11	14	16	8
One man and one woman, three children	[3]	4	3	5	2
Two adults, four or more children	[1]	[0]	[1]	[1]	1
Three adults	8	12	13	11	6
Three adults, one or more children	5	4	7	6	3
All other households without children	7	8	11	13	6
All other households with children	[1]	[2]	4	[2]	2
All compositions	100	100	100	100	100
Age of household reference person					
15 and under 20 years	[1]	[0]	–	–	[0]
20 and under 25 years	[2]	[3]	[1]	[1]	3
25 and under 30 years	9	9	10	[3]	6
30 and under 35 years	11	12	9	9	8
35 and under 40 years	14	13	15	15	10
40 and under 45 years	15	14	15	14	10
45 and under 50 years	11	12	17	18	10
50 and under 55 years	10	13	13	18	10
55 and under 60 years	8	7	8	12	8
60 and under 65 years	8	8	7	7	9
65 and under 70 years	4	5	[3]	[2]	6
70 and under 75 years	[3]	[2]	[1]	[0]	6
75 and under 80 years	[2]	[0]	[1]	[1]	6
80 and under 85 years	[1]	[1]	[0]	–	4
85 and under 90 years	[0]	[0]	[0]	[0]	3
90 years or more	[0]	–	[0]	[0]	1
All ages	100	100	100	100	100

Note: Please see page xiii for symbols and conventions used in this report.
1   Mainly dependent on state pensions and not economically active - see Appendix B.

Table A55

Percentage of households by economic activity, tenure and socio-economic classification in each gross income decile group, 2008

based on weighted data

	Lowest ten per cent	Second decile group	Third decile group	Fourth decile group	Fifth decile group	Sixth decile group
Lower boundary of group (£ per week)		146	224	305	408	522
Weighted number of households (thousands)	2,570	2,570	2,570	2,570	2,570	2,570
Number of households in the sample	550	580	610	630	590	600
Number of economically active persons in household						
No person	79	80	64	42	28	14
One person	19	17	29	42	43	41
Two persons	[2]	4	6	14	25	40
Three persons	–	–	–	[1]	[3]	5
Four or more persons	–	–	–	[0]	[1]	[0]
All economically active persons	100	100	100	100	100	100
Tenure of dwelling[1]						
Owners						
Owned outright	28	46	44	42	37	28
Buying with a mortgage	4	6	12	25	34	46
All	32	52	56	66	71	74
Social rented from						
Council	36	21	17	10	8	5
Registered social landlord[2]	15	16	16	10	6	7
All	50	37	33	20	15	12
Private rented						
Rent free	4	[1]	[1]	[1]	[2]	[1]
Rent paid, unfurnished	10	9	9	11	11	9
Rent paid, furnished	4	[1]	[2]	[2]	[1]	[4]
All	18	11	12	14	14	14
All tenures	100	100	100	100	100	100
Socio-economic classification						
Higher managerial and professional						
Large employers/higher managerial	–	[0]	[0]	[1]	[1]	[2]
Higher professional	[2]	[1]	[1]	[1]	[3]	6
Lower managerial and professional	[1]	[2]	4	8	16	19
Intermediate	[1]	[2]	3	9	8	8
Small employers	[3]	[3]	4	5	6	8
Lower supervisory	[1]	[1]	[3]	6	9	12
Semi-routine	5	3	10	11	11	12
Routine	4	4	6	10	12	11
Long-term unemployed[3]	8	4	[2]	[2]	[2]	[1]
Students	[3]	[2]	[1]	[1]	[1]	[1]
Occupation not stated[4]	73	77	65	46	32	21
All occupational groups	100	100	100	100	100	100

Note: Please see page xiii for symbols and conventions used in this report.
1 See footnotes in Table A34.
2 Formerly housing association.
3 Includes those who have never worked.
4 Includes those who are economically inactive - see definitions in Appendix B.

Table A55

Percentage of households by economic activity, tenure and socio-economic classification in each gross income decile group, 2008 (cont.)

based on weighted data

	Seventh decile group	Eighth decile group	Ninth decile group	Highest ten per cent	All house-holds
Lower boundary of group (£ per week)	664	817	1026	1356	
Weighted number of households (thousands)	2,570	2,560	2,570	2,560	25,690
Number of households in the sample	590	570	550	580	5,850
Number of economically active persons in household					
No person	8	4	[2]	[2]	32
One person	31	21	15	15	27
Two persons	49	57	58	55	31
Three persons	9	14	16	18	7
Four or more persons	[3]	[4]	8	11	3
All economically active persons	100	100	100	100	100
Tenure of dwelling[1]					
Owners					
Owned outright	24	20	20	23	31
Buying with a mortgage	56	64	69	72	39
All	79	84	89	94	70
Social rented from					
Council	4	[2]	[1]	[0]	11
Registered social landlord[2]	4	[2]	[2]	[1]	8
All	8	5	[3]	[1]	18
Private rented					
Rent free	[1]	[0]	[2]	–	1
Rent paid, unfurnished	8	8	5	4	8
Rent paid, furnished	[3]	[3]	[1]	[1]	2
All	13	12	8	5	12
All tenures	100	100	100	100	100
Socio-economic classification					
Higher managerial and professional					
Large employers/higher managerial	4	8	10	19	5
Higher professional	8	11	17	25	8
Lower managerial and professional	28	34	32	35	18
Intermediate	6	6	6	[2]	5
Small employers	8	6	9	6	6
Lower supervisory	11	11	12	4	7
Semi-routine	10	7	[4]	[3]	7
Routine	8	6	4	[1]	7
Long-term unemployed[3]	[0]	–	[1]	[0]	2
Students	[2]	[1]	[1]	[1]	1
Occupation not stated[4]	14	9	5	5	35
All occupational groups	100	100	100	100	100

Note: Please see page xiii for symbols and conventions used in this report.
1   See footnotes in Table A34.
2   Formerly housing association.
3   Includes those who have never worked.
4   Includes those who are economically inactive - see definitions in Appendix B.

Table A56

Average weekly household expenditure by OAC supergroup, 2008
based on weighted data and including children's expenditure

		OAC Super-group 1	OAC Super-group 2	OAC Super-group 3	OAC Super-group 4	OAC Super-group 5	OAC Super-group 6	OAC Super-group 7	All house-holds
Weighted number of households (thousands)		4,180	1,520	3,450	5,480	3,290	4,890	2,890	25,690
Total number of households in sample		990	290	880	1,360	740	1,080	500	5,850
Total number of persons in sample		2,480	560	2,130	3,430	1,500	2,430	1,300	13,830
Total number of adults in sample		1,800	480	1,650	2,680	1,170	1,930	930	10,640
Weighted average number of persons per household		2.5	1.9	2.4	2.5	2.0	2.3	2.6	2.4
Commodity or service					Average weekly household expenditure (£)				
1	Food & non-alcoholic drinks	48.50	45.30	56.70	59.00	37.80	50.60	48.70	50.70
2	Alcoholic drinks, tobacco & narcotics	11.80	10.40	11.40	11.30	10.70	10.10	9.00	10.80
3	Clothing & footwear	17.60	24.40	22.00	27.20	15.20	21.50	22.10	21.60
4	Housing (net)[1], fuel & power	46.20	95.20	54.00	47.20	46.40	48.60	65.70	53.00
5	Household goods & services	23.60	29.80	36.80	42.80	17.20	30.80	21.20	30.10
6	Health	4.80	5.90	5.70	6.50	3.20	5.10	4.30	5.10
7	Transport	52.60	55.90	79.10	83.40	35.50	68.90	48.80	63.40
8	Communication	11.30	13.10	12.10	12.50	10.50	12.20	12.40	12.00
9	Recreation & culture	50.50	54.20	76.80	87.60	38.70	55.30	37.20	60.10
10	Education	2.20	19.70	11.00	7.70	2.00	3.50	5.80	6.20
11	Restaurants & hotels	31.20	48.70	41.90	47.70	22.60	38.30	33.70	37.70
12	Miscellaneous goods & services	27.20	48.60	41.50	47.10	20.90	36.00	28.50	35.60
1–12	All expenditure groups	327.50	451.40	448.90	479.90	260.80	380.70	337.50	386.30

Note: Please see page xiii for symbols and conventions used in this report.

1   Excluding mortgage interest payments, council tax and Northern Ireland rates.

Table A57

Average weekly household expenditure by OAC group, 2008

based on weighted data and including children's expenditure

	OAC group 1A	OAC group 1B	OAC group 1C	OAC group 2A	OAC group 2B	OAC group 3A	OAC group 3B	OAC group 3C	OAC group 4A	OAC group 4B	OAC group 4C
Weighted number of households (thousands)	1,090	1,760	1,340	560	960	1,430	960	1,050	1,140	1,540	1,790
Total number of households in sample	250	410	330	100	200	350	280	260	310	390	410
Total number of persons in sample	600	1,040	840	170	390	820	730	590	830	960	960
Total number of adults in sample	460	720	620	160	330	630	560	460	610	770	780
Weighted average number of persons per household	2.5	2.6	2.5	1.8	2.0	2.4	2.4	2.3	2.7	2.4	2.4

Commodity or service	Average weekly household expenditure (£)										
1 Food & non-alcoholic drinks	45.20	47.60	52.20	41.90	47.20	55.70	57.90	57.10	57.00	61.20	53.80
2 Alcoholic drinks, tobacco & narcotics	11.50	13.10	10.50	10.60	10.30	11.80	10.50	11.70	11.40	12.30	10.20
3 Clothing & footwear	17.10	18.30	16.90	30.80	20.70	18.70	26.10	22.50	35.90	28.00	21.40
4 Housing (net)[1], fuel & power	44.30	48.10	45.30	91.60	97.30	55.10	54.90	51.80	45.50	48.50	42.80
5 Household goods & services	18.00	21.00	31.60	25.70	32.30	31.50	38.70	42.40	44.30	42.10	36.10
6 Health	3.50	6.50	3.80	4.40	6.80	3.90	5.60	8.20	4.50	6.40	7.10
7 Transport	52.10	41.50	67.60	51.60	58.50	72.60	89.70	78.10	100.80	82.80	64.70
8 Communication	10.20	11.80	11.60	13.30	12.90	11.70	12.50	12.20	14.30	11.90	11.00
9 Recreation & culture	54.80	43.70	55.90	50.60	56.30	62.60	92.00	82.30	94.90	116.20	63.80
10 Education	1.20	3.10	1.70	10.20	25.20	10.00	13.60	9.90	12.40	8.60	2.60
11 Restaurants & hotels	25.80	33.20	33.10	45.40	50.70	35.80	38.80	53.00	54.80	50.40	37.90
12 Miscellaneous goods & services	23.80	25.50	32.30	39.80	53.80	40.10	39.30	45.40	54.00	45.00	42.70
1–12 All expenditure groups	307.50	313.40	362.40	415.90	472.00	409.40	479.50	474.60	529.70	513.20	394.10

Note: Please see page xiii for symbols and conventions used in this report.

1 Excluding mortgage interest payments, council tax and Northern Ireland rates

Table A57

Average weekly household expenditure by OAC group, 2008 (cont.)

based on weighted data and including children's expenditure

	OAC group 4D	OAC group 5A	OAC group 5B	OAC group 5C	OAC group 6A	OAC group 6B	OAC group 6C	OAC group 6D	OAC group 7A	OAC group 7B	All house-holds
Weighted number of households (thousands)	1,020	480	2,070	730	1,340	1,390	1,120	1,040	1,740	1,150	25,690
Total number of households in sample	260	100	470	170	290	310	240	240	330	180	5,850
Total number of persons in sample	680	170	940	400	670	670	510	580	880	420	13,830
Total number of adults in sample	530	150	760	270	540	540	410	440	620	310	10,640
Weighted average number of persons per household	2.6	1.7	2.0	2.2	2.4	2.1	2.1	2.4	2.8	2.5	2.4

Commodity or service					Average weekly household expenditure (£)						
1 Food & non-alcoholic drinks	66.90	33.60	38.80	37.90	54.10	48.20	43.80	56.50	51.50	44.60	50.70
2 Alcoholic drinks, tobacco & narcotics	11.60	9.40	10.30	12.90	11.30	9.30	10.10	9.70	9.00	9.10	10.80
3 Clothing & footwear	26.80	11.00	15.00	18.70	20.90	18.50	20.70	27.20	22.50	21.60	21.60
4 Housing (net)[1], fuel & power	55.00	46.40	47.00	44.70	42.20	50.60	43.80	59.30	63.30	69.30	53.00
5 Household goods & services	54.10	13.00	19.00	15.00	34.30	28.10	19.40	42.20	21.80	20.40	30.10
6 Health	7.60	5.00	2.90	2.60	4.70	5.30	4.00	6.20	5.70	2.00	5.10
7 Transport	97.40	31.40	39.70	26.60	77.30	60.70	54.80	84.00	51.10	45.20	63.40
8 Communication	14.10	8.40	10.70	11.10	12.30	11.70	11.80	13.00	12.30	12.40	12.00
9 Recreation & culture	77.80	38.10	41.40	31.50	54.00	55.60	47.20	65.20	40.80	31.80	60.10
10 Education	9.80	3.20	1.80	1.80	1.10	2.90	2.10	8.80	4.00	8.50	6.20
11 Restaurants & hotels	52.80	21.00	23.10	22.30	35.70	33.40	34.90	51.90	33.90	33.40	37.70
12 Miscellaneous goods & services	50.40	17.20	23.40	16.10	39.30	30.80	32.50	42.20	30.70	25.10	35.60
1–12 All expenditure groups	524.40	237.60	273.10	241.10	387.20	355.20	325.20	466.20	346.60	323.60	386.30

Note: Please see page xiii for symbols and conventions used in this report.

1 Excluding mortgage interest payments, council tax and Northern Ireland rates

Table A58

Average gross normal weekly household income by OAC supergroup, 2008

based on weighted data

	OAC Super-group 1	OAC Super-group 2	OAC Super-group 3	OAC Super-group 4	OAC Super-group 5	OAC Super-group 6	OAC Super-group 7	All house-holds
Weighted number of households (thousands)	4,180	1,520	3,450	5,480	3,290	4,890	2,890	25,690
Total number of households in sample	990	290	880	1,360	740	1,080	500	5,850
Total number of persons in sample	2,480	560	2,130	3,430	1,500	2,430	1,300	13,830
Total number of adults in sample	1,800	480	1,650	2,680	1,170	1,930	930	10,640
Weighted average number of persons per household	2.5	1.9	2.4	2.5	2.0	2.3	2.6	2.4
Gross normal weekly household income	**527.80**	**1226.70**	**819.70**	**899.60**	**413.90**	**683.60**	**620.90**	**713.10**

Note: Please see page xiii for symbols and conventions used in this report.

Methodology

Page

- Description and response rate of the survey   184

- Uses of the survey   186

- Standard errors and estimates of precision   187

- Definitions   190

- Changes in definitions, 1991 to 2008   200

- Weighting   203

- Index to tables in reports on the FES/EFS
  1996–97 to 2008   206

Appendix B

Description and response rate of the survey

The survey

A household expenditure survey has been conducted each year in the UK since 1957. From 1957 to March 2001, the Family Expenditure and National Food Surveys (FES and NFS) provided information on household expenditure patterns and food consumption. In April 2001 these surveys were combined to form the Expenditure and Food Survey (EFS).

In 2008, selected Government household surveys, on which ONS leads, were combined into one Integrated Household Survey (IHS) (known as the Continuous Population Survey in the public domain). In anticipation of this, the EFS moved to a calendar-year basis in January 2006. The EFS questionnaire became known as the Living Costs and Food (LCF) module of the IHS in 2008 to accommodate the insertion of a core set of IHS questions. In addition to the LCF, the other surveys incorporated into the IHS were the General Household Survey (GHS), the Omnibus Survey (OMN) and the English Housing Conditions Survey (EHCS). These surveys are now called the General Lifestyle Survey (GLF), Opinions Survey (OPN) and the English Housing Survey (EHS) respectively.

The LCF is a voluntary sample survey of private households. The basic unit of the survey is the household. The LCF (in line with other Government household surveys) uses the harmonised definition of a household: a group of people living at the same address with common housekeeping, that is sharing household expenses such as food and bills, or sharing a living room (see 'Definitions'). The previous definition (used on the FES) differed from the harmonised definition by requiring both common housekeeping **and** a shared living room.

Each individual aged 16 or over in the household visited is asked to keep diary records of daily expenditure for two weeks. Information about regular expenditure, such as rent and mortgage payments, is obtained from a household interview along with retrospective information on certain large, infrequent expenditures such as those on vehicles. Since 1998-99 the results have also included information from simplified diaries kept by children aged between 7 and 15. The effects of including children's expenditure were shown in Appendix F of *Family Spending* for 1998-99 and again for 1999-2000. Inclusion of the data is now a standard feature of the survey.

Detailed questions are asked about the income of each adult member of the household. In addition, personal information such as age, sex and marital status is recorded for each household member. Paper versions of the computerised household and income questionnaires can be obtained from ONS at the address given in the Introduction.

The survey is continuous, interviews being spread evenly over the year to ensure that seasonal effects are covered. From time to time changes are made to the information sought. Some changes reflect new forms of expenditure or new sources of income, especially benefits. Others are the result of new requirements by the survey's users. An important example is the re-definition of housing costs for owner occupiers in 1992 (see 'Changes in definitions, 1991 to 2008').

The sample design

The LCF sample for Great Britain is a multi-stage stratified random sample with clustering. It is drawn from the Small Users file of the Postcode Address File - the Post Office's list of addresses. All Scottish offshore islands and the Isles of Scilly are excluded from the sample because of excessive interview travel costs. Postal sectors are the primary sample unit. Until 2006, 672 postal sectors were randomly selected during the year after being arranged in strata defined by Government Office Regions (sub-divided into metropolitan and non-metropolitan areas) and two 2001 Census variables – socio-economic group of head of household and ownership of cars. These were new stratifiers introduced for the 1996-97 survey. For 2007, a decision was taken to reduce the EFS sample by 5 per cent, resulting in 34 postal sectors being removed from the sample. The Northern Ireland sample is drawn as a random sample of addresses from the Land and Property Services Agency list.

Response to the survey

Great Britain

Around 11,484 households were selected in 2008 for the LCF in Great Britain, but it is never possible to get full response. A small number cannot be contacted at all, and in other households one or more members decline to co-operate. 5,091 households in Great Britain co-operated fully in the survey in 2008; that is they answered the household questionnaire and all adults in the household answered the full income questionnaire and kept the expenditure diary. A further 180 households provided sufficient information to be included as valid responses. The overall response rate for the 2008 LCF was 51 per cent in Great Britain. This represented a 2 per cent decrease in response from the 2007 survey year.

Details of response are shown in the following table.

Response in 2008 – Great Britain

		No of households or addresses	Percentage of effective sample
i.	Sampled addresses	11,484	–
ii.	Ineligible addresses: businesses, institutions, empty, demolished/derelict	1,147	–
iii.	Extra households (multi-household addresses)	82	–
iv.	Total eligible (i.e. i less ii, plus iii)	10,419	100.0
v.	Co-operating households (which includes 180 partials)	5,271	50.6
vi.	Refusals	3,735	35.8
vii.	Households at which no contact could be obtained	1,413	13.6

Northern Ireland

In the Northern Ireland survey, the eligible sample was 1,065 households. The number of co-operating households who provided usable data was 574, giving a response rate of 54 per cent. Northern Ireland is over-sampled in order to provide a large enough sample for some separate analysis. The weighting procedure compensates for the over-sampling.

The fieldwork

The fieldwork is conducted by the Office for National Statistics (ONS) in Great Britain, and by the Northern Ireland Statistics and Research Agency (NISRA) of the Department of Finance and Personnel in Northern Ireland, using almost identical questionnaires. Households at the selected addresses are visited and asked to co-operate in the survey. In order to maximise response, interviewers make at least four separate calls, and sometimes many more, at different times of day on households which are difficult to contact. Interviews are conducted by Computer Assisted Personal Interviewing (CAPI) using portable computers. During the interview, information is collected about the household, about certain regular payments such as rent, gas, electricity and telephone accounts, about expenditure on certain large items (for example vehicle purchases over the previous 12 months), and about income. Each individual aged 16 or over in the household is asked to keep a detailed record of expenditure every day for two weeks. Children aged between 7 and 15 are also asked to keep a simplified diary of daily expenditure. In 2008 a total of 1,712 children aged between 7 and 15 in responding households in the UK were asked to complete expenditure diaries; 281 or about 16 per cent, did not do so. This number includes both refusals and children who had no expenditure during the two weeks. Information provided by all members of the household is kept strictly confidential. Each person aged 16 and over in the household who keeps a diary (and whose income information is collected) is subsequently paid

£10, as a token of appreciation. Children who keep a diary are given a £5 payment.

In the last two months of the 1998-99 survey, as an experiment, a small book of postage stamps was enclosed with the introductory letter sent to every address. It seemed to help with response and the measure has become a permanent feature of the survey. It is difficult to quantify the exact effect on response but the cognitive work that was carried out as part of the EFS development indicated that it was having a positive effect.

A new strategy for reissues was adopted in 1999-2000 and has continued since. Addresses where there had been no contact or a refusal, but were judged suitable for reissue, were accumulated to form complete batches consisting only of reissues. The interviewers dealing with them were specially selected and given extra briefing. In 2008 some 135 addresses were reissued, of which 17 were converted into responding households. This added 0.2 percentage points to the response rate.

Eligible response

Under LCF rules, a refusal by just one person to respond to the income section of the questionnaire invalidates the response of the whole household. Similarly, a refusal by the household's main shopper to complete the two-week expenditure diary also results in an invalid response.

Proxy Interviews – while questions about general household affairs are put to all household members or to a main household informant, questions about work and income are put to the individual members of the household. Where a member of the household is not present during the household interview, another member of the household (e.g. spouse) may be able to provide information about the absent person. The individual's interview is then identified as a proxy interview.

In 2001-02, the EFS began including households that contained a proxy interview. In that year, 12 per cent of all responding households contained at least one proxy interview. In 2008, the percentage of responding households with a proxy interview was 21 per cent. Analysis of the 2002-03 data revealed that the inclusion of proxy interviews increased response from above average income households. For the 2002-03 survey, the average gross normal weekly household income was some 3 per cent higher than it would have been if proxy interviews had not been accepted. The analysis showed a similar difference for average total expenditure.

Reliability

Great care is taken in collecting information from households and comprehensive checks are applied during processing, so that errors in recording and processing are minimised. The main factors that affect the reliability of the survey results are sampling variability, non-response bias and some incorrect reporting of certain items of expenditure and income. Measures of sampling variability are given alongside some results in this report and are discussed in detail in 'Standard errors and estimates of precision'.

The households which decline to respond to the survey tend to differ in some respects from those which co-operate. It is therefore possible that their patterns of expenditure and income also differ. A comparison was made of the households responding in the 1991 FES with those not responding, based on information from the 1991 Census of Population (*A comparison of the Census characteristics of respondents and non-respondents to the 1991 FES by K Foster, ONS Survey Methodology Bulletin No. 38, Jan 1996*). Results from the study indicate that response was lower than average in Greater London, higher in non-metropolitan areas and that non-response tended to increase with increasing age of the head of the household, up to age 65. Households that contained three or more adults, or where the head was born outside the United Kingdom or was classified to an ethnic minority group, were also more likely than others to be non-responding. Non-response was also above average where the head of the household had no post-school qualifications, was self-employed, or was in a manual social class group. The data were re-weighted to compensate for the main non-response biases identified from the 1991 Census comparison, as described in 'Weighting'. ONS has completed a similar comparative exercise, with the 2001 Census data, which resulted in an update of the non-response weights for the 2007 and 2008 calendar year EFS/LCF estimates.

Checks are included in the CAPI program, which are applied to the responses given during the interview. Other procedures are also in place to ensure that users are provided with high quality data. For example, quality control is carried out to ensure that any outliers are genuine, and checks are made on any unusual changes in average spending compared with the previous year.

When aspects of the survey change, rigorous tests are used to ensure the proposed changes are sensible and work both in the field and on the processing system. For example, in 1996-97 an improved set of questions was introduced on income from self-employment. This was developed by focus groups and then tested by piloting before being introduced into the main survey.

Income and expenditure balancing

The LCF is designed primarily as a survey of household expenditure on goods and services. It also gathers information about the income of household members, and is an important

and detailed source of income data. However, it is not possible to draw up a balance sheet of income and expenditure either for individual households or groups of households.

The majority of expenditure information collected relates to the two week period immediately following the interview, whereas income components can refer to a much longer period (the most recent 12 months). LCF income does not include withdrawal of savings, loans and money received in payment of loans, receipts from maturing insurance policies, proceeds from the sale of assets (e.g. a car) and winnings from betting or windfalls, such as legacies. Despite this, recorded expenditure might reflect these items, as well as the effects of living off savings, using capital, borrowing money or income - either recent or from a previous period.

Hence, there is no reason why income and expenditure should balance. In fact measured expenditure exceeds measured income at the bottom end of the income distribution. However, this difference cannot be regarded as a reliable measure of savings or dis-saving.

For further information of what is included in income on the LCF see Income headings on page 197.

Imputation of missing information

Although LCF response is generally based on complete households responding, there are areas in the survey for which missing information is imputed. This falls into two broad categories:

(i)   Specific items of information missing from a response. These missing values are imputed on a case by case basis using other information collected in the interview. The procedure is used, for example, for council tax payments and for interest received on savings.

(ii) Imputation of a complete diary case. Where a response is missing a diary from a household member, this information is imputed using information from respondents with similar characteristics.

Uses of the survey

LCF expenditure data

Retail Prices Index – The main reason, historically, for instituting a regular survey on expenditure by households has been to provide information on spending patterns for the Retail Prices Index (RPI). The RPI plays a vital role in the uprating of state pensions and welfare benefits and in general economic policy and analysis. The RPI measures the change in the cost of a selection of goods and services representative of the expenditure of the vast majority of households. The pattern of expenditure gradually changes from one year to the next, and the composition of the basket needs to be kept up-to-date. Accordingly, regular information is required on spending patterns and much of this is supplied by the LCF. The expenditure weights for the general RPI need to relate to people within given income limits, for which the LCF is the only source of information.

Household expenditure and GDP – LCF data on spending are an important source used in compiling national estimates of household final consumption expenditure which are published regularly in *United Kingdom National Accounts (ONS Blue Book)*. Household final consumption expenditure estimates feed into the National Accounts and estimates of GDP. They will also provide the weights for the Consumer Price Index (CPI), and for Purchasing Power Parities (PPPs) for international price comparisons. LCF data are also used in the estimation of taxes on expenditure, in particular VAT.

Regional accounts – LCF expenditure information is one of the sources used by ONS to derive regional estimates of consumption expenditure. It is also used in compiling some of the other estimates for the regional accounts.

The Statistical Office of the European Communities (Eurostat) collates information from family budget surveys conducted by the member states. The LCF is the UK's contribution to this. The UK is one of only a few countries with such a regular, continuous and detailed survey.

HM Revenue and Customs (HMRC) have had early access to LCF expenditure data for 2008 quarter 1 (Jan-Mar). This data is used for the Spirits Tax Gap analysis.

Other Government uses – The Department of Energy and Climate Change and the Department for Transport, both use LCF expenditure data in their own fields, e.g. - relating to energy, housing, cars and transport. Several other Government publications include LCF expenditure data, such as *Social Trends*, *Regional Trends* and the *Social Focus* series.

Non-Government uses – There are also numerous users outside Central Government, including academic researchers and business and market researchers.

LCF income data

Redistribution of income – LCF information on income and expenditure is used to study how Government taxes and benefits affect household income. The Government's interdepartmental tax benefit model is based on the LCF and enables the economic effects of policy measures to be analysed across households. This model is used by HM Treasury and HM Revenue and Customs to estimate the impact

on different households of possible changes in taxes and benefits.

Non-Government users – As with the expenditure data, LCF income data are also studied extensively outside Government. In particular, academic researchers in the economic and social science areas of many universities use the LCF. For example the Institute for Fiscal Studies uses LCF data in research it carries out both for Government and on its own account to inform public debate.

Other LCF data

The Department for Environment, Food and Rural Affairs (Defra) publishes separate reports using LCF data on food expenditure to estimate consumption and nutrient intake.

The Department for Transport uses LCF data to monitor and forecast levels of car ownership and use, and in studies on the effects of motoring taxes.

Note: Great care is taken to ensure complete confidentiality of information and to protect the identity of LCF households. Only anonymised data are supplied to users.

Standard errors and estimates of precision

Because the LCF is a sample of households and not a census of the whole population, the results are liable to differ to some degree from those that would have been obtained if every single household had been covered. Some of the differences will be systematic, in that lower proportions of certain types of household respond than of others. That aspect is discussed in 'Description and response rate of the survey' and 'Weighting'. This section discusses the effect of sampling variability that is the differences in expenditure and income between the households in the sample and in the whole population that arise from random chance. The degree of variability will depend on the sample size and how widely particular categories of expenditure (or income) vary between households. The sampling variability is smallest for the average expenditure of large groups of households on items purchased frequently and when the level of spending does not vary greatly between households. Conversely, it is largest for small groups of households, and for items purchased infrequently or for which expenditure varies considerably between households. A numerical measure of the likely magnitude of such differences (between the sample estimate and the value of the entire population) is provided by the quantity known as the standard error.

The calculation of standard errors takes into account the fact that the LCF sample is drawn in two stages, first a sample of areas (primary sampling units) then a sample of addresses within each of these areas. The main features of the sample design are described in 'Description and response rate of the survey'. The calculation also takes account of the effect of weighting. The two-stage sample increases sampling variability slightly, but the weighting reduces it for some items.

Standard errors for detailed expenditure items are presented in relative terms in Table A1 (standard error as a percentage of the average to which it refers). As the calculation of full standard errors is complex, this is the only table where they are shown. Tables B1 and B2 in this section show the design factor (DEFT), a measure of the efficiency of the survey's sample design. The DEFT is calculated by dividing the 'full' standard error by the standard error that would have applied if the survey had used a simple random sample ('simple method').

Table B1

Percentage standard errors of expenditure of households and number of recording households, 2008

Commodity or service		Percentage standard error		Percentage standard error	Households recording expenditure	
	Weighted average weekly household expenditure (£)	Simple method	Design factor (DEFT)	Full method	Recording households in sample	Percentage of all households
All expenditure groups	386.30	1.1	1.1	1.2	5,845	100
Food and non-alcoholic drinks	50.70	0.8	1.0	0.8	5,804	99
Alcoholic drink, tobacco & narcotics	10.80	2.1	1.0	2.0	3,602	62
Clothing and footwear	21.60	2.2	1.0	2.2	3,939	67
Housing, fuel and power	53.00	1.4	1.3	1.9	5,821	100
Household goods and services	30.10	3.1	1.0	3.2	5,354	92
Health	5.10	5.6	1.2	6.5	2,936	50
Transport	63.40	1.9	1.0	2.0	5,003	86
Communication	12.00	1.2	1.1	1.2	5,566	95
Recreation and culture	60.10	3.6	1.0	3.6	5,786	99
Education	6.20	9.8	1.3	12.8	467	8
Restaurants and hotels	37.70	2.0	1.1	2.1	5,093	87
Miscellaneous goods and services	35.60	2.2	1.1	2.5	5,710	98

Table B2

Percentage standard errors of income of households and numbers of recording households, 2008

Source of income		Percentage standard error		Percentage standard error	Households recording expenditure	
	Weighted average weekly household expenditure (£)	Simple method	Design factor (DEFT)	Full method	Recording households in sample	Percentage of all households
Gross household income	713	2.6	1.6	4.1	5,839	100
Wages and salaries	476	2.7	1.6	4.2	3,488	60
Self-employment	66	11.9	0.8	9.9	686	12
Investments	28	18.3	1.8	33.0	3,030	52
Annuities and pensions (other than social security benefits)	49	4.0	0.9	3.4	1,737	30
Social security benefits	89	1.4	0.8	1.2	4,283	73
Other sources	6	7.3	1.4	10.5	735	13

Using the standard errors – confidence intervals

A good way of using standard errors is to calculate 95% confidence intervals from them. Simplifying a little, these can be taken to mean that there is only a 5% chance that the true population value lies outside that confidence interval. The 95% confidence interval is calculated as 1.96 times the standard error on either side of the mean. For example the average expenditure on food and non-alcoholic drinks is £50.70 and the corresponding percentage standard error (full method) is 0.8%. The amount either side of the mean for 95% confidence is then:

1.96 x (0.8 ÷100) x £50.70 = £0.80 (rounded to nearest 10p)
Lower limit is 50.70 – 0.80 = £49.90 (rounded to nearest 10p)
Upper limit is 50.70 + 0.80 = £51.50 (rounded to nearest 10p)

Similar calculations can be carried out for other estimates of expenditure and income. The 95% confidence intervals for main expenditure categories are given in Table B3.

Table B3

95 per cent confidence intervals for average household expenditure, 2008

Commodity or service	Weighted average weekly household expenditure (£)	95% confidence interval	
		Lower limit	Upper limit
All expenditure groups	**386.30**	**377.00**	**395.70**
Food and non-alcoholic drinks	50.70	49.90	51.50
Alcoholic drink, tobacco & narcotics	10.80	10.40	11.20
Clothing and footwear	21.60	20.60	22.50
Housing, fuel and power	53.00	51.10	55.00
Household goods and services	30.10	28.30	32.00
Health	5.10	4.50	5.80
Transport	63.40	60.90	65.90
Communication	12.00	11.70	12.20
Recreation and culture	60.10	55.80	64.30
Education	6.20	4.60	7.70
Restaurants and hotels	37.70	36.20	39.30
Miscellaneous goods and services	35.60	33.90	37.40

Calculation of standard errors

Simple method

This formula treats the LCF sample as though it had arisen from a much simpler design with no multi-stage sampling, stratification, nor differential sampling and no non-response weights. The weights are used but only to estimate the true population standard deviation in what is, in fact, a weighted design. The method of calculation is as follows: Let n be the total number of responding households in the survey, x_r the expenditure on a particular item of the r-th household, w_r be the weight attached to household r, and $\overline{x}$ the average expenditure per household on that item (averaged over the n households). Then the standard error $\overline{x}$, sesrs is given by:

$$sesrs = \sqrt{\frac{\sum_{r=1}^{n} w_r (x_r - \overline{x})^2}{(n-1)\sum_{r=1}^{n} w_r}}$$

Full method

In fact, the sample in Great Britain is a multi-stage, stratified, random sample described further in 'Description and response rate of the survey'. First a sample of areas, the Primary Sampling Units (PSUs), is drawn from an ordered list. Then within each PSU a random sample of households is drawn. In Northern Ireland, however, the sample is drawn in a single stage and there is no clustering. The results are also weighted for non-response and calibrated to match the population separately by sex, by 5-year age ranges, and by region, as described in 'Weighting'.

The method for calculating complex standard errors for the weighted estimates used on this survey is quite complex. First, we apply methods that take account of the clustering, stratification and differential sampling (and initial non-response weights) used in the design. Then we modify these to allow for the calibration weighting used on the survey. The exact formulae also depend on whether we are estimating standard errors for an estimated total or a mean or proportion. Here we outline the method for a total.

Consecutive PSUs in the ordered list are first grouped up into pairs, or triples at the end of a regional stratum. The standard error of a weighted total is estimated by:

$$sedes = \sqrt{\sum_h \frac{k_h}{k_h - 1} \sum_i (x_{hi} - \overline{x}_h)^2}$$

where the h denotes the stratum (PSU pairs or triples), k_h is the number of PSUs in the stratum h (either 2 or 3), the x_{hi} is the weighted total in PSU$_i$ and the $\overline{x}_h$ is the mean of these totals in stratum h. Further details of this method of estimating sampling errors are described in *A Sampling Errors Manual* (B Butcher and D Elliot, ONS 1987).

The effect of the calibration weighting is calculated using a jackknife linearisation estimator. It uses the formula given above but with each household's expenditure, x_r, replaced by a residual from a linear regression of expenditure on the number of people in each household in each of the regions and age by sex categories used in the weighting.

The formulae have been expressed in terms of expenditures on a particular item, but of course they can also be applied to expenditures on groups of items, commodity groups and incomes from particular sources.

Definitions

Major changes in definitions since 1991 are described in 'Changes to definitions, 1991 to 2008'. Changes made between 1980 and 1990 are summarised in Appendix E of *Family Spending* 1994–95. For earlier changes see Annex 5 of Family Expenditure Survey 1980.

Contents	Page
Household	**190**
Retired households	190
Household reference person (HRP)	190
Members of household	191
Household composition	191
Adult	191
Children	191
Spenders	191
Economically active	**191**
Economically inactive	**192**
NS-SEC	**192**
Regions	**192**
Urban/rural areas	**192**
Expenditure	**193**
Goods supplied from a household's own shop or farm	193
Hire purchase, credit sales agreements and loans	193
Club payments	193
Credit card transactions	193
Income tax	194
Rented dwellings	194
Rent-free dwellings	194
Owner-occupied dwellings	194
Second-hand goods and part-exchange transactions	194
Business expenses	194
Income	**194**
Wages and salaries of employees	195
Income from self-employment	195
Income from investment	195
Social security benefits	196
Quantiles	**196**
Income headings	**197**
Region diagram	**199**

Household

A household comprises one person or a group of people who have the accommodation as their only or main residence and (for a group):

> share the living accommodation, that is a living room or sitting room, or
> share meals together or have common housekeeping

Resident domestic servants are included. The members of a household are not necessarily related by blood or marriage. As the survey covers only private households, people living in hostels, hotels, boarding houses or institutions are excluded. Households are not excluded if some or all members are not British subjects, but information is not collected from households containing members of the diplomatic service of another country or members of the United States armed forces.

Retired households

Retired households are those where the household reference person is retired. The household reference person is defined as retired if 65 years of age or more and male or 60 years of age or more and female, and economically inactive. Hence if, for example, a male household reference person is over 65 years of age, but working part-time or waiting to take up a part-time job, this household would not be classified as a retired household. For analysis purposes two categories are used in this report:

- 'A retired household mainly dependent upon state pensions' is one in which at least three-quarters of the total income of the household is derived from national insurance retirement and similar pensions, including housing and other benefits paid in supplement to or instead of such pensions. The term 'national insurance retirement and similar pensions' includes national insurance disablement and war disability pensions, and income support in conjunction with these disability payments.

- 'Other retired households' are retired households which do not fulfil the income conditions of 'retired household mainly dependent upon state pensions' because more than a quarter of the household's income derives from occupational retirement pensions and/or income from investments, annuities etc.

Household reference person (HRP)

From 2001-02, the concept of household reference person (HRP) was adopted on all government-sponsored surveys, in place of head of household. The household reference person is the householder, i.e. the person who:

- owns the household accommodation, or

- is legally responsible for the rent of the accommodation, or

- has the household accommodation as an emolument or perquisite, or

- has the household accommodation by virtue of some relationship to the owner who is not a member of the household.

If there are joint householders the household reference person will be the one with the higher income. If the income is the same, then the eldest householder is taken.

Members of household

In most cases the members of co-operating households are easily identified as the people who satisfy the conditions in the definition of a household, above, and are present during the record-keeping period. However difficulties of definition arise where people are temporarily away from the household or else spend their time between two residences. The following rules apply in deciding whether or not such persons are members of the household:

- married persons living and working away from home for any period are included as members provided they consider the sampled address to be their main residence; in general, other people (e.g. relatives, friends, boarders) who are either temporarily absent or who spend their time between the sampled address and another address, are included as members if they consider the sampled address to be their main residence. However, there are exceptions which override the subjective main residence rule:

  i.   Children under 16 away at school are included as members;

  ii. Older persons receiving education away from home, including children aged 16 and 17, are excluded unless they are at home for all or most of the record-keeping period;

  iii. Visitors staying temporarily with the household and others who have been in the household for only a short time are treated as members provided they will be staying with the household for at least one month from the start of record-keeping.

Household composition

A consequence of these definitions is that household compositions quoted in this report include some households where certain members are temporarily absent. For example, 'two adult and children' households will contain a few households where one parent is temporarily away from home.

Adult

In the report, persons who have reached the age of 18 are classed as adults. In addition, those aged 16–18 who are not in full-time education, or who are married, are classed as adults.

Children

In the report, persons who are under 18 years of age, in full-time education and have never been married are classed as children.

However, in the definition of clothing, clothing for persons aged 16 years and over is classified as clothing for men and women; clothing for those aged five but under 16 as clothing for boys and girls; and clothing for those under five as babies clothing.

Main Diary Keeper (MDK)

The MDK is the person in the household who is normally responsible for most of the food shopping. This includes people who organise and pay for the shopping although they do not physically do the shopping themselves.

Spenders

Members of households who are aged 16 or more, excluding those who for special reasons are not capable of keeping diary record-books, are described as spenders.

Absent spenders

If a spender is absent for longer than seven days they are defined as an 'absent spender'. Absent spenders do not keep a diary and consequently are not eligible for the monetary gift that is paid to diary keepers.

Non-spenders

If a household member is completely incapable of contributing to the survey by answering questions or keeping a diary, then they are defined as a 'non-spender'. However, incapable people living on their own cannot be designated as non-spenders as they comprise the whole expenditure unit. If this is the case, the interviewer should enlist the help of the person outside of the household who looks after their interests. If there is no-one able or willing to help, the address should be coded as incapable.

Economically active

These are persons aged 16 or over who fall into the following categories:

- Employees at work – those who at the time of interview were working full-time or part-time as employees or were away from work on holiday. Part-time work is defined as normally working 30 hours a week or less (excluding meal breaks) including regularly worked overtime.

- Employees temporarily away from work – those who at the time of interview had a job but were absent because of illness or accident, temporary lay-off, strike etc.

- Government supported training schemes – those participating in government programmes and schemes who in the course of their participation receive training, such as Employment Training, including those who are also employees in employment.

- Self-employed – those who at the time of interview said they were self-employed.

- Unemployed – those who at time of interview were out of employment, and have sought work within the last four weeks and were available to start work within two weeks, or were waiting to start a job already obtained.

- Unpaid family workers – those working unpaid for their own or a relative's business. In this report, unpaid family workers are included under economically inactive in analyses by economic status (Tables A19 and A48) because insufficient information is available to assign them to an economic status group.

Economically inactive

- Retired – persons who have reached national insurance retirement age (60 and over for women, 65 and over for men) and are not economically active.

- Unoccupied – persons under national insurance retirement age who are not working, nor actively seeking work. This category includes certain self-employed persons such as mail order agents and baby-sitters who are not classified as economically active.

In this report, unpaid family workers are classified as economically inactive in analyses by economic status, although they are economically active by definition. This is because insufficient information is available to assign them to an economic status group.

National Statistics Socio-economic classification (NS-SEC)

From 2001, the National Statistics Socio-economic classification (NS-SEC) was adopted for all official surveys, in place of Social Class based on Occupation and Socio-economic group. NS-SEC is itself based on the Standard Occupational Classification 2000 (SOC2000) and details of employment status. Although NS-SEC is an occupationally based classification, there are procedures for classifying those not in work.

The main categories used for analysis in *Family Spending* are:

1 Higher managerial and professional occupations, sub-divided into:

    1.1 Large employers and higher managerial occupations

    1.2 Higher professional occupations

2 Lower managerial and professional occupations

3 Intermediate occupations

4 Small employers and own account workers

5 Lower supervisory and technical occupations

6 Semi-routine occupations

7 Routine occupations

8 Never worked and long-term unemployed

9 Students

10 Occupation not stated

11 Not classifiable for other reasons

The long-term unemployed are defined as those unemployed and seeking work for 12 months or more. Members of the armed forces, who were assigned to a separate category in Social Class, are included within the NS-SEC classification. Individuals that have retired within the last 12 months are classified according to their employment. Other retired individuals are assigned to the 'Not classifiable for other reasons' category.

Regions

These are the Government Office Regions as defined in 1994. See the region map on page 161 for more details.

Urban and rural areas

This classification replaces the previous Department for Transport, Local Government and the Regions (DTLR) 1991 Census-based urban and rural classification, which was used in previous editions of *Family Spending*. The new classification is applied across Great Britain (GB) and is an amalgamation of the Rural and Urban Classification 2004 for England and Wales and the Scottish Executive Urban Rural Classification. These classifications are based on 2001 Census data and have been endorsed as the standard National Statistics Classifications for identifying urban and rural areas across GB.

It should be noted that the Rural and Urban Classification 2004 for England and Wales and the Scottish Executive Urban Rural Classification use different definitions, as the nature of rurality is different in these countries. Within Tables A38, A45 and A48 of this publication, households in Scotland have been classified using the Scottish Classification for rural and urban areas and households in England and Wales have been classified using the England and Wales Classification. Nonetheless, in broad terms, both classifications define an area as urban or rural depending on whether the population falls inside a settlement of population 10,000 or more. For further details concerning these classifications please refer to the ONS website: www. statistics.gov.uk/geography/nrudp.asp.

Expenditure

Any definition of expenditure is to some extent arbitrary, and the inclusion of certain types of payment is a matter of convenience or convention depending on the purpose for which the information is to be used. In the tables in this report, total expenditure represents current expenditure on goods and services. Total expenditure, defined in this way, excludes those recorded payments which are really savings or investments (e.g. purchases of national savings certificates, life assurance premiums, contributions to pension funds). Similarly, income tax payments, national insurance contributions, mortgage capital repayments and other payments for major additions to dwellings are excluded. Expenditure data are collected in the diary record-book and in the household schedule. Informants are asked to record in the diary any payments made during the 14 days of record-keeping, whether or not the goods or services paid for have been received. Certain types of expenditure which are usually regular though infrequent, such as insurance, licences and season tickets, and the periods to which they relate, are recorded in the household schedule as well as regular payments such as utility bills.

The cash purchase of motor vehicles is also entered in the household schedule. In addition, expenditure on some items purchased infrequently (thereby being subject to high sampling errors) has been recorded in the household schedule using a retrospective recall period of either three or 12 months. These items include carpets, furniture, holidays and some housing costs. In order to avoid duplication, all payments shown in the diary record-book which relate to items listed in the household or income schedules are omitted in the analysis of the data irrespective of whether there is a corresponding entry on the latter schedules. Amounts paid in respect of periods longer than a week are converted to weekly values.

Expenditure tables in this report show the 12 main commodity groups of spending and these are broken down into items which are numbered hierarchically (see 'Changes to definitions, 1991 to 2008' which details a major change to the coding frame used from 2001-02). Table A1 shows a further breakdown in the items themselves into components which can be separately identified. The items are numbered as in the main expenditure tables and against each item or component

are shown the average weekly household expenditure and percentage standard error.

Qualifications which apply to this concept of expenditure are described in the following paragraphs:

- **Goods supplied from a household's own shop or farm**

  Spenders are asked to record and give the value of goods obtained from their own shop or farm, even if the goods are withdrawn from stock for personal use without payment. The value is included as expenditure.

- **Hire purchase and credit sales agreements, and transactions financed by loans repaid by instalments**

  Expenditure on transactions under hire purchase or credit sales agreements, or financed by loans repaid by instalments, consists of all instalments which are still being paid at the date of interview, together with down payments on commodities acquired within the preceding three months. These two components (divided by the periods covered) provide the weekly averages which are included in the expenditure on the separate items given in the tables in this report.

- **Club payments and budget account payments, instalments through mail order firms and similar forms of credit transaction**

  When goods are purchased by forms of credit other than hire purchase and credit sales agreement, the expenditure on them may be estimated either from the amount of the instalment which is paid or from the value of the goods which are acquired. Since the particular commodities to which the instalment relates may not be known, details of goods ordered through clubs, etc. during the month prior to the date of interview are recorded in the household schedule. The weekly equivalent of the value of the goods is included in the expenditure on the separate items given in the tables in this report. This procedure has the advantage of enabling club transactions to be related to specific articles. Although payments into clubs, etc. are shown in the diary record-book, these entries are excluded from expenditure estimates.

- **Credit card transactions**

  From 1988 purchases made by credit card or charge card have been recorded in the survey on an *acquisition* basis rather than the formerly used payment basis. Thus, if a spender acquired an item (by use of credit/charge card) during the two week survey period, the value of the item would be included as part of expenditure in that period whether or not any payment was made in this period to the credit card account. Payments made to the card account are ignored. However any payment of credit/charge card *interest* is included in expenditure if made in the two week period.

- **Income Tax**

  Amounts of income tax deducted under the PAYE scheme or paid directly by those who are employers or self-employed are recorded (together with information about tax refunds). For employers and the self-employed the amounts comprise the actual payments made in the previous twelve months and may not correspond to the tax due on the income arising in that period, e.g. if no tax has been paid but is due or if tax payments cover more than one financial year. However, the amounts of tax deducted at source from some of the items which appear in the Income Schedule are not directly available. Estimates of the tax paid on bank and building society interest and amounts deducted from dividends on stocks and shares are therefore made by applying the appropriate rates of tax. In the case of income tax paid at source on pensions and annuities, similar adjustments are made. These estimates mainly affect the relatively few households with high incomes from interest and dividends, and households including someone receiving a pension from previous employment.

- **Rented dwellings**

  Expenditure on rented dwellings is taken as the sum of expenditure on rent, rates, council tax, water rates etc. For local authority tenants the expenditure is gross rent less any rebate (including rebate received in the form of housing benefit), and for other tenants gross rent less any rent allowance received under statutory schemes including the Housing Benefit Scheme. Rebate on Council Tax or rates (Northern Ireland) is deducted from expenditure on Council Tax or rates. Receipts from sub-letting part of the dwelling are not deducted from housing costs but appear (net of the expenses of the sub-letting) as investment income. Average payments by households renting accommodation for repairs, maintenance and decorations are shown separately in the estimates of expenditure by such households in Table A34 which gives housing expenditure by tenure type. Accommodation rented from a housing association is shown separately.

- **Rent-free dwellings**

  Rent-free dwellings are those owned by someone outside the household and where either no rent is charged or the rent is paid by someone outside the household. Households whose rent is paid directly to the landlord by the DWP do not live rent-free. Payments for Council Tax, water rates etc., are regarded as the cost of housing. Rebate on rates (Northern Ireland)/Council Tax/water rates(Scotland) (including rebate received in the form of housing benefit), is

deducted from expenditure on rates/Council Tax/water rates. Receipts from sub-letting part of the dwelling are not deducted from housing costs but appear (net of the expenses of the sub-letting) as investment income.

- **Owner-occupied dwellings**

  In the LCF payments for water rates, ground rent, fuel, maintenance and repair of the dwelling, and other miscellaneous services related to the dwelling etc., are regarded as the cost of housing. Receipts from letting part of the dwelling are not deducted from housing costs but appear (net of the expenses of the letting) as investment income. Mortgage capital repayments and amounts paid for the outright purchase of the dwelling or for major structural alterations are not included as housing expenditure, but are entered under 'other items recorded', as are Council Tax, rates (Northern Ireland), and mortgage interest payments. Structural insurance is included in Miscellaneous goods and services.

- **Second-hand goods and part-exchange transactions**

  The survey expenditure data are based on information about actual payments and therefore include payments for second-hand goods and part-exchange transactions. New payments only are included for part-exchange transactions, i.e. the costs of the goods obtained less the amounts allowed for the goods which are traded in. Receipts for goods sold or traded in are not included in income.

- **Business expenses**

  The survey covers only private households and is concerned with payments made by members of households as private individuals. Spenders are asked to state whether expenditure which has been recorded on the schedules includes amounts which will be refunded as expenses from a business or organisation or which will be entered as business expenses for income tax purposes, e.g. rent, telephone charges, travelling expenses, meals out. Any such amounts are deducted from the recorded expenditure.

Income

The standard concept of income in the survey is, as far as possible, that of gross weekly cash income current at the time of interview, i.e. before the deduction of income tax actually paid, national insurance contributions and other deductions at source. However, for a few tables a concept of disposable income is used, defined as gross weekly cash income less the statutory deductions and payments of income tax (taking refunds into account) and national insurance contributions. Analysis in Chapter 3 of this volume and some other analyses of LCF data use 'equivalisation' of incomes - i.e. adjustment of household income to allow for the different size and composition of each household. For more information see Chapter 3 of this volume. The cash levels of certain items of income (and expenditure) recorded in the survey by households receiving supplementary benefit were affected by the Housing Benefit Scheme introduced in stages from November 1982. From 1984 housing expenditure is given on a strictly net basis and all rent/council tax rebates and allowances and housing benefit are excluded from gross income.

Although information about most types of income is obtained on a current basis, some data, principally income from investment and from self-employment, are estimated over a 12-month period.

The following are excluded from the assessment of income:

- money received by one member of the household from another (e.g. housekeeping money, dress allowance, children's pocket money) other than wages paid to resident domestic servants;

- withdrawals of savings, receipts from maturing insurance policies, proceeds from sale of financial and other assets (e.g. houses, cars, furniture, etc.), winnings from betting, lump-sum gratuities and windfalls such as legacies;

- the value of educational grants and scholarships not paid in cash;

- the value of income in kind, including the value of goods received free and the abatement in cost of goods received at reduced prices, and of bills paid by someone who is not a member of the household;

- loans and money received in repayment of loans.

Details are obtained of the income of each member of the household. The income of the household is taken to be the sum of the incomes of all its members. The information does not relate to a common or a fixed time period. Items recorded for periods greater than a week are converted to a weekly value.

Particular points relating to some components of income are as follows:

- **Wages and salaries of employees**

  The normal gross wages or salaries of employees are taken to be their earnings. These are calculated by adding to the normal 'take home' pay amounts deducted at source, such as income tax payments, national insurance contributions and other deductions, e.g. payments into firm social clubs, superannuation schemes, works transport, benevolent funds etc. Employees are asked to give the earnings actually received including bonuses and commission the last time payment was made and, if different, the amount

usually received. It is the amount usually received which is regarded as the normal take-home pay. Additions are made so as to include in normal earnings the value of occasional payments, such as bonuses or commissions received quarterly or annually. One of the principal objects in obtaining data on income is to enable expenditure to be classified in ranges of normal income. Average household expenditure is likely to be based on the long-term expectations of the various members of the household as to their incomes rather than be altered by short-term changes affecting individuals. Hence if employees have been away from work without pay for 13 weeks or less they are regarded as continuing to receive their normal earnings instead of social security benefits, such as unemployment or sickness benefit, that they may be receiving. Otherwise, normal earnings are disregarded and current short-term social security benefits taken instead. Wages and salaries include any earnings from subsidiary employment as an employee and the earnings of HM Forces.

- **Income from self-employment**

  Income from self-employment covers any personal income from employment other than as an employee; for example, as a sole trader, professional or other person working on his own account or in partnership, including subsidiary work on his own account by a person whose main job is as an employee. It is measured from estimates of income or trading profits, after deduction of business expenses but before deduction of tax, over the most recent 12-month period for which figures can be given. Should either a loss have been made or no profit, income would be taken as the amounts drawn from the business for own use or as any other income received from the job or business. Persons working as mail order agents or baby-sitters, with no other employment, have been classified as unoccupied rather than as self-employed, and the earnings involved have been classified as earnings from "other sources" rather than self-employment income.

- **Income from investment**

  Income from investments or from property, other than that in which the household is residing, is the amount received during the 12 months immediately prior to the date of the initial interview. It includes receipts from sub-letting part of the dwelling (net of the expenses of the sub-letting). If income tax has been deducted at source the gross amount is estimated by applying a conversion factor during processing.

- **Social security benefits**

  Income from social security benefits does not include the short-term payments such as unemployment or sickness benefit received by an employee who has been away from work for 13 weeks or less, and who is therefore regarded as continuing to receive his normal earnings as described on page 198.

Quantiles

The quantiles of a distribution, e.g. of household expenditure or income, divide it into a number of equal parts; each of which contains the same number of households.

For example, the median of a distribution divides it into two equal parts, so that half the households in a distribution of household income will have income more than the median, and the other half will have income less than the median. Similarly, quartiles, quintiles and deciles divide the distribution into four, five and ten equal parts respectively.

Most of the analysis in *Family Spending* is done in terms of quintile groups and decile groups.

In the calculation of quantiles for this report, zero values are counted as part of the distribution.

Income headings

Headings used for identifying 2008 income information

Source of income

References in tables	Components separately identified	Explanatory notes
a. Wages and salaries	Normal 'take-home' pay from main employment 'Take-home' pay from subsidary employment Employees' income tax deduction Employees' National Insurance contribution Superannuation contributions deducted from pay Other deductions	(i) In the calculation of household income in this report, where an employee has been away from work without pay for 13 weeks or less his normal wage or salary has been used in estimating his total income instead of social security benefits, such as unemployment or sickness benefits that he may have received. Otherwise such benefits are used in estimating total income (see notes at reference e) (ii) Normal income from wages and salaries is estimated by adding to the normal 'take-home' pay deductions made at source last time paid, together with the weekly value of occasional additions to wages and salaries (see page 195). (iii) The components of wages and salaries for which figures are separately available amount in total to the normal earnings of employees, regardless of the operation of the 13 week rule in note (i) above. Thus the sum of the components listed here does not in general equal the wages and salaries figure in tables of this report.
b. Self-employment	Income from business or profession, including subsidiary self-employment	The earnings or profits of a trade or profession, after deduction of business expenses but before deduction of tax
c. Investments	Interest on building society shares and deposits Interest on bank deposits and savings accounts including National Savings Bank Interest on ISAs Interest on TESSAs Interest on Gilt-edged stock and War Loans Interest and dividends from stocks, shares, bonds, trusts, PEPs, debentures and other securities Rent or income from property, after deducting expenses but inclusive of income tax (including receipts from letting or sub-letting part of own residence, net of the expenses of the letting or sub-letting). Other unearned Income	

Income headings (cont.)

Headings used for identifying 2008 income information

Source of income

d. Annuities and pensions, other than social security	Annuities and income from trust or covenant Pensions from previous employers Personal pensions	
e. Social security benefits	Child benefit Guardian's allowance Carer's allowance (formerly Invalid care allowance) Retirement pension (National Insurance) or old person's pension Pension credit Widow's pension/bereavement allowance or widowed parent's allowance War disablement pension or war widow/widower's pension Severe disablement allowance Care component of disability living allowance Mobility component of disability living allowance Attendance allowance Job seekers allowance Winter fuel allowance Cold Weather Payment Income support Working tax credit Child tax credit Incapacity benefit Statutory sick pay (from employer) Industrial injury disablement benefit Maternity allowance Statutory maternity pay Statutory paternity pay Statutory adoption pay Any other benefit including lump sums and grants Social security benefits excluded from income calculation by 13 week rule	(i) The calculation of household income in this report takes account of the 13 week rule described at reference a, note (i) (ii) The components of social security benefits for which figures are separately available amount in total to the benefits received in the week before interview. That is to say, they include amounts that are discounted from the total by the operation of the 13 week rule in note i. Thus the sum of the components listed here differs from the total of social security benefits used in the income tables of this report. (iii) Housing Benefit is treated as a reduction in housing costs and not as income
f. Other sources	Married person's allowance from husband/wife temporarily away from home Alimony or separation allowances; allowances for foster children, allowances from members of the Armed Forces or Merchant Navy, or any other money from friends or relatives, other than husband outside the household Benefits from trade unions, friendly societies etc., other than pensions Value of meal vouchers Earnings from intermittent or casual work over 12 months, not included in a or b above Student loans and money scholarships received by persons aged 16 and over and aged under 16. Other income of children under 16	e.g. from spare-time jobs or income from Trusts or investments

STANDARD STATISTICAL REGION

GOVERNMENT OFFICE REGION

STANDARD STATISTICAL REGION		GOVERNMENT OFFICE REGION
NORTH	Cleveland Durham Northumberland Tyne and Wear	NORTH EAST
	Cumbria	
NORTH WEST	Cheshire Greater Manchester Lancashire Merseyside	NORTH WEST
YORKSHIRE AND HUMBERSIDE	Humberside North Yorkshire South Yorkshire West Yorkshire	YORKSHIRE AND THE HUMBER
EAST MIDLANDS	Derbyshire Leicestershire Lincolnshire Northamptonshire Nottinghamshire	EAST MIDLANDS
WEST MIDLANDS	Hereford and Worcester Shropshire Staffordshire Warwickshire West Midlands	WEST MIDLANDS
EAST ANGLIA	Cambridgeshire Norfolk Suffolk	EAST OF ENGLAND
	Bedfordshire Essex Hertfordshire	
	Greater London	LONDON
SOUTH EAST	Berkshire Buckinghamshire East Sussex Hampshire Isle of Wight Kent Oxfordshire Surrey West Sussex	SOUTH EAST
SOUTH WEST	Avon Cornwall Devon Dorset Gloucestershire Somerset Wiltshire	SOUTH WEST

Changes in definitions, 1991 to 2008

1991

No significant changes.

1992

Housing – Imputed rent for owner occupiers and households in rent-free accommodation was discontinued. For owner occupiers this had been the rent they would have had to pay themselves to live in the property they own, and for households in rent-free accommodation it was the rent they would normally have had to pay. Up to 1990 these amounts were counted both as income and as a housing cost. Mortgage interest payments were counted as a housing cost for the first time in 1991.

1993

Council Tax – Council Tax was introduced to replace the Community Charge in Great Britain from April 1993.

1994–95

New expenditure items – The definition of expenditure was extended to include two items previously shown under 'other payments recorded'. These were:

- gambling payments;
- mortgage protection premiums.

Expenditure classifications – A new classification system for expenditures was introduced in April 1994. The system is hierarchical and allows more detail to be preserved than the previous system. New categories of expenditure were introduced and are shown in detail in Table 7.1. The 14 main groups of expenditure were retained, but there were some changes in the content of these groups.

Gambling Payments – data on gambling expenditure and winnings are collected in the expenditure diary. Previously these were excluded from the definition of household expenditure used in the FES. The data are shown as memoranda items under the heading 'Other payments recorded' on both gross and net bases. The net basis corresponds approximately to the treatment of gambling in the National Accounts. The introduction of the National Lottery stimulated a reconsideration of this treatment. From April 1994, (gross) gambling payments have been included as expenditure in 'Leisure Services'. Gambling winnings continued to be noted as a memorandum item under 'Other items recorded'. They are treated as windfall income. They do not form a part of normal household income, nor are they subtracted from gross gambling payments. This treatment is in line with the PRODCOM classification of the Statistical Office of the European Communities (SOEC) for expenditure in household budget surveys.

1995–96

Geographical coverage – The FES geographical coverage was extended to mainland Scotland north of the Caledonian Canal.

Under 16s diaries – Two-week expenditure diaries for 7–15 year olds were introduced following three feasibility pilot studies which found that children of that age group were able to cope with the task of keeping a two-week expenditure record. Children are asked to record everything they buy with their own money but to exclude items bought with other people's money. Purchases are coded according to the same coding categories as adult diaries except for meals and snacks away from home which are coded as school meals, hot meals and snacks, and cold meals and snacks. Children who keep a diary are given a £5 incentive payment. A refusal to keep an under 16's diary does not invalidate the household from inclusion in the survey.

Pocket money given to children is still recorded separately in adult diaries; and money paid by adults for school meals and school travel is recorded in the Household Questionnaire. Double counting is eliminated at the processing stage.

Tables in *Family Spending* reports did not include the information from the children's diaries until the 1998–99 report. Appendix F in the 1998–99 and 1999–2000 reports show what difference the inclusion made.

1996–97

Self-employment – The way in which information about income from self-employment is collected was substantially revised in 1996–97 following various tests and pilot studies. The quality of such data was increased but this may have lead to a discontinuity. Full details are shown in the Income Questionnaire, available from the address in the introduction.

Cable/satellite television – Information on cable and satellite subscriptions is now collected from the household questionnaire rather than from the diary, leading to more respondents reporting this expenditure.

Mobile phones – Expenditure on mobile phones was previously collected through the diary. From 1996/97 this has been included in the questionnaire.

Job seekers allowance (JSA) – Introduced in October 1996 as a replacement for Unemployment Benefit and any Income Support associated with the payment of Unemployment Benefit. Receipt of JSA is collected with NI Unemployment

Benefit and with Income Support. In both cases the number of weeks a respondent has been in receipt of these benefits is taken as the number of weeks receiving JSA in the last 12 months and before that period the number of weeks receiving Unemployment Benefit/Income Support.

Retrospective recall – The period over which information is requested has been extended from 3 to 12 months for vehicle purchase and sale. Information on the purchase of car and motorcycle spare parts is no longer collected by retrospective recall. Instead expenditure on these items is collected through the diary.

State benefits – The lists of benefits specifically asked about was reviewed in 1996–97. See the Income Questionnaire for more information.

Sample stratifiers – New stratifiers were introduced in 1996–97 based on standard regions, socio-economic group and car ownership.

Government Office Regions – Regional analyses are now presented using the Government Office Regions (GORs) formed in 1994. Previously all regional analyses used Standard Statistical Regions (SSRs). For more information see Appendix F in the 1996–97 report.

1997–98

Bank/Building society service charges – Collection of information on service charges levied by banks has been extended to include building societies.

Payments from unemployment/redundancy insurances – Information is now collected on payments received from private unemployment and redundancy insurance policies. This information is then incorporated into the calculation of income from other sources.

Retired households – The definition of retired households has been amended to exclude households where the head of the household is economically active.

Rent-free tenure – The definition of rent-free tenure has been amended to include those households for which someone outside the household, except an employer or an organisation, is paying a rent or mortgage on behalf of the household.

National Lottery – From February 1997, expenditure on National lottery tickets was collected as three separate items: tickets for the Wednesday draw only, tickets for the Saturday draw only and tickets for both draws.

1998–99

Children's income – Three new expenditure codes were introduced: pocket money to children; money given to children for specific purposes and cash gifts to children. These replaced a single code covering all three categories.

Main job and last paid job – Harmonised questions were adopted.

1999–2000

Disabled Persons Tax Credit replaced Disability Working Allowance and Working Families Tax Credit replaced Family Credit from October 1999.

2000–01

Household definition – the definition was changed to the harmonised definition which has been in use in the Census and nearly all other government household surveys since 1981. The effect is to group together into a single household some people who would have been allocated to separate households on the previous definition. The effect is fairly small but not negligible.

Up to 1999–2000 the FES definition was based on the pre–1981 Census definition and required members to share eating and budgeting arrangements as well as shared living accommodation.

The definition of a household was:

One person or a group of people who have the accommodation as their only or main residence

and (for a group)

> share the living accommodation, that is a living or sitting room
> **and**
> share meals together (or have common housekeeping).

The harmonised definition is less restrictive:

One person or a group of people who have the accommodation as their only or main residence and (for a group)

> share the living accommodation, that is a living or sitting room
> **or**
> share meals together or have common housekeeping.

The effect of the change is probably to increase average household size by 0.6 per cent.

Question reductions – A thorough review of the questionnaire showed that a number of questions were no longer needed by government users. These were cut from the 2000–01 survey to reduce the burden on respondents. The reduction was fairly small but it did make the interview flow better. All the questions needed for a complete record of expenditure and income were retained.

Redesigned diary – The diary was redesigned to be easier for respondents to keep and to look cleaner. The main change of substance was to delete the column for recording whether each item was purchased by credit, charge or shop card.

Ending of MIRAS – Tax relief on interest on loans for house purchase was abolished from April 2000. Questions related to MIRAS were therefore dropped. They included some that were needed to estimate the amount if the respondent did not know it. A number were retained for other purposes, however, such as the amount of the loan still outstanding which is still asked for households paying a reduced rate of interest because one of them works for the lender.

2001–02

Expenditure and Food Survey (EFS) introduced, replacing the Family Expenditure and National Food Surveys (FES and NFS).

Household reference person – this replaced the previous concept of head of household. The household reference person is the householder, i.e. the person who:

- owns the household accommodation, or
- is legally responsible for the rent of the accommodation, or
- has the household accommodation as an emolument or perquisite, or
- has the household accommodation by virtue of some relationship to the owner who is not a member of the household.

If there are joint householders the household reference person is the one with the higher income. If the income is the same, then the eldest householder is taken.

A key difference between household reference person and head of household is that the household reference person must always be a householder, whereas the head of household was always the husband, who might not even be a householder himself.

National Statistics Socio-economic classification (NS-SEC) – the National Statistics Socio-economic classification (NS-SEC) was adopted for all official surveys, in place of Social Class based on Occupation and Socio-economic group. NS-SEC is itself based on the Standard Occupational Classification 2000 (SOC2000) and details of employment status.

The long-term unemployed, which fall into a separate category, are defined as those unemployed and seeking work for 12 months or more. Members of the armed forces, who were assigned to a separate category in Social Class, are included within the NS-SEC classification. Residual groups that remain unclassified include students and those with inadequately described occupations.

COICOP – From 2001–02, the Classification Of Individual COnsumption by Purpose (COICOP/HBS, referred to as COICOP in this volume) was introduced as a new coding frame for expenditure items. COICOP has been adapted to the needs of Household Budget Surveys (HBS) across the EU and, as a consequence, is compatible with similar classifications used in national accounts and consumer price indices. This allows the production of indicators which are comparable Europe-wide, such as the Harmonised Indices of Consumer Prices (computed for all goods as well as sub-categories such as food and transport). The main categorisation of spending used in this volume (namely 12 categories relating to food and non-alcoholic beverages; alcoholic beverages, tobacco and narcotics; clothing and footwear; housing, fuel and power; household goods and services; health, transport; communication; recreation and culture; education; restaurants and hotels; and miscellaneous goods and services) is only comparable between the two frames at a broad level. Table 4.1 in this volume has been produced by mapping COICOP to the FES 14 main categories. However the two frames are not comparable for any smaller categories, leading to a break in trends between 2000–01 and 2001–02 for any level of detail below the main 12-fold categorisation. A complete listing of COICOP and COICOP plus (an extra level of detail added by individual countries for their own needs) is available on request from the address in the introduction.

Proxy interviews – While questions about general household affairs are put to all household members or to a main household informant, questions about work and income are put to the individual members of the household. Where a member of the household is not present during the household interview, another member of the household (e.g. spouse) may be able to provide information about the absent person. The individual's interview is then identified as a proxy interview. From 2001–02, the EFS began accepting responses that contained a proxy interview.

Short income – From 2001–02, the EFS accepted responses from households that answered the short income section. This was designed for respondents who were reluctant to provide more detailed income information.

2002–03

Main shopper – At the launch of the EFS in April 2001, the respondent responsible for buying the household's main shopping was identified as the 'Main Diary Keeper''. From 2002–03, this term has been replaced by the 'Main Shopper'.

The importance of the Main Shopper is to ensure that we have obtained information on the bulk of the shopping in the household. Without this person's co-operation we have insufficient information to use the other diaries kept by members of the household in a meaningful way. The main shopper must therefore complete a diary for the interview to qualify as a full or partial interview. Without their participation, the outcome will be a refusal no matter who else is willing to complete a diary.

2003–04

Working Tax Credit replaced Disabled Persons Tax Credit and Working Families Tax Credit from April 2003.

Pension Credit replaced Minimum Income Guarantee from October 2003.

Child Tax Credit replaced Children's Tax Credit and Childcare Tax Credit from April 2003.

2004–05

No significant changes.

2005–06

Urban and rural definition – A new urban and rural area classification based on 2001 Census data has been introduced onto the EFS dataset and is presented in Tables A38, A45 and A48 of this publication. The classification replaces the Department for Transport, Local Government and the Regions (DTLR) 1991 Census-based urban and rural classification that was used in previous editions of Family Spending. The new classification is the standard National Statistics classification for identifying urban and rural areas in England and Wales, and Scotland. Please refer to 'Definitions' for further details.

Motor vehicle road taxation refunds – Questions on road tax refunds were inadvertently omitted from the 2005–06 questionnaire. Within the Appendix A tables of the 2005–06 report, the heading for category 13.2.3 'Motor vehicle road taxation payments less refunds', has been changed to reflect this omission.

Purchase of vehicles – During April to December 2005, respondents who had sold a vehicle were not asked whether they had bought that same vehicle in the previous year. This was corrected from January 2006, but means that some expenditure on vehicles may have been missed.

2006

No significant changes.

2007

An improvement to the imputation of mortgage interest payments has been implemented and applied to 2006 and 2007 data in this publication, which should lead to more accurate figures. This will also lead to a slight discontinuity.

An error was discovered in the derivation of mortgage capital repayments which was leading to double counting. This has been amended for the 2006 and 2007 data in this publication, which will cause a minor discontinuity.

2008

The LCF question used to derive the student category for NSSECB was changed in 2008 due to the introduction of the Integrated Household Survey (IHS). Prior to the IHS, respondents were asked if they were currently in full-time education and those who responded yes to this question were classified as students. Since 2008, respondents have been asked if they are enrolled on any full-time or part-time education course and those who respond yes have then been asked to select the course they are attending from a set of options. Respondents who select any of the full-time course options have been classified as students under NSSEC. This more stringent definition of full-time student has resulted in a decrease in the number of people classified as students.

Weighting

Since 1998-99 the FES/EFS/LCF has been weighted to reduce the effect of non-response bias and produce population totals and means. The weights are produced in two stages. First, the data are weighted to compensate for non-response (sample-based weighting). Second, the sample distribution is weighted so that it matches the population distribution in terms of region, age group and sex (population-based weighting).

Sample-based weighting using the Census

Weighting for non-response involves giving each respondent a weight so that they represent the non-respondents that are similar to them in terms of the survey characteristics. From 1998-99 the EFS has used results from the 1991 Census-linked study of non-respondents to carry out non-response weighting[1]. From 2007 onwards the EFS/LCF non-response classes and weights have been annually updated using 2001 Census-linked data

The Census-linked studies matched Census addresses with the sampled addresses of some of the large continuous surveys, including FES for 1991 link study and EFS for the 2001 link study. In this way it was possible to match the address details of the respondents as well as the non-respondents with corresponding information gathered from the Census for the same address. The information collected during the 1991 and then the 2001 Census/FES/EFS matching work was then used to identify the types of households that were being under-represented in the survey.

For the 1991 Census based non response weights a combination of household variables were analysed with the software package AnswerTree (using the chi-squared statistics CHAID)[2], to identify which characteristics were most significant in distinguishing between responding and non-responding households. These characteristics were sorted by the program to produce ten weighting classes with different response rates. For the updated 2001 Census based non-response weights a combination of household variables were analysed using a mixed model approach. The mixed model is a combined approach to modelling, to benefit from the underlying statistical model of logistic regression as well as utilising AnswerTree. Updated weighting classes were produced and households within each of the weighting classes were assigned an updated non-response weight.

Population-based weighting

The second stage of the weighting adjusts the non-response weights so that weighted totals match population totals. As the LCF sample is based on private households, the population totals used in the weighting need to relate to people living in private households. For 2008, 2007 and 2006 (reweighted) data, the EFS/LCF used population projections from the 2001 Census. These estimates exclude residents of institutions not covered by the EFS/LCF, i.e. those living in bed-and-breakfast accommodation, hostels, residential homes and other institutions.

The non-response weights were calibrated[3], so that weighted totals matched population totals for males and females in different age groups and for regions. An important feature of the population-based weighting is that it is done by adjusting the factors for households not individuals.

The weighting is carried out separately for each quarter of the survey. The main reason is that sample sizes vary from quarter to quarter more than in the past. This is due to re-issuing addresses where there had been no contact or a refusal to a new interviewer after an interval of a few months, which results in more interviews in the later quarters of the year than in the first quarter. Quarterly weighting therefore counteracts any potential bias from the uneven spread of interviews through the year. Quarterly weighting also results in small sample numbers in some of the age/sex categories that were used in previous years. The categories have therefore been widened slightly to avoid this.

Table B4

The effect of weighting on expenditure, 2008

Commodity or service	Average weekly household expediture		Absolute difference	Percentage difference
	Unweighted	Weighted as published		
All expenditure groups	388.80	386.30	-2.47	-0.6
Food and non-alcoholic drinks	51.80	50.70	-1.06	-2.0
Alcoholic drink, tobacco & narcotics	10.90	10.80	-0.15	-1.4
Clothing and footwear	22.20	21.60	-0.65	-2.9
Housing, fuel and power	50.80	53.00	2.21	4.3
Household goods and services	30.90	30.10	-0.80	-2.6
Health	5.20	5.10	-0.09	-1.7
Transport	64.10	63.40	-0.68	-1.1
Communication	11.80	12.00	0.16	1.4
Recreation and culture	61.50	60.10	-1.42	-2.3
Education	6.00	6.20	0.16	2.7
Restaurants and hotels	37.50	37.70	0.19	0.5
Miscellaneous	36.00	35.60	-0.34	-0.9
Weekly household income:				
Disposable	572	582	10	1.7
Gross	699	713	14	2.0

Effects of weighting on the data

Table B4 shows the effects of the weighting by comparing unweighted and weighted data from 2008.

The weighting reduced the estimate of total average expenditure by £2.47 a week; that is by 0.6 per cent. It had the largest impact on average weekly expenditure on housing, fuel and power, increasing the estimate by 4.3 per cent; on education, increasing the estimate by 2.7 per cent; and on communication, increasing the estimate by 1.4 per cent. It reduced the estimate of spending on clothing and footwear by 2.9 per cent and reduced the estimate of spending on household goods and services by 2.6 per cent. Weighting also increased the estimates of average income, by £10 a week (1.7 per cent) for disposable household income and by £14 a week (2.0 per cent) for gross household income, which is the income used in most tables in the report.

Re-weighting also has an effect on the variance of estimates. In an analysis on the 1999-2000 data, weighting increased variance slightly for some items and reduced for others. Overall the effect was to reduce variance slightly.

Further information

Further information on the method used to produce the weights is available from the contacts given on page ii of this publication

Notes

1   See Foster, K. (1994) *Weighting the FES to compensate for non-response, Part 1: An investigation into Census-based weighting schemes*, London: OPCS.

2   CHAID is an acronym that stands for Chi-squared Automatic Interaction Detection. As is suggested by its name, CHAID uses chi-squared statistics to identify optimal splits or groupings of independent variables in terms of predicting the outcome of a dependent variable, in this case response.

3   Implemented by the CALMAR software package before 2007 and GES for 2006-2008 (updated weights).

Index to tables in reports on the Family Expenditure Survey in 1997–98 to 2000–01 and the Living Costs and Food Survey 2001–02 to 2008

2008 tables		2007	2006	2005-06	2004-05	2003-04	2002-03	2001-02[1]	2000-01	1999-2000
Detailed expenditure and place of purchase										
A1	Detailed expenditure with full–method standard errors	A1	A1	A1	A1	A1	7.1	7.1	7.1	7.1
A2	Expenditure on alcoholic drink by type of premises	A2	A2	A2	A2	A2	7.2	7.2	7.2	7.2
A3	Expenditure on food by place of purchase	A3	A3	A3	A3	A3	7.3	7.3	7.3	7.3
..	Expenditure on alcoholic drink by place of purchase	..	..	..	..	..	–	–	–	7.4
A4	Expenditure on selected items by place of purchase	A3	A3	A4	A4	A4	7.4	7.4	7.4	–
..	Expenditure on petrol, diesel and other motor oils by place of purchase	..	..	..	..	..	–	–	–	7.5
..	Selected household goods and personal goods and services by place of purchase	..	..	..	..	..	–	–	–	7.6
..	Selected regular purchases by place of purchase	..	..	..	..	..	–	–	–	7.7
A5	Expenditure on clothing and footwear by place of purchase	A5	A5	A5	A5	A5	7.5	7.5	7.5	7.8
Expenditure by income										
A6	Main items by gross income decile	A6	A6	A6	A6	A6	1.1	1.1	1.1	1.1
A7	Percentage on main items by gross income decile	A7	A7	A7	A7	A7	1.2	1.2	1.2	1.2
A8	Detailed expenditure by gross income decile	A8	A8	A8	A8	A8	1.3	1.3	1.3	1.3
..	(Housing expenditure in each tenure group)	–	–	..	..	..	–	–	–	–
A9	Main items by disposable income decile	A9	A9	A9	A9	A9	1.4	1.4	1.4	1.4
A10	Percentage on main items by disposable income decile	A10	A10	A10	A10	A10	1.5	1.5	1.5	1.5
Expenditure by age and income										
A11	Main items by age of HRP	A11	A11	A11	A11	A11	2.1	2.1	2.9	–
..	Main items by age of head of household	..	..	..	..	..	–	–	2.1	2.1
A12	Main items as a percentage by age of HRP	A12	A12	A12	A12	A12	2.2	2.2	2.2	2.2
A13	Detailed expenditure by age of HRP	A13	A13	A13	A13	A13	2.3	2.3	2.3	2.3
A14	Aged under 30 by income	A14	A14	A14	A14	A14	2.4	2.4	2.4	2.4
A15	Aged 30 and under 50 by income	A15	A15	A15	A15	A15	2.5	2.5	2.5	2.5
A16	Aged 50 and under 65 by income	A16	A16	A16	A16	A16	2.6	2.6	2.6	2.6
A17	Aged 65 and under 75 by income	A17	A17	A17	A17	A17	2.7	2.7	2.7	2.7
A18	Aged 75 or over by income	A18	A18	A18	A18	A18	2.8	2.8	2.8	2.8
Expenditure by socio–economic characteristics										
A19	By economic activity status of HRP	A19	A19	A19	A19	A19	3.1	3.1	3.9	–
..	By economic activity status of HoH	..	..	..	..	..	–	–	3.1	3.1
..	By occupation	..	..	..	..	..	–	–	3.2	3.2
A20	HRP is a full–time employee by income	A20	A20	A20	A20	A20	3.2	3.2	3.3	3.3
A21	HRP is self–employed by income	A21	A21	A21	A21	A21	3.3	3.3	3.4	3.4
..	By social class	..	..	..	..	..	–	–	3.5	3.5
A22	By number of persons working	A22	A22	A22	A22	A22	3.4	3.4	3.6	3.6
A23	By age HRP completed continuous full–time education	A23	A23	A23	A23	A23	3.5	3.5	3.7	3.7
..	By occupation of HRP	..	..	..	..	..	–	–	3.8	–
A24	By socio–economic class of HRP	A24	A24	A24	A24	A24	3.6	3.6	–	–
Expenditure by composition, income and tenure										
A25	Expenditure by household composition	A25	A25	A25	A25	A25	4.1	4.1	4.1	4.1
A26	One adult retired households mainly dependent on state pensions	A26	A26	A26	A26	A26	4.2	4.2	4.2	4.2
A27	One adult retired households not mainly dependent on state pensions	A27	A27	A27	A27	A27	4.3	4.3	4.3	4.3
A28	One adult non–retired	A28	A28	A28	A28	A28	4.4	4.4	4.4	4.4
A29	One adult with children	A29	A29	A29	A29	A29	4.5	4.5	4.5	4.5
A30	Two adults with children	A30	A30	A30	A30	A30	4.6	4.6	4.6	4.6

Notes
.. Tables do not appear in these publications
1 Previously known as the Expenditure and Food Survey (2001–02 to 2007)

Index to tables in reports on the Family Expenditure Survey in 1997–98 to 2000–01 and the Living Costs and Food Survey 2001–02 to 2008   (cont.)

							Table numbers in reports for		
2008 tables	2007	2006	2005–06	2004–05	2003–04	2002–03	2001–02[1]	2000–2001	1999–00
Expenditure by composition, income and tenure (cont.)									
A31 One man one woman non-retired	A31	A31	A31	A31	A31	4.7	4.7	4.7	4.7
A32 One man one woman retired mainly dependent on state pensions	A32	A32	A32	A32	A32	4.8	4.8	4.8	4.8
A33 One man one woman retired not mainly dependent on state pensions	A32	A32	A33	A33	A33	4.9	4.9	4.9	4.9
A34 Household expenditure by tenure	A33	A33	A34	A34	A34	4.10	4.10	4.10	4.10
.. Household expenditure by type of dwelling	..	..	..	..	..	-	-	-	-
Expenditure by region									
A35 Main items of expenditure by GOR	A35	A35	A35	A35	A35	5.1	5.1	5.1	5.1
A36 Main items as a percentage of expenditure by GOR	A36	A36	A36	A36	A36	5.2	5.2	5.2	5.2
A37 Detailed expenditure by GOR	A37	A37	A37	A37	A37	5.3	5.3	5.3	5.3
.. (Housing expenditure in each tenure group)	..	..	..	..	..	-	-	-	-
.. Expenditure by type of administrative area	..	..	..	..	..	-	-	5.4	5.4
A38 Expenditure by urban/rural areas (GB only)	A38	A38	A38	A38	A38	5.4	5.4	5.5	-
Household income									
A40 Income by household composition	A40	A40	A40	A40	A40	8.1	8.1	8.1	8.1
A41 Income by age of HRP	A41	A41	A41	A41	A41	8.2	8.2	8.10	-
.. By age of head of household	..	..	..	..	..	-	-	8.2	8.2
A42 Income by income group	A42	A42	A42	A42	A42	8.3	8.3	8.3	8.3
A43 Income by household tenure	A43	A43	A43	A43	A43	8.4	8.4	8.4	8.4
.. Income by economic status of HoH	..	..	..	..	..	-	-	8.5	8.5
.. Income by occupational grouping of HoH	..	..	..	..	..	-	-	8.6	8.6
A44 Income by GOR	A44	A44	A44	A44	A44	8.5	8.5	8.7	8.7
A45 Income by GB urban/rural areas	A45	A45	A45	A45	A45	8.6	8.6	8.8	-
A46 Income by socio-economic class	A46	A46	A46	A46	A46	8.7	-	-	-
A47 Income 1970 to 2006	A47	A47	A47	A47	A47	8.8	8.7	8.9	8.8
.. Income by economic activity status of HRP	..	..	..	..	..	-	-	8.11	-
.. Income by occupation of HRP	..	..	..	..	..	-	-	8.12	-
Households characteristics and ownership of durable goods									
A48 Household characteristics	A48	A48	A48	A48	A48	9.1	9.1	9.1	9.1
A49 Person characteristics	A49	A49	A49	A49	A49	9.2	9.2	9.2	9.2
A50 Percentage with durable goods 1970 to 2006	A50	A50	A50	A50	A50	9.3	9.3	9.3	9.3
A51 Percentage with durable goods by income group & hhld composition	A51	A51	A51	A51	A51	9.4	9.4	9.4	9.4
A52 Percentage with cars	A52	A52	A52	A52	A52	9.5	9.5	9.5	9.5
A53 Percentage with durable goods by UK Countries and Government Office Regions	A53	A53	A53	A53	A53	9.6	9.6	9.6	9.6
A54 Percentage by size, composition, age, in each income group	A54	A54	A54	A54	A54	9.7	9.7	9.7	9.7
.. Percentage by occupation, economic activity, tenure in each income group	..	..	..	..	..	-	-	9.8	9.8
A55 Percentage by economic activity, tenure and socio-economic class in each income group	A54	A54	A55	A55	A55	9.8	9.8	-	-
Output Area Classification									
A56 Average weekly household expenditure by OAC supergroup	..	..	..	..	..	..	..	..	..
A57 Average weekly household expenditure by OAC group	..	..	..	..	..	..	..	..	..
A58 Average gross normal weekly household income by OAC supergroup	..	..	..	..	..	..	..	..	..
Trends in household expenditure (moved to Chapter 4)									
4.1 FES main items 1984 - 2006	4.1	4.1	4.1	4.1	4.1	6.1	6.1	6.1	6.1
4.2 FES as a percentage of total expenditure 1984 - 2006	4.2	4.2	4.2	4.2	4.2	6.2	6.2	6.2	6.2
.. by Region	..	..	..	..	..	-	-	6.3	6.3
4.3 COICOP main items 2001-02 to 2006	4.3	4.3	4.3	..	..	..	..	..	..
4.4 COICOP as a percentage of total expenditure 2001-02 to 2006	4.4	4.4	4.4	..	..	..	..	..	..
4.5 Household expenditure 2002-03 to 2008 COICOP based current prices	..	..	..	..	..	..	..	..	..

Notes
.. Tables do not appear in these publications
1 Previously known as the Expenditure and Food Survey (2001–02 to 2007)